"Here is a trustworthy guide through the theological thicket in which Western culture encounters Jesus. Readers wearied by the recent parade of Jesus-debunkers will find clarity and inspiration for new understanding. With the mind of a scholar and the heart of a believer, Yoder Neufeld surveys a wide range of perspectives in language a non-specialist can understand."

—**J. Nelson Kraybill,** Associated Mennonite Biblical Seminary

"For too long, students of the New Testament were forced to choose between the Jesus of scholarship and the Christ of faith. In lively and accessible prose, Dr. Yoder Neufeld skillfully integrates both courses into a helpful road map for those serious about negotiating the tortuous turns on their way to rediscovering Jesus. He presents all possible historical and theological options available to his readers with competence, never shrinking back from questions that might scandalize the believer or embarrass the scholar. His greatest virtue, however, is that though he is quite clear about his personal convictions on Jesus, he never imposes his views on his readers, content with leaving them with enough directions to find their way home. This is the text I will use next time I teach a course on Jesus."

—**Sze-kar Wan,** Andover Newton Theological School

"A superb guide—unmatched for clarity and accessibility—into an 'encounter' with the Jesus of the New Testament and other early Christian writings, offered in gentle, engaging prose by a seasoned teacher whose scholarship and faith complement each other, to the benefit of believers and inquirers/seekers alike. Thanks to its comprehensiveness, sound scholarship, and excellent organization, with subsections clearly labeled, it will also serve as a valuable reference work after the first engrossing read."

—**Harold Remus,** Wilfrid Laurier University, Waterloo, Ontario (Emeritus)

"Respected scholar, masterful teacher, man of faith—Tom Yoder Neufeld has combined these qualities to produce a solid, eminently readable, and informative study of the New Testament witness for the man, Jesus, and for the early development of christological reflection in the second century.

Using the analogy of archaeology, Yoder Neufeld examines carefully the different layers of New Testament evidence, giving particular emphasis to the historical context of the world of the first century and then following the biographical framework of Jesus's life from birth to death and resurrection. He puts at the center, as well it should be, Jesus's proclamation of the kingdom of God, and in successive chapters he treats 'Announcing the Kingdom,' 'Teaching the Kingdom,' 'Enacting the Kingdom,' and 'Living the Kingdom.' His is a sensitive and nuanced handling of such difficult issues as the virgin birth and the challenges of understanding well the meaning of resurrection. As every good teacher does, he provides an abundant use of analogies and explanatory examples. Never have I read a more skillful presentation of the organic growth of New Testament Christology from low to high, with fine treatment of the origin and function of the various titles applied to Jesus in the New Testament and beyond. The text is unencumbered by laborious footnotes, while clearly reflective of the diverse, ongoing scholarly dialogue of which this book is part. Each chapter concludes with a summary box of 'Key Terms and Concepts' and suggestions for further reading. This is a superb text—one I will surely use with seminary students to their certain profit and delight."

—**Barbara E. Bowe,** Catholic Theological Union

"A lucid, engaging treatment of Jesus and the Gospels, attending well to sources and methods. Yoder Neufeld laudably combines faith and scholarship. His lists of reading sources at the end of each chapter are valuable for further study. This book is well designed for introducing Jesus and current scholarship to university students, and to laypeople who want to understand how we know what we know about Jesus."

—**Willard M. Swartley,** Associated Mennonite Biblical Seminary

RECOVERING JESUS

THE WITNESS OF THE NEW TESTAMENT

Thomas R. Yoder Neufeld

BrazosPress
Grand Rapids, Michigan

©2007 by Thomas R. Yoder Neufeld

Published by Brazos Press
a division of Baker Publishing Group
P.O. Box 6287, Grand Rapids, MI 49516-6287
www.brazospress.com

Printed in the United States of America

Library of Congress Cataloging-in-Publication Data
Neufeld, Thomas R.
    Recovering Jesus : the witness of the New Testament / Thomas R. Yoder Neufeld.
        p.   cm.
    Includes bibliographical references and index.
    ISBN 10: 1-58743-202-1 (pbk.)
    ISBN 978-1-58743-202-6 (pbk.)
    1. Jesus Christ—Biography. 2. Bible. N.T.—Criticism, interpretation, etc. I. Title.
    BT301.3.N48 2007
    232.9′01—dc22   2007001798

First published in Great Britain in 2007 by
Society for Promoting Christian Knowledge
36 Causton Street
London SW1P 4ST

British Library Cataloguing-in-Publication Data
A catalogue record for this book is available from the British Library

ISBN 978-0-281-05972-0

10 9 7 8 6 5 4 3 2 1

For my companion for life, Rebecca,
and our children, David and Miriam,
with whom to follow Jesus together is a gift too great to measure.

Contents

Preface

THIS BOOK GROWS out of years of teaching undergraduate students about Jesus. Sometimes they have been religious studies majors, but more typically their fields of study have been some other area of the arts, science, computer science, or engineering. For many the course on Jesus has been the one religion course they have taken while at university. Most, whether or not Jesus has figured in a personal faith, have been primarily interested in learning about Jesus and not in learning about the problems of learning about Jesus, least of all in learning about one particular scholar's take on Jesus. The pedagogical challenge in this is how to enter into the academic study of Jesus while responding to the primary interest of students to learn about the Jesus the New Testament presents. How do I as an academic, trained in critical scholarship, who has at the same time a deep faith and trust in the biblical witnesses and who himself confesses Jesus as Lord, present the fruit of scholarship hospitably, inviting students to engage the data for themselves, all in the interests of facilitating an encounter with the Jesus to whom the New Testament writers give witness?

This book is the fruit of attempting to respond to those demands and to work within such constraints. Pedagogical rather than methodological interests predominate. Those wishing for a carefully argued historical reconstruction of the Jesus of history or for a literary critical study of the gospels may be frustrated. And those wishing for an explicitly faith-centered Bible study may be equally frustrated. I empathize with both as one who is himself active within both contexts. At the same time, I have discovered that the teaching of Jesus within a pluralistic context such as the university classroom, in which I may not privilege any particular set of students, whether religiously indifferent, highly skeptical, or passionately Christian, does not prevent an encounter with the Jesus presented in the New Testament. More, it encourages such an encounter.

I thus wish to thank those many students, whether at the Bienenberg Seminary outside Basel, Switzerland, who sat through German versions of these chapters during a sabbatical in 2001, or at Conrad Grebel University College at the University of Waterloo, Canada, who have road tested this book and given sharp and gracious feedback. I am most grateful too for the attentive care the good folks at Brazos Press have given this project, most especially Rodney Clapp and Rebecca Cooper, but also Steve Ayers, who many years ago planted the seed of writing this book during a typically friendly visit to my office.

In John 1:44–46, Jesus's newly enrolled disciple Philip excitedly seeks to recruit his friend Nathanael with the good news that the one promised by Moses and the prophets has been found in Jesus of Nazareth. Nathanael's skepticism is met with the simple straightforward words: "Come and see!" Indeed, that is my invitation to the reader.

1

One Jesus or Many Jesuses?

F EW FIGURES IN history are as well known as Jesus. As Dan Brown's *Da Vinci Code* and Tom Harpur's *Pagan Christ* have shown recently, Jesus is big business, regardless of or perhaps especially because of how outlandish the claims are. However much or little Jesus's teachings actually shape how people live, he is venerated by millions. The sounds of such veneration range from simple singing without the accompaniment of instruments to loud worship bands, from Johann Sebastian Bach's *St. Matthew Passion* to Andrew Lloyd Weber's *Jesus Christ Superstar*. Jesus plays well at the movies too—from Denis Arcand's *Jesus of Montreal* to Mel Gibson's *The Passion of the Christ*.

Even a quick search of the internet for images of Jesus illustrates an exciting and also bewildering diversity of depictions, from high art to folk art, from the obviously devotional to the irreverent. Too often Jesus looks European, but he can also be African, Asian, and occasionally also Middle Eastern. "He" is sometimes even depicted as a woman. Portraits of Jesus range from laughing friend of children, to ethereal epitome of piety, to fierce warrior on behalf of the poor and downtrodden. In other words, Jesus is both an unthreatening omnipresent cultural and religious icon and an inspiration for radical and sometimes violent struggle against power and privilege. Some Jesuses are emotionally accessible, intensely human, much like any normal, vulnerable human being: sometimes sad, pensive, or impatient, at other times joyful and laughing, and sometimes tormented. Other Jesuses are austere and distant, virtually nonphysical, nonmaterial, and transcendent, like the

11

divine ruler of the cosmos many believe him to be. Jesus seems to look like whatever anyone wishes him to look like.

Does Jesus Get Lost in the Crowd?

Is this diversity a problem? After all, who knows what Jesus really looked like? We have no eyewitness descriptions of him. To complicate matters, the Christian tradition itself insists that Jesus was "just like us," that is, representative of humanity as a whole (e.g., Hebrews 2). Mother Teresa spoke often and movingly of seeing Christ in the face of the poorest of the poor, echoing Jesus's unforgettable words in his parable of the great judgment:

> I was hungry and you gave me food, I was thirsty and you gave me something to drink, I was a stranger and you welcomed me, I was naked and you gave me clothing, I was sick and you took care of me, I was in prison and you visited me. . . . Truly I tell you, *just as you did it to one of the least of these who are members of my family, you did it to me.* (Matt. 25:35–36, 40, emphasis added)

Indeed, one of the central Christian convictions is that Jesus as the Christ encompasses *all* of liberated humanity in himself, regardless of race, sex, or social and economic status:

> There is no longer Jew or Greek, there is no longer slave or free, there is no longer male and female. (Gal. 3:28)

Paul of Tarsus, one of the most important of the early leaders in the Jesus movement and the writer of those words, went so far as to call the many diverse people making up the community of Jesus's followers "the body of Christ" (Rom. 12:4–5; 1 Cor. 12:12–27). Should we be surprised, given the diversity of the human community, that Jesus would be represented in a countless variety of ways?

That raises an urgent question: is there anything about Jesus that is distinct? Is there something that draws our attention not only to ways in which Jesus looks like us, but also to what makes him special and distinct? Are we not interested in what makes Jesus *Jesus*, and not simply a projection of a community's highest ideals or its most fervent wishes? Such a desire is often put today in terms of getting at the real Jesus.

Will the Real Jesus Please Stand Up!

Perhaps the first thing we should acknowledge is that "real" is itself a loaded term when it comes to the study of Jesus. For example, for some "real" refers to the Jesus we can reconstruct on the basis of strict historical investigation. Most people today use the term in that way, and much contemporary Jesus scholarship goes about its work with that objective in mind. At the other end of the spectrum are those who look upon the work of such scholars with suspicion. The real Jesus is in fact the Christ that the Christian community believes in, confessed in the creeds, and celebrated in worship. In the broad middle are many, both scholars and ordinary folk (and you will find me among them), who care about Jesus precisely because he matters religiously or theologically, but who do not consider historical investigation to be the enemy of such a perspective. In their view it is the Son of God, Savior, and risen Lord who is the real Jesus, the Jesus who also lived, taught, and died in Palestine some two millennia ago, that is, who lived a very specific historical existence as a first-century Jew in Palestine. Such a real Jesus can be *both* believed in *and* investigated with the tools of the historian. But even among these people the arguments are often heated.

Just Read the Bible!

Some might think that we can settle who Jesus was and why he matters by going back to the sources, which means, for the most part, going to the Bible, specifically the New Testament. At first glance that appears to be a good solution. After all, here we have a set of documents that come from the very time in which Jesus lived, give or take a few decades. We do not often have such excellent sources for figures of the distant past. However, the moment we set out to use the Bible, we encounter several problems.

First, people view the Bible in very different ways. Some view the Bible as a sacred text and understand that to mean that it must be read straight up as a historically accurate depiction of what once happened. Others view the Bible as a collection of religious documents that have to be evaluated much the way one evaluates any documents from ancient history. Just as in the case of ancient accounts of Alexander the Great or Julius Caesar, fact must be separated from fiction. Not surprisingly, many view the biblical depiction of Jesus to contain more fiction than fact, especially when it comes to reports of virgin birth, miracles, and resurrection. There are many others, scholars and nonscholars, who consider the Bible to be sacred Scripture, but not a historically reliable record in any simple sense. So, the first difficult issue we encounter in the search for Jesus is how the Bible should be viewed and approached.

Second, the biblical sources themselves present us with a set of difficulties. To begin with, the New Testament contains not one record of Jesus, but four gospels, each of which to varying degree tells the story of Jesus in a distinctive way and from a particular perspective. Three of them depict things roughly the same way, which is why we call Matthew, Mark, and Luke the Synoptic Gospels (*syn* = "together with" and *optic* = "look"). The Gospel of John is very different from the three look-alikes. To complicate matters further, Jesus is centrally important to the Apostle Paul, the New Testament author who wrote years, perhaps even decades, earlier than any of the gospel writers. But stories of Jesus's ministry and most of his teachings are largely absent from Paul's correspondence. It is the death, resurrection, and imminent return of Jesus that take center stage. Should Paul count in the search for the real Jesus?

Third, all four gospels and the other writings in the New Testament were written with matters of faith being absolutely central. They were written with a concern to communicate who Jesus *was*, but from a view to who Jesus *is*, from a belief in a Jesus who is *presently* alive and who communicates with his followers through his "spirit." That does not mean that the New Testament writers did not have an interest in telling what actually took place. Indeed, that was one of their chief concerns. But they were not historians; they were witnesses, preachers, evangelists (to use the technical term for the authors of the New Testament gospels), relating the past in order to persuade readers of Jesus's *present* significance. That is why their documents are called "gospels" (Greek *euangelion* = "evangel, good news") and not "archives" or even "biographies."

Fourth, the writers of the gospels wrote in order to help out the fledgling communities of Jesus's followers who needed guidance. A historian will thus easily recognize that one of the factors in the selection and transmission of Jesus's teachings and actions was to provide a community that venerated him with an example to follow. An excellent example of this is the Sermon on the Mount in Matthew 5–7 (see chapter 10 below).

Fifth, for all their desire to convince readers of the *present* importance of Jesus for them and their world, the gospel writers, or evangelists, are concerned to tell a story of what happened *in history*. At the same time, they tell the story of Jesus in such a way as to indicate that Jesus's followers did not comprehend who he *really* was until after Easter. In other words, as much as the evangelists intend to recall the pre-Easter Jesus, they also signal that it is only after Easter that his followers caught on to his true and full identity. Contemporary search for the historical Jesus is largely restricted to that pre-Easter Jesus. The New Testament writers would insist that this search stops well short of a full appreciation of who Jesus turned out to really be, namely, the Christ, the Son of God, fully revealed in both identity and significance with the resurrection and exaltation.

Sixth, the existence of nonbiblical ancient sources dealing with Jesus has become an embattled part of the contemporary search for Jesus. Among the most well known are the Dead Sea Scrolls at Qumran, the gnostic library found at Nag Hammadi in the Egyptian desert, and especially the *Gospel of*

Thomas (see the next chapter). Most recently, in 2006 a manuscript of the second-century *Gospel of Judas* came to light. Just as scholars differ on how to use the Bible as a source for the study of Jesus, so there are significant differences of opinion about what status to give these nonbiblical ancient writings in the search for a full understanding of Jesus. With the possible yet limited exception of the *Gospel of Thomas*, none of these sources give us more information on Jesus per se.

It is not hard to see why this state of affairs regarding the sources renders the search of the real Jesus rather difficult. Can one trust the sources we have, even those within the New Testament? In what sense? Are they historically reliable sources? Or are they theologically reliable? Even when scholars have restricted themselves to a search for a pre-Easter or pre-Christian Jesus, results have been frustratingly diverse.

Searching for the Jesus of History

The nature of the sources and the troubled relationship between religious commitment and historical enquiry have marked what is often called the "quest for the historical Jesus" since that search began with the Enlightenment. The first to attempt a historical investigation of Jesus was Hermann Samuel Reimarus, whose fragmentary work *The Aims of Jesus and His Disciples* was published posthumously in 1778. Under the impact of a new interest in history and historical research, the church's official portrait of Jesus was largely ignored in favor of one of Jesus as teacher of ethics, captured in the phrase *kingdom of God* and parsed largely as "the fatherhood of God and the brotherhood of man," as it was commonly known.

The first quest came to an end with the German publication in 1906 of *The Quest of the Historical Jesus: A Critical Study of Its Progress from Reimarus to Wrede* by the famous Alsatian physician, organist, and New Testament scholar Albert Schweitzer. Schweitzer insisted that, far from being a liberal teacher of brotherhood, Jesus would have been a stranger to contemporary sensibilities. Jesus was an apocalyptic prophet, anticipating the end of this present world at any moment. By giving himself over to death, Jesus intended to hasten its end. Schweitzer's dismissal of the "lives of Jesus" up to that point was joined by a very thoroughgoing skepticism that the gospels, given their prime concern for matters of faith, would divulge much of anything historically reliable about Jesus. Schweitzer's work ushered in a time of severe skepticism among many scholars regarding the New Testament as a historical source for Jesus. The name most often identified with this radical historical skepticism is Rudolf Bultmann, arguably the most influential New Testament scholar of the first half of the twentieth century. He wedded his historical skepticism with an existentialist theological approach where what truly matters is the authentic "decision of faith," not whether one can verify something historically. In his view, the New Testament provides much more historical information about the early church, its traditions, and its beliefs than it does about Jesus.

Several of Bultmann's students broke rank and began what has come to be known as the new quest or second quest for the historical Jesus. These scholars recognized that the gospels make access to Jesus difficult, but they insisted that at least in the most theologically important ways, they do provide access. Well known from this period is the work of Günther Bornkamm, simply titled *Jesus of Nazareth* (1960; original German, 1956).

A so-called third quest has emerged on the scene in the last few decades, marked by renewed interest in the Jewish matrix of Jesus's life, identity, and teachings, as well as a renewed debate over the historical value of the gospels and extrabiblical writings. As part of this effort, scholars like James Dunn and N. T. Wright attempt to show the continuity between Jesus and his Jewish matrix, as well as continuity between Jesus and the community that venerated him as Messiah and Son of God.

Who Was Jesus?

There is today little consensus among scholars who have attempted to recover and reconstruct the Jesus of history. Paula Fredriksen, a leading Jewish scholar of Jesus, puts it well:

> Jesus the charismatic leader; Jesus the existential religious thinker; Jesus the hypnotic healer; Jesus the witty, subversive sage; Jesus the passionate social revolutionary; Jesus the prophet of the End—all these diverse images of Jesus populate the most recent books; all are presented with the same flourish of authority; all are constructed by appeals to the same data. . . . *If this is progress, we might wish for less of it.* (*Jesus of Nazareth, King of the Jews*, 4, emphasis added)

Scholars are used to this diversity of opinion. Indeed, their work is energized by it. They take it as an inevitable consequence of the nature of the data with which they must work. At the risk of serious oversimplification, we can distill the diversity of proposals or portraits into the following categories.

Jesus the Healer and Exorcist

Some believe that Jesus best fits the profile of a first-century wonder worker, healer, and exorcist. In short, Jesus was a magician. That does not imply agreement among these scholars as to what actually happened in Jesus's activity as a healer and exorcist. However, they recognize that his contemporaries would have explained his activity as acting with divine power in dramatic fashion to change people's experience of illness and spiritual bondage.

Jesus the Sage

Particularly popular at present is a view of Jesus as a teacher of wisdom, as a sage. Focusing less on his powerful deeds and even less on his fate at the hands of his enemies, this portrait highlights Jesus's use of parables and pithy sayings, often expressing very nonconformist or even subversive wisdom. Not surprisingly, such scholars give great weight to ancient documents not found in the New Testament itself, such as the *Gospel of Thomas*, which show little interest in the death or resurrection of Jesus. Members of the well-known and rather notorious Jesus Seminar have championed this interpretation.

Jesus the Prophet

Others, as did Schweitzer a century ago, view Jesus as a prophet who came to announce the kingdom or reign of God and with it to bring history to an end—at least history as we know it. Some propose that Jesus was mistaken in this conviction, but that it was nonetheless the basis of his actions and his teachings, even his death. Some see social revolutionary traits in Jesus's words and actions, traits we today might dub political. Others think of Jesus as a prophet who announced and indeed inaugurated the reign of God and in the process set the scene for the subsequent developments of the church as the embodiment of the kingdom.

Jesus the Messiah

Whereas many scholars have serious reservations about whether Jesus saw himself as a messiah, as a king or deliverer, there are those who believe he and especially his followers would have seen him as such. By itself, his death at the hand of the Roman imperial authorities would have made such claims difficult to sustain. Most scholars thus consider the claims to messiahship, and the related claim that Jesus was "Son of God," to be respect accorded him by those who believed that God raised him to life following his execution at the hands of the Romans (see chapters 12–13 below).

Jesus (the Son of) God

If many scholars have reservations about whether Jesus saw himself as a messiah, they will have even more difficulty with attributing the traditional

Christian claim of his divinity to Jesus himself. Many (most?) scholars view this as an emerging conviction among the followers of Jesus in the years following his life in Palestine. This claim is thus typically bracketed out when getting at the historical Jesus. Christian claims are viewed as post-Easter phenomena. As a result, Christology, the study of the theological meaning and identity of Jesus as the Christ, has largely become a separate field of enquiry. The very nature of the sources, however, as well as the interest that brings most readers to this book, requires an account of christological beginnings (see chapter 13 below).

This brief menu of profiles greatly oversimplifies the scholarly proposals, as Fredriksen's comments quoted earlier suggest. Plenty of data in the sources give rise to each of these profiles, and many scholars rightly combine elements of each of them in their reconstructions of who Jesus was. Of particular importance in contemporary scholarship is the question of the Jewishness of Jesus as it relates to each of these portraits. The debate is a lively one, not least due to important Jewish participation in the study of Jesus (see the work of Jewish scholars like Paula Fredriksen, Geza Vermes, and David Flusser).

But We Do See Jesus!

These words were penned by an anonymous preacher whose sermon we know as the letter to the Hebrews (2:9), one of the writings that make up the New Testament. They express the conviction of the writers of the New Testament that in the end "seeing Jesus," the man from Nazareth, is essential to any full appreciation of him, regardless of how exalted his status and great his significance.

It would be the height of arrogance to say that in this study we truly will get at the real Jesus, if by that we mean *the* definitive portrait of what he was truly like. But it is not, in my opinion, arrogant in the least to believe that in the honest listening to and wrestling with the testimony of his first-century followers—and of more recent witnesses, scholarly and popular—we are in a position to "see" the Jesus the writers of the New Testament give witness to. That is the conviction informing this book. I trust the biblical witnesses to provide windows on Jesus. True, fingerprints, smudges of scribes, and the dust kicked up by the struggles of early followers of Jesus with each other and their detractors are found all over these windows. But I do not believe that these witnesses, with their deep and profound convictions about Jesus, pulled the blinds on those windows, preventing us from seeing Jesus. Even so, much room remains for testing and evaluating the sources, for diversity of insight, even for serious disagreement. Indeed, any truly attentive, inquisitive, and honest reading of the gospels will raise questions about *them* as sources, about *Jesus*, and, importantly, about *our* cherished views of Jesus.

Goals for This Book

This book treats the scholarly task respectfully and empathetically. Students should know what kinds of issues the academic search for Jesus has raised. The workshop of scholarship is a sometimes raucous place. And we can be grateful that through the work done in that noisy workshop we have been alerted in our day to such crucially important issues as the Jewishness of Jesus, the subversiveness and wonder of his wisdom, and the creativity of those who saw to his legacy. Most importantly, however, this book is intended to be an introduction to the Jesus we encounter in the New Testament, not primarily the one that modern historians attempt to reconstruct. So, whereas readers will necessarily come to understand some of those problems associated with the study of Jesus, it is the encounter with the New Testament witnesses, our primary sources for Jesus, that constitutes the heart of this effort. This book is therefore no substitute for reading the raw data, the New Testament. This is so not only because this book will often make sense only in light of a direct reading of the Bible, in particular the gospels, but also because only so will readers be able to engage this book critically and to form their own considered opinions.

About the Author

In the interests of inviting readers to be honest about themselves and the perspectives they bring to the study of Jesus, I will introduce myself. I come to the study of Jesus both as a believer and as a scholar. The first has much to do with the respect with which I come to the task, the energy with which I engage it, and the intensity of interest I have in the outcome. In addition to a career in teaching, I have been a pastor as well as a hospital and prison chaplain; I preach and teach often in church settings. So the "stuff" of Jesus matters a great deal to me as a believer. As much as I am a believer, I am at the same time a scholar. I do not experience faith and scholarship to be in tension with each other, even if they often ask each other terribly hard and vexatious questions. I believe that it is appropriate and illuminating to bring to the study of Jesus the tools of a scholar who is trained not only in theology, but in the study of history and literature, especially as they relate to the biblical literature.

I am not naïve about my biases, conscious and unconscious. Everyone has biases. As will be the case with many readers of this book, I have a deep and abiding interest in Jesus, one that is rooted in heritage and tradition, in the rich deposit of faith, and in culturally nurtured convictions and perspectives. The specific church tradition in which I have been nurtured is the Mennonite church, within the Anabaptist part of the Christian tradition. I am also conscious of my social location as a North American, specifically Canadian, scholar and that there are many within North America and certainly around the globe whose access to Jesus is from a very different set of convictions, experiences, and perspectives and who therefore do not share either the vistas or the limitations of my location.

That said, I undertake the study of the gospels and of the New Testament, as well as of the scholarship dealing with Jesus, with an openness to be estranged from cherished notions and perspectives. Nothing is gained by holding up a mirror to already existing convictions and having them substitute for a fresh examination of the sources, as illustrated by titles of recent books, such as Marcus Borg's *Meeting Jesus Again for the First Time*, Philip Yancey's *The Jesus I Never Knew*, and Michael J. McClymond's *Familiar Stranger: An Introduction to Jesus of Nazareth*. Bias, interest, and heritage need not prevent us from meeting on the common ground of the New Testament and wrestling there together to come to fuller understanding of who Jesus was and how he matters.

Suggested Exercise

In preparation for the next few chapters, begin reading the gospels rapidly, *each one at one sitting*. Originally the gospels were written without chapter and verse divisions and were meant to be heard at one sitting. They were meant first and foremost to work as a whole story rather than as a collection of snippets. To read it this way will mean that you will not comprehend nearly everything or be able to linger at favorite passages. It will, however, open up new vistas and insights.

For Further Reading

Following are only a few select resources that can point the way to further reading. Readers should mine the voluminous and accessible information on virtually every topic in encyclopedias like the six-volume *Anchor Bible Dictionary* (ed. David Noel Freedman et al.; 6 vols.; New York: Doubleday, 1992) and in one-volume encyclopedias like the *Dictionary of Jesus and the Gospels* (ed. Joel B. Green and Scot McKnight; Downers Grove, IL: InterVarsity, 1992). These resources have excellent articles on the issues, themes, and personalities raised in this book, most often with extensive bibliographies. Even larger bibliographies are to be found in the major studies listed below. The web has a wealth of academically respectable and scholarly resources as well (New Testament Gateway [www.ntgateway .com] is an excellent portal to many relevant websites).

Primary Sources

Most of the primary sources such as the Bible and noncanonical literature are available in various translations and editions online at sites like Early Christian Writings (www.earlychristianwritings.com). See also the following:

Apocrypha or Deuterocanonical writings (e.g., Wisdom of Solomon [or Book of Wisdom] and Wisdom of Jesus ben Sirach [Ecclesiasticus]); found in all Catholic translations (Jerusalem Bible/New Jerusalem Bible and New American Bible) and in most Protestant translations (except New International Version), where they are called Apocrypha.

New Testament Apocrypha. Edited by Edgar Hennecke and Wilhelm Schneemelcher. Translated by R. M. Wilson. 2 vols. Philadelphia: Westminster, 1964.

Gospel of Thomas. In *The Nag Hammadi Library*. Edited by Bentley Layton and James M. Robinson. San Francisco: Harper & Row, 1977.

Josephus. Translated by William Whiston. Edited by Paul Meier. Revised edition. Grand Rapids: Kregel, 1999.

The Dead Sea Scrolls Translated: The Qumran Texts in English. By Florentino García Martínez. Translated by Wilfred G. E. Watson. Leiden: Brill, 1994.

Overviews of Contemporary Jesus Scholarship

Borg, Marcus J. *Jesus in Contemporary Scholarship*. Harrisburg, PA: Trinity, 1994.

Evans, Craig A., and Stanley E. Porter. *The Historical Jesus*. Sheffield, UK: Sheffield Academic Press, 1995.

Powell, Mark Allan. *Jesus as a Figure in History: How Modern Historians View the Man from Galilee*. Louisville: Westminster/John Knox, 1998.

Tatum, Barnes W. *In Quest of Jesus*. Revised edition. Nashville: Abingdon, 1999.

Witherington, Ben, III. *The Jesus Quest: The Third Search for the Jew of Nazareth*. 2nd edition. Downers Grove, IL: InterVarsity, 1997.

Major Jesus Studies

All introductions to the New Testament treat the gospel literature; many also have a section on Jesus per se. Commentaries (analysis and interpretation of biblical texts) on each of the gospels are too numerous to list. All of them take up virtually every issue related to the study of Jesus, but within the context of the particular gospel being interpreted. Following are some major works devoted to the study of Jesus:

Crossan, John Dominic. *The Historical Jesus: The Life of a Mediterranean Jewish Peasant*. San Francisco: Harper, 1993. A leading Jesus scholar, Crossan has, together with Marcus Borg (cited above), been an important member of the Jesus Seminar. Under the direction of Robert W. Funk, the Jesus Seminar has published *The Five Gospels: What Did Jesus Really*

Say? The Search for the Authentic Words of Jesus (San Francisco: Harper, 1997) and *The Acts of Jesus: What Did Jesus Really Do?* (San Francisco: Harper, 1998).

Dunn, James D. G. *Jesus Remembered*. Christianity in the Making, vol. 1. Grand Rapids: Eerdmans, 2003. Dunn has been a major force in the so-called third quest and one of the most prolific Jesus scholars working in the United Kingdom. His work provides a very readable and at the same time thoroughly scholarly treatment of the Jesus the New Testament presents.

Meier, John P. *A Marginal Jew: Rethinking the Historical Jesus*. 3 vols. New York: Doubleday, 1991–2001. The three volumes are subtitled *The Roots of the Problem and the Person*; *Mentor, Message, and Miracles*; and *Companions and Competitors*. Erudite and comprehensive, Meier is one of the leading contemporary Catholic Jesus scholars. An excellent reference work.

Wright, N. T. *Christian Origins and the Question of God*. 3 vols. Minneapolis: Fortress, 1992–2003. The three volumes are subtitled *The New Testament and the People of God*; *Jesus and the Victory of God*; and *The Resurrection of the Son of God*. Always a pleasure to read, Wright, the Bishop of Durham in the United Kingdom, is one of the most prolific and engaging New Testament scholars today, keenly appreciative of the evangelical tradition of the church.

Shorter Studies of Jesus

The following is a small sample of the many books on Jesus accessible to the nonspecialist. They reflect quite different methodological and theological perspectives:

Allison, Dale C. *Jesus of Nazareth: Millenarian Prophet*. Minneapolis: Fortress, 1998.

Bockmuehl, Markus. *This Jesus: Martyr, Lord, Messiah*. Downers Grove, IL: InterVarsity, 1994.

Borg, Marcus. *Meeting Jesus Again for the First Time: The Historical Jesus and the Heart of Contemporary Faith*. San Francisco: Harper, 1995.

Borg, Marcus, and N. T. Wright. *The Meaning of Jesus: Two Visions*. San Francisco: Harper, 1999.

Burridge, Richard A., and Graham Gould. *Jesus Now and Then*. Grand Rapids: Eerdmans, 2004.

Crossan, John Dominic. *Jesus: A Revolutionary Biography*. San Francisco: Harper, 1995.

Herzog, William R., II. *Jesus, Justice, and the Reign of God: A Ministry of Liberation*. Louisville: Westminster John Knox, 2000.

McClymond, Michael J. *Familiar Stranger: An Introduction to Jesus of Nazareth*. Grand Rapids: Eerdmans, 2004.

Pope-Levison, Priscilla, and John R. Levison. *Jesus in Global Contexts*. Louisville: Westminster John Knox, 1992.

Senior, Donald C. P. *Jesus: A Gospel Portrait*. Mahwah, NJ: Paulist, 1992.

Soelle, Dorothee, and Luise Schottroff. *Jesus of Nazareth*. Louisville: Westminster John Knox, 2002.

Stein, Robert H. *Jesus the Messiah: A Survey of the Life of Christ*. Downers Grove, IL: Inter-Varsity, 1996.

———. *The Method and Message of Jesus' Teachings*. Revised edition. Louisville: Westminster John Knox, 1994.

Wright, N. T. *Who Was Jesus?* Grand Rapids: Eerdmans, 1993.

Yancey, Philip. *The Jesus I Never Knew*. Grand Rapids: Zondervan, 1995.

Jewish Studies of Jesus

Flusser, David. *Jesus*. Translated by R. Steven Notley. Jerusalem: Magnes, 1997.

Fredriksen, Paula. *Jesus of Nazareth, King of the Jews*. New York: Vintage, 1999.

Vermes, Geza. *Jesus the Jew: A Historian's Reading of the Gospels*. Minneapolis: Fortress, 1981.

———. *The Religion of Jesus the Jew*. Minneapolis: Fortress, 1993.

2

Development of Jesus Traditions

S EVERAL YEARS AGO I spent half a year in Israel and the Occupied Territories (the West Bank). I was fascinated by the work of archeologists,
by the skill with which they meticulously dig down through the layers of
accumulated debris that time and events have deposited. Often the surface
gives an indication that underneath might lie the leftovers of an important
past. Using archeology as a metaphor for beginning our study of Jesus, we
will begin in this chapter from the present and dig down through the layers
of history on our way to the bedrock of the first century.

Surface

We begin by observing a highly diverse "surface," a wide variety of views of
Jesus informed by personal taste and conviction, but also by church traditions
and theology, by the results of scholarship informed by academic research,
by geography, race, class, gender, and politics. We find recognizable religious
traditions, from orthodox and mainline Christianity to charismatic renewal
movements and Pentecostalism. But we also find species of piety that do
not easily fit any of these categories or that run right through them, such
as so-called liberation theologies, whether black or feminist, and New Age
religious movements. Given that Christianity is a truly global phenomenon,

25

Chart 1
Development of Jesus Traditions
An "Archeological" Exploration

Surface _

surface marked by great **diversity** due to multiple factors: movements and personalities, both present and past

Enlightenment (18th century)
the rise of modernity (rise of critical scholarship)

Reformation (16th century)
diversification of Christian community; growth of interest in Bible and diversity of traditions of biblical interpretation

The Great Creeds (4th and 5th centuries)
Nicea and Chalcedon
Trinitarian identification of Jesus as part of the Godhead; became the lens through which most Christians have viewed Jesus, even if critically

Canon of the New Testament (2nd to 4th centuries)
Apparent unity of the canon also preserves a remarkable diversity of traditions and perspectives

Development of New Testament Writings (1st and 2nd centuries)

(For an elaboration of the last item please see chart 2 on page 31, Written Sources Related to Jesus.)

a consequence of missionary efforts in the early decades and centuries, later aided by imperial and colonial aspirations of Western powers, perceptions and veneration of Jesus are strongly marked by geographical and cultural diversity.

The Jesus who is so diversely studied, believed in, prayed to, and sometimes followed seems hardly to be the one and the same Jesus. And yet, all of these Jesuses stem in one way or another, to a greater or lesser degree, from the Jesus who once lived in Palestine. To unearth that Jesus, to continue the archeological metaphor, would thus require not one probe, but many. What we would discover, however, is that the deeper we dig the closer the probes come to each other. However strenuous the effort to get to the Jesus who actually existed, we must humbly acknowledge that this is only one probe among many that could be undertaken. Such humility should not, even so, make us shy of digging down as far as we can.

Enlightenment

On the way to digging down through the layers of history we would find many important artifacts, representing events, struggles, and movements, such as, for example, the Enlightenment of the seventeenth and eighteenth centuries in Europe. The Enlightenment represented the birth of critical thinking free of church control, sometimes hostile to the Christian religion. The shape of the present debate over the historical Jesus owes much to the questions the Enlightenment first raised about the nature of historical enquiry, about the nature of the biblical writings (e.g., should they be subjected to the kind of historical enquiry directed at other ancient writings?), about the possibility of miracles (e.g., is it possible for a dead man to live again?), and, most fundamentally, about what "God" means and how that explains Jesus.

Reformation

As we dig down we begin to unearth the artifacts of the Reformation of the sixteenth century. For the study of Jesus, the Reformation and the preceding Renaissance represent two very important things: the breaking up of monolithic Christendom and renewed interest in the Bible itself, aided and abetted by renewed competence in the biblical languages of Greek and Hebrew and Johannes Gutenberg's invention of movable type.

It is difficult to overestimate the importance of access to the Bible to believer and scholar alike for our understanding of Jesus. While representing the breakup of Christendom and opening the way for the mushrooming of denominations and movements, the Reformation and its aftermath represented also the democratizing of the study of and belief in Jesus. Just as important, it raised, especially among some of the marginal movements of the larger Reformation, the critical importance of following Jesus practically, spawning radical attempts to shape individual and communal life in accordance with what was believed to be Jesus's teaching (e.g., Anabaptists, Quakers, early Methodists).

Without direct access to the Bible in everyday language, such developments are hardly imaginable, let alone explicable. In short, the Reformation and its attending events and movements put the story (or stories) of Jesus into the hands of the masses. As in the first century, this would have profoundly unsettling consequences for entrenched interests, whether cultural, political, or religious.

Creeds

As we continue our dig through a millennium of church history preceding the Reformation, we encounter the birth of religious orders, mystical movements, and countless groups and individuals persecuted for their desire to follow Jesus. We meet the likes of Thomas of Kempen, Peter Chelcicky, Jan Huss, Peter Waldo, Julian of Norwich, Meister Eckhart, Francis of Assisi, Martin of Tours, to name only a few of the illustrious and significant persons who influenced the way that people have come to think about Jesus.

Our interest spikes when we dig down to the fifth and fourth centuries. Here we find a rich deposit that helps to explain much of subsequent developments regarding the understanding of Jesus. We unearth the great creeds, most notably and famously those formulated at the Council of Chalcedon in 451 CE and more than a hundred years earlier at the Council of Nicea in 325 CE.

A word of background: by the time the Emperor Constantine the Great called the council at Nicea in 325, some significant changes had come about in the church and its relation to the world around it. Shortly after Constantine's so-called conversion in 312, the Christian religion was first tolerated and then became the official religion of the empire. Constantine could not abide disagreements in the new imperial religion, especially of a fundamental kind that threatened to tear apart the fabric of the newly established religion and thus of society. The most virulent controversies had to do with how to think about Jesus: was he divine or was he human, or perhaps both?

The emperor demanded that the leaders of the church settle the issue and come to a formulation on which they could agree. The Council of Nicea in 325 CE developed such a formulation, or creed, quoted here in the amended form approved at Council of Constantinople in 381 CE:

> We believe in one God the Father Almighty, Maker of all things visible and invisible; and in one Lord Jesus Christ, the only begotten of the Father, that is, of the substance of the Father, God of God, light of light, true God of true God, begotten not made, of the same substance with the Father, through whom all things were made both in heaven and on earth; who for us and our salvation descended, was incarnate, and was made human, was crucified also for us under Pontius Pilate, suffered and was buried; and the third day rose again according to the Scriptures. And ascended into heaven, sits at the right hand of the Father, and shall come again with glory to judge the living and the dead, of whose kingdom there shall be no end. And in the Holy Ghost.

The Council of Chalcedon in 451 CE expressed the same thoughts in similar form:

Our Lord Jesus Christ: the same perfect in divinity and perfect in humanity, the same truly God and truly man, of a rational soul and a body; consubstantial with the Father as regards his divinity, and the same consubstantial with us as regards his humanity; like us in all respects except for sin; . . . one and the same Christ, Son, Lord, only-begotten, known in two natures without confusion, change, division, or separation; . . . he is not parted or divided into two persons, but is one and the same only-begotten Son, God, Word, Lord Jesus Christ, just as the prophets taught from the beginning about him, and as the Lord Jesus Christ himself instructed us, and as the creed of the fathers handed it down to us.

Even if one has never heard of Nicea or Chalcedon, some of these phrases and ideas may sound quite familiar. They have left their mark on subsequent Christianity, distilling the concepts and defining the language with which Christians have talked and argued about Jesus.

The central interest lies in defining the relationship between Jesus and God, between Father and Son. Whereas Jesus is identified as being the "only-begotten son," vocabulary taken from the New Testament (e.g., Heb. 1:5; 5:5), we now have the further claim that he is "true God of true God, . . . of one substance with the Father." But this rather abstract assertion is related to the historical narrative of being born of Mary, of suffering under Pilate, and of rising on the third day. The creeds claim that Jesus *was* a man with a particular history, at a particular time, and in a particular place. They claim also that Jesus *is* an essential aspect of the Godhead. The Christian tradition since has, for the most part, continued to insist on both. That has sometimes made *theology* difficult, because it always has to contend with a person who lived at a particular time and place and who lived a certain way, wanting others to follow him. In short, *theology has had to contend with history*. It has also made history writing a nightmare for many Christians, since this is not just any man whose story we are telling but the second person of the Trinity. *History has had to contend with theology*.

These brief excerpts from the creeds show what is *not* stressed—Jesus's life and teachings—and thus the creeds exhibit a corresponding lack of emphasis on a central theme in the gospels, namely, following and imitating Jesus, called "discipleship" in some Christian traditions. Perhaps that is not what creeds are about. It is true that ethical issues, especially those pertaining to clergy, were spoken to in the canons (or rules) attached to what we read above. But what if correct belief *and* correct action—orthodoxy *and* orthopraxy—had been linked within the great creeds from the very outset, linked precisely at the point of defining the character and meaning of Jesus? What if they stated something like this: "We hold that to believe in Jesus Christ as 'true God of true God' means that we too must love our enemies and take up our own cross." What might "Jesus culture" have been like in the centuries that followed had the good bishops been willing to pick a fight with the emperor on the point of loving enemies, for example? Past and present are full of examples of orthodox—that is, right-believing and right-thinking—Christians who oppress the poor, hold slaves, go to war, and even persecute other Christians. Even traditions that stress the Bible's authority over the creeds travel, for the most part, much the same road.

The point is not to take issue with what the creeds affirm so much as to point out what has *not* been considered central to them. This has often led to a tension, if not outright opposition, between those who stress Jesus's life and teaching as relevant to ethics and who often see the creeds as a distraction or even an impediment to following Jesus practically and those who, on the basis of the creedal traditions of the church, place the emphasis on Jesus's atoning death and who define his identity as divine. This is a tension that also afflicts contemporary Jesus research, notably in the widespread suspicion that the church with its doctrines has obscured the radical this-worldly ethics of a Palestinian sage and prophet. It is a tension the writers of the New Testament would not have recognized.

New Testament Canon

As archeologists we want to keep scratching and digging, not least because our interest has been piqued by references in the creeds to Jesus, the prophets, and the Scriptures. The formulators of the creeds quite consciously intended to summarize, clarify, and crystallize something prior, namely, the tradition of the apostles as captured in the New Testament. So, as we dig deeper, we encounter a treasure trunk we call the New Testament canon (to be distinguished from the church canons mentioned above).

The word *canon* literally means "rule, standard, or measure," a criterion by which one tests, evaluates, and accredits something. The process of accrediting writings as Holy Scripture is called "canonization." Documents from the first century of the church's existence came to be included in the Scriptures of the church, based on such criteria as apostolic authorship, consistency with apostolic teaching, and proven use within church worship. The word *canon* has come to refer more commonly to the collection of approved biblical documents itself.

The process of canonization was a long one, some two hundred years or more of sometimes acrimonious sifting and sorting before the lid on the trunk was closed, to continue our metaphor. The process was, to put it mildly, dynamic and organic. Strewn about the vicinity of the trunk are documents and pieces of document—gospels, letters, and apocalypses—that were not placed into the canonical box. By the middle of the fourth century the debate about what should go into it had subsided, and a consensus was established.

We have thus finally arrived at the earliest sources of information on Jesus. We have a treasure box containing the earliest documents dealing with Jesus. This should now settle all arguments—right? Hardly, because, as chapter 1 already indicated, when we open the treasure box we find *four* gospels. We also find letters, all of which talk about Jesus as the Christ but seldom in the way we see done in the gospels. Within the canonical box we also find a very strange document called the Apocalypse or Revelation of John, which depicts Jesus as a lamb and a lion or as a fierce warrior apparently engaged in a final cosmic battle with the forces of evil, whose victory is won through his own death.

Digging inside the Canon

So, as archeologists we have our work cut out for us, even once we have dug down to the prize find. As we begin to explore the contents of the trunk, we discover many things that have a significant impact on our study of Jesus.

Chart 2
Written Sources Related to Jesus

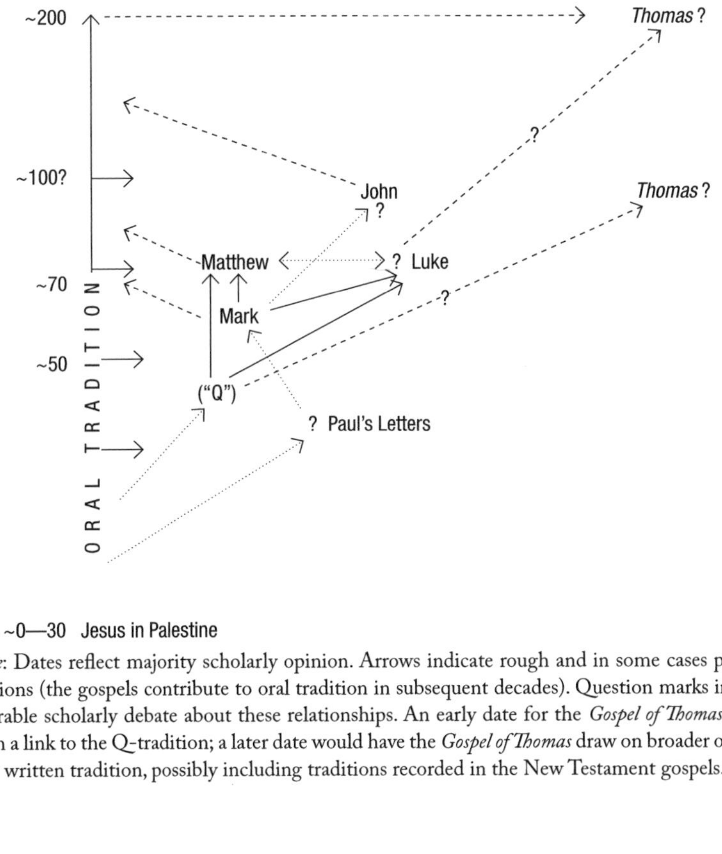

~0—30   Jesus in Palestine

Note: Dates reflect majority scholarly opinion. Arrows indicate rough and in some cases possible connections (the gospels contribute to oral tradition in subsequent decades). Question marks indicate considerable scholarly debate about these relationships. An early date for the *Gospel of Thomas* would establish a link to the Q-tradition; a later date would have the *Gospel of Thomas* draw on broader oral and perhaps written tradition, possibly including traditions recorded in the New Testament gospels.

Four Gospels

We find four documents that are called "gospels." Each of them carries a superscription such as "The Gospel according to Matthew." The others are ascribed to Mark, Luke, and John. The superscriptions look very much like they were not part of the gospels themselves, so we are safe to think of the gospels, strictly speaking, as anonymous. They likely did not stay that way for long.

We speak typically of *gospels* (plural). The superscriptions should remind us that the evangelists (i.e., the writers of the gospels) and those who pre-served their writings and added the superscriptions would have been happier if we spoke of a "fourfold gospel." They would have insisted that they were each in their own way telling the one story, the one gospel. They recognized that the only gospel that counts is that "of" Jesus Christ, both in the sense that Jesus is the center of the good news, but also in that he is the ultimate proclaimer of the *euangelion* that God's kingdom is becoming reality. With that in mind, and over their protestations, we will follow common practice and refer to their writings as gospels.

What is a gospel? When we open the ones we find in the New Testament, they appear to be a story, a narrative depicting the high points of Jesus's brief life, but also his teachings and deeds. While they are similar to a biography, they seem to have a purpose well beyond telling the story of Jesus. They seem to want to tell not only *about* Jesus, what he said and did, notably about his death and resurrection, but *why* Jesus matters. They are similar in some ways to ancient lives of famous people (*bios*, to use the ancient term), but they have an obvious intention to preach, to persuade the reader of the world-altering importance of Jesus. They are called, not inappropriately, "good news" (*euangelion*, to use the Greek term), a favorite way that early followers of Jesus talked about their proclamation (*kerygma*) of Jesus as the Messiah.

One of the first surprises we encounter is that the gospels are found close to the top of the pile of documents we find in the box, to continue our ar-cheological metaphor. This means that they were written *after* Paul's letters that tell us next to nothing of Jesus's acts and words. Might we not have expected the opposite? Would not the *earliest* writings contain many more reminiscences of Jesus sayings and miracles? Is it not more likely that through the years Jesus's significance would be distilled into some central doctrinal convictions, highlighting the importance of Good Friday and Easter?

We might also wonder why there are four gospels. Given how long the process of selection took, we might have expected the church to sift more thoroughly and to preserve one narrative. Who were the four different au-thors? Did they know each other? Did they rely on each other's accounts? Apparently several of them did. The gospels of Matthew, Mark, and Luke are quite similar, setting them apart from John. But what sets these gospels apart from each other? Did these writers have different agendas? Or might the authors have had different sources of information? These are just a few tantalizing questions that have been occupying scholars for centuries.

Oral Tradition(s)

As we sit around the trunk at the bottom of our archeological dig and compare these gospels with each other, we very quickly suspect that these authors drew on memories, stories, and reminiscences and maybe even written sources that *preceded* their written records. In other words, they themselves seem to have done some digging!

We often refer to this prewritten material as "oral tradition." Our metaphor of archeology is being stretched somewhat, since in this case we have nothing to scrape at. We infer only from the nature of the texts we have in hand that their authors utilized traditions that were passed by word of mouth for some time before they were put into writing. As chart 2 indicates, we have to assume that this phenomenon of passing things on by word of mouth would have continued alongside the early production of written documents. People did not, of course, stop talking the moment when something was written down, especially in a time when the majority of people could not read and write. So, whereas oral tradition as a phenomenon continued for decades, even centuries, it very particularly marks the early decades of the church when many of the traditions about Jesus were passed on orally in unwritten form: controversy stories, miracle stories, teachings, and, of course, the crucially important story of Jesus's death and resurrection.

Who would have remembered such stories and passed them on, and for what purpose? We might think first of those followers of Jesus who knew themselves to have been entrusted with spreading the news about Jesus in the years after his departure—the apostles (literally "sent ones"). These folks, many of whom were no doubt Jesus's former companions, were missionaries and pastors; they were decidedly not archivists. While we must be careful not to overstress this point, we also must take it into account. The raw data the evangelists had at their disposal were not neutral reminiscences or archival records. They were more likely stories, teachings, and sayings of Jesus that were, at the risk of oversimplification, recalled for two purposes. The first was the need to remember and to recount the teachings and deeds of Jesus in order to give guidance to groups of Jesus followers, no doubt often urgently needing answers to pressing problems. The second was to persuade others to join the community of believers in Jesus. Our four gospels are thus called good news—news intended to be heard and passed on.

We should not think only of early leaders, including former companions and students of Jesus. No doubt the movement spread through the witness of countless ordinary followers of Jesus as well. And who would most naturally tell and retell stories of Jesus reaching out to outcasts such as lepers and demoniacs, befriending prostitutes and tax collectors, and taking care of the hungry, if not those on the margins themselves? So when we speak of oral tradition, we should not have in mind a club of accredited oral-tradition experts, archivists, or historians, but rather people telling the stories of their own experiences and those of others in conversations, in gathered worship settings, and also in witnessing to their neighbors, friends, and opponents. Especially prominent among them were no doubt eyewitnesses who may well include those persons remembered by name in the gospels.

Some scholars consider semiliterate societies like Jesus's to have been very good at memory and faithful recollection. They view oral tradition as remarkably trustworthy at preserving authentic materials. Perhaps scholarship has been too quick to judge oral tradition by present-day abilities at retention and communication, aided as they are by technology. Today we rely almost completely on written, photographic, or electronic records of what needs to be preserved.

One important factor, however, should make us a bit cautious about overstressing this point: early followers of Jesus were not interested in simply preserving the past; they believed themselves to be in direct communication with a presently living divine master who continued to communicate with them through the Holy Spirit. Moreover, this Jesus who communicated through the Spirit was eagerly expected to appear again as judge and liberator. They called being in touch with this risen and exalted Messiah "prophecy." We can well imagine that this makes it often difficult for a historian to adjudicate the historical reliability of the oral tradition about Jesus.

To repeat, early witnesses were not simply reminiscing; they told stories about Jesus and recalled his teachings for a purpose. They intended to evangelize, to let people know of the good news of Jesus. They also intended to give guidance for how to live, whether to individuals seeking to follow Jesus or to communities seeking to order communal life in such a way as to conform to Jesus's way. That too has left its traces all over the tradition.

Early Written Sources: The Case of Q

Carefully comparing the existing gospels with each other suggests that, in addition to oral traditions, the gospel writers utilized written sources. Even a quick look at illustration 2.2 suggests that Matthew, Luke, and John could easily have used Mark. A majority of scholars think that they did, especially Matthew and Luke. That is one reason for calling them Synoptic Gospels. But close comparison of the first three gospels also shows that Matthew and Luke quite often agree word for word with each other where they have no relation to Mark.

The most widely held, although not unanimous, explanation is that Luke and Matthew were both dependent on Mark and also on a written source to which Mark may not have had access. The material that Matthew and Luke uniquely share consists almost exclusively of things Jesus *said*. The Christmas story does not count in this case since Matthew and Luke each have a rather distinct version, as we shall see. In the minds of many scholars, there must have been some earlier written source that consisted of a collection of Jesus's teachings. German scholars dubbed this collection Q, the first letter of the German word *Quelle*, which means "source." This hypothetical document has retained that nickname ever since.

Serious doubts about Q persist among a significant minority of scholars. The overlap between Matthew and Luke can be explained by borrowing, e.g., Matthew from Luke. Or perhaps there was a variety of collections of tradition, some written, some not. The majority of scholars believe, however, there to have been such a written collection of Jesus's sayings, a position I see no reason to challenge, even if one should always be wary of any claims to certainty.

Here is where things get interesting. We might be content to leave Q as a symbol for what looks like shared written material unique to Matthew and Luke. We should be very cautious, however, about claiming to know all the contents of such a hypothetical written source or about what the views of the author of this hypothetical document might have been. Since we "see" it only in the overlap between Matthew and Luke, we cannot know the extent of Q. Perhaps we see only the tip of the iceberg. Maybe Mark also contains some Q material that we cannot see, since Matthew and Luke both use so much of Mark. Humility about how much we can know would seem to be the wise approach in the case of Q.

More recently, however, some scholars have claimed to know a great deal about Q and the views of Jesus that gave it shape. They treat Q as a complete gospel. This has enormous implications. Matthew, Mark, Luke, and John all combine Jesus's sayings and deeds with an account of his death and resurrection. *If* Q existed and *if* the overlapping similarities unique to Matthew and Luke are the full extent of Q (big "ifs," indeed), then we have some basis for proposing that *some* early followers of Jesus believed in him not as a dying and rising messiah, but as a teacher and revealer of truth. Jesus may well have healed people and the Romans may well have executed him, but his deeds and his death were of little if any significance to the author(s) of Q and those whose views it reflects.

Most scholars who believe that Q actually existed date it roughly at mid-first century CE. That is also when Paul was writing his letters. For him the death, resurrection, and return of Jesus were the essence of why Jesus matters. Do we then see here a "clash of gospels" between Q and Paul at the very beginning of the Jesus movement, a clash of two very different ways of understanding, confessing, and proclaiming Jesus? The New Testament gospels would then, interestingly, represent a combination of these two once-distinct approaches, combining traditions about Jesus's teachings and deeds with traditions about his death and resurrection.

A question emerges: supposing there really was such a document as Q, is it possible that it gives us a more accurate picture of what Jesus was really like than do the four canonical gospels? Such is, roughly, the claim made by those who speak not of a Q-source, but of a Q-gospel. They suggest that the evangelists, following Mark's lead, took up the traditions of Jesus as a sage and wonder worker, as we find them collected in Q, and fused them with Paul's emphasis on a dying and rising Savior. In the process, the gospel genre we now find in the New Testament emerged, and with it the Jesus we encounter in the New Testament. We should wonder whether the thin ice of a hypothetical document, the extent or stand-alone significance of which no one can do more than guess at, can bear the full weight of this theory.

Two-Source Hypothesis

If we employ the Q hypothesis and, along with a majority of scholars, hold the Gospel of Mark to be the earliest of the Synoptic Gospels, then the relationship of Matthew, Mark, and Luke to each other can be summarized as the two-source hypothesis (see illustration 2.3). If, as some scholars suggest, Matthew and Luke each had another source available to them, their relationship could be called a four-source hypothesis ("M" stands for Matthew's special source, and "L" for Luke's).

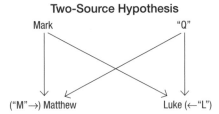

Digging around the Periphery of the Canon

Noncanonical Gospels

Digging down to where we have found the canonical box, we would also have encountered other documents called gospels, some of which have become quite famous as of late. For example, the so-called *Infancy Gospel of Thomas* figures in Anne Rice's 2005 novelization of Jesus's early life (*Christ the Lord: Out of Egypt*). The *Gospel of Mary*, a late-second-century gnostic document in which Jesus reveals to Mary Magdalene the divine mystery, figures improbably in Dan Brown's *Da Vinci Code*. Most recently, just before Easter 2006, the National Geographic Society published the *Gospel of Judas*, another second-century gnostic writing. After having been discovered several decades earlier, it languished in dealers' bank vaults, falling prey to the ravages of time and greed. In its fragmentary state it nevertheless presents a fairly clear portrayal of a conversation between Jesus and his disciples, in particular Judas. Much as in the case of Mary in the gospel named after her, Jesus reveals to Judas secret wisdom, predicting that he will play the central role of "saving" Jesus from his corporeal existence by handing him over to his enemies. "You will sacrifice the man that clothes me," Jesus tells Judas. In this document Judas is clearly Jesus's favored disciple—and not the epitome of treachery. We should expect that this newly discovered and published gospel will tell us more about second-century gnostic believers in Jesus than about either Jesus or Judas.

More relevant to the traditions recorded in the canonical gospels are the *Gospel of Peter*, a little-known second-century document quite possibly containing very early traditions of Jesus's death and resurrection, and the so-called *Secret Gospel of Mark*, claimed to have been discovered by now-deceased New Testament scholar Morton Smith in a monastery in the Judean desert in 1958. A small fragment, it describes Jesus's raising of a young man from the dead, reminiscent of the raising of Lazarus in John 11, and Jesus's subsequent initiation of the youth into the "mystery of the kingdom of God." Arguments persist as to whether this is a fragment of an early version of what we know as the Gospel of Mark or whether it is a clever forgery.

Gospel of Thomas

The most significant of these noncanonical writings is the *Gospel of Thomas*, not least because it is one of the main supports for treating the hypothetical Q as a gospel. As chart 2 shows, there is little agreement among scholars on when to date the *Gospel of Thomas* or, for that matter, what importance to give it. Some date it late in the second century, others at the same time the New Testament gospels were written, late in the first century.

What is at stake? First, unlike Q, the *Gospel of Thomas* is not a hypothetical document. It really does exist. It purports to be a record of Didymus Judas Thomas, believed in some circles to be the twin brother of Jesus, of the "hidden" (literally "apocryphal") sayings that the living Jesus spoke and that Thomas wrote down. Second, like the hypothetical Q, this gospel is a collection of 114 *logoi* ("sayings") of Jesus, a good number of which, such as some parables, have parallels in the canonical tradition. But it is without a discernable structure, order, or story line. This is significant. Jesus's birth, ministry, death, resurrection, and his coming again as judge and savior are absent. The implied claim about Jesus is that he is important as a revealer of secret wisdom, or raiser of consciousness, as we might say today. Jesus is a divine savior, but not because he gives his life for humanity on the cross or because he has defeated the powers of death through his resurrection or because he will usher in the kingdom of God when he comes again. He saves by revealing the truth, by awakening the consciousness of believers about who they are, from whence they have come, and to where they will return, thereby freeing them from the shackles of numbing ignorance, as seen in these quotations (from Patterson and Meyer, "Scholars' Translation"):

> Jesus said, "Those who seek should not stop seeking until they find. When they find, they will be disturbed. When they are disturbed, they will marvel, and will reign over all." (*Gospel of Thomas* 2)

> Jesus said, . . . "When you know yourselves, then you will be known, and you will understand that you are children of the living Father. But if you do not know yourselves, then you live in poverty, and you are the poverty." (*Gospel of Thomas* 3)

The theme of "knowing yourself" is familiar from Greek philosophy. While some sayings are very similar to those found in the canonical gospels (e.g., the parable of the sower and the seed in *Gospel of Thomas* 9), other sayings are extremely obscure:

> The disciples said to Jesus, "Tell us, how will our end come?" Jesus said, "Have you found the beginning, then, that you are looking for the end? You see, the end will be where the beginning is. Congratulations to the one who stands at the beginning: that one will know the end and will not taste death." (*Gospel of Thomas* 18)

The emphasis on enlightenment runs parallel with a sense that material, embodied existence is part of the poverty, leading to what is likened to being in a drunken stupor:

> Jesus said, "I took my stand in the midst of the world, and in flesh I appeared to them. I found them all drunk, and I did not find any of them thirsty. My soul ached for the children of humanity, because they are blind in their hearts and do not see, for they came into the world empty, and they also seek to depart from the world empty. But meanwhile they are drunk. When they shake off their wine, then they will change their ways." (*Gospel of Thomas* 28)

> Jesus said, "If the flesh came into being because of spirit, that is a marvel, but if spirit came into being because of the body, that is a marvel of marvels. Yet I marvel at how this great wealth has come to dwell in this poverty." (*Gospel of Thomas* 29)

Jesus said, "How miserable is the body that depends on a body, and how miserable is the soul that depends on these two." (*Gospel of Thomas* 87)

One might get the impression that the point of some of these sayings is to confuse and bewilder. But, as in much gnostic literature (*gnosis* = "knowledge"), such bewilderment is intended to serve true enlightenment.

The question of the date of the *Gospel of Thomas* takes on central importance in relation to Q. Those who hold to the Q-gospel hypothesis (as opposed to simply a Q-source, the extent of which we do not know), usually also hold to an early date for the *Gospel of Thomas*. That is because both the *Gospel of Thomas* and Q are collections of sayings with no interest in Jesus's birth, life, death, and resurrection. So, an early date for the *Gospel of Thomas*, roughly at the same time as the composition of the canonical gospels, and a theory of Q as a complete gospel tend to go together and reinforce each other.

Others, in my view more persuasively, consider the *Gospel of Thomas* to be a second-century document that recasts traditions, including some we also find in the canonical gospels, in keeping with a gnostic view of Jesus as a gnostic revealer. While such scholars may believe that a source of sayings called Q may best explain the non-Markan overlap between Matthew and Luke, they also typically reject the hypothesis of a *Thomas*-like Q-gospel.

One important caution: it is important not to confuse the two documents. The *Gospel of Thomas* exists; we have copies of it. Q is a hypothetical document, whose existence and extent is debated. The two are related in the scholarly debate chiefly because the actual existence of the *Gospel of Thomas* lends some support to the hypothesis that Q was a gospel in its own right and gives evidence of a community for whom Jesus was important as a revealer of divine wisdom.

To return to our archeological metaphor, we can perhaps now better understand why there is so much controversy down our archeological shaft and why the noise of debate and argumentation gets louder the closer we come to the time when Jesus himself walked the highways and back roads of Palestine. The noise is not likely to subside soon, if ever.

Josephus

All the sources for our study of Jesus mentioned so far share the belief that Jesus is the Christ, however differently they might understand that confession. In digging for evidence of Jesus outside the New Testament we also come upon the works of a Jewish historian of that time named Flavius Josephus. He was a general in the Jewish army in Galilee who defected to the Roman side during the Jewish war against Rome in 66–70 CE. He went to Rome and subsequently spent much of the rest of his life writing voluminously about Jewish traditions and history. Josephus is relevant to the study of Jesus not because he has much to say about Jesus—he does not, even though he was a contemporary of the gospel writers—but because he has so much to say about first-century Judaism.

There are two brief mentions of Jesus in his famous *Jewish Antiquities*. One is found in a retelling of the death of James, who is referred to as "the brother of Jesus who is called Christ" (*Jewish Antiquities* 20.9.1 §200). This tells us little if anything about Jesus, other than that Josephus appears to know about him. The other reference is more extensive:

> At this time there appeared Jesus, a wise man, *if indeed one should call him a man*. For he was a doer of startling deeds, a teacher of people who received the truth with pleasure. And he gained a following both among many Jews and among many of Greek origin. *He was the Messiah*. And when Pilate, because of an accusation made by the leading men among us, condemned him to the cross, those who had loved him previously did not cease to do so. *For he appeared to them on the third day, living again, just as the divine prophets had spoken of these and countless other wondrous things about him*. And up until this very day the tribe of Christians, named after him, has not died out. (*Jewish Antiquities* 18.3.3 §§63–64, quoted from Meier, *Marginal Jew*, 1.60, emphasis added)

This text, known historically as the *Testimonium Flavianum* ("Flavius's Testimony"), played an important role in the history of Christianity, representing an outsider's validation of Christian belief in Jesus. This supposed testimony looks, on closer inspection, suspiciously like it was either redacted (i.e., edited) or interpolated (i.e., injected) in its entirety into Josephus's history of the Jewish people. Josephus's writings were, after all, preserved chiefly in Christian circles, and it is therefore not unimaginable that somebody wanted Josephus to validate Christian belief in Jesus. Most scholars today consider the passage authentic, but think it has been extensively altered to reflect core Christian beliefs (italic type in the quotation above indicates those parts of the *Testimonium* that are usually considered obvious additions by a Christian hand). So, whereas Josephus gives us no meaningful information directly regarding Jesus, he remains important as a source for helping to flesh out the picture of the world in which Jesus lived.

Interpreting the Data

Having surveyed briefly the variety of literature we have found in our "dig," it is accurate to say that the New Testament gospels represent the mother lode of information on Jesus. But what kind of sources are these gospels?

The Gospels as Historical Sources

What are the interpretive options for dealing with the complex data we have assembled, especially with respect to the primary sources for Jesus, the gospels? At the cost of oversimplifying the positions scholars hold, let me first identify the two options at opposite ends of the interpretive spectrum.

OPTION A: THE GOSPELS AS DIRECT LINKS TO JESUS

At one end of the spectrum, the gospels are viewed not only as an invaluable source of information on how early followers of Jesus viewed him, but also as a *direct link* to the pre-Easter Jesus. Many assumptions usually go with such a view. One of them is that eyewitnesses wrote down their reminiscences much earlier than most scholars assume or, if they were written later, that they are at least in direct dependence on *eyewitnesses* who preserved traditions very accurately. The creativity factor in the development of tradition is played down. Many within this line of interpretation also hold to a view of biblical inspiration that understands the Holy Spirit as exercising rather direct divine control over the memory and the recording of memory. In other words, because of the role of God in the process as revealer and overseer, the gospels provide us with historically accurate record.

There may well be good *scholarly* reasons for wondering whether majority opinion has been correct in dating the gospels as late as is normally held or whether scholars have been too skeptical of how reliable tradition, even oral tradition, can be in preserving history faithfully. All dating of ancient documents is more or less informed guesswork. No doubt the scholarly consensus will shift in the future. But it is important to acknowledge that in many instances the argument in favor of the reliability of the gospels as historical sources rests less on scholarly investigation than on religious or theological conviction.

OPTION B: THE GOSPELS AS QUESTIONABLE LINKS TO JESUS

At the other end of the spectrum scholars are deeply suspicious of the control that Christian theology has—and had!—over what we have been told about Jesus. As those who wish to get at the real (by which they mean historical) Jesus, they extend their suspicion to the gospels and their authors, who make no secret of their desire to proclaim and persuade persons to place their faith in Jesus.

Whereas option A would have us bore a hole directly to the gospels and there find the real Jesus of history, in option B we have an attempt to bore a hole to Jesus *through* the gospels, attempting to *get past* the witnesses. In other words, we have to get past the contaminating or at least obscuring effect of beliefs *about* Jesus that shape the gospels if we want to get to the real historical Jesus. This has a tendency to pit historical investigation against faith, the real Jesus against belief in him. A central assumption of this approach is a radical distinction, even disjunction, between Jesus and what his followers claimed about him. Encrusting what Jesus himself said, did, and believed, and impairing our access to him, are "laminated layers of development and interpretation," as John Dominic Crossan, a prominent member of the Jesus Seminar, puts it. The gospels are thus the best of sources (the only ones we really have) and the worst of sources (all of them are profoundly compromised as historical sources by belief in Jesus).

OPTION C: GOSPELS AS RELIABLE HISTORICAL LINKS TO JESUS

Many students of Jesus, including myself, locate themselves somewhere between these two polar-opposite approaches. They view the gospels as having come about in history, with all that implies for the role of memory, culture, worldview, and tradition. They share with their more skeptical colleagues the working assumption that one has to be able to read between the lines of the gospels, to read past or through the traditions about Jesus, the beliefs about him as savior and lord, all the while paying respectful and appreciative attention to the gospels themselves. But such scholars see no reason on historical grounds (even less on theological grounds) to question or even reject the possibility, even likelihood, of considerable continuity and consistency between the beliefs of Jesus and those of his followers. To put it crudely, Jesus had some sense of who he was and what he was about. His followers learned about that from him, even if it took Easter to get them to understand fully, and even if the impact of that experience unleashed considerable creativity in how they articulated their message. The very nature of the gospels suggests that his followers believed their proclamation to be of a piece with Jesus's own mission (e.g., Matt. 10 and Luke 10 on the sending out of the messengers).

For scholars to see such continuity between Jesus and the early church does not mean that they believe that Jesus and his early followers thought they were starting a new religion called Christianity. Early devotees of Jesus held that he was the long-hoped-for *Jewish* Messiah whose coming was ushering in the long-hoped-for renewal of the world. In other words, they believed they were witnessing the culmination, or at least the beginning of the culmination, of all that for which the people of God had been hoping for centuries; and they shared that good news with Jew and Gentile alike. To recognize continuity between Jesus and his followers also leaves room for the significant impact of the Gentile followers on the memory and recollection of Jesus.

Scholars who consciously share the faith of the writers of the New Testament not surprisingly take the accounts of Jesus's miracles seriously, even if they also recognize that the evangelists or the traditions they drew on may have embellished their accounts to the extent that it is difficult to tell where memory gives way to legend. Some scholars in this camp do not dismiss as legend such unusual phenomena as Jesus's birth of a virgin or of his resurrection, even if they are honest about the limits of historical investigation and verification when it comes to these aspects of the Jesus story. For these scholars, and I number myself among them, the interplay between scholarly investigation and theological conviction is much more complex than it is for either of the two polar opposites mentioned earlier.

The Toolbox for Sifting the Evidence

Scholars who believe that it is not only permissible but important to evaluate the traditions about Jesus for their historical value have developed many tools with which to sift through the material. The toolbox has become rather large. It includes anthropological and social scientific methods of analysis in order to answer questions on how ancient societies work and how individuals work within those societies. More specifically, what was Judaism like in the first century? What was the Roman occupation like? How would religious figures in the first century behave, or how would they be viewed?

Today scholars also apply sophisticated literary analysis to the gospels and the traditions they contain. What shaped the oral traditions in the process of transmission? How did writers exercise their craft in the first century? What is the literary character of the gospels? Answering questions such as these has helped us to develop a much greater appreciation for the creativity of the gospel writers and for the way in which they employed the oral and written traditions they inherited. While benefiting from such work, we will not in this book be able to explore many of these important avenues of study thoroughly.

Criteria of Authenticity or Historicity

As we rummage through the toolbox many Jesus scholars bring to their task, we come upon a set of tools that are of particular importance and notoriety, especially for the question of what in the gospels really goes back to Jesus. The discussion of oral tradition and the creative role of the evangelists (see the next chapter) will have prepared the ground for considerable understanding for why a historian will want to know how to evaluate the data. What did Jesus himself say? What did Jesus himself do? What actually happened to him? In the attempt to answer these questions, scholars have developed some special scalpel-like tools, called "criteria of authenticity." I will list only some of the best known and widely used of these criteria.

CRITERION OF DISSIMILARITY

The criterion of dissimilarity is on the lookout for ways in which Jesus was *unlike* his Jewish contemporaries and those who came to believe in him. It stipulates that, if there is a saying of Jesus that cannot be explained either as an invention of the church or as a common Jewish tradition, then it likely goes back to Jesus. To illustrate: it is highly unlikely that anyone would invent something as difficult and troubling as the statement: "Love your enemies!" (Matt. 5:44 || Luke 6:27). We might expect to find a more conventional: "Treat your enemies with respect!" But such counsel is widespread in the ancient world, in pagan and Jewish circles (see Paul's quotation of Prov. 25:21–22 in Rom. 12:20). Jesus's demand that people *love* their enemies exceeds anything they would want to invent for themselves. Not surprisingly, this saying is widely considered to be authentic even by the most skeptical of scholars.

This is a very sharp scalpel indeed. Many quite rightly think it cuts too deep. Surgery quickly becomes autopsy. It eliminates from our understanding of Jesus ways in which he would have been like his fellow Jews; it also blinkers out all the ways in which Jesus would have been like or agreed with his followers. We end up with a Jesus who fits neither the world out of which he came, in which he worked and attracted persons to himself, nor the community that was devoted to him. Why would anyone have cared about such a Jesus? Could anyone have made sense of him and of what he said and did? The use of this tool by itself is thus hardly adequate.

CRITERION OF MULTIPLE ATTESTATION

The second authenticity tool, the criterion of multiple attestation, stipulates that if one can find the same saying or deed attributed to Jesus in several different sources, especially different kinds of sources and different layers of tradition, confidence in its authenticity is greatly strengthened. In other words, if you have the same saying in Mark, Matthew, and Luke, you might explain Matthew and Luke simply as having borrowed it from Mark. But, if you find the same saying or similar saying in several different layers of tradition or documents that show no evidence of being dependent on each other, then it has a good chance of going back to Jesus—especially if it has survived the application of the first criterion as well. Both the first and second criteria are acid tests.

CRITERION OF COHERENCE

The third tool, the criterion of coherence, is largely dependent on the acid bath of the first two for its utility. Is a particular saying consistent with sayings we have determined elsewhere to be authentic? Is it coherent with what we have thus far distilled from the tradition as reliably authentic? If so, then we can add it to our collection of authentic sayings.

CRITERION OF PALESTINIAN COLORING

With the fourth criterion we are on the lookout for linguistic and cultural features that fit what we know of first-century Palestine. From very early on, people who believed in Jesus could be found just about anywhere in the Roman Empire, far beyond the Semitic world of first-century Palestine. Some of the gospels might well have been written far from Palestine. Mark's Gospel, for example, is often thought to have been written in Rome. If, in a document likely written outside of Palestine, we find features that clearly reflect rural Palestinian culture and language, then we might have an indication of authenticity or at least an indication that the tradition is very old.

CRITERION OF REJECTION AND EXECUTION

Several scholars propose that we should pay particular attention to the death of Jesus as a means of sorting out what goes back to Jesus. There is no doubt that Jesus died a very specific death: crucifixion. This was a manner of execution the Romans chose for political troublemakers. Moreover, the sources all agree that there was some sort of connivance on the part of Jewish authorities in bringing about Jesus's violent end. In other words, Jesus must have done something or said something for him to have met that kind of death. What sayings and deeds are attributed to Jesus that cohere with the kind of end he met?

CRITERION OF DOUBLE SIMILARITY/DOUBLE DISSIMILARITY

The criteria listed above, especially the first, give a sharp set of scalpels to those scholars who believe that the real Jesus emerges most clearly when we can distinguish him from his world and the world of his followers and who treat the sources accordingly. However, while virtually all scholars today employ these tools to one extent or another, many correctly no longer want to separate Jesus either from his Jewish milieu or from his followers, viewing the attempt itself as fatal to a historically useful representation of Jesus. In this view, signs in the gospels of Jesus's Jewishness count as evidence of authenticity, even if the gospels reflect a Jesus movement increasingly in tension with its Jewish roots. Just as much, points of contact between Jesus's words and deeds and the beliefs and manner of life of his followers count as evidence of authenticity and historicity, even if one needs to be cautious about imposing later Christian theology onto Jesus.

Noted British scholar N. T. Wright attempts to articulate this concern with his *criterion of double similarity/double dissimilarity*. Something can be reliably attributed to Jesus if it *both* fits the Jewish matrix of Jesus's activity *and* provides the basis of subsequent development of the community of his followers (hence "double similarity"), *but* is at the same time not simply identical with either (hence "double *dis*similarity"). In other words, Jesus was a Jew, through and through, regardless of how much he disagreed with fellow Jews about important topics like purity, law, temple, or the kingdom of God. Just as true, a community emerged that believed in Jesus, recalled his teachings, and attempted to emulate his own way of living in how they comported themselves. His followers learned from Jesus to love God, each other, and their enemies, to share their goods with each other, to establish communities where persons of low degree socially were valued, and more. The real Jesus has the best chance of being found at the intersection between those two sets of "facts." Whereas for the criterion of dissimilarity, similarity is the enemy of authenticity, here it is a condition of authenticity.

There are, of course, all kinds of ways in which one can criticize any and all of these criteria. Even so, the judicious use of these tools—even the acid bath of dissimilarity—has allowed certain characteristics of Jesus and his words and work to emerge clearly. Among these is the central emphasis on the kingdom of God or the importance of Jesus's teaching by means of parables. As much as the critical historical investigation of the sources has often introduced undue skepticism into the picture, it has also had a very profound and important positive effect on our appreciation of who Jesus was. In the process of helping us to make a distinction between Jesus and those who tell us about him, these tools have also often enhanced our appreciation of the creativity and insightfulness of the early witnesses, including the evangelists.

Conclusion

I conclude this chapter by making explicit the stance I take in this book. First, I treat the gospels as *historical documents*. I take them to have emerged in the real life of real communities existing in time and place. I see plenty of evidence in the gospels and in the rest of the New Testament of very active use and development of traditions of and about Jesus. To respect the historical nature of the development of traditions, and within that larger picture the historical nature of the gospels themselves, does not need to lead to a thoroughgoing skepticism about whether they provide access to the Jesus who actually existed.

Second, I believe it important to treat Jesus himself as a *historical person*, as a first-century Jew living in Palestine. His first followers were Jews; they experienced Jesus within the context of Jewish hopes, fears, and expectations. The authentic Jesus will be found only within that context.

I also believe, third, that it is important to look for continuity between Jesus and the traditions about him. It is often said that Jesus did not found the church, that he was not a Christian. That is obviously true. But that insight does not require the *assumption* that his followers betrayed Jesus in the very act of getting excited about him, living and dying for their belief in him.

That said, the primary interest in this book is not to argue with fellow scholars or to second-guess the sources in an attempt to reconstruct the real Jesus. It is to facilitate an encounter with the Jesus to whom the New Testament writers witness.

Key Terms and Concepts
canon
creeds
criteria of authenticity
Gospel of Thomas
oral tradition
Q
Trinitarian definition

For Further Reading

The dictionaries and encyclopedias and the major Jesus studies listed in chapter 1 all provide ample further reading on the topics raised in this chapter. In addition, see the following:

Bauckham, Richard. *Jesus and the Eyewitnesses: The Gospels as Eyewitness Testimony.* Grand Rapids: Eerdmans, 2006.

Dunn, James D. G. A New Perspective on Jesus: What the Quest for the Historical Jesus Missed. Grand Rapids: Baker Academic, 2005.

Funk, Robert W., Roy W. Hoover, and the Jesus Seminar. *The Five Gospels: The Search for the Authentic Words of Jesus.* New York: Macmillan, 1993.

Johnson, Luke Timothy. *The Real Jesus: The Misguided Quest for the Historical Jesus and the Truth of the Traditional Gospels.* San Francisco: HarperCollins, 1996.

Koester, Helmut. *Introduction to the New Testament,* vol. 2: *History and Literature of Early Christianity.* New York: de Gruyter, 1982.

Theissen, Gerd, and Annette Merz. *The Historical Jesus: A Comprehensive Guide.* Translated by John Bowden. Minneapolis: Fortress, 1996.

3

One Jesus—Four Gospels

A LL NEW TESTAMENT writers share the conviction that Jesus lived, died by crucifixion, and was raised from the dead. But if we want to have specific information of what Jesus said and did while living in Palestine we typically go to the gospels and their authors, the evangelists. What kind of sources are these gospels—histories, biographies, archival records, religious fiction? Nonspecialists are likely to read them as historical accounts, as small biographies of Jesus. Specialists are greatly divided as to how much actual historical information they offer, as already indicated in the previous chapter. The differences of opinion are occasioned by the very nature of the gospels as sources. In this chapter we will explore their nature and character more closely.

Nature and Character of the Gospels

Similarity and Diversity

Even a hasty reading of the New Testament gospels will have alerted you to several features. On the one hand, the first three gospels share roughly the same outline: Jesus begins his ministry in Galilee and then, after some time, goes to Jerusalem where he confronts the authorities, is killed, and is raised from the dead. These three very similar gospels are called the "Synoptic Gospels." But in the Fourth Gospel—the one ascribed to John—Jesus moves in and out of Jerusalem repeatedly, usually in some connection with the great Jewish annual festivals. Galilee figures as a place of refuge as much as a place of ministry. But, despite the distinctness of the Fourth Gospel, the central elements of death and resurrection in Jerusalem are present also.

For all their similarities, the Synoptic Gospels often differ exactly at those places where they share material. These similarities and differences may be seen in the Beatitudes, where Luke balances his beatitudes (blessings) with dire words of judgment:

Matthew 5:3–12	Luke 6:20–26
Blessed are the poor in spirit, for theirs is the kingdom of heaven.	Blessed are you who are poor, for yours is the kingdom of God.
Blessed are those who mourn, for they will be comforted.	Blessed are you who are hungry now, for you will be filled.
Blessed are the meek, for they will inherit the earth.	Blessed are you who weep now, for you will laugh.
Blessed are those who hunger and thirst for righteousness, for they will be filled.	Blessed are you when people hate you, and when they exclude you, revile you, and defame you on account of the Son of Man.
Blessed are the merciful, for they will receive mercy.	Rejoice in that day and leap for joy, for surely your reward is great in heaven; for that is what their ancestors did to the prophets.
Blessed are the pure in heart, for they will see God.	But woe to you who are rich, for you have received your consolation.
Blessed are the peacemakers, for they will be called children of God.	Woe to you who are full now, for you will be hungry.
Blessed are those who are persecuted for righteousness' sake, for theirs is the kingdom of heaven.	Woe to you who are laughing now, for you will mourn and weep.
Blessed are you when people revile you and persecute you and utter all kinds of evil against you falsely on my account. Rejoice and be glad, for your reward is great in heaven, for in the same way they persecuted the prophets who were before you.	Woe to you when all speak well of you, for that is what their ancestors did to the false prophets.

Similarities and differences may also be seen in the Lord's Prayer (see ch. 10): Matthew includes his Lord's Prayer in his Sermon on the Mount (Matt. 6:9–13), whereas in Luke it is not part of his version of the Sermon, the Sermon on the Plain, but Luke 11:2–4. Mark does not include the prayer at all, even though it is clear he knows of Jesus's instructions on prayer and forgiveness (Mark 11:25).

One last example: in recounting the Last Supper of Jesus with his followers, the Gospel of John says nothing about the wine and the bread, which play a central role in the rituals of Christianity, as seen in these quotations from the Synoptic accounts of the words of Jesus at the Last Supper (compare the [earlier?] tradition that the Apostle Paul rehearses in 1 Cor. 11:23–25):

Matthew 26:26–29	Mark 14:22–25	Luke 22:15–20
While they were eating, Jesus took a loaf of bread, and after blessing it he broke it, gave it to the disciples, and said, "Take, eat; this is my body." Then he took a cup, and after giving thanks he gave it to them, saying, "Drink from it, all of you; for this is my blood of the covenant, which is poured out for many for the forgiveness of sins. I tell you, I will never again drink of this fruit of the vine until that day when I drink it new with you in my Father's kingdom."	While they were eating, he took a loaf of bread, and after blessing it he broke it, gave it to them, and said, "Take; this is my body." Then he took a cup, and after giving thanks he gave it to them, and all of them drank from it. He said to them, "This is my blood of the covenant, which is poured out for many. Truly I tell you, I will never again drink of the fruit of the vine until that day when I drink it new in the kingdom of God."	He said to them, "I have eagerly desired to eat this Passover with you before I suffer; for I tell you, I will not eat it until it is fulfilled in the kingdom of God." Then he took a cup, and after giving thanks he said, "Take this and divide it among yourselves; for I tell you that from now on I will not drink of the fruit of the vine until the kingdom of God comes." Then he took a loaf of bread, and when he had given thanks, he broke it and gave it to them, saying, "This is my body, which is given for you. Do this in remembrance of me." And he did the same with the cup after supper, saying, "This cup that is poured out for you is the new covenant in my blood."

Instead, John includes something that the other gospels do not—Jesus's washing the feet of the disciples (John 13:1–20). John does have something like the tradition of the Last Supper in relation to his account of Jesus's feeding of the crowd (see esp. 6:51–58).

How should we explain these phenomena? Several possible explanations suggest themselves.

Jesus Said Things More Than Once in Different Ways

One obvious explanation might be that Jesus said things more than once, especially if he thought them important. Could it have been any other way? I know of no teacher or preacher who does not stress things through repetition. I know of no good teacher who does not also vary the way important things are said. We might then still ask whether the followers of Jesus remembered Jesus's words in exactly these various ways and committed them to memory verbatim. That strikes me as less than likely, even if the gospel writers and those they relied on wanted very much to relay the words of *Jesus* and not their own.

The Gospel Writers Employed Different Sources

A second explanation, as in the case of the Beatitudes, is that Matthew and Luke had two different sources, each of which reflects a diversity of teaching occasions or a diversity of how those words were remembered and passed on over the years. Perhaps we have found our answer, perhaps not. Such an explanation has a better chance in the case of the Christmas story, for example, which is missing in two of the gospels and quite different in the two that contain it. It seems a little less plausible in the cases where the gospel writers cite teachings of Jesus in an identical fashion, except for the occasional divergence of words or in cases where the words appear in different sequence (e.g., the Lord's Prayer).

The Tradition Was Passed on in More Than One Way

A third possibility is that the evangelists got their material from the same source(s) but adapted and edited them to suit their purposes. Every good communicator has a sense of his or her purpose in communicating and also a keen sense of his or her audience. Should we be surprised to find a similar dynamic in the writing of these gospels? The evangelists employed what we call "tradition." That makes it sound like the gospel writers were conservationists involved chiefly in preservation. Not quite. While the evangelists were no doubt interested in collecting and preserving, their writings were from the beginning engaged in proclaiming gospel, which is to say that their writings are good news and not archival records. News is shaped, then as now, by a complex mix of urgent information, audience interest, and creativity in communication.

All of the Above!

In the end we are safe to assume that all of the above are to varying degrees fitting explanations for what we find in the gospels. Good and important things are said more than once, even with some variation, and there is every reason to think that was true of Jesus; sayings and deeds are remembered variously by various and numerous witnesses, and there is every reason to think that this was true of the witnesses who contributed to the Jesus tradition(s); and important things are couched in ways to serve the interests and objectives of a particular writer addressing a particular audience, and there is every reason to think that was true of the gospel writers. To recognize this does not make it easy to know when and to what degree each of these explanations fits a particular set of texts. We seldom if ever know enough to make such judgments with certainty.

One more comment regarding audience: the New Testament gospels are news, even if news that has been well digested. News is by its very nature intended to be spread. Unlike the letters of Paul, for example, which are with some notable exceptions addressed to a particular local readership, the gospels are by their very nature literature to be disseminated, to be passed on. They are clearly gospel, meant to persuade those not yet believing in Jesus to do so. But they are surely also a rich collection of instruction for the many communities of Jesus's followers eager to know more, eager to shape their lives in accordance with their savior, teacher, and lord. While these are two quite different objectives, they nevertheless intersect at the point where a gospel writer wants the community of believers to get its witness and its life right. The faith and life of the church, then as now, is deeply related to the clarity and truthfulness of its witness to the surrounding world. We should be careful, then, not to define and limit the intended audience of these gospels too closely. We will never know with certainty how much the gospel writers assumed their readers were familiar with other gospels. We will never know how closely the views of the evangelists reflect the views of the communities out of which they came or to whom they were addressing their writing. We must assume, however, that the gospels and their authors were historically rooted, both reflecting and addressing, sometimes critically, the diversity of perspectives and agendas that marked the house churches, worship and prayer circles, and wandering missionaries in the first century of the Jesus movement.

Character of the Gospels

Given even just the very little we have already observed about the gospels, it would be difficult to make the claim that the evangelists were historians in a modern sense of the term. Today, historians are very much aware that they are conditioned by their own time, class, race, and gender. For the most part, however, they work hard at being objective, to use a very problematic term, not least so that their work can be evaluated and tested by others not conditioned by the same factors. That is what makes scholarship a collaborative and collegial enterprise, cutting across cultural and confessional lines.

The evangelists did not see their work in such terms. They were, after all, first and foremost evangelists or preachers of good news, not historians, let alone archivists. They were propagandists, in the best sense of the term. The raw material for writing their gospels consisted of the diverse testimonies of "eyewitnesses and servants of the word" (Luke 1:2), such as apostles, prophets, teachers, evangelists (Eph. 4:11), and the many unrecognized shapers of the oral tradition—evangelistic tellers and retellers of events, sayings, and encounters with Jesus. Such raw materials are reminiscences recalled in order to make Jesus real *today*—their "today." If that is true of the raw data the evangelists had at their disposal, it is just as true of their gospels. That does not mean, of course, that the evangelists were not interested in what happened. After all, the news they wrote is a *story*, the story of Jesus's life, work, death, and resurrection. They wrote a life of Jesus. Even if they did not do so in terms of modern biography, their way of presenting the life and teachings of Jesus did conform in some important ways to ancient biographies (*bios*). They wrote a *story* because they believed firmly that it is in the events, deeds, and words of *Jesus the man* from Nazareth that the significance of *Jesus the Christ* is to be found. We might therefore think of the gospels as a *fusion of sermon and biography*.

The Evangelists as Creative Writers

If we are correct in characterizing the gospels in this way, then they tell us a great deal not only about Jesus but also about the authors and the communities to which they were writing. In other words, we can see in the gospels the fingerprints of the early Christian carriers and shapers of the traditions about Jesus. The gospel writers themselves then also put their stamp on the material. It has become a very important part of New Testament scholarship to enquire about the perspectives of the gospel writers themselves, to pay attention to their style of writing and their theological perspective, to treat them as authors in their own right. We call this, rather clumsily, "redaction criticism."

The idea that the gospel writers themselves played a significant role in shaping the material is not a modern one, even if that insight has been developed to a highly sophisticated extent in our day. The great fourth-century church historian Eusebius refers to a second-century bishop named Papias on the origin of the Gospel of Mark. Defending the reliability and trustworthiness of Mark, Papias relates what he believes to be traditions that go back to the time of the writing of the gospel:

> Mark became the interpreter of Peter and he wrote down accurately, but not in order, as much as he remembered of the saying and doing of Christ. For he was not a hearer or a follower of the Lord but of Peter who adapted his teachings to the needs of the moment and did not make an ordered exposition of the sayings of the Lord. And so Mark made no mistake when he thus wrote down some things as he remembered them, for he made it his special care to omit nothing of what he heard and to make no false statement therein. (Papias in Eusebius, *Ecclesiastical History* 3.39.15)

This is an extremely interesting comment, even if we will want to be careful about the historical trustworthiness of Papias on the details of Mark's authorship and his reliance on the great Apostle Peter. Clearly people were aware of differences between these gospels, and it must have been troubling for some. So Papias defends the trustworthiness of the Gospel of Mark by insisting that Mark was *not* himself an eyewitness of Jesus. He was, rather, an interpreter of Peter, likely in his view Jesus's most important companion during his ministry in Galilee. Papias does *not* say that Mark sat down with Peter and learned exactly what happened when and where in the correct chronological sequence. Papias knows that Mark's sequence of events and teaching is not identical to that found in the other gospels. That does not trouble Papias. He imagines Mark as acquiring his information on Jesus from what he heard Peter preach or teach.

Here we have another important bit of information: according to Papias, Peter did not give a series of sermons on Jesus's life in biographical order, but rather "adapted" the teachings, as Papias puts it, to "the needs of the moment." In short, Mark derived his information about Jesus not by interviewing Peter the way a modern biographer might, but by interpreting his teachings that clearly did not have a biographical purpose. Papias implies that we should not demand of Mark's Gospel what neither Mark nor Peter were concerned to provide, namely, a strictly biographical rehearsal of Jesus's life.

A tantalizing passage within the New Testament, the famous prologue to the Gospel of Luke itself, helps flesh out this picture further:

> Since many have undertaken to set down an orderly account of the events that have been fulfilled among us, just as they were handed on to us by those who from the beginning were eyewitnesses and servants of the word, I too decided, after investigating everything carefully from the very first [or for a long time], to write an orderly account for you, most excellent Theophilus, so that you may know the truth concerning the things about which you have been instructed. (Luke 1:1–4)

First, Luke knows that "many" others have also set themselves the task of writing presentations of what Jesus did, said, and experienced and why it matters. This alone should alert us that the four gospels we have in the New Testament are not all the gospels that were written. We know of others, such as the later *Gospel of Thomas* and the *Gospel of Peter*, but we will never know how many "many" is.

Second, Luke refers to "eyewitnesses" and to "servants of the word." Might he be thinking, much like Papias does of Peter, of those who pass on the teachings and deeds of Jesus so as to serve the interests of the word as good news?

What makes Luke's account orderly? Is he a more careful biographer and chronicler than, say, Mark? Should we give pride of place to Luke as the trustworthy historian? Interestingly, the early church never felt compelled to understand Luke in this way. Or could it be that "orderly" has to do with how to write the story so that Theophilus might know the truth? In other words, might "orderly" have to do with getting the story right, *not* from a strictly biographical point of view, but from a theological or evangelistic point of view, in this case in order to persuade Theophilus of the truth about Jesus? Here, I believe, we are closer to the truth. This interpretation of "orderly" would conform to Papias's view that already Peter taught in response to "the needs of the moment." Luke, and with him the other gospel writers, wrote to respond in an orderly fashion to the needs, not of the moment, but of their audience(s).

Both Luke's and Papias's views anticipate those held by most scholars today, namely, that the biographical shape of the gospels is supplied in large measure by the gospel writers themselves. More, that biographical shape reflects the *theological* interests of the gospel writers as much or more than it does the life of Jesus. The one-year Galilee-to-Jerusalem sequence of the

Synoptics might then reflect the theological interests of the writers, who see Jerusalem as the location of the grand finale, the place of final struggle, death, and resurrection. The Gospel of John, on the other hand, has Jesus in and out of Jerusalem throughout a three-year ministry, connecting the great festivals with important discourses by Jesus. The order of events in the gospels may then not give us a great deal of biographical information, even if there is no reason to doubt on historical grounds that Jesus was from Nazareth in the Galilee, spent a good deal of his active ministry there, and died in Jerusalem.

If what we have just said is correct and respectful of the nature and character of the gospels, then we should want to pay close attention to the intentions, perspectives, and creativity of the gospel writers themselves. The evangelists are like artists: they want us to see what they see, but in the process infuse their subject with much of themselves. This book is not about the artists, to be sure. There are plenty of books that deal with the perspectives of the evangelists in great depth. Nevertheless, it is worth knowing something about the art of the evangelist so as to read the story of Jesus more intelligently and appreciatively.

Before going on to a brief consideration of the artists and their work of art, if we can refer to the evangelists and their gospels that way, we recall that all four gospels are anonymous. Strictly speaking, we do not know who wrote them. Early on, the church connected the gospels with certain persons: Matthew, Mark, Luke, and John. There may be historical validity to the ascriptions, but we cannot be certain. Whoever they were, the evangelists had distinctive voices and particular perspectives. We will refer to the authors by the names the tradition has ascribed to them.

In this chapter we want to get a sense of the character of each of the gospels, and the Jesus we encounter there. We are standing in a gallery, as it were, and are paying special attention to the artists through whom we come to know Jesus. So, for now let us pay attention to the brush strokes, the organizational features, and the particular perspectives of the evangelists *cum* artists. What follows are thumbnail sketches of the four gospels.

Profiles of the Gospels

Mark: Jesus—Suffering Prophet of the Kingdom

We begin first with the Gospel of Mark, by majority opinion the earliest of the gospels. Many students of the gospels think, correctly in my view, that Mark provided the pattern for at least Matthew and Luke. It is right, then, that we should begin with Mark. Most introductions to the New Testament date this gospel somewhere close to the catastrophic Jewish war against Rome in 66–70 CE. While one should never take majority opinion as equivalent to an assured result of scholarly enquiry, I see no reason to argue against the prevailing opinion on the date of the gospel. That says nothing about the age of the traditions the writer of Mark uses, to be sure. Many scholars think a good case can be made that the home of this gospel was Rome, but we cannot be sure. Since Matthew and Luke appear to have made use of Mark, we should assume it was quickly read well beyond the confines of Rome or any other community of believers in Jesus.

BIOGRAPHY OF A PROPHET

Especially if you have previously read the other gospels, or come to the reading of Mark after reading Matthew, you will be startled that Mark's Gospel does not begin with a Christmas story, but with an adult Jesus. After being briefly introduced by a prophetlike figure called John the "Baptizer" (or "Dipper"), Jesus appears on stage announcing the kingdom or reign of God. Were we first-century readers we would recognize Jesus himself to be a prophet—a prophet of the kingdom. And with that introduction, the reader is also alerted to a likely script for the drama. A biblical prophet is God's mouthpiece; prophets generate excitement with words of hope and deliverance; they also generate intense opposition and hostility with their words of confrontation and judgment. In the Bible prophets who speak truth from God can expect a turbulent life. That is very much how Mark presents Jesus.

Haste and Urgency

Given the script, we are not surprised to see the great urgency and haste that marks the first chapters of Mark. One storytelling device the evangelist employs is the repeated use of the small Greek word *euthys* ("immediately"). *Euthys* appears forty-one times in Mark, which is 80 percent of its occurrences in the New Testament (by comparison, Matthew uses the word five times, John three times, and Luke once). In Mark's first chapter alone, *euthys* appears eleven times (1:10, 12, 18, 20, 21, 23, 28, 29, 30, 42, 43; English translations vary the vocabulary for stylistic reasons and thereby obscure the deliberate repetitiveness of the style). Clearly Mark wants us to notice the urgency marking Jesus's activity.

Authority and Vulnerability

This note of haste is augmented by a strong emphasis on Jesus's authority. Jesus impresses the crowds as someone who acts and speaks with great authority (e.g., Mark 1:22, 27; 2:10). As readers we are meant to share Jesus's original audience's sense of wonder and awe at the power of God present in Jesus's words and deeds. The script may be that of a prophet, but we are given intimations that something more is at work in the words and deeds of Jesus. While the note of power and authority is strong in the narrative of

Jesus's actions and words, so is the note of vulnerability. His activities draw the charge that he is possessed and out of his mind (3:19b–30).

Popularity and Hostility

Haste and authority are accompanied by a growing popularity among the masses but also increasing hostility among the religious leadership. This mix of urgency, power and authority, and popularity and hostility is volatile chemistry. As readers, we quickly develop a sense of both anticipation and foreboding. This will not be a comfortable story to follow, nor will it have an easy and happy ending.

THE PROBLEM WITH POWER: THE MESSIANIC SECRET

The early chapters of Mark contain many acts of power, such as exorcisms and healings. Frequently, after important miracles (e.g., 1:44; 3:12; 5:43), Jesus tells people not to talk about what they have just seen or experienced. Of course, this command is usually highly ineffectual. After all, it is very difficult to keep under wraps the healing of a visible illness such as leprosy, deformation, or blindness. Everyone will notice that those once afflicted are now clean of a disease that kept them ostracized, as in the case of the skin disease the ancients called leprosy. Is Jesus then expecting the impossible? How should we understand his repeated orders to keep his identity secret?

The solution to this puzzle may not lie so much with Jesus as with the evangelist. Perhaps we should see the gag order as a device of the storyteller. Why would Mark employ it? Surely he did so not in order to downplay what he considered beyond question, namely, that Jesus not only announced the kingdom or reign of God, but enacted it with startling power. Why then does Mark include these statements?

We get an answer to this question in the very center of Mark's narrative, in 8:27–33. At this point in the story Jesus is traveling with his disciples in the north of Galilee, high up in the area of Caesarea Philippi. He turns to his followers and asks them: "Who do people say I am?" This is a question Mark's readers are being asked as well, of course. We, along with those early readers, have been following the breathtaking course of Jesus's ministry; we have heard him speak like no other; we have seen him act as no other. With those who sat in the boat with him when he tamed the violent storm, we will have asked: "Who then is this, that even the wind and the sea obey him?" (4:41). And like the disciples in the gospel story itself, we will by now have our own thoughts as to Jesus's identity.

The answer of his followers is instructive, giving us a window on how such a life as Mark recounts would be viewed during Jesus's time: "[Some say] John the Baptist, and others, Elijah; and still others, one of the prophets" (8:28). This gospel has already indicated that John the Baptist had met with a violent end (6:14–29). There were evidently those who thought Jesus was none other than John having come back to life. John and the famous ancient prophet Elijah (see 1 Kings 17–2 Kings 10) were viewed as prophets of a God who has it within his power to bring his messengers back to life—an important theme also for Mark's story of Jesus.

Jesus then asks the pivotal question of his followers: "But who do *you* say that I am?" (emphasis added). Peter, who at the time of the writing of the gospel enjoyed great, perhaps unequaled, prominence in the early Jesus movement (as seen in Papias's relating a tradition regarding Peter's relation to the Gospel of Mark), has the honorable role of responding for the Twelve and, we might add, for the readers of the gospel: "You are the Messiah!" To use the Greek equivalent to the Hebrew *meshiach*: "You are the Christ!" Peter passes the exam—or does he?

Jesus responds in a puzzling fashion: "And he sternly ordered them not to tell anyone about him" (8:30). Why the gag order? The clue lies in the immediately following verses, where Jesus predicts his suffering and refers to himself as "Son of Man." On the one hand, this common phrase may mean no more than "human being." On the other hand, it alludes to the strange heavenly but humanlike figure mentioned in Daniel 7:13, to whom is promised rule over the whole cosmos. It thus functions like the title *Christ* as a way of capturing the widely held hope among Jews that God will at some point finally act to remake the universe and end the torment of sin and mortality (see chapter 13 below).

The tension between Jesus's identity as Messiah and as Son of Man and the suffering he predicts for his future is unbearable for Peter. So Peter, who has just passed the exam with flying colors, now speaks again, expressing the consternation that the others would also have felt and that we as readers of the gospel are to feel as well. Peter protests that this is not the way the story line of the Messiah goes. The Messiah is a powerful victor, most assuredly not a victim. The Messiah is God's agent to make the world right, not to fall victim to it!

The scene has a harsh climax. The same Jesus who just commended Peter now scolds him in the most brutal fashion: "Get behind me, *Satan*! You do not know what God has in mind; you think the way humans do" (8:33, my translation, emphasis added).

With this scene, played out at the very center of the gospel, Mark says to his readers: do not mistake Jesus's impressive acts of power and his authoritative way of teaching as the key to the meaning of his messiahship. If you want to understand what Jesus's messiahship is about you are going to have to come to terms with his suffering and with the cross. The shock to readers, then as now, does not end there. Jesus turns to his already troubled audience: "If any want to become my followers, let them deny themselves and take up *their* cross and follow me!" (8:34, emphasis added). To get excited about Jesus is costly in the extreme.

The story has taken an unexpected but pivotal turn. Like the dark gongs of a bell, this prediction of suffering is now repeated two more times in 9:31 and 10:33. Significantly too, the scene now shifts to Judea and Jerusalem. If Galilee was the place of ministry, Jerusalem now becomes the place of suffering and, in the view of Mark, the location of Jesus's greatest ministry.

THE LAST AND GREATEST ACT IN THE DRAMA: JERUSALEM

Typical of the way Mark tells the story, Jesus's arrival in Jerusalem is initially greeted with both great public enthusiasm and growing hostility from the leadership (11:1–10). Jesus does nothing to lessen the controversy surrounding his person and activity. In fact, he provokes the leadership with sayings and parables and prophetic condemnations. But nothing expresses his prophetic authority and outrages the leadership as keenly as his prophetic demonstration in the temple. This is often called the "temple cleansing" (11:15–18), but this term sanitizes the act too much. It must have been nothing short of a demonstration of outrage on Jesus's part over what he considered to be a defilement of God's house. He is depicted as driving out those doing the usual commerce associated with the massive sacrificial system, kicking over the tables of the moneychangers, and shutting down any further commercial activity. The Jewish leadership now decides to remove him. The dramatic tension in the story only increases when one of Jesus's followers, Judas, agrees to hand him over to the authorities (14:10, 43).

Mark paints the last events of Jesus's life in very dark colors. Indeed, he has no interest in brightening the picture. The cross is, after all, the high point of the story of the Messiah. Nothing should be allowed to soften that harsh image.

The events described in Mark's last chapters are familiar in their broad outline: in his public speeches, Jesus increases his tone of judgment, leaving the reader with a deep sense of unease. His entry into the city, accompanied by enthusiastic crowds, and his dramatic disruptive action in the temple are making it impossible for the authorities to ignore Jesus. A woman anoints him, a remarkable act of coronation (kings were anointed in Israel) and an anticipation of his impending death (anointing was part of the ritual of burial). His last meal with his followers is a Passover meal, when Jews celebrate the deliverance from Egypt by eating a lamb. It is not a joyous meal. It is marked by a deep sense of foreboding. The focus this time is not on deliverance from Egypt but the impending death of Jesus himself. Then there are the two tragic figures of Judas, who facilitates Jesus's arrest, and Peter, who at the crucial moment denies any knowledge of his friend, teacher, and Lord.

Jesus, following an excruciating personal struggle with what he knows is about to happen, is subjected to an extraordinary miscarriage of justice and is finally crucified—a horrific, if all too familiar, form of Roman state terror. Jesus is tortured and executed by the imperial authorities as a political troublemaker—"King of the Jews" is the charge they nail to his cross—with the connivance of at least some Jewish leaders. In the end, Jesus is alone in his torment. The terrified men of his inner circle are in hiding. Only the women who have come with Jesus from Galilee are present, and they stand at a distance. Nothing captures the loneliness of the moment better than Jesus's only words on the cross: "My God, my God, why have you forsaken me?" (15:34). It is left to a Roman soldier to offer a verbal epitaph: "Truly this man was [a] son of God" (15:39, my translation).

An Abrupt and Wrenching Conclusion

The darkness of the story is accentuated by the way Mark's Gospel apparently ends. Many modern translations end at 16:8 or at least supply a marginal note indicating that the manuscripts usually considered the most reliable conclude the gospel at the end of this verse. The problem is that 16:8 ends on an incomplete note. After coming to the tomb in order to care for Jesus's body and being informed by a mysterious "young man" that Jesus had risen from the dead, the women "went out and fled from the tomb, for terror and amazement had seized them; and they said nothing to anyone, for they were afraid."

Can we imagine a gospel—good news—ending on such a note? The incompletion is even more striking in Greek, since the sentence is not grammatically complete. Not surprisingly, then, several endings were supplied to the gospel, likely in the second century, which provide a more palatable conclusion to the gospel. Today many scholars are intrigued by the possibility that Mark quite deliberately intended the story to end exactly as abruptly and disturbingly as the best manuscripts have it.

Why Write Such a Biography? Why Preach This Sermon?

Given the narrative structure of Mark's Gospel and the striking features of his narrative portrait, what would have prompted him to write the gospel this way? Why would he have preached this sermon? Since every sermon has an intended audience, every sermon has a context in which it makes sense. What might it have been in this case?

A great deal of the oral tradition reflects the energetic efforts to recruit persons to belief in Jesus. The stories of Jesus's wise sayings, and especially the stories of his powerful deeds of exorcism and healing, would have played an important role in efforts to impress people. To put it crassly, evangelism, then as now, tends to accentuate the ways Jesus can solve problems better than anyone. Apparently many in that day tended to think and talk about Jesus as a divinely empowered miracle worker. Still others may have wished to stress Jesus's special teachings and viewed him as the greatest sage (see the previous chapter).

Mark in no way denies that Jesus is *the* enactor of the reign of God. Jesus is *the* teacher and preacher par excellence. We sense Mark's own excitement when he has the crowd exclaim with wonder: "A new teaching—with authority!" (1:27). It is also emphasized in the account of the transfiguration: "This is my beloved Son; *listen* to him!" (9:7, emphasis added). But Mark's good news rests not on that so much as on the scandal of Jesus's death and its ironic expression of the power of God. In writing his gospel this way, Mark is stressing the cross as the heart of the good news. In doing so, Mark is not only proclaiming that as gospel for the world, but he is also taking issue with fellow followers of Jesus who are enamored with a successful and powerful Messiah. To them Mark says: "Let's make sure we understand what is truly important about Jesus's messiahship. Because if we do not come to grips with *his* cross, we will never understand what it means to follow him, namely, that it requires us to take up *our* cross." For Mark, as for Paul before him, the center of the story of Jesus is the cross. That is why, particularly if the gospel originally ended so abruptly, he makes so little in this gospel of the resurrection, even though he surely had no desire to downplay its significance. Mark's Gospel is a Good Friday sermon rather than an Easter Sunday sermon.

Matthew: Jesus—Teacher of Righteousness

The Gospel of Matthew was likely written a decade or two after Mark. As in the case of Mark, we do not know who wrote this gospel. Early tradition attributes it to Matthew, presumably one of Jesus's disciples, identified in this gospel with the tax collector in 9:9 and 10:3. It has been suggested that there is a wordplay in the name *Matthew*, since the term for "disciple" in Greek is *mathetes*. Be that as it may, we will continue to use the name tradition has assigned to the author.

Many scholars think the home of this gospel was the great city of Antioch, then the capital of Syria, with a vibrant Jewish community, but also the place from which Paul and others first began their mission to Gentiles. This gospel, regardless of where it first emerged, quickly became the most widely favored of the gospels.

Matthew shares with Mark a basic set of convictions: Jesus was a teacher and a healer; Jesus died on the cross and was raised from the dead; Jesus is the Messiah, the living Lord. Further, Matthew adopts Mark's basic story line. But in reading Matthew we discover some new features that help us to identify the distinctive character of this gospel's portrait of Jesus.

First of all, many readers of this gospel are immediately impressed by how Jewish it feels. There is good reason for that, as we will see. But it is important not to downplay the Jewishness of the other gospels, which were quite possibly *all* written by Jews who thought they were writing the story of a Jewish Messiah, even if they were doing so for a mixed or Gentile audience. Even so, some features of this gospel strike us as particularly rooted in Judaism. Matthew 13:52 may provide the clue for how Matthew understands himself and his task. He quotes Jesus as concluding his parables of the kingdom this way: "Every scribe who has been trained for the kingdom of heaven is like the master of the household who brings out of his treasure what is new and what is old."

This verse combines three important emphases we see in the Gospel according to Matthew: respect for Scriptures, discipleship, and openness to the kingdom of God. The word *scribe* refers to someone able to communicate in writing and, more importantly, someone versed in the Scriptures. The word *trained* (*matheteuo*) translates a verb form of the noun *disciple*. In this instance it is someone who has been "discipled" in the values of God's reign or kingdom and "walks" that way. Such a person is able to retrieve from the treasury of Scripture, tradition, and kingdom both the new and the old. A scribe "trained for the kingdom" is both appreciative of tradition and alert to the new ways in which God's presence and power make themselves felt. Matthew's Gospel can be quite justly characterized as a *scribal gospel* by a scribe who has become a disciple of the kingdom. That more than anything may account for its feel as a Jewish gospel.

How does a kingdom scribe treat the gospel story? The more we know of the Scriptures and its major figures, such as Abraham, Moses, David, and the figure of Wisdom, the more we can appreciate the allusions that Matthew makes.

A New Genesis—a Genealogy for Jesus, Son of David

"The book of the genesis of Jesus Christ, the son of David, the son of Abraham" (my translation). So begins the Gospel of Matthew. It also introduces Jesus's genealogy, a rather boring way to start a story, we might think. The genealogy might also strike us as rather peculiar, since Matthew goes on to relate that Jesus did *not* have an earthly father! However boring to modern ears and however peculiar, given the story Matthew relates, it is a very deliberate signal that the story of Jesus began a long time ago, that Jesus fits into Israel's long family history, and that he is related to those who were there at the most central moments of that history. Most important, by highlighting persons like Abraham and David, Matthew draws attention to the promises of God, promises that faithful Jews were yearning to see fulfilled—hence Matthew's frequent use of the phrase *so that the Scriptures might be fulfilled* (e.g., 1:22; 2:15, 17, 23).

Alert and patient readers will also notice that Matthew has constructed the genealogy very carefully. In 1:17 Matthew explicitly draws attention to having divided the genealogy into three groups of fourteen generations (that our counting might not quite correspond to his does not change the point he intends to make). Why? For one thing the divisions highlight the two great figures—Abraham and David. The last may be especially important in that the numerical value of the name *David* is fourteen (using the older spelling *dwd*: *d*/4 + *w*/6 + *d*/4 = 14). We should see in this a rather clever way to associate Jesus with the Davidic line and make the implicit claim that he is the new King David—the Messiah.

JESUS, A NEW MOSES

Birth Story

The allusions to central biblical figures continue in the birth narrative. It is easy to see the numerous allusions to Moses, for example. Apart from Abraham and David, the most important figure in the story of Israel is surely Moses, the one who led enslaved Israel to freedom and the one through whom they received the Torah, the law of God. The broad outline of Moses's life would have been familiar to first-century Jews. They would have known of his birth taking place during a particularly violent crackdown by the Egyptian Pharaoh and how his sister Miriam hid him in a basket in the reeds on the shore of the Nile. In Matthew's account of Jesus's birth, it is now the evil King Herod who intends to kill him along with all the little boys of Bethlehem. Jesus's mother Miriam (= Hebrew "Mary") and Joseph have to flee with their child *to* Egypt.

Five Blocks of Teaching or Discourses

The allusions to Moses extend well beyond the story of Jesus's birth and infancy. We can see it in the very way in which Matthew shapes his gospel as a whole. For example, Matthew collects Jesus's sayings, some of which we find also in Mark, others of which he shares with Luke, and some of which only he records, into five major blocks:

- the Sermon on the Mount (Matt. 5–7)
- the commissioning of his disciples (Matt. 10)
- a collection of parables of the kingdom (Matt. 13)
- a set of instructions for internal church matters (Matt. 18)
- prophetic utterances and warnings regarding the future (Matt. 24–25)

Each of these blocks concludes with the phrase "now when Jesus finished these things" (7:28; 11:1; 13:53; 19:1; 26:1). Might this be an allusion to the Torah? The first five books of the Bible, also known as the Pentateuch (Genesis, Exodus, Leviticus, Numbers, Deuteronomy), are and were often called "the law" or "the five books of Moses." Is Matthew signaling to readers that Jesus is a new Moses, the authoritative interpreter of the law?

The first block of teaching is called the Sermon on the Mount (Matthew 5–7). Comparing the gospels with each other shows that Luke shares some of the material found in the Sermon on the Mount, only he places it on a "level place" (Luke 6:17; see chapter 10 below). Whatever Luke's reasons for placing his material into this setting, should we not see in Matthew's placing of Jesus on a mount another allusion to Moses, who received the law on Mount Sinai?

Second, Jesus proclaims that he did not come to abolish but to *fulfill* the law. His words are unambiguous:

> For truly I tell you, until heaven and earth pass away, not one letter, not one stroke of a letter, will pass from the law until all is accomplished. Therefore, whoever breaks one of the least of these commandments, and teaches others to do the same, will be called least in the kingdom of heaven; but whoever does them and teaches them will be called great in the kingdom of heaven. For I tell you, unless your righteousness exceeds that of the scribes and Pharisees, you will never enter the kingdom of heaven. (Matt. 5:18–20)

In effect, Matthew's Jesus asks his hearers to *outdo* the Pharisees at righteousness, that is, at faithful obedience to Torah. As we will discover when we discuss the Sermon on the Mount (chapter 10 below), Matthew has Jesus radically sharpen what it means truly to obey the law of God. He calls it the "righteousness of the kingdom of God" (6:33). In doing so, Matthew insists that it is *Jesus*, not the Pharisees, who is the authoritative interpreter of the law.

As indicated earlier, the evangelists wrote in a particular time and setting. They were prompted to preach in a particular fashion. We are probably on safe ground to see in Matthew's strong emphasis on the validity of the law and Jesus's authoritative if controversial interpretation of it a reflection of a debate that would have taken place in the years after the destruction of Jerusalem in 70 CE. That was the fateful year in which the Romans destroyed Jerusalem and, with it, the great temple. The Pharisees, practiced in the law and its application to life, were in a position following that catastrophe to pick up the pieces and refocus the identity of Jews around the law. If they could no longer have the temple, Jews certainly could be true to the Torah. We can well imagine two related arguments that Jews who believed in Jesus carried on with those many more who did not. One was whether it made any sense to call Jesus God's Messiah in light of the calamity the Jewish people had experienced. The other argument was one that evidently already raged around Jesus during his ministry, namely, whether he was faithful to Judaism, that is, whether he was faithful to the law. This question was given an added edge in the years and decades after the crucifixion of Jesus, when many Gentiles joined the Jesus movement, many of whom did not see themselves as subject to the law and were, moreover, making it difficult for Jews to remain law abiding (e.g., Galatians 1–2 and Romans 14–15). In

making the allusions to Moses and in stressing Jesus to be *the* authoritative teacher of true righteousness, Matthew seems to be caught up in this
complex debate.

Jesus, the Wisdom of God

Matthew's stress on Jesus's continuity with Judaism's valuing of the law
comes to creative expression in Matthew 11. In order to appreciate this
creativity, we need briefly to place this discussion into the context of Jewish
tradition (see chapter 13 below). Wisdom is an important dimension of the
biblical tradition. Among the most familiar examples of wisdom literature are
Proverbs, Ecclesiastes, and Job. We could add many of the Psalms and also
documents such as the Wisdom of Solomon (the Book of Wisdom) or the
Wisdom of Jesus ben Sirach (Ecclesiasticus), found in the Catholic canon of
the Bible and frequently published in Protestant versions as Apocrypha.

Of special importance in this tradition is the personification of Wisdom
as a female figure, a poetic and creative celebration of God's wisdom as experienced in creation and in law. She is wonderfully described in Proverbs
7–9, Wisdom of Solomon 6–9, and Sirach 6 and 24. Wisdom, or Sophia in
the Greek Scriptures, is God's daughter or God's companion, who is there
at creation participating in the process of bringing the world into being
(Prov. 8:22–31). She is also, importantly, a gracious instructor in the law
(Prov. 8:1–21; Sirach 6:18–31; 51:26); more, she *is* the law (Sirach 24:23)!
Creation is the expression of God's wisdom.

The purpose of such poetic creativity is to express the conviction that the
law is God's way of drawing near to humanity. Wisdom herself speaks in
Sirach 24 (see also Proverbs 8–9):

> Come to me, you who desire me,
>   and eat your fill of my fruits.
> For the memory of me is sweeter than honey,
>   and the possession of me sweeter than the honeycomb.
> Those who eat of me will hunger for more,
>   and those who drink of me will thirst for more.
> Whoever obeys me will not be put to shame,
>   and those who work with me will not sin. (Sirach 24:19–22)

A close relationship with Wisdom is commended elsewhere in Sirach:

> Put your feet into her fetters,
>   and your neck into her collar.
> Bend your shoulders and carry her,
>   and do not fret under her bonds.
> Come to her with all your soul,
>   and keep her ways with all your might.

> Search out and seek, and she will become known to you;
>> and when you get hold of her, do not let her go.
> For at last you will find the rest she gives,
>> and she will be changed into joy for you.
> Then her fetters will become for you a strong defense,
>> and her collar a glorious robe.
> Her yoke is a golden ornament,
>> and her bonds a purple cord. (Sirach 6:24–30)

> Put your neck under her yoke,
>> and let your souls receive instruction;
>> it is to be found close by. (Sirach 51:26)

Compare this with what Jesus says in Matthew:

> Come to me, all you that are weary and are carrying heavy burdens, and I will give you rest. Take my yoke upon you, and learn from me; for I am gentle and humble in heart, and you will find rest for your souls. For my yoke is easy, and my burden is light. (Matt. 11:28–30)

These words, a startling echo of Sirach, are found only in Matthew among the New Testament gospels (a briefer version is found in *Gospel of Thomas*, 90). The evangelist clearly wants us to view Jesus as Wisdom come in the flesh, to borrow language from John 1:14. Matthew wants us to see Jesus as *more than* Moses! Jesus is God's will incarnate, God's law having come to live with the people. Sophia has appeared as the man from Nazareth. One can see Matthew's intention in the way he edits a saying also found in Luke: in response to accusations against both John the Baptizer and himself, Luke 7:35 has Jesus respond, "Wisdom is vindicated [*or* justified] by all her *children*" (emphasis added), implying that John and Jesus are Sophia's offspring. In Matthew, on the other hand, Jesus identifies himself not just as Wisdom's offspring, but as Sophia herself: "Wisdom is vindicated by *her* deeds" (Matt. 11:19, emphasis added).

We will have occasion to return to this identification of Jesus with Wisdom in chapter 13 below. Here it is sufficient to see the connection between the Jesus who preaches the Sermon on the Mount and the Wisdom that comes to be with those who are prepared to follow the way of righteousness, however few there might be: "Where two or three are gathered in my name, I am there among them" (Matt. 18:20).

WHY WRITE SUCH A BIOGRAPHY? WHY PREACH THIS SERMON?

Matthew's Gospel was relevant not only to debates among Jews who differed fiercely with each other over Jesus, as I suggested earlier. This gospel also places before *all* followers of Jesus—Jews and Gentiles alike—the importance not only of Jesus's deeds, of his death and resurrection, but of the need to be his students, his followers, his disciples. To believe in Jesus is to follow him in the path of righteousness, says Matthew. That is what it means to "strive first for the kingdom of God and [its] righteousness" (6:33). If Matthew's narration of Jesus's life and work begins roughly with the great Sermon on the Mount, it concludes with the equally famous Great Commission, where the resurrected Jesus commissions his followers to "make disciples of all nations, . . . teaching them to obey everything that I have commanded you" (28:19–20). Matthew's is a disciple's—a student's—gospel.

Luke: Jesus—Friend and Advocate of Those on the Margins of Society

As we saw earlier, Luke introduces his gospel with the guarantee that his is a trustworthy and "orderly" account (1:1–4). The author makes it very clear that he is aware of "many" other attempts to write the good news. It appears that, like Matthew, Luke relies on Mark for the basic outline of the story. It appears also, based on comparison with Matthew, that Luke shares with that author access to distinct material perhaps not known to Mark (see chapter 2 above). Luke's deliberate drawing of attention to the "sequential orderliness" of his account invites us to pay attention to the particular or distinctive shape and emphasis of his gospel.

We remind ourselves that we do not know who wrote this anonymous gospel or where it was written. Tradition ascribes it to Luke, perhaps the physician and companion of Paul (Col. 4:14; 2 Tim. 4:11; Philemon 24). It is also fairly safe to say that the author intends his gospel for a predominantly Gentile audience.

VOLUME ONE

Luke's Gospel is the first of a two-volume work. We know the second volume as the Acts of the Apostles. The present order of the New Testament obscures that relationship in that the Gospel of John comes between Luke and Acts. The relationship of Luke's Gospel to Acts goes beyond the purpose of our study. Briefly, the gospel traces the life of Jesus from his birth as the liberator of the downtrodden and oppressed to his ascension. The second volume, the Acts of the Apostles, picks up the narrative where the gospel left off and traces the spread of "the Way," as Jesus's followers are repeatedly called in Acts, from Jerusalem to Rome, from the city of God to the capital of the Roman Empire. Especially prominent in that second part of the story are the two great apostles of the first decades of the Jesus-centered movement, Peter and Paul.

AN APOLOGY

Some scholars believe that Luke wrote his two-volume work as an apology—*apology* in this case not referring to an expression of regret but rather to a *defense*, specifically of Jesus and belief in him vis-à-vis potentially suspicious

Roman authorities. Relatedly, they view Luke as having been motivated by a desire to make the news of Jesus as attractive as possible to a wide reading public. In other words, in Luke's presentation, neither Jesus nor the movement devoted to him is a threat to Rome. Luke is saying to his educated Gentile readers: there is no need to fear or to be suspicious of the followers of Jesus. Conversely, some scholars view him as saying to his fellow believers in Jesus, there is no need to fear the empire.

As much as the catastrophic Jewish war with Rome in 66–70 might well have put anything Jewish in a bad light, the evidence in both Luke's Gospel and Acts is too ambiguous to lend credence to the idea that Luke is principally concerned to distance the Jesus movement from association with that violent chapter in Jewish history. That he is concerned to render the story of a Jewish messiah intelligible to a wide largely Gentile reading public is more compelling.

Luke, just about everyone agrees, is an excellent storyteller. He employs literary means that render the stories unforgettable. To illustrate, my informal surveys suggest that in the vast majority of cases it is Luke's Christmas story—and not Matthew's—that is read around the Christmas tree. Further, travel reports always make good reading, and, not surprisingly, it was a favorite motif in Hellenistic writing. Anyone familiar with the Acts of the Apostles knows how prominently the travels of Paul feature in the story. This travel motif also marks Luke's Gospel. Most of the material that is unique to Luke is found between Luke 9 and Luke 19, often referred to as the "Great Insertion." In those chapters Luke greatly expands the trip from Galilee to Jerusalem, the story line he inherited from Mark. This is where we find the remarkable parables unique to Luke's Gospel, like the good Samaritan or the prodigal son. The author excels at the kind of good storytelling that would render the good news of Jesus attractive to a wide reading public.

Jesus in the History of Salvation

Other scholars draw attention to the way Luke orders his gospel in relation to the "history of salvation," as it is often called. Luke, so the argument goes, imagines salvation history as consisting of three periods: first, the period of *Israel* up to John the Baptist, who represents an important bridge between the story of God's people and the coming of the Messiah; second, the period of *Jesus*, marked off by the Spirit *descending* on him as a dove at his baptism (3:21–22) and *ascending* again at his death (23:46); and, third, the period of the *church*, beginning when the Spirit is *poured out* again, now not on a solitary individual or on special leaders, but, in keeping with ancient prophecy, on the whole community. We know this event as Pentecost (Acts 2; see also Joel 2). The Acts of the Apostles then narrates the good news of that third, as-yet-unfinished period, where the Messiah, rooted in and emerging out of the long history of Israel, becomes the Lord of *all* peoples.

GOOD NEWS FOR THE OPPRESSED

No doubt both Luke's relationship to the broader Hellenistic culture and his placing of Jesus within the context of the larger story of God's saving of the world constitute the elements of the orderliness of his account of Jesus. I see little evidence, however, that Luke intends to make his gospel safe or even palatable, however compelling a storyteller he is. For example, his Christmas story places the birth of Jesus into the context of Roman imperial oppression, into the context of the way the big world impacts the lives of little people yearning for liberation (2:1–5). The Song of Mary, also known as the *Magnificat*, powerfully evokes the yearnings of the oppressed (1:46–55), but the savior of the world—the liberator of the oppressed—does not even have a proper place to be born! And who witnesses Jesus's birth? That honor is given to none other than lowly shepherds.

In the first century, there were as yet no Hallmark cards or shopping mall crèches to render romantic this compelling story of the powerless and the poor being buffeted about by imperial might. Augustus's birth, the Roman emperor mentioned in 2:1, was certainly celebrated very differently by Roman poet Virgil in his *Fourth Eclogue*.

> Now the last age by Cumae's Sibyl sung
> has come and gone, and the majestic roll
> of circling centuries begins anew:
> justice returns, . . .
> with a new breed of men sent down from heaven.
> Only do thou, at the boy's birth in whom
> the iron shall cease, the golden race arise,
> befriend him, chaste Lucina; 'tis thine own
> Apollo reigns. . . .
> Under thy guidance, what tracks remain
> of our old wickedness, once done away,
> shall free the earth from never-ceasing fear.
> He shall receive the life of gods, and see
> heroes with gods commingling, and himself
> be seen of them, and with his father's worth
> reign o'er a world at peace. (trans. James Rhoades)

Luke knows full well the irony of Jesus's humble beginnings. By deliberately drawing attention to Augustus, he signals to his readers that he is narrating the birth of the one who is infinitely greater than the one Romans called *divi filius* ("son of a god"). And Luke does so by giving the reader a clue what Jesus will be like. Jesus is good news for those who suffer—for the poor, the powerless, the sick, and the rejected. In keeping with this emphasis, Jesus's first sermon in Luke's Gospel has him identifying himself with the prophecy of Isaiah (61:1–2) regarding the great day of liberation:

> The Spirit of the Lord is upon me,
>> because he has anointed me
>>> to bring good news to the poor.
> He has sent me to proclaim release to the captives
>> and recovery of sight to the blind,
>>> to let the oppressed go free,
> to proclaim the year of the Lord's favor. (Luke 4:18–19)

That this good news for those marginalized by oppression, poverty, and illness will not come easy is illustrated in Luke's much shorter version of Matthew's Sermon on the Mount, often called the Sermon on the Plain (6:17–49). The good news for the poor and oppressed is mixed with dire warnings—"woes"—for those who oppress them (6:20–26; see also 1:51–53). Luke's point is clear: in Jesus, God is acting to set things right. Jesus is God's agent of liberation.

Thus, throughout his gospel Luke shows Jesus as being particularly sensitive to the poor, to the disadvantaged, to those marginalized through social rejection due to work (tax collection) or illness (leprosy), and to the women who form an important part of his entourage (8:2). Luke is particularly concerned to draw from the traditions about Jesus those elements that accentuate Jesus's immediate relevance to everyday social justice, as seen in the parables of Jesus that Luke retells, such as the good Samaritan (10:30–36), the shrewd manager (16:1–9), or Lazarus and the rich man (16:19–31).

Why Write Such a Biography? Why Preach This Sermon?

Luke wrote this gospel for several reasons. Like the other evangelists, Luke desires first and foremost to introduce Jesus to his audience as crucified and risen Lord. He does so in a style and with emphases that may well have been particularly compelling to a wide readership well beyond the confines of the Jewish community. But if we want to listen for the distinctive voice of Luke as author in his own right, then we will also hear a preacher of social justice and peace, who stresses Jesus's passionate concern for wholeness, justice, and peace, individually and socially. The arena of salvation encompasses both, in Luke's view. In writing his gospel as he did, Luke may thus also have wanted to address believers in Jesus, who then as now like to ignore the often deeply irksome dimensions of the good news as it relates to social injustice.

John: Jesus—the Word Made Flesh

We come now to the last of our four portraits of Jesus, the Gospel of John. Strictly speaking, this gospel is anonymous, as are the others in the New Testament. We find mention of a mysterious eyewitness referred to as "the disciple whom Jesus loved" (19:26; 21:20, 24), commonly identified in the tradition of the church as John, the son of Zebedee, brother of James, and one of Jesus's disciples. Tradition has this John writing the gospel in Ephesus, where he is said to have moved, together with Jesus's mother, Mary. Today, the vast majority of scholars takes the anonymous nature of the gospel seriously and continues to debate whether the Beloved Disciple was an actual historical figure or a symbol of a faithful follower of Jesus and, if he was an actual historical figure, whether he was the evangelist who wrote the gospel or the chief source for whoever did write the gospel. Whereas some scholars argue for an early date of composition, most date it late in the first century.

As with the Gospel of Mark, we come up against some striking features at the end of the gospel. It appears to come to a close at the end of John 20. Is John 21, then, an addition by a later hand? Does the reference to the Beloved Disciple in 21:20, 24 imply that he wrote the gospel or only that the traditions that have been added to the gospel come from him? We will not settle such questions here. They are a reminder of the living and dynamic process by which these documents came about and were edited, preserved, and disseminated. The majority of scholars place this gospel, in its present form at least, in the last decade of the first century.

A Unique Gospel

John differs from the Synoptic Gospels in several ways.

Historical Chronology and Travel Pattern

Most folks think of Jesus as having had a three-year ministry. We have John's Gospel to thank for that. The Synoptics would leave the impression of a much shorter period of activity. The travel pattern or schema in John is also different from that found in the Synoptic Gospels. Instead of a pattern in which Galilee is the place of Jesus's ministry and Jerusalem the place of his death, John has Jerusalem and environment as the principal arena of Jesus's work. Jesus moves back and forth between Galilee and Judea, usually because of opposition in Judea. Jesus seems to be rather familiar to the authorities at the time of his death. A striking illustration is the famous incident of the so-called temple cleansing. In the Synoptics it is the event that precipitates Jesus's arrest and crucifixion (Matt. 21:12–13 || Mark 11:15–17 || Luke 19:45–46). In contrast, John places the event toward the beginning of Jesus's public ministry (2:13–17). In having Jesus visit Jerusalem more frequently throughout his period of activity, John may well reflect historical reality as much as or more closely than the Synoptics. There is nothing implausible about a Jew from Galilee spending time in Jerusalem during several of the important festivals such as Pessach (Passover) and Succoth (Feast of Booths). We should, at the same time, recognize that the evangelist uses those major festivals as occasions with which to frame major blocks of Jesus's teaching. The travel schema may thus be less history than literary device, serving the purpose of "ordering," to use Luke's term, the traditions of Jesus's teachings.

Kingdom of God

Apart from a few references in one exchange between Jesus and a Jewish leader named Nicodemus in John 3, there is not one reference to the kingdom or reign of God. How can that be? Can we imagine the ministry of Jesus apart from this key term? The fourth evangelist evidently could.

Parables

Relatedly, while we find metaphors, analogies, cryptic sayings, and riddles (see, for example the collection of sheep, sheepfold, and shepherd sayings in John 10), there are none of the familiar parables we associate with Jesus. Did John not know of them? Can we imagine an account of Jesus's teaching without them? John evidently could.

Miracles

The first half of the Gospel of John has some well-known miracles such as changing water into wine (2:1–11) or the healing of the man born blind (John 9). There are no accounts of Jesus driving out demons. Not only are the miracles for the most part different than those described in the Synoptics (an important exception is the feeding of the multitude in John 6), they appear to serve a different purpose than in Mark, for example. Mark's Jesus typically places a gag order on the one who has been healed or exorcized, intending, as suggested earlier, to deflect attention to the miracles as the key to Jesus's messiahship. In John the miracles are not hushed up; in fact, they are called "signs," intentionally public demonstrations of Jesus's true identity.

View of the Future (Eschatology)

The Gospel of John has a rather unique way of speaking of future hopes and expectations as already realized in Jesus. For example, whereas we might expect that "to be lifted up" is a way of speaking of Jesus's resurrection and/or his exaltation after the resurrection, the Fourth Gospel (as it is also often called) speaks repeatedly of his being put on the cross as Jesus's being "lifted up" (3:14; 8:28; 12:30–36; compare Acts 1:9). Perhaps even more dramatically, whereas in the Synoptic Gospels, as in much of the New Testament, "eternal life" is something anticipated either beyond death or after the present evil age comes to an end, in John's Gospel we read sentences like this:

> Very truly, I tell you, anyone who hears my word and believes him who sent me has eternal life, and does not come under judgment, but has passed from death to life. (John 5:24)

This is sometimes called "realized eschatology," that is, future or final events are spoken of as already realized in the life and death of Jesus or in the faith of those who believe in him.

John does not, somewhat bewilderingly, give up on a future expectation completely. We can see this by reading on from the verse just quoted:

> Very truly, I tell you, the hour is coming, and is now here, when the dead will hear the voice of the Son of God, and those who hear will live. For just as the Father has life in himself, so he has granted the Son also to have life in himself; and he has given him authority to execute judgment, because he is the Son of Man. Do not be astonished at this; for the hour is coming when all who are in their graves will hear his voice and will come out—those who have done good, to the resurrection of life, and those who have done evil, to the resurrection of condemnation. (John 5:25–29)

To be sure, not everything in the Fourth Gospel is different from the three other gospels. Like the other evangelists, John knows about the feeding of the multitude, although rather typically he uses that occasion to attach a tradition of Jesus being the bread of life (John 6). John also agrees in important ways with the Passion Narrative in the Synoptics, even if striking differences emerge also there. For example, there is no mention in John's narrative of Jesus's last meal with his followers of wine and bread and their symbolic significance. Further, like Luke, John knows of appearances of the risen Christ in and around Jerusalem. At the same time, the addition of John 21 also adds traditions associating those appearances with Galilee, as in Matthew and suggested by Mark. To go back to the beginning of the gospel narrative, like Mark but unlike Matthew and Luke, John does not contain an account of Jesus's birth. It is here, in fact, that some of distinctness of this gospel comes to clearest expression.

THE WORD BECAME FLESH

John begins his account not with a birth narrative but with a hymn or poem on the Word becoming flesh—incarnation. While mysterious and abstract, John's opening is so striking that it has provided the glasses through which many view the birth of Christ and specifically the virgin birth. John's prologue, as it is usually called, is more than likely an adapted hymn to wisdom (see above). True, in John we find not "wisdom" (*sophia*) but a virtual synonym: "word" (*logos*). The opening poetic words of this gospel are breathtaking in their scope:

> In the beginning was the Word, and the Word was with God, and the Word was God. He was in the beginning with God. All things came into being through him, and without him not one thing came into being. What has come into being in him was life, and the life was the light of all people. The light shines in the darkness, and the darkness did not overcome it. (John 1:1–5)

Echoes of the great celebrations of Wisdom cited earlier are unmistakable (see especially Prov. 8:22–31 and Wisdom of Solomon 7:15–8:1). Now John takes our breath away:

> And the Word became flesh and lived among us, and we have seen his glory, the glory as of a father's only son, full of grace and truth. . . . From his fullness we have all received, grace upon grace. . . . No one has ever seen God. It is God the only Son, who is close to the Father's heart, who has made him known. (John 1:14, 16, 18)

We hear echoes of Sirach 24, where Wisdom resides with God and then comes to find a home in Israel. In John, God's wisdom, now as word (*logos*), comes into the world as light comes into the darkness. But the darkness does not receive the light gladly. Those who are attuned and receptive to the word are drawn to the light; many others are repelled. The poem thus anticipates much like an overture the basic shape and ingredients of John's Gospel. The entry of Jesus is nothing less than the entry of God's wisdom, God's word, into the world that the Word created. The Word has come home. But the encounter is met with fierce resistance, leading finally to Jesus's death. But just as the darkness does not win out over light, so Jesus's death is not the final word. In John, in fact, the victory of light over darkness is spoken of as Jesus's being "lifted up" (12:32–33). In John, Easter invades Good Friday, so strong is the victory of light over darkness.

The Word Is God

Having read the Synoptic Gospels, we are by now used to thinking of Jesus as very significant and very special. He is the Christ, the Son of God. But the Gospel of John pushes the language to the very limit and beyond. Any Jew familiar with the Bible would have known that a statement beginning with "I am," especially within a very loaded context, would have evoked the name God gives himself. When in Exodus 3:14 Moses asks God what his name is, God answers, "I AM WHO I AM" (see also, e.g., Isa. 43:10, 25). In John, Jesus repeatedly uses this divine self-designation as a way of signaling his divinity:

I am the bread that came down from heaven. (6:41)

I am the light of the world. (8:12)

Very truly, I tell you, before Abraham was, I am. (8:58)

I am the gate. (10:9)

I am the good shepherd. (10:11)

I am the resurrection and the life. (11:25)

I am the way, and the truth, and the life. (14:6)

I am the vine. (15:5)

Such assertions would have been heard within Jesus's and the evangelist's Jewish world as implying a bracing claim to divinity, forcing a decision between belief or the charge of blasphemy.

JESUS THE REVEALER

The collisions of word and world, light and darkness, truth and falsity, insight and blindness, mark the portrayal of Jesus's life and ministry in John. Given the emphasis on word and light, we should expect that the central feature of John's portrait of Jesus is that of a *revealer*, a bringer of insight, knowledge, and revelation. The emphasis on hearing, understanding, and knowing is much more prominent in John than in the other gospels. A rare exception in the Synoptic Gospels is the Q-saying in Matthew 11:25–27 || Luke 10:21–22. Most concentrated is the expression in John 17:3: "And this is eternal life, that they may know you, the only true God, and Jesus Christ whom you have sent." To know God is to have eternal life now, in the present.

Scholars have wondered whether this emphasis on knowing moves this gospel into the orbit of early Christian Gnosticism (*gnosis*, "knowledge"). It is not difficult to see the gnostic-like elements in this remarkable portrait of Jesus. Even so, and this needs to be stated very strongly, John places those very distinctive emphases within the context of the recognizable story line of the Jesus who speaks and acts as an agent of God, who as a consequence goes to the cross, and who is then raised to life. So, with all its differences, the author of the Fourth Gospel does not lose touch with that earthy story of the man from Nazareth. The Word did, after all, become *flesh*.

WHY WRITE SUCH A BIOGRAPHY? WHY PREACH THIS SERMON?

How could such a gospel have come about? We can account for the differences among the Synoptic Gospels by recognizing different stresses, emphases, and perhaps audiences. But, with the exception of a few obvious points of contact between John and the other three gospels, or at least traditions recorded there, the Fourth Gospel appears to be based on a remarkably distinct body of tradition. What was the origin of these traditions? How could they have taken shape as they did?

Beloved Disciple

A tantalizing hint may well lie in the mysterious figure of the Beloved Disciple (19:26; 21:20, 24). While, as indicated above, Christian tradition typically identifies him as John, a disciple of Jesus, he is strictly speaking not identified, leaving the door open, of course, to speculation, including the proposal that he was Lazarus (the friend whom Jesus raised back to life in John 11) or that "he" was actually Mary Magdalene. Women do play a significant role in this gospel at pivotal moments in the narrative. It may even be that the Beloved Disciple is no more than a symbol of the ideal disciple.

Many scholars nevertheless think that "the disciple whom Jesus loved" represents an important leader in the community in which this gospel emerged. Perhaps not a member of the Twelve, this follower seems to have had a very significant relationship with Jesus. He may also have had a distinct perspective on Jesus. The Gospel of John as we have it before us would in that case reflect the Beloved Disciple's memories, traditions, and interpretations of Jesus. This disciple's followers would have further developed this material. Like the others, this gospel might well have undergone considerable editing in the early years and decades of its transmission (a set of traditions seems to have been added in John 21).

Samaritan Connection

Samaritans are another piece of the puzzle, even if scholars differ as to where or how this piece fits. Samaria is a region wedged between Judea and Galilee. During Jesus's day there was much hostility and mutual suspicion between Jews and Samaritans (see the next chapter). Jews living in Judea or Galilee would have found the designation "good Samaritan" highly ironic, if not oxymoronic. Apparently some of the early followers of Jesus had great success in drawing converts from within the Samaritan community, possibly reflected in the prominence given the famous story of Jesus and the Samaritan woman in John 4. Was some of the intensity of hostility from the larger Jewish community, reciprocated quite freely in John's Gospel, fueled by a significant presence of Samaritans in the Jesus movement? Does some of the special character of this gospel reflect traditions and perspectives nurtured within such circles? This too remains strictly conjecture.

Theology with a Difference

The majority of scholars today imagine the home of this gospel to have been a "Johannine community," with its own very particular character. They also see the gospel directed not so much at the wider world or even the wider circles of devotees of Jesus, but at that community itself. Some have seen hints in the gospel that the Johannine believers may have only recently been ejected from the synagogue, perhaps because of their high Christology or the presence among them of Samaritans (John 9). The gospel is then seen as intended to nurture the community's sense of identity in a hostile world.

These students of the Fourth Gospel may be right. Other significant scholarly voices, however, see this gospel as very much intended for the wider world. More, they see it quite intentionally written to be read by those *already familiar* with gospel traditions as recorded in the Synoptic Gospels. That would mean that this gospel should *not* be viewed as an island but as a particularly striking and distinct feature in the *shared* geography of gospel writings. Not, "Here is a different Jesus!" Or, "Here is additional material on Jesus!" Rather, "Here is a deeper way to view the Jesus you already know!"

That does not mean that the evangelist is interested only in addressing fellow Jesus believers. This gospel is, as are all of the gospels in the New Testament, a rich and full-voiced invitation to the wider world to encounter the living Jesus. Its pride of place in the church's evangelism over the years gives ample evidence.

We can be certain that the answers to these intriguing and bewildering questions are and will remain shrouded in mystery for a long time to come. Anyone proposing answers should do so with the utmost care and reticence. The church eventually incorporated this unique gospel into its approved collection or canon. But rather than meld it together with the other gospels, the church allowed it to stand alongside the other three gospels in all its glorious distinctiveness. That remains a remarkable and courageous decision, respectful of the evangelist and the tradition he represented.

The gospel's distinctiveness, especially the absence of significant elements of the portrait of Jesus found in the Synoptic Gospels (e.g., kingdom of God, parables), has led to a tendency to disregard it in the attempts to reconstruct a so-called historical Jesus. More recently, scholars have again taken up this question, as thorny as it is for historians and gospel critics. As with so much of biblical study, the jury's deliberations are not likely to end soon.

Conclusion: Four Gospels or Fourfold Gospel?

We have briefly attempted to consider four portraits of Jesus: Mark's Christ on the cross, Matthew's Christ as Wisdom teaching righteousness, Luke's Christ as friend and liberator of the marginalized, and John's Christ as the revealing Word in the flesh. All four portraits hang together side by side in one room, the New Testament canon, together teaching us who Jesus was and is. We can hardly imagine Jesus without the influence of each one of the artists we might dub the "Group of Four." We have thereby become aware that our access to Jesus himself is via these very particular and creative sources, whether we like it or not. Moreover, we have come to see how deeply these portraits are marked by faith, devotion, and a deep desire to persuade us of Jesus's importance. Lastly, we have come to appreciate more fully the distinctive contribution of each of the evangelists to our understanding of Jesus.

Regardless of our thoughts and convictions about Jesus, we can empathize with the historian's difficulty in answering the question: "Who then was Jesus?" Do we have to settle for understanding the artist, that is, the evangelist, or the particular community out of which we think he emerged and within which he worked? Will it always be only "Matthew's Jesus" or

"John's Jesus"? Not if we understand the role of the artist in opening our eyes to reality, in this case to Jesus. Even so, regardless of religious orientation, we are likely to be more humble about being able to write a life of Jesus in a modern biographical sense. In my opinion the nature of the sources make such a biography difficult, if not impossible. We get to Jesus only through the witness of those who were not interested in writing a modern biography. They were interested not in themselves as writers either and would be exasperated if we were satisfied with an encounter with them. They were interested in having us encounter Jesus.

That said, in our study of the New Testament we are never alone with Jesus. The witnesses—the evangelists, those they learned from, and those who preserved and edited their writings—are always there with him. If we send the witnesses out of the room, the interview with Jesus is over, because he turns out to have left with them! How frustrating for the scholar who wishes it were different. But, from the perspective of a believer, should it be any different?

Key Terms and Concepts
Beatitudes
destruction of Jerusalem and its temple in 70 CE
evangelist
gospel
messianic secret
realized eschatology
redaction criticism
Sermon on the Mount
Sermon on the Plain
signs
Synoptic Gospels
Wisdom/Sophia
Word/Logos

For Further Reading

In addition to articles in the dictionaries listed in chapter 1, see also the excellent articles on each of the gospels in the many introductions to the New Testament, as well as the introductions to the many excellent commentaries on each of the gospels. In addition, consult the following works:

Baukham, Richard, ed. *The Gospels for All Christians: Rethinking the Gospel Audiences*. Grand Rapids: Eerdmans, 1998.

Burridge, Richard A. *Four Gospels, One Jesus? A Symbolic Reading*. Grand Rapids: Eerdmans, 1994; 2nd ed., 2005.

Hengel, Martin. *The Four Gospels and the One Gospel of Jesus Christ*. Harrisburg, PA: Trinity, 2000.

Sanders, E. P., and Margaret Davies. *Studying the Synoptic Gospels*. Philadelphia: Trinity, 1989.

4

Jesus's World

T HE WORLD INTO which Jesus was born and in which he lived and died was one marked by several important factors reflected in the narratives of his life in the gospels. Pervasive, even in varying degrees of oppressiveness, was Roman imperial domination, the sporadic violence of resistance to it, and the callous brutality of the empire's response. While there were wealthy landowners and those whose wealth and power were tied to the temple in Jerusalem, many people were poor, working as day laborers, or more likely peasants eking out a living in small villages, vulnerable to illness and violence. Piety was an ever-present source of conflict between those attempting to live lives of purity and righteousness (or fidelity to the Torah) or of those many more who were not. Fidelity to the law and its requirements of purity and holiness was for many an expression of urgent hope that God would bring liberation to his people, freeing them from oppression, disease, and sin.

This social setting has been excavated, sometimes quite literally, by archeologists and social scientists in recent decades (see bibliography at the end of this chapter). In this chapter I will provide little more than some thumbnail sketches of some of the groups we encounter in the gospels.

Historical Background

The contemporary study of Jesus, whether in order to reconstruct a historical Jesus or to fully understand the gospel portraits of him, takes the context of first-century Judaism very seriously. While scholars disagree on exactly how to understand the Judaism of Jesus's day, they have no doubt that our understanding of Jesus, what he said, why he acted as he did, and how others would have viewed him and spoken about him, is greatly enhanced by knowing something about his world.

We begin with the first question: Who were Jews? In order to answer that question it is useful to begin with a very brief historical sketch of the Jewish people and a few of the major historical events.

Exodus

First, we begin the story of the Jews with the Israelites (or the Hebrews). To oversimplify greatly, the Israelites believed themselves to be descendents of Abraham, a Semite originally from what is today Iraq. Their family history indicates that they were enslaved in Egypt, but then, approximately a millennium and a half prior to the time of Jesus, they emerged out of Egypt as a liberated community of slaves, sharing not so much family or tribal ties as a belief in and adherence to a god they believed had liberated them from slavery. In Hebrew one would write the name of this deity with four consonants, transliterated YHWH.

An aside: today most scholars believe that the tetragrammaton (or "four-letter-word") YHWH should be pronounced "Yahweh." In Hebrew, vowels are not written, however. During the Middle Ages rabbinic scribes added "pointing" under the consonants as equivalents to vowels in order to teach the faithful how to pronounce the words correctly. But, out of great respect for God they did not say his name, preferring rather to use the title *Lord* (Hebrew *adonai*). So, underneath the consonants YHWH they placed the vowel points of *adonai* instead, indicating that the reader should say "Adonai" and not "Yahweh." Centuries ago Christian scholars, apparently not knowing this, read the consonants of the word YHWH with the vowels of Adonai and came up with "Jehovah," thus producing in effect a hybrid of God's name and "Lord." The NRSV and the NIV follow Jewish practice and render YHWH as "Lord," using small caps to distinguish it from "lord" or "Lord." The Jerusalem Bible, on the other hand, does not. Many Jewish writers today will express this sensitivity by leaving out the vowel in the name *God*, hence "G-d."

David, Jerusalem, and the Temple

King David forged the various tribes or communities that shared this faith in YHWH into a nation with a capital city and a cult center, Jerusalem, at around a millennium before Jesus. It was left up to his famous son Solomon to build the temple. In popular Israelite and later Jewish thinking, David remained the ideal king. He played a large role in the expectations many

Jews had during the time of Jesus: when God finally liberates his people he will send someone in David's lineage—a messiah. In fact, Jesus is sometimes called "son of David" (e.g., Matt. 1:1; 9:27; 22:42; Luke 1:32).

Northern and Southern Kingdoms

Catastrophe struck quickly. Immediately after the reign of Solomon the Israelite Empire broke in two kingdoms. To the north was what is often called the northern kingdom, sometimes referred to as Israel or Ephraim, with a capital in Samaria. The southern kingdom, made up largely of the tribe of Judah, thus often called Judah, had its capital in Jerusalem. It is from the name *Judah* that the term *Jew* derives.

The northern kingdom disappeared as a recognizable political entity in 722 BCE, when the Assyrians destroyed it. Their policy was to decimate the population by removing a large part of the resident population and then repopulating the area with colonists from outside. In essence, they practiced a kind of ethnocide, destroying the recognizable cultural identity of the people who were there. They succeeded in large measure. One theory is that the Samaritans whom we encounter in the gospels are descendants of northern Israelites who survived and mixed with Assyrian colonists in the years following the destruction of the northern kingdom. Whereas Samaritans viewed themselves as a remnant of the tribes of Manasseh and Ephraim, that is, of Israel, Jews (descendents of those living in the southern kingdom) viewed them as a mongrel people. Their view is reflected in the Old Testament (see 2 Kings. 17). This history of mutual hostility serves as a background for the famous story of Jesus's conversation with the Samaritan woman at the well in John 4, as well as for Jesus's even more famous parable of the good Samaritan in Luke 10.

Exile

The pivotal event for the kingdom of Judah, the historical home of Jews, happened in 587 BCE, when the Babylonians laid siege to Jerusalem, taking the cream of the population off to exile in Babylon. It is impossible to measure fully the impact this event had on Jewish culture and religion. On the one hand, it was a major disaster, in that it uprooted the religious and the political leadership from the land Jews believed firmly God had given them. On the other hand, exile in Babylon represented a major step toward the kind of Judaism we encounter during the time of Jesus. The exile forced Jews to come to terms with the experience of traumatic loss.

The exiles had to take stock and ask themselves what had led to their exile in Babylon. It forced them to go back to the roots: Where did we come from? Who are we as a people? Where did we go wrong? It also raised to a new critical level the urgent need to preserve a memory of home, of passing on the legacy, of ensuring that this people would remain a people and that something as terrible as the exile would never happen again.

Hebrew Bible

This was, then, the time when Jews began to collect their writings into what eventually became the Hebrew Bible. It was during this time of great upheaval that they paid special attention to collecting and codifying the Torah—legal traditions, some of which may well go back to Moses. In the absence of their own land, in the absence of the temple as a center of their culture and of their worship, Jews became aware of the central importance of living the law as the central defining feature of being a Jew.

The writings of the great prophets such as Isaiah of Jerusalem, Jeremiah, Amos, and Hosea, to name only a few, were also collected and, likely, edited and added to. Whereas in their own day the prophets' warnings of dire consequences for the moral and spiritual failings of the people and their kings were not always welcomed, and sometimes violently resisted, in Babylon they were later recalled as all too true.

Exile was also a time in which Jews began to develop what we today might call a "theology of hope," a hope that at some point in the future God would be true to the promises made to Abraham and to David to restore the nation, to restore Jerusalem as the center of leadership and worship. This hope comes to forceful expression in the writings of Ezekiel or of some later parts of the book of Isaiah. Jews began to dream of a new king in the line of David, one who would truly judge the people in fairness and in mercy, one who would lead the people in a way faithful to the will of God. In other words, people began to hope for a perfect king, one whom God would send. This is the time period out of which emerges what we call messianic hopes:

> The people who walked in darkness
>   have seen a great light;
> those who lived in a land of deep darkness—
>   on them light has shined. . . .
> For the yoke of their burden,
>   and the bar across their shoulders,
>   the rod of their oppressor,
>   you have broken as on the day of Midian.
> For all the boots of the tramping warriors
>   and all the garments rolled in blood
>   shall be burned as fuel for the fire.
> For a child has been born for us,
>   a son given to us;

> authority rests upon his shoulders;
>> and he is named
> Wonderful Counselor, Mighty God,
>> Everlasting Father, Prince of Peace.
> His authority shall grow continually,
>> and there shall be endless peace
> for the throne of David and his kingdom.
>> He will establish and uphold it
> with justice and with righteousness
>> from this time onward and forevermore.
> The zeal of the LORD of hosts will do this. (Isa. 9:2, 4–7)

In 538 BCE, King Cyrus of Persia permitted the Jews to return to Judea and to rebuild Jerusalem and its temple. This caused a great deal of excitement and anticipation that finally God would reestablish Israel to its rightful place, and no doubt many decided to return home. But many Jews decided to remain in Babylon. It had become home for them; they had not only survived, but prospered. Babylon would continue to be a center of Jewish culture centuries long after the time of Christ.

The situation in Judea was not a particularly a happy one. Not only was the reconstruction of Jerusalem extremely difficult and long, life in general did not measure up to the high hopes of the returnees. One of the most vexing issues was that, with the exception of a relatively brief interruption (see below), Judea remained under the thumb of great empires until and including the time of Jesus.

Alexander the Great and Hellenism

One of the most decisive events in the history of Jews was the conquest of the eastern Mediterranean area by Alexander the Great of Macedonia early in the fourth century before the time of Jesus. Alexander was born in Macedonia in 356 BCE, son of Philip II, and died a young man in 323 BCE in Babylon and was buried in the city to which he gave his name, Alexandria in Egypt.

Alexander is important for many reasons. First, he was an enthusiast for Greek culture. His father, Philip of Macedonia, made sure he had the best education, arranging to have Alexander tutored by none other than the great Greek philosopher Aristotle. As a young general, Alexander enjoyed enormous military success, acquiring an empire that reached from Egypt to what today is India and China. Among the results of Alexander's military exploits was his bequeathal to the Mediterranean world, including Judea, of a world culture—a fusion between Greek and local cultures. This culture is referred to as Hellenism, which we should translate most literally as "Greekishness."

The importance of this can hardly be overstated for an understanding of the world of Jesus and his followers. Hellenism, emerging some three hundred years before the time of Jesus, would constitute the world culture well into the Roman period, allowing for an unprecedented level of commerce in goods and ideas, facilitated by a common language, which many people could speak in addition to their local tongues. We call it "common" or Koine Greek. In short, Alexander the Great provided the Mediterranean world with a medium of communication that helps to account for how a religious movement centered on a Galilean woodworker from Palestine could so quickly become a world religion.

One Hundred Years of Independence—the Maccabees

The history of Jewish subjugation to foreign empires was interrupted in the second century before Jesus. In and around 167 BCE a guerilla war was precipitated through some very insensitive and hostile actions by the Hellenistic Syrian monarch just to the north of Judea, Antiochus IV Epiphanes. He issued harsh legislation prohibiting Jews from faithful adherence to their laws, resulting in immense tensions between Jews and their Syrian overlords, but also among themselves on how to respond to edicts of Syria. The straw that broke the camel's back was this pagan king's entering the holy of holies in the temple in Jerusalem, thereby defiling the temple. The response on the part of observant Jews was swift and violent. The Maccabees (named after the leader of the revolt, Judas Maccabeus) led a successful guerilla campaign in 166–160 BCE, finally establishing the independence of Judea in 142 BCE (an ancient account of the struggle can be found in 1–2 Maccabees, present in Catholic versions of the Bible or in the Apocrypha in Protestant versions that contain these books).

One of the important accomplishments of the Maccabees, or Hasmoneans, as they are also called, was to purify the temple, an event still celebrated in the Jewish community with the festival called Hanukkah. In 140 BCE the Hasmoneans, specifically Judas's brother Simon, fused the role of high priest and king (or ethnarch) into one. Many Jews, believing that God had given the priesthood to the descendants of Zadok, considered the priesthood of the Hasmoneans to be illegitimate. For this and other reasons, the reign of the Hasmonean dynasty, which lasted approximately one hundred years, was marked by much strife and violence.

The Romans and Herod

Due to these circumstances Palestine became vulnerable to conquest yet again. The empire to exert its power over Palestine this time was Rome. Roman imperial control arrived in the person of General Pompey in 63

BCE. After some decades, Rome appointed as puppet ruler a half-Jew named Herod, whose wife, Mariamne, was a Hasmonean. Herod undertook a massive building program, including the complete rebuilding of the temple, earning him the title "Great." His reign, especially in his later years, was marked by brutality toward any who would challenge his rule, including anyone he suspected within his own family (he had one wife and three sons executed). His brutality and paranoia is remembered in Matthew's famous account of the slaughter of the infants in Bethlehem (Matt. 2:16).

After Herod's death Palestine was divided among his sons. One of them was the Herod (his full name was Herod Antipas) who had John the Baptist beheaded (Matthew 14 || Mark 6) and who is recorded as having been present at the time of Jesus's trial (Luke 23). He ruled Galilee with the title "Tetrarch."

In Judea Herod the Great's son Archelaus was soon deposed and replaced by direct Roman rule by an administrator who would later come to be called a "procurator." At the time of Jesus's death this was none other than the infamous Pontius Pilate. We shall encounter him again when we come to discuss Jesus's death. Here it is enough to say that Pilate was known as a very brutal and capricious ruler.

Whereas we speak of the political power of this era as the Roman Empire, centered in the great imperial city of Rome, the world culture we call Hellenism still very much shaped the common culture of the time. Greek, not Latin, was the linguistic means of communicating across cultures and regions. So, when we come to the time of Jesus, Palestine had been under Hellenistic cultural influence for more than three hundred years. It had been under Roman rule for more than half a century and endured the rather uneven and often brutal rule of puppet rulers doing Rome's bidding. Bluntly put, Palestine was occupied territory during the time of Jesus. And, as is typical in such circumstances, some flourish, many more suffer terribly, and a large number of folk simply wish to survive from one day to the next. So also in the time of Jesus.

A calamity of far-reaching consequence would come four decades after Jesus's death at the hands of the Romans. A Jewish war against Roman rule took place between 66 and 70, which resulted in the sacking of Jerusalem and the destruction of the temple in 70 CE. It was out of this catastrophe that a law-centered rather than temple-centered Judaism emerged.

Hopes and Fears

We have discussed in very sketchy terms the rough contours of Jewish history up to the time of Jesus. But what was going on among Jews as they attempted to live out their social, religious, and cultural life as individuals and as communities? As stated at the beginning of the chapter, many Jews hoped intensely that at some point, possibly very soon, God would live up to the promises made to their forebears, that Israel would be reestablished in freedom and glory, and that an offspring of David—a messiah—would ascend the throne. Messianic hopes were very much alive during the time of Jesus and mark much of the excitement and also the resistance to Jesus. Such hopes would have been particularly intense among those who were disfranchised from social, economic, and religious life. But they were also alive among those sectors in society deeply committed to fidelity to the law. Many Jews saw Hellenism as the encroachment of a paganism odious to God and thus to be resolutely resisted.

But there were also those who benefited greatly from the state of affairs, who profited from the Roman occupation, culturally and economically. There may even have been "moderns," to speak anachronistically, who welcomed the cultural influence of Hellenism as the breaking in of a new day, superseding the parochialism of the old Jewish ways.

It is not difficult to see that these constituted huge tensions within the Jewish community. Some of these factors were at work in the emergence of identifiable movements and social groupings we encounter in the gospels.

Palestine in Jesus's Time

Geography

The geography of Palestine (see illustration 4.1) figures in many important ways, as we already saw in comparing the Synoptic Gospels with John. According to the Synoptic Gospels, after growing up in Nazareth Jesus did the bulk of his work in Galilee, with a home base in Capernaum at the Sea of Galilee or Kinneret (also called Sea of Tiberias). In the first three gospels, Jesus decides to go to Jerusalem to face death and travels through Samaria to get there.

The way the author of the Fourth Gospel tells it, Jesus made numerous trips between Jerusalem and Galilee, having to travel through Samaria on the way. The schema of conflict with the authorities in Judea, in particular Jerusalem, is thus retained, but it is made more constant by the repeated clashes of Jesus with the powerful in the capital.

Each of these regions was rather different. Judea was in Jesus's day the heartland of Palestinian Judaism, indeed of world Jewry, being home to the central cultic or worship institution of Judaism, the temple. Galilee, on the other hand, had a much more mixed population of Jews and Gentiles. Scholars are not sure what the proportions were or how deep the Jewish roots of the population went. Just a very few kilometers from Nazareth,

Illustration 4.1. Geography of Palestine

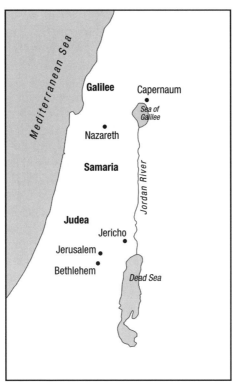

for example, was a Greek-speaking city named Sepphoris (Zippori). The influence of Hellenism on architecture and culture is evident throughout the region. Along the shores of the lake where Jesus appears to have been active was Tiberias, the imposing new city named after Roman Emperor Tiberius. If we can draw any inferences from his parables, it would appear that Jesus largely avoided the cities, relating primarily to people living on the land or in small villages.

Between Galilee and Judea was Samaria. The longstanding hostility between Jews and Samaritans is epitomized perhaps most strongly by the actions of the Hasmonean ruler John Hyrcanus. In 128 BCE he destroyed the Samaritan temple and, a scant nineteen years later, their capital Samaria. Then, in the early years of the Common Era, Samaritans snuck into the Jerusalem temple and defiled it with bones. No doubt pilgrims making their way through the territory between Galilee and Judea had good reason to be on the lookout for trouble. Special poignancy is lent to the episode of Jesus's talking to the Samaritan woman in John 4 and to the parable of the good Samaritan in Luke 10.

Groups in Palestinian Society

In his writings, Jewish historian Josephus names four "philosophies" as particularly important in Jewish society: Pharisees, Sadducees, Essenes, and Zealots. We know of Pharisees and Sadducees from the New Testament, but Essenes and Zealots, as well as another group we encounter repeatedly in the gospels, the scribes, are also relevant.

PHARISEES

Perhaps the most important movement or group in Jewish society, and the most prevalent within the gospel narratives, are the Pharisees. We are not exactly sure how or when they emerged. In fact, there is a great deal of ambiguity around much of what we think we know about the Pharisees, first, because we have relatively little information on them and, second, because the sources we do have give historians much the same difficulties they have with the gospels as sources for historical information on Jesus. That is, we have sources that have very strong interests, either to commend the Pharisees (Josephus speaks of them as a "philosophy" akin to Gentile "schools" that commended a particular way of life) or to discredit them (New Testament writers show them with few exceptions in opposition to Jesus). To complicate matters, our sources are sometimes of uncertain date (traditions preserved in rabbinic literature). So everything that follows should be considered as at best a distillation of majority opinion under sharp review.

The Pharisees likely emerged during the Hasmonean period as a group of law-abiding Jews committed to observing God's ways, perhaps with designs of changing society to conform to their views on what that might mean, especially with regard to tithing and purity laws. Their name is likely a derivative of the root *prsh* ("to separate, interpret"). Some of them might have been priests, but many were likely laypeople who, nevertheless, took on the discipline of priestly purity as a life of piety. They were not likely members of the ruling class, but may well have attempted to play a political role as educators, judges, and officials. The extent of their impact on the rest of society is a matter of some dispute among scholars. According to Josephus, who identifies himself as having been a Pharisee, they numbered around six thousand during the time of Jesus. Paul the apostle identifies himself as a Pharisee (Phil. 3:5; see also Acts 23:6; 26:5), which indicates that there were Pharisees in regions beyond Palestine. However great or small their importance in the larger story, there is little question that Pharisees played a very significant role in relation to the Jesus movement.

If later rabbinic traditions go back to the Pharisees, and rabbinic literature does indicate a strong connection, then we might see among Pharisees the beginnings of a tradition of interpretation of Torah called *halakah*, a kind of "oral Torah." This is sometimes also called a "hedge" around the Torah:

Moses received the Torah from Sinai and committed it to Joshua, and Joshua to the elders, and the elders to the prophets; and the prophets committed it to the men of the Great Congregation. These said three things:
"Be deliberate in judgment";
"Raise up many disciples"; and
"Make a hedge for the Torah." (Mishnah, tractate *Aboth* 1.1)

The *halakah* was an ever-growing collection of more or less binding interpretations of the law intended to make the Torah livable within the changing circumstances of life, but also to safeguard the Torah from human manipulations and infractions. These traditions of interpretation and application were gathered up some centuries later in the Talmud (made up of Mishnah and Gemara [i.e., rules and interpretive discussion]). This may be what in the New Testament is referred to as "the tradition of the elders" (e.g., Mark 7:3–4). One source of controversy between Jesus and the Pharisees appears to have been over the status and function of this oral law, in effect, over how to interpret the Torah in relation to everyday life.

It was apparently in Pharisaic circles that some of the most intense hopes for divine intervention, as well as some of the most radical visions for the future, were nurtured and formulated. One of the most striking of these hopes was the belief in the resurrection of the dead. (For an example that not all Jews held to such ideas, see the account of Paul's arraignment before Jewish leaders in Acts 23:1–10.) In this the Pharisees and the movement around Jesus were close indeed.

Due to the largely negative portrayal they receive in the New Testament, Pharisees have become in Christian circles, at least until recent times, a virtual byword for legalism and intolerance. Is this fair? Hardly. Whereas there were tensions between Pharisees and a less observant population, Pharisees were generally respected. A measure of their importance for Jewish society is that after the terrible calamity of the war with Rome in 66–70 CE, when Jerusalem and the temple were destroyed, it was Pharisees, practiced in devotion to the Torah, who were in a position to help the Jewish people get back on their feet and to find a new center in Torah observance. Rabbinic Judaism has its roots in the traditions of the Pharisees.

However unfair the stereotype of legalism is, it is also true that *any* group, regardless of religion, that is deeply committed to living a life of faithfulness is vulnerable to legalism, hypocrisy, and intolerance—or at least of being suspected of being intolerant and hypocritical. The history of Christianity, for example, provides numerous examples of legalism and intolerance. Might legalism, hypocrisy, and intolerance be occupational hazards of all who try hard (harder than those in the surrounding culture) to be good, holy, and acceptable to God?

The desire of Pharisees to please God through meticulous observance, especially of purity rules, would have necessarily put them on a collision course with less strict and nonobservant Jews. Perhaps we can empathize with the extreme discomfort of some of them at Jesus's touching lepers who were ritually contaminated or at his consorting with "sinners" like tax collectors and prostitutes at mealtime. Was he not thereby endangering the fate of the people as a whole by drawing God's displeasure on them? Since the gospels were written by those who took Jesus's side in these controversies, we should hardly be surprised that Pharisees do not get what a historian would consider a fair shake.

Yet another factor helps us to understand the negative press the Pharisees get in the gospels: the war with Rome in 66–70 CE (see above). It appears that the traditions of the Pharisees left an ever-stronger mark on the Judaism that began to take shape in the decades following that calamity. This was also precisely the period in which the Jesus movement was coming to greater definition. We should not be surprised that there would have been intense debates between Jews who believed Jesus to be the Messiah and the true interpreter of Torah and those who felt that the Roman destruction of Jerusalem was proof enough that Jesus could not possibly be the fulfillment of God's promises and was thus also not to be trusted regarding the interpretation of Torah. Such relations appear to have been acrimonious during Jesus's own life and would only become more so in the years that followed, as seen in the harsh words of judgment against the Pharisees that Matthew attributes to Jesus (Matthew 23). There is reason to think that at least some of that harshness reflects the post-70 CE hostility between, on the one hand, pro-Jesus Jews and their non-Jewish associates and, on the other, the vast majority of Jews, who rejected Jesus and his followers as misguided at best and blasphemously unfaithful to Judaism at worst. The gospels were written exactly during this time.

To summarize: the rather one-sidedly negative depiction of the Pharisees in the gospels may reflect less the battles Jesus himself had with them than the struggles of his followers with those leading the Jewish people after the destruction of Jerusalem. It is even suggested by Jewish Jesus scholar David Flusser that the tensions between Jesus and the Pharisees in the New Testament likely reflect tensions *among* Pharisees and that Jesus himself was a Pharisee. However that may be, it is caution enough not to take the one-sidedly negative portrayal of Pharisees in the gospels at face value.

SADDUCEES

The Sadducees are another first-century Palestinian group mentioned in the New Testament, albeit much more rarely. We know even less about this group. It is difficult to be sure either about who they were or where they came from. Most scholars think that we should think of them as a largely aristocratic, priestly leadership group or persons in charge of the affairs of the temple. Their name may have derived from the character of Zadok, whose descendants appear to have constituted the Jerusalem priesthood from the time of King David's son Solomon up until the exile, after which those eligible to serve as priests appear to have included the descendants of Aaron. Even so, Zadokites seem to have held on to the high priesthood until Antiochus IV Epiphanes, after which the Hasmoneans arrogated that role to themselves. Sadducees appear to have been socially well placed.

Sadducees do not get a particularly sympathetic press from either Josephus or the later Jewish tradition. According to ancient records, they did not believe in divine determinism; that is, they believed God had bestowed free will on human beings. This had implications for how God's sovereignty was understood. More importantly, especially for the early Jesus movement, ancient witnesses testify that they did not believe in immortality or resurrection (the issue with which they are identified in most of the instances in which they are mentioned in the New Testament; e.g., Mark 12:18 || Luke 20:27 || Matthew 22:23; Acts 4:2; 23:6–8). Belief in resurrection was important to Pharisees and, of course, to followers of Jesus. Resurrection was an essential component of a belief in God's sovereign intervention in the affairs of an evil world (see chapter 6 below). If our few morsels of information are correct, we can see why Sadducees would have been opponents of both Pharisees and followers of Jesus.

ESSENES AND THE DEAD SEA COMMUNITY AT QUMRAN

One important group we do not meet directly in the New Testament is the Essenes. But Josephus, Philo of Alexandria, the great first-century Jewish philosopher, and pagan writer Pliny the Elder witness to their existence during the time of Jesus. Once again the scholarly debates are, to say the least, heated as to the origin, character, and extent of the Essene movement, especially with respect to their relationship to the site at Qumran at the Dead Sea. Even whether the site at Qumran housed a religious community or whether it was a factory is up for debate. What follows must therefore be seen as, once again, tentative.

The Essenes can be thought of as true separatists. Whereas the Pharisees kept separate from impure or contaminated elements within Jewish society, they were not separatists; they were public figures, as the gospels correctly depict them. Apparently the Essenes believed in living apart, in chosen poverty, as well as in celibacy. Josephus estimates their size at four thousand.

Since the discovery in 1947 of the Dead Sea Scrolls at what may have been an Essene monastery at Qumran in the immediate vicinity of the Dead Sea south of Jericho, Essenes have been linked to that community. If that is correct, and there are scholars who not only doubt but reject the connection, then not all Essenes lived at Qumran, because that site would have had room for only several hundred people.

Further, if that connection holds and if the famous scrolls give us some insight into their thinking, then we can surmise some other features of the movement: first, they were deeply alienated from the temple in Jerusalem and those presently in charge of its worship, hoping for a day when a new temple would be built in which proper sacrifices would once again be offered (one of the Dead Sea Scrolls is known as the Temple Scroll). They may well have viewed themselves as the true priesthood for such a temple. Second, they believed that God would act in a very dramatic way in the very near future to bring about an end to Roman domination and reestablish the kingdom of Israel. They may even have believed that they would join God's heavenly troops in the war against Rome (one scroll is entitled "War of the Sons of Light against the Sons of Darkness"). In short, they appear to have had very strongly eschatological, even apocalyptic views (for the meaning of these terms, see chapter 6 below). Third, the scrolls suggest that they were led by a "righteous teacher," suggesting similarities to the movement centered on Jesus.

We introduce the Essenes in this study of Jesus not because Jesus had ties to this group, but because John the Baptist may reflect some of their thinking and some of their values (see chapter 7 below). Even that remains very much at the level of conjecture, however. Whatever the connection between the Essenes and the Dead Sea community might have been, they represent important evidence that people like John the Baptist or Jesus, or some of their radical followers, were not the only Jews who believed that God would act in very dramatic fashion very soon to bring about a new time of justice and peace. This is thus an important reminder also not to think of the Judaism of Jesus's time as a uniform phenomenon from which Jesus and his followers were the lone dissenters.

ZEALOTS

Zealots are often listed among the identifiable groups of Jesus's day. Josephus refers to them as the "fourth philosophy." They are often characterized as religiously motivated opponents of the Roman occupation and those who collaborated with it. The term Zealots is synonymous, then, with revolutionaries, guerilla warriors, and even assassins. Today most scholars think that during the time of Jesus there certainly were groups of radicals, guerillas, bandits, or brigands who fought Romans, wealthy landholders, and collaborators in sporadic battles and hit-and-run attacks. There may have been radical elements also among Pharisees, whose vision of the coming reign of God would have moved them to take a very hostile stance toward the present order.

However, as an identifiably cohesive movement, Zealots really came into existence only during the war with the Romans in 66–70 CE, a good three decades after Jesus's public ministry. They likely derived their nickname from association with the priest Phineas, whose "zeal" for God led to his killing an Israelite and his Gentile woman companion (Num. 25:7–13). Even if we should be very cautious about using the designation *Zealot* for those who in Jesus's day were willing to exercise violence in their zeal for God, there are tantalizing hints that Jesus did not befriend only "sinners and tax collectors," but may have drawn followers from among some radical sectors of society. One of Jesus's disciples is named Simon the Zealot (Luke 6:15; Acts 1:13). That may simply be a nickname referring to Simon's own zeal as a follower of Jesus or as a pious Jew; it might also be an indication, however, that Jesus drew into his inner circle those with an intense impatience to see God establish his kingdom. Also among his inner circle are two brothers, James and John, to whom Jesus is said to have given the nickname "Sons of Thunder" (Mark 3:17). One can only guess what sort of hotheads they were. Speculation has also included Judas Iscariot, whose second name some have linked to the Sicarii ("assassins").

Scribes

Often in the gospels Jesus's opponents are summarized as "the scribes and the Pharisees." A scribe in Jesus's world was not a member of a movement or philosophy so much as a midlevel official—or bureaucrat, we would say today—serving the structures of power, whether political or religious. Some were high officials, wielding considerable power, others were local village officials. The Hebrew Bible knows of scribes like Ezra, the most famous of them, who are learned in the law and trusted as leaders. Scribes must be credited with the formation of the Scriptures of Israel. In Matthew Jesus is quoted as speaking favorably of a "scribe who has been trained for the kingdom of heaven" (Matt. 13:52). We might in that sense think of the writers of the New Testament as "scribes of the kingdom." For the most part, however, in the gospels they are typically suspicious of Jesus's activity and teaching and often hostile.

Sectors in Palestinian Society

We become aware of other groups in reading the gospels. It would be more accurate to refer to these as sectors of society. They are identified in the stories about Jesus and play a significant role in the controversies that surrounded his actions. A full picture of their importance would require a fuller treatment of Palestinian society. A few generalizations will need to suffice.

The Palestine of Jesus's time was a region under the imperial thumb of Rome via either its own governors (e.g., Pontius Pilate) or puppet rulers like Herod and his descendants. Most immediately, they enforced their control through the military, whose responsibilities often extended to policing and tax enforcement. These forces were often mercenary or local armies lent to the Romans to secure their interests (e.g., the armies of Herod and his offspring).

As always in such circumstances, there were sectors of society quite willing to collaborate with this imperial occupation, others fiercely opposed, and many more simply trying to make it from one day to the next.

Rich and Poor

At the cost of oversimplifying the diverse conditions in Judea and Galilee, for example, it is safe to say that the vast majority of the population of Palestine was made up of rural and urban poor, with Jesus generally relating to the rural poor. Many were peasants, making their living off land increasingly owned by a wealthy elite. This only increased the rural population's economic and social vulnerability. Many were driven off the land into the cities, into yet deeper desperation of poverty and disease. Many others were left to work as day laborers and sharecroppers on large estates owned by often-absentee landlords. Through such breaking of ties to land and place, kinship and family ties were also severely strained and often broken, leaving persons isolated and without a network of support that would have provided some security. Not to own land set one apart from those who did, even if that might be only a small plot.

Jesus's parables take on special resonance within this world, a world of unequal wealth and power, of economic vulnerability, of fierce competition, as well as of wily survivors. The sometimes-dark humor of the parables reflects the yearnings and sense of injustice that people would have experienced. We should imagine that Jesus's popularity was in no small measure owing to his understanding of the vulnerability and everyday suffering of "little people" and of his care for their everyday welfare, illustrated in the gospel accounts by his feeding of the multitudes (e.g., Mark 6 || John 6) and by his challenge to the rich to give their wealth to the needy (Matt. 19:16–22 || Mark 10:17–22 || Luke 18:18–23).

Women

The status of women in Jesus's society was not high, even if we should be careful not to overgeneralize. Women were, for the most part, not greatly respected. Women lived within a patriarchal context, with few, if any, rights. Widows were particularly vulnerable. Some were driven into prostitution (see below). We meet many such women in the narratives of Jesus's activity.

The presence of women in the stories of Jesus should be taken as an indicator of the character of Jesus's relationships with people and also of his message. Jesus seems to have had a high degree of concern for their well-being and little concern for whether his openness to them compromised his public standing. Their presence in the gospel stories, especially at the high points in the narrative such as Jesus's death and resurrection, is all the more noteworthy if, as many scholars believe, the early church became increasingly *less* open to women's full participation as years and decades passed. We might therefore guess that, if we find plenty of evidence of the importance of women in the circle around Jesus in accounts written decades after Jesus's Palestinian ministry, then their importance to Jesus and his movement may have been even greater than the gospels suggest!

The gospel accounts show Jesus's special care for widows (e.g., Mark 12:40–44; Luke 18:2–8) and women afflicted with illness or rejection by others, whether the raising of his disciple Peter's mother-in-law (Matt. 8:14–15 || Mark 1:29–31 || Luke 4:38–39) or the raising of Jairus's daughter and the healing of the woman with hemorrhage (Mark 5:22–43 || Luke 8:41–56). Jesus is depicted as reaching out to women scorned by others, illustrated wonderfully in the episode of Jesus talking to the Samaritan woman at the well (John 4) and of his treatment of the woman caught committing adultery (John 8:3–11).

Women seemed to reciprocate with respect and loyalty, whether in what is often referred to as his anointing (compare the various accounts in Matt. 26:6–13 || Mark 14:3–9; Luke 7:36–50; John 12:1–8), financial support of Jesus's ministry (Luke 8:2–3, where some of the women are identified by name and social status), and most dramatically by being present when the men had fled at Jesus's crucifixion; they were also the very first to be at the grave as witnesses to the resurrection.

Notable are also the several women named Mary, among them his mother, who continues to play a role in the narrative after his birth (Acts 1:14); Mary, the sister of Martha and Lazarus (especially John 11); and perhaps most notably Mary Magdalene. She is referred to repeatedly at pivotal points in the story by all four evangelists, especially in connection with Jesus's crucifixion and resurrection. Her prominence in the story testifies to her importance to Jesus, but also to the movement in the decades following, as witnessed to by her prominence in the tradition. Parenthetically, there is no textual evidence, not even a hint, that she was a prostitute, as tradition has often painted her. Rather, she was a particularly well-known beneficiary of Jesus's healing and exorcism ministry and without doubt an important member of his inner circle of followers.

This short inventory illustrates why there is a growing consensus that Jesus's ministry was characterized by deliberate openness to women. How much this set him apart from his contemporaries—or even from the movement that bore his name in decades to follow—continues to be a matter of debate. We do not need to demonize his contemporaries to see and appreciate that openness.

PROSTITUTES

The evangelist Matthew lists two groups of social rejects—tax collectors and prostitutes (21:31–32). Prostitutes, then as now, bore the brunt of social opprobrium. Why would Jesus have reached out to such persons, thereby repeatedly putting a cloud on his reputation? He clearly did not think that commerce in sex was a morally indifferent issue. Perhaps, as in the case of tax collectors (see below), Jesus saw that their means of earning a living was an expression of their own victimization by an unjust social system. It is clear that prostitution victimizes women first and foremost, doubly so when the context is one of extreme economic distress. So also in Palestine. Without approving of illicit sexual behavior, especially of those abusing the women (John 8:3–11), Jesus seems to have been able to provide the kind of respect and acceptance that allowed them to value themselves as daughters of God. The gospels are clear that he was willing to do so at the cost of his reputation among the religious elites.

TAX COLLECTORS

In reading the gospels we frequently encounter tax or toll collectors (the King James Version calls them "publicans"). One of them is numbered among Jesus's followers (Matt. 10:3; Mark 2:14). Toll collectors were ubiquitous within the Palestinian context and had been for all the centuries of foreign domination. At the cost of oversimplification, the system ran roughly like this: apart from the temple tax that every Jew was obligated to pay, the Romans exacted taxes from the population in the form of tribute and poll taxes. In addition, tolls were collected for commerce along roads and in towns. The collecting of at least some of these taxes and tolls was given to tax "farmers," who in turn would hire collectors to do the dirty work. These collectors were not paid a salary; it was assumed that they would make their livelihood by raising money that exceeded the amount that they would then have to turn in to their superiors. Such a system would leave plenty of room for abuse, graft, and theft. Tax collectors, who no doubt sometimes took the jobs for their own survival, were naturally the target of suspicion and hostility. They also bore the brunt of anti-Roman anger, especially in Judea.

Jesus appears to have recognized the exceedingly vulnerable situation of these tax collectors by reaching out to them. The gospels suggest that he was accused over and over again of eating with tax collectors and sinners (Matt. 11:19 || Luke 7:34–35; Matt. 9:11–13 || Mark 2:14–17 || Luke 5:27–31). The episode in Jericho with the famous tax collector Zacchaeus, recounted in Luke 19:1–10, is a particularly instructive and moving account of how Jesus reached out to those on the margins, even if what put them there was their own participation in an oppressive system. It is highly instructive that Jesus's drawing close to tax collectors is remembered as having a direct impact on that oppression. After Jesus invites himself to the tax collector's home for a meal, Zacchaeus promptly assures Jesus he will make things right with those he has wronged. Luke concludes the narrative and in the process sums up the importance of Jesus's engagement with those caught up on the structures and systems of oppression and injustice with Jesus's startling utterance, "Today salvation has come to this house!"

SICK PEOPLE

The absence of medical knowledge and attention and the ever-present poverty insured that among the crowds that constantly surrounded Jesus were many who struggled with illness. Many of the sick were doubly ill, as it were, because certain illnesses marked people as being ritually impure and thus to be avoided by the pious. Most dramatic among these was leprosy—a disfiguring disease that brought with it radical ostracism. Lepers were typically banished to the edges of society. So, in incidents and stories where Jesus reaches out to lepers and heals them, we should pay close attention to exactly how Jesus interacts with them. He gets close to them, he touches them, eats with them, and he addresses them with respect (e.g., Matt. 8:2–4 || Mark 1:40–44; Matt. 26:6 || Mark 14:3; Luke 17:12–19). Jesus's behavior would have shocked both lepers and those who avoided them.

POSSESSED PEOPLE

Another phenomenon prevalent in first-century Palestine leading to social ostracism was what is even today often called possession by evil spirits or demons. Unlike in many parts of the world, in which such phenomena are understood in spiritual categories, in North American and European cultures many of these phenomena are typically identified as psychological disorders and misunderstood physical ailments, such as epilepsy. Others see in these phenomena the effects of social and political oppression as well.

In Jesus's day people would not have debated about whether there are evil spirits and whether spirits can inhabit and possess people. They viewed human life as caught up in a great battle between good and evil forces, a battle that extended from the struggle between nations at war with each other, to the struggle with illness, poverty, and powerlessness, and into the personal sphere of demonic possession of individuals (for a fascinating glimpse of the interplay between these various spheres, see the remarkable incident of the Gerasene demoniac in Mark 5:1–20, where the name of the demons is "Legion," a barely veiled allusion to the imperial military presence of Rome). For Jesus's contemporaries the issue was rather how one can be liberated from the control of such oppressive spiritual forces.

Jesus appears to have been known in many circles as an exorcist, that is, as someone who could liberate people from evil spirits. Jesus's success at exorcism was perceived to be an act of great power and begged for some explanation as to the nature and origin of such power. We catch some of the excitement around this question in Matthew 12:22–32 and parallel passages in the other gospels (see chapter 9 below).

Conclusion

The Palestine of the first century was caught up in intense religious, political, and social ferment. We find a population struggling under the heavy lid of imperial control and economic oppression. Many were pushed to the margins of society, either because of extreme poverty or because of debilitating and ostracizing illnesses of a physical and spiritual nature. Others struggled mightily to practice fidelity to the will of God as expressed in the Torah and sometimes fell victim to the vices that easily beset the virtuous, namely, intolerance and hypocrisy. Not surprisingly, many Jews in the first century had an intense desire to see God rectify the situation. Many of those expectations centered around the hope that God would bring about his long-promised kingdom or reign, that God would send a new David, a messiah who would set things right.

I have described Jesus's society in this way in order to awaken the awareness that it is impossible for Jesus not have evoked great excitement in his contemporaries, given his teachings, actions, healings, and exorcisms: hostility from suspicious leadership and intense enthusiasm among needy folk who saw him as potentially God's Messiah. The Jewish community into which Jesus was born and within which he worked had a long history. That history of liberation, promise, failure, and hope predisposed many Jews to have profound expectations of what God might do in the future. That is the world in which Jesus acted; that is the world in which he spoke about the kingdom of God. It would be impossible

Key Terms and Concepts
Alexander the Great
Babylon
demon possessed (demoniac)
Essenes
exile
exodus
Hasmoneans
Hellenism
Herod the Great
Israelites/Hebrews
Jews
lepers
Maccabees
Messiah
northern kingdom/Israel/Ephraim
oral law/*halakah*
Pharisees
Pompey
prostitutes
Qumran
Sadducees
southern kingdom/Judah
Talmud
tax collectors
YHWH
Zealots

for that society to be nonchalant about this man—as his history bears out amply.

For Further Reading

Crossan, John Dominic, and Jonathan L. Reed. *Excavating Jesus: Beneath the Stones, behind the Texts*. San Francisco: Harper, 2001.

Horsley, Richard A. *Galilee: History, Politics, People*. Philadelphia: Trinity, 1995.

———. *Jesus and the Spiral of Violence: Popular Jewish Resistance in Roman Palestine*. San Francisco: Harper & Row, 1987.

Malina, Bruce J. *The Social Gospel of Jesus: The Kingdom of God in Mediterranean Perspective*. Minneapolis: Fortress, 2001.

———. *Windows on the World of Jesus: Time Travel to Ancient Judea*. Louisville: Westminster John Knox, 1993.

Rousseau, John, and Rami Arav. *Jesus and His World: An Archaeological and Cultural Dictionary*. Minneapolis: Fortress, 1995.

Schüssler Fiorenza, Elisabeth. *In Memory of Her: A Feminist Theological Reconstruction of Christian Origins*. New York: Crossroad, 1983.

Stegeman, Wolfgang, Bruce J. Malina, and Gerd Theissen, eds. *The Social Setting of Jesus and the Gospels*. Minneapolis: Fortress, 2002.

Witherington, Ben, III. *Women in the Ministry of Jesus: A Study of Jesus's Attitudes to Women and Their Roles as Reflected in His Earthly Life*. New York: Cambridge University Press, 1987.

5

Birth of Jesus

At first glance, it seems quite obvious why, following the introductory chapters, we would begin our consideration of Jesus with an exploration of the accounts of his birth and their significance. After all, life begins at birth. Having read all four gospels and knowing something about how the traditions of Jesus's life and teachings were collected and put into writing, we will know why that is *not* obvious, however. Apart from two of the gospels, Matthew and Luke, no one among New Testament authors says anything about Jesus's birth. Paul does know of a tradition that Jesus is of the line of David (Rom. 1:3), but he mentions neither his birth to a virgin nor of it happening in Bethlehem. I mention Paul because his writings are the earliest in the New Testament. But the same might be said of Mark and John, evangelists whose gospels *begin* with an account of the adult Jesus's ministry, not with his birth. Their silence on this might startle us.

The birth story of Jesus is, even so, a well-known part of the tradition about Jesus and clearly important in the gospels of Matthew and Luke. Indeed, their accounts are intended to set the scene for their story of Jesus. So it is only fitting that we should take up this part of the Jesus story at this point. We will treat each of the accounts in Matthew and Luke and then ask some difficult questions. This discussion will be of greatest value if it is read *after* a careful comparative reading of the infancy narratives in Matthew 1–2 and Luke 1:1–2:52 and 3:23–38.

Matthew's Account of Jesus's Birth and Infancy

We begin with Matthew's account, not because it is earlier and more reliable than Luke's (there is no reason to think that it is), but only because Matthew comes first in the sequence of gospels in the New Testament.

Genealogy of Jesus

He will shortly inform us that Jesus's birth was from a virgin named Mary. So why does Matthew provide a genealogy through the father? Is there a purpose other than to trace genetic lineage?

The answer may already be hidden in the two names given in the very first sentence: "the son of *David*, the son of *Abraham*." These are two of the most important names in the family history of Israel. Abraham was the father of the nation, the one to whom God made the promises of nationhood. David, on the other hand, was the father of the royal house to whom God had promised the throne forever. Jews believed the Messiah, the Christ, the Anointed One, to come from the house of David. At the outset of the story, then, Matthew places Jesus into the very center of the history of Israel, identifying him with promise and liberation, with nationhood and kingship.

In Greek, Matthew 1:1 literally begins, "The book of *genesis* of Jesus [the] Christ." English translations obscure this clear allusion to the first Genesis found at the beginning of the Bible. By making this allusion, Matthew is insisting that this new "genesis," this "starting over," has deep historical roots that go back to the very beginning of the family story, not only, but especially of the people of Israel.

The highly symbolic nature of this genealogy is seen in other ways as well. The genealogy is stylistically shaped around three groups of fourteen generations (see chapter 3 above). The number fourteen is prominent, and the numerical value of the name David adds up to fourteen—indicating that Matthew uses the genealogy to point to the connection between Jesus and David. Jesus is "Son of David" (see also 9:27; 12:23; 15:22; 20:30; 21:9). Jesus is King, "Messiah," in the lineage of David.

Some scholars divide this genealogy into six groups of seven—the number seven being the biblical number for completeness—symbolizing that when history had come to its fullness, Jesus appeared on the scene. Such a reading appears to impose on the structure of the genealogy something to which it does not draw attention. The allusion to David is much clearer.

Listed among the progenitors of Jesus are four rather unusual women: Tamar, Rahab, Ruth, and Bathsheba (referred to not by name, but as the "wife of Uriah"). All of them are to one degree or another ill suited for an official family portrait. But here they play an important symbolic role in this highly symbolic genealogy: Tamar, daughter-in-law to the patriarch Judah, conceived a child by disguising herself as a prostitute and then tricking her father-in-law into sleeping with her (Genesis 38), the kind of episode usually covered up in a family history. We can only assume that the Rahab listed here is none other than the Gentile prostitute in Jericho who protected the Israelite spies, thus saving herself and her family (Joshua 2; 6). Ruth is another Gentile woman, married to an Israelite. Her story is wonderfully retold in the biblical book bearing her name. Finally, there is Bathsheba, associated with a very dark chapter in the life of King David, a story of lust, murder, confrontation, and contrition recounted in the biblical record (2 Samuel 11–12).

Why are these women part of this genealogy? We are quite legitimately invited to ask the question, especially given the symbolic nature of the genealogy. One reason might be to highlight the ultimate and mysterious agency of God: God brings about salvation regardless of historical circumstances; God's way of being true to the promises made to Abraham may well find very surprising and circuitous, even morally ambiguous, routes. A second reason for the inclusion of these women might be that they would have been the subject of rumor and suspicion. It would not take much to draw some parallels to the way in which Jesus's own birth might well have been greeted within the larger Jewish community, given that he was conceived out of wedlock. Is Matthew, by drawing attention to Tamar, Rahab, Ruth, and Bathsheba, telling readers, both friendly and hostile, that God's ways have always been unusual and not seldom accompanied by the whiff of scandal?

There is a contemporary twist to this issue. In the decades following Jesus's earthly life, the charge was made that Jesus was illegitimate, a charge no doubt intended to discredit him and his devotees. Recently, however, the same has been proposed, not to discredit Jesus, to be sure, but to see both Matthew's and Luke's narrative as insisting on God's agency in the midst of a scandalous circumstance, just as in the case of the four women in the genealogy (see the controversial work of feminist biblical scholar Jane Schaberg, *The Illegitimacy of Jesus: A Feminist Theological Interpretation of the Infancy Narratives* [San Francisco: Harper & Row, 1987]).

In my view such a proposal is consistent with the notion that God can bring good out of any situation, a conviction expressed often in the Bible, one that comes to expression not least in the presence of the four women in the genealogy. That said, this specific proposal rests heavily on an imaginative reading between the lines. It may rest also on a scientifically informed conviction that a virgin birth simply cannot happen, a perspective the author of the Gospel of Matthew would not have shared. It is worth pondering that, in terms of miracle, birth from a virgin pales in comparison to the arrival of salvation, which is, finally, the heart of both Matthew's and Luke's accounts. Both assert intrusive, reality-altering, prediction-shattering action on the part of God.

Birth of Jesus

Symbol and allusion characterize Matthew's birth narrative as much as they do the genealogy. Matthew introduces Jesus's birth in a very straightforward fashion: "The birth of Jesus the Messiah took place in this way" (1:18). There follows a discussion of Mary and the circumstances of her engagement to Joseph and the statement that she was found to be with child by or from the Holy Spirit. Matthew allows the reader to appreciate how scandalous all this would seem. Joseph, a "just man," that is, one who lives a pious, law-abiding life, is clearly puzzled and embarrassed by this circumstance. He wants to distance himself from Mary and possibly also protect Mary from further embarrassment by breaking off their engagement. All this is described in the tersest terms possible. But as terse as is the account, first-century readers would have been more than aware that they were witnessing a potential disaster in which Mary would bring a child to birth out of wedlock. In the nick of time, Joseph has a dream in which a divine messenger (that is what the term *angel* means) informs him that he is to take Mary as his wife and that the child is of the Holy Spirit. He is told to name the boy "Jesus" (Hebrew "Yeshua"), which means "liberator" or "savior." This is the same name as "Joshua." Thereby another link to the story of Israel is established.

To the links in the genealogy and in the naming of Jesus we can now add another in the form of a characteristic feature of Matthew's storytelling: he quotes a Bible verse. "All this took place to fulfill what had been spoken by the Lord through the prophet" (1:22). References to fulfilling scripture occur repeatedly in Matthew's way of rehearsing the story of Jesus, not least in his infancy narrative. In this particular instance Matthew is referring to Isaiah, a favorite mine of scriptural support for believers in Jesus. He quotes Isaiah 7:14 in Matthew 1:23, here given the way Matthew quotes it:

> Look, the virgin shall conceive and bear a son,
>   and they shall name him Emmanuel,
> which means, "God is with us."

But in Isaiah 7:14 we find the term *young woman* rather than *virgin*:

> Look, the young woman is with child and shall bear a son, and shall name him Immanuel.

True, the NIV and a few other versions retain "virgin" in their rendition of Isaiah, but the Hebrew *almah* would normally mean "woman of marriageable age."

Did Matthew inject the term *virgin* into the text, in effect altering Isaiah? Do some translations like the NIV then allow Matthew to rewrite Isaiah?

Not really. Like most Jews in the Hellenistic period, early believers in Jesus most frequently used a Greek translation of the Hebrew Bible known as the Septuagint (abbreviated LXX). This Greek version of the Bible translates Hebrew *almah* with *parthenos* in Isaiah 7:14. *Parthenos* is typically translated "virgin," even if it too need not necessarily mean more than "young woman." Despite that semantic stretch, it is clear that Matthew understands the term to mean "virgin" and quotes Isaiah as a biblical prophecy pointing to the unusual circumstances of Jesus's birth. Did Matthew come to believe in the virgin birth because of this verse? We should be careful not to draw this conclusion too quickly, given that Luke too holds this view and nowhere makes reference to Isaiah 7:14.

The quotation from Isaiah 7 adds, or at least supports, yet another element in the narrative, namely, the name *Emmanuel*, which means "God is with us." Allusions to the hopes and dreams of Israel continue to pile up.

Herod and the Visit of the Magi from the East

Herod

Beginning with Matthew 2, the story takes a particularly poignant turn. Jesus's birth is placed into the time of King Herod. We know from historical sources that Herod was a brutal and demanding monarch, ruling at the behest of the Roman Empire. He was paranoid about anyone he thought might want to wrest power from him, including members of his own family, a number of whom he had murdered. Matthew very deliberately makes a connection between the birth of Jesus and this ruler, who would have been remembered by Matthew's readers as brutal, power hungry, and paranoid.

Magi

What draws Herod's attention to the events in Bethlehem is the curious visit of some *magoi* (Greek) from the East. They are sometimes referred to as "kings," sometimes as "wise men." We are probably safest simply to refer to them with the conventional Latinized *magi*. Matthew might think of them as *magi*cians, but more likely as astrologers, given the reference to the star in 2:2. Importantly, the distinction between astrology and astronomy was unknown at the time.

We are not told how many magi there were; we are told only that there were three gifts. Later tradition obliges us by filling in the blanks: in Western tradition there were three "kings," and their names were Caspar, Melchior, and Balthazar. Syrian and Armenian traditions give them different names, some even suggesting that they represent the three families of Noah. But this is pure, if delightful, fantasy.

The location of "east" too is left rather vague. Does if refer to Persia, Babylon, or more immediately to the Arabian or Syrian deserts? More than likely

Matthew has Babylon in mind. Babylon was remembered as both the place of exile for the Jewish people and as a major center of learning, especially of astrology and astronomy. There is great likelihood that with this allusion to Babylon, Matthew wants us to be aware that these are *pagan* astrologers who have come to inquire about the birth of the new *Jewish* monarch.

STAR

Figuring strongly in Matthew's narrative is the famous "star of Bethlehem." Not surprisingly, many scholars consider this to be little more than a pious tradition. We are permitted, even so, to ask what the origin of the tradition might have been. Might it be an ingenious allusion to the story in Numbers 22–24 of a Gentile prophet from the east named Balaam? Balaam was hired to bring curses on Israel; but at the critical moment he instead pronounced a blessing with these words: "A star shall come out of Jacob, and a scepter shall rise out of Israel" (24:17). In Jewish biblical interpretation that text was understood as an unambiguous reference to the monarchy, most particularly to the Messiah. Some therefore suggest that Matthew shaped his narrative around that biblical allusion. That would fit Matthew's love of making connections to already known biblical stories and prophecies. Just as the pagan Balaam pronounced the promise of God to send a star—a messiah—so now the pagan magi come to see the promise realized.

Scholars also point out, however, that underlying Matthew's narrative may be some actual astronomical events of that era. Haley's Comet, for example, made an appearance 12–11 BCE. Some four to five years later there was a planetary conjunction between Saturn, Jupiter, and Mars. These would have been viewed as major astronomical events, with great astrological significance. Might Matthew be alluding both to those events and to the biblical story of Balaam?

It is also possible that Matthew has in mind to impress on his readers that the birth of the Christ is nothing less than cosmic in significance and scope. Two other accounts of the birth of the Messiah, both even more symbolic in style than Matthew's, make much of stars in their presentation. The first comes from the Apocalypse of John (or the book of Revelation), usually dated late in the first century CE:

A great portent appeared in heaven: a woman clothed with the sun, with the moon under her feet, and on her head a crown of twelve stars. She was pregnant and was crying out in birthpangs, in the agony of giving birth. Then another portent appeared in heaven: a great red dragon, with seven heads and ten horns, and seven diadems on his heads. His tail swept down a third of the stars of heaven and threw them to the earth. Then the dragon stood before the woman who was about to bear a child, so that he might devour her child as soon as it was born. And she gave birth to a son, a male child, who is to rule all the nations with a rod of iron. But her child was snatched away and taken to God and to his throne; and the woman fled into the wilderness, where she has a place prepared by God, so that there she can be nourished for one thousand two hundred sixty days. (Rev. 12:1–6)

The second is from Bishop Ignatius of Antioch, written likely in the second decade of the second century CE:

And the Prince of this world was in ignorance of the virginity of Mary and her childbearing and also of the death of the Lord—three mysteries loudly proclaimed to the world, though accomplished in the stillness of God! How, then, were they revealed to the ages? A star blazed forth in the sky, outshining all the other stars, and its light was indescribable, and its novelty provoked wonderment, and all the starry orbs, with the sun and the moon, formed a choir round that star; but its light exceeded that of all the rest, and there was perplexity as to the cause of the unparalleled novelty. This was the reason why every form of magic began to be destroyed, every malignant spell to be broken, ignorance to be dethroned, an ancient empire to be overthrown—God was making His appearance in human form to mold the newness of eternal life! Then at length was ushered in what God had prepared in His counsels; then all the world was in an upheaval because the destruction of death was being prosecuted. (Ignatius of Antioch, *Ephesians* 19)

HEROD'S PLOT TO KILL THE INFANTS

In Matthew's account the star brings the magi to Jerusalem, specifically to Herod's court. After all, an important person would have been born in an important place. After some deliberation, the magi are given directions on how to get to Bethlehem, the rather surprising birthplace of the new monarch-to-be. But Herod undertakes a plan to slaughter all boys two years and under. Attention is often drawn to this order, which implies that in Matthew's mind this visit did not happen immediately following Jesus's birth. That would fit with something else in Matthew's account, namely, that the family appears to be at home in Bethlehem from the very start. There is no indication in Matthew's story that this family ever came from anywhere else.

Joseph now receives another dream in which an unnamed messenger warns him that he is to take the mother and the child and to flee to Egypt. And so they flee to Egypt as refugees from the wrath of Herod.

The allusion to David in the genealogy indicates that Jesus is a messiah in the line of David. Bethlehem as birthplace would have strengthened that association. Here now enter allusions to that other great figure in Jewish history—Moses. Exodus 2 tells of a Hebrew couple that has a boy child who has to be hidden in a basket because the evil monarch (Pharaoh) has commanded that every boy born to the Hebrews shall be killed. The infant is watched over by his sister, Miriam, after whom Jesus's mother is named ("Mary" and "Miriam" are the same name). Quite ironically, the boy Moses finds refuge in Egypt itself, in that Pharaoh's daughter finds him and raises him in the palace. Matthew's narrative of Jesus's infancy has remarkable echoes of that famous story known to every Jew. It is difficult to imagine that Matthew was not intentional about placing these allusions in his narrative.

Matthew tells us nothing about what happened in Egypt. Later lore filled in or invented many details about the events that transpired on the journey through the Sinai desert on the way to Egypt. It is enough for Matthew to make the connection to Egypt and follow that up with another quotation from Scripture, this time from Hosea 11:1: "Out of Egypt I have called my son."

The story of the "massacre of the innocents" is associated with a poignant lament from Jeremiah 31:15:

> Thus says the LORD:
> A voice is heard in Ramah,
>   lamentation and bitter weeping.
> Rachel is weeping for her children;
>   she refuses to be comforted for her children,
>   because they are no more.

Jesus's own safety from the wrath of Herod is thereby set into the context of terrible suffering on the part of other children.

Return to Palestine

The narrative of Jesus's birth and infancy concludes with a final visitation of a messenger to Joseph in a dream. Joseph is given permission to return to Palestine with Mary and the baby, but they are warned not to return home to Bethlehem, because the situation is still unsafe. Instead, they are to go to Nazareth in Galilee, far to the north of Bethlehem. Nazareth becomes their second place of refuge, after Egypt, from the ongoing danger in Judea. This shift to Nazareth is grounded in what looks like yet one more biblical reference: "He will be called a Nazorean." The text is not identifiable, however, but has multiple allusions. No doubt it is an intentional pun on the name of the town Nazareth. It may, in addition, suggest a connection between Jesus and one who has taken Nazarite vows, like Samson in Judges 13 (in some ways more fitting for John the Baptist; see chapter 7 below). And, finally, it may be a play on the Hebrew term for branch (*nazer*) and thus an allusion to Isaiah 11:1: "A branch shall grow out of [Jesse's] roots."

Observations

First, by narrating the birth of Jesus as having taken place within the context of both human vulnerability (the potential of social ostracism for Mary, Herod's brutal rule, flight first to Egypt and then to Nazareth), on the one hand, and of intense yearning for liberation, on the other, Matthew has told the story of Jesus's birth in a way that is anything but romantic or sweet. This is a story of God's response to intense human suffering. By telling the story this way, Matthew is also preparing his readers for how to read the rest of the gospel. Like Moses and David, and much more yet, Yeshua has come to set his people free!

Second, Matthew may envision Jesus's life as a reenactment of Israel's story. Matthew is telling the story of Jesus, signaled by the allusions to both Moses and David, as the story of Israel's liberation, but a story of Israel's liberation that encompasses the broader Gentile world. That is why we find not only Moses and David, but also the Gentile women in the genealogy and the magi from the East. This mix of the particularity of the Jewish story and the universality of its relevance to the whole world marks the gospel writers generally, but also Matthew's very Jewish gospel.

Third, time and again parts of the story are grounded in a biblical reference. This raises important questions: what are the building blocks of this narrative? Are there historical reminiscences that Matthew draws on that he then grounds in the biblical story by means of these biblical references? Or is he constructing a narrative out of texts he believes are relevant? Given how tenuous some of those scriptural supports appear to be at times, I suspect it is more often the former than the latter. Nevertheless, whatever historical data lie beneath this story, the presentation of these data is heavily shaped and influenced by Matthew's desire to relate the birth of Jesus to the biblical traditions of Israel. Matthew is interested in relating the story with as much scriptural resonance as possible. To recognize that is not to dismiss these data as unhistorical, even if it is exceedingly difficult if not impossible to test, let alone prove, such historicity.

Fourth, anyone familiar with the Christmas story will, with a careful reading of Matthew's narrative by itself, have noticed both the presence and the absence of familiar features. For example, Mary plays almost no role in Matthew's narrative. It is Joseph who is prominent in the narrative. Where are the shepherds? Where is the visit between Mary and Elizabeth? Where is the birth of John the Baptist? And what about the census of Augustus, the trip from Nazareth to Bethlehem, and the birth in the barn? All of those familiar features of the Christmas story as it is reenacted over and over again each year in churches are found not in the Matthean Christmas story, but rather in the story we will turn to next, namely, the one found in the Gospel of Luke.

Luke's Account of Jesus's Birth and Infancy

Luke (1:1–2:52; 3:23–38) does not simply retell Matthew's account. Nor is it likely that Matthew has rewritten Luke's. Having said that, the two accounts have many common features:

- Jesus's parents have the same names: Mary and Joseph.
- Joseph is Jesus's father, but not biologically.
- Mary has conceived a child by the Holy Spirit.
- Jesus is born in Bethlehem.
- Jesus's birth occurs during Herod's reign.
- Jesus then comes to reside in Nazareth.

These are the basic features shared by these two gospels. There are of course other features Luke shares with Matthew, but they happen more at the level of theology or at the level of biblical interpretation than at the level of narrative or historical data.

Distinctive Features

GENEALOGY

Unlike Matthew, Luke does not begin with the genealogy. Luke does include one in 3:23–38, between Jesus's baptism and his temptation. In other words, the genealogy is related to Jesus's ministry, not, significantly, to his birth.

This should tell us something: the genealogy, just as it did in Matthew, serves not principally to prove a bloodline, but rather to show which story Jesus is a part of and how that story is intended to spin itself out. Matthew began his genealogy with Abraham, followed it through David, through the exile, to liberation. Luke goes in the other direction: he begins with Jesus and moves backward, all the way past Abraham to Adam, indeed all the way back to God. In short, Jesus's significance is rooted in the Jewish story of God's dealings with Israel. But in Luke's mind its significance goes well beyond the confines of the Jewish community, in the end encompassing all of humanity. That is why Luke arrives at that very primal relationship between human and divine, namely, Adam and God.

When the genealogies in Matthew and Luke are placed next to each other and one of them is inverted in order to make comparison easier, the genealogical line between David and Joseph is different. Should that trouble us? These genealogies were no doubt put together very carefully but differently from modern genealogies. As we have said, symbolism rather than biology seems to play an equal if not greater role. This would have been obvious to the first readers, just as it should be to contemporary readers.

Despite both Matthew and Luke telling us that Joseph was *not* Jesus's biological father, attempts have been made to deal with the potential contradictions in the genealogies. A favorite suggestion is that the genealogy in Matthew is through Joseph's line, in Luke through Mary's. That would make a convenient explanation; it attempts to preserve the historical usefulness of both genealogies by suggesting that they come through two different lines. No evidence within the text itself, however, provides a basis for this otherwise clever suggestion. More likely is that both genealogies intend to place Jesus in the story of God's involvement with his people—a story every Jew knew would finally climax in salvation and liberation—and that is all the weight we should place on them.

Two Births

Even a quick reading of Luke alerts the reader to two birth narratives, the one centered on John the Baptist, the other on Jesus. In some respects the births parallel each other: both of them are highly unusual; both witness to God's dramatic intervention. John is born to elderly folks who *no longer* expect that they will be blessed with a child. Jesus is born to someone who has not had sexual relations and who does *not yet* expect to bear a child. Both births are highly extraordinary. Both witness to the dramatic intervention of God to bring liberation or salvation (biblically both terms mean the same thing). Luke connects the two accounts by noting that Mary and Elizabeth are cousins, thereby creating a link between John and Jesus already at infancy.

Prominence of Women

In Matthew, Joseph plays a major role in the narrative. While in Luke's account Zechariah plays some role in the birth narrative of John the Baptist, Joseph plays virtually no role at all in the story of Jesus's birth. The women, Mary and Elizabeth, are much more prominent.

No Explicit Biblical References

Luke's account contains few if any direct biblical quotations. The formula "this happens so that Scripture might be fulfilled," so frequent in Matthew, is not present in Luke. Instead, we find long, beautiful psalmlike poems or hymns that are full of biblical allusions and evocations:

Traditional Latin Name	Speaker/Singer	Reference
Magnificat	Mary	1:46–55
Benedictus	Zechariah	1:68–79
Gloria	heavenly hosts	2:14
Nunc Dimittis	Simeon	2:29–32

No doubt a biblically informed reader in the first century would have made all kinds of connections between Luke's narrative and biblical stories. The birth of John the Baptist to a mother long past childbearing years would immediately have brought to mind the births of both Isaac to Abraham and Sarah (Genesis 15–21) and Samuel to Hannah and Elkanah (1 Samuel 1–2). The wonderful characters of Simeon and Anna in the temple would have brought to mind the great prophets of old. The song of Mary (*Magnificat*) would have echoed not only recent revolutionary songs sung around the campfires of guerillas during the struggles of the Maccabees (see chapter 4 above), but also the songs of the first Miriam, sister to Moses (Exodus 15), and Hannah (1 Samuel 2), celebrating God as a divine warrior bringing liberation to his oppressed people. No doubt the shepherds who are the first to witness the birth of the Messiah in Luke's account will have reminded readers of that earlier shepherd from Bethlehem who became the most important king in the history of Israel, David (1 Samuel 17). While in a very different way, Luke's account is no less soaked in biblical allusion than is Matthew's.

Zechariah and Elizabeth and the Birth of John

Luke begins his infancy narrative with the story of Zechariah and Elizabeth, an old couple of priestly lineage who have been surprised late in life by the announcement that Elizabeth will bear a child—a magical story filled with wonder, surprise, and delight.

Of central importance is the unusualness of John's birth. Really old people, especially those who have given up after a lifetime of trying, do not have babies. As unusual as the birth is, such an account would not, as I said earlier, have been unfamiliar to the readers and hearers of Luke's account. This story has many points of contact with earlier spectacular births in the long story of salvation, such as the rather remarkable story of Abraham and Sarah (Genesis 15–21). They too are old folks who no longer expect to have an heir, given their age. For them this represents a massive challenge to their trust in God. But as the narrative in Genesis shows so forcefully, Sarah's natural *in*ability to have children is necessary to show that God is true to his promises and not bound by what is humanly possible. As Gabriel says to Mary: "Nothing will be impossible with God!" (Luke 1:37).

This principle also comes to expression in the birth story of Samuel to Hannah and Elkanah (1 Samuel 1–2). In Hannah's case it is a young woman who has wanted a child desperately, and finally God blesses her with a child. Like Mary does in Luke's story, Hannah celebrates the birth of her child and at the same time God's intervention as liberator and savior of the downtrodden by singing a song.

Opinions today vary quite radically on such centrally important questions as to how God intervenes in human affairs, that is, whether there are miracles of this kind. What is important, regardless of how one answers such questions for oneself, is to recognize that in Luke's view the central issue in this narrative of birth is that it is *God* who acts to bring about salvation. And Luke has learned from Scripture that God's faithful intervention on behalf of suffering humanity is as often as not intrusive, surprising, even shocking, and thus by definition miraculous.

Such convictions do not, of course, set Luke (or Matthew) apart from his contemporaries. Unlike many in the modern West, Luke and his contemporaries expected the unexpected, as it were. Early readers would not have entertained our scientific questions. Instead, they would have zeroed in immediately on the central claim: not, "Can old women long past menopause bear children?" but rather, "Is God finally keeping his promise? Is salvation finally here?"

Why does Luke bother to tell us the story of John's birth? After all, neither Matthew nor, of course, the other evangelists tell us anything about it. We can venture several possible reasons: for one, John figures prominently at the beginning of *all* the gospel accounts of Jesus's life and ministry (see chapter 7 below). John appears to have been a very prominent figure in his own right, perhaps as widely or more widely known than was Jesus. He no doubt had a major impact on Jesus's early development. He baptized Jesus. Further, there is a strong possibility that many of John's followers eventually made their way into the Jesus movement. As all the evangelists see it, John had the role of forerunner or messenger, announcing the coming intervention of God, preparing the way for Jesus. This is reflected in the way Luke structures his twin birth stories. John's birth is narrated first, but in relation to Jesus's. When Mary goes to visit a very pregnant Elizabeth, the child in Elizabeth's womb leaps with great excitement, and she utters words to Mary that have come to enjoy great importance in the liturgy of the church: "Blessed are you among women, blessed is the fruit of your womb!" (1:42).

Songs of Mary and Zechariah

At this Mary breaks into song, known as the *Magnificat*. Comparing this with Hannah's song in 1 Samuel 2 reveals that a central theme running through this hymn is the praise of a God who pays attention to the needs of the poor and the oppressed. God is depicted as a mighty, victorious warrior who looks after the powerless. Mary's song is a song of revolution. Some suggest that this poetry may well have emerged in the Maccabean period, a time of revolutionary struggle of Jews against their oppressors a century and a half prior to Jesus (see chapter 4 above). However that may be, the song's allusions to the biblical narrative and its rootedness in the conviction that God looks after the poor is a very important signal of how Luke wishes us to read his whole gospel.

Mary's song is followed by Zechariah's well-known hymn, the *Bene-dictus*. This song or poem connects the birth of both John and Jesus ("the Lord") to the story of God's intervention on behalf of his suffering people (1:78). In short, both hymns set the births of John and Jesus into the context of Jewish hopes for liberation and redemption. As celebratory as they are, they leave no doubt in the minds of the hearers and readers of this story that this is not a romantic story, but nothing less than a revolutionary assertion of hope and liberation. God the liberator is living up to his promises! As such, the story of John's birth, Elizabeth's blessing of Mary, and the songs of Mary and Zechariah serve as a prelude to the birth of Jesus.

Birth of Jesus

After the announcement that salvation and liberation is on the way, Luke 2 sets the story in the temporal and political context of Roman Emperor Augustus. For first-century readers this would have been enough to conjure up the full grandeur and terror of Roman imperial might. The irony would not have been lost on early readers: on the one hand, the impending birth of Jesus has already been announced with great fanfare as *the* significant moment at which God is intervening to bring about liberation and peace on earth; on the other hand, the birth itself is now narrated as the story of an insignificant, vulnerable, easily victimized little family—Mary and Joseph from Nazareth.

Most contemporaries of Luke would have imagined Mary as a young woman, perhaps even a girl of twelve or thirteen years of age. It is difficult to say much about Joseph. No doubt we should imagine him somewhat older. We cannot be sure. He plays only a minor role in Luke's narrative. We should imagine a young couple, Mary and Joseph, needing to make an arduous journey from Nazareth in Galilee all the way to Bethlehem; they must go there because the emperor wants to know who his subjects are for reasons of control, information, and no doubt taxation. That is how Luke's contemporaries would have heard his story—a story of little people getting caught up in events engineered by callous rulers—eerily similar to the contemporary experience of Palestinians in our day. Nothing in Luke's narrative would have struck his readers as romantic.

True, we have no evidence apart from Luke for such a "worldwide" census during this time, even allowing for the possibility of exaggeration on Luke's part. It is possible that we simply do not have all the information. We should be cautious about "knowing" that no census dislocated this family from their home. At the same time, it is also possible that Luke, or his sources, invented this feature of the story for the purpose of making clear that Jesus has come for those whose lives are not only marked by sin, that is, by alienation from

God, but by real, material, historical, and political depravation and oppression, in this case at the hands of a callous and mighty empire. To narrate the birth of Jesus in relation to such realities speaks volumes about the kind of salvation that Luke believes Jesus will bring. Jesus's bringing of salvation will have relevance, says Luke, to real material, political, social, economic needs, in addition to what we might refer to as the religious needs of a restored relationship to God.

Returning to the narrative, we continue to be confronted with a high degree of tension-filled irony. When Mary and Joseph finally make it to Bethlehem, there is no room anywhere for them other than with the animals. The tension we feel grows out of the sense that we already know who it is that will be born: the Messiah of Israel, the Savior of the world. For modern Christmas shoppers, it is difficult to appreciate this in any way other than as romantic. But for first-century readers the contrast would have been nothing short of shocking. Israel's king, born in a stable? Watch out, Caesar, your challenger has been born to an insignificant woman in an out-of-the-way village in a stable! How absurd!

Further, in Matthew's account it is the magi from the East—wealthy, educated Gentiles—who come to pay homage. In Luke it is not wealthy or intellectual foreigners, but poor and lowly locals who come to show their respect. As the shepherds are out with their flocks, suddenly the heavens tear open and the heavenly armies shout at the top of their voices that God's liberator has appeared, that he has been born in Bethlehem, and that they can find him in a manger with the animals. Who else would possibly have believed such an account other than people already living on the margins of respectable society?

Prophets in the Temple

As Luke narrates the story, eight days after Jesus's birth Mary and Joseph have Jesus circumcised according to the Torah. They then take their newborn and go to the temple, there to offer some turtle doves and young pigeons, purifying themselves and consecrating Jesus to God (see Lev. 12:6–8).

At the temple they encounter two old people. One is named Simeon, a man who has for his whole long life been yearning to see the liberation of his people or, as it is put so beautifully in the text, for "the consolation of Israel" (2:25). When he sees the young couple and their child, he takes Jesus into his arms and breaks into song. As in the case of the other hymns in Luke's narrative, Simeon's song is usually referred to by its Latin name, *Nunc Dimittis*, translating the first two Greek words: "*Now you are dismissing your servant in peace*" (2:29).

Simeon then turns to Mary and gives her an ominous "blessing," which may be paraphrased this way:

Your son will be a sword of both judgment and liberation for Israel, laying bare what is hidden in the hearts of people (a highly concentrated summation of Jesus's ministry about to be rehearsed in Luke's Gospel).

You too will have a sword pierce your soul (unmistakably anticipating the grief Mary as a mother will experience when her son is tortured and executed). (Luke 2:34–35)

Luke introduces yet one more woman in this story, an eighty-four-year-old prophet by the name of Anna. We are told that she has been in the temple since being widowed after seven years of marriage, which, we should assume, would have widowed her young. As Simeon has hoped and prayed for "the consolation of Israel," so too has Anna spent her life praying for "the redemption of Jerusalem" (2:38).

The presence of these two old prophets in the story makes it very clear that Luke understands the birth of Jesus as bringing liberation to a people living in poverty and oppression. By making this point over and over again, Luke leaves no doubt that he wants us to read the whole of the gospel through such a lens. That does not, of course, mean that we, as readers, know what such liberation will look like. Simeon's ominous "blessing" suggests that our euphoria will give way to shock and surprise. Nonetheless, the Messiah has come to bring consolation and redemption to Israel. Those who have hoped ceaselessly can now rest in the confidence that God is finally acting.

From Judea to Nazareth

Luke concludes his narrative of Jesus's birth and early life by having the family return to Nazareth. He then attaches a brief story about Jesus coming back to the temple when he is twelve, clearly intended to illustrate Jesus's precocious commitment to God and his singleness of purpose in being at God's beck and call: "[Jesus] said to [his parents], Why were you searching for me? Did you not know that I must be in my Father's house?" (2:49).

Matthew mentions nothing of that boyhood experience in the temple, and he has a different accounting for the family's move to Nazareth. In Matthew's narrative, after Jesus's birth the family goes from Bethlehem to Nazareth, because it is still too dangerous to return to Bethlehem. As Matthew puts it, they "made [their] home in a town called Nazareth" (Matt. 2:23). In Luke they "returned . . . to their own town of Nazareth" (2:39). There have been endless attempts to harmonize these two narratives, an effort not to be disparaged, to be sure. At the same time, did we not have both accounts, we would assume on the basis of Matthew that Bethlehem was the family's home and on the basis of Luke that their home was Nazareth. There may be some historical circumstance that might explain this, but at the present time it will need to remain one of those puzzling aspects of the story.

Concluding Questions and Observations

We are now in a position to step back and ask some questions. Can the infancy narratives in Matthew and Luke be harmonized? How come only Matthew and Luke tell us anything about Jesus's birth? Are these accounts myth or history?

Harmonizing Matthew and Luke

Can the accounts in Matthew and Luke be harmonized? If so, how? Luke introduces his gospel by assuring his readers that he has written a trustworthy and orderly account based on a good deal of research (see chapter 3 above). Should we then give preferential treatment to Luke's version and see how we might fit Matthew's into it? On the surface that might seem like a good solution. The first obstacle to such an endeavor is surely that we have two quite different accounts, each fleshing the story out in different ways and with different episodes and features. Each account has a good deal of material unique only to it and features that serve its own specific purpose. It would seem unwise to privilege one account over another. That is why we took them in the sequence they are given in the New Testament.

But that raises a further question: Is this one story in two versions that augment each other, or do Matthew and Luke narrate two different traditions? The siglum Q refers to material that Matthew and Luke share and is not present in Mark. The accounts of Jesus's birth are too different for them to fit that category. Yes, there are some common features, as shown earlier. Both insist that Jesus was born in Bethlehem. I see little good reason to doubt that Jesus was indeed born there, as both evangelists claim. After all, Luke works hard to get Jesus there (Augustus's census), and Matthew has to explain why he did not stay. Both gospel writers claim Mary to be his mother. There is plenty of evidence in the gospels that show that Mary was widely known to be Jesus's mother. Third, both claim that Joseph was the husband to Mary and link the genealogy of Jesus to him (even if those genealogies diverge significantly). Interestingly, Joseph does not play a role in the story of Jesus other than in the birth narratives, which suggests that he too is a historical figure who could not quite be ignored, even if his presence is somewhat complicating. Lastly, both gospel writers claim that Joseph was not the biological father of Jesus, but that Mary conceived of the Holy Spirit. Beyond that, the stories diverge considerably.

One approach to dealing with the different accounts is theologically driven: many Christians hold that because the gospels of Matthew and Luke are part of divine revelation, their accounts are both to be taken as historically accurate and are by definition harmonious. They simply augment each other in their diversity. The special and difficult task for someone holding such a perspective is how to explain the divergences in the two accounts. The temptation for this approach is not to see the differences or to dismiss them as unimportant. The two accounts are simply melded, as they have largely been meshed in popular imagination for two millennia. Check any crèche or Christmas card: there are always both shepherds and magi at the manger, with the star overhead.

More critical readers see Matthew and Luke as two accounts rather than as one account in two versions. But divergent accounts of what? Are we talking of two accounts of one historical event, accounts shaped by the divergent ways that traditions developed in the early church or shaped more directly by two creative evangelists? Or should we take them simply to be two theologically informed traditions that have little if any historical reality behind them, other than a birth, even an unusual birth?

I find it most plausible to see a historical core at the basis of these two accounts, which was likely given distinct and unique shape both by a diverse processes of tradition and by the distinctness of the gospel writers.

The Silence of the Rest of the New Testament

How do we explain the silence of the other New Testament writers on this matter? Did Paul, Mark, and John not know about Jesus's special birth and infancy? Is it conceivable that a tradition so important to Matthew and Luke was known to only a few? Was this tradition so limited that there would have been people within the Jesus movement who would not have known of the Christmas story some four decades after Jesus's death? If they knew of it, how do we explain their silence? Was this tradition not important for a significant segment of the early Jesus communities? Would that not indicate quite a different sense of what is important about Jesus than that which has existed in much of Christian history over the past two thousand years?

These questions may be impossible to answer satisfactorily, but they force us minimally to recognize that the development of early Christian traditions was evidently quite varied. And they invite us to ask what was important to the evangelists who *do* give an account of Jesus's birth and infancy, Matthew and Luke.

Myth or History or Both

When we use the word *myth* in common parlance, we usually imply that something did not really happen in history, but that it is a set of beliefs that people find very important, that shapes their view of reality. So, in the case

of the story of Jesus's being born of a virgin, many today, including Christians, consider it a myth, rather than an actual event. It is, in their view,
simply impossible for someone to be born without a sperm from a human
father. It may express some important theological insights, but they are not
dependent on this actually having taken place.

Others consider it to have happened, insisting at the same time that it
was a miracle and thus an event that by definition falls outside what we
consider scientifically possible. They might even agree that it is myth, in the
sense that it is a story that, while having taken place in history, nevertheless
has become part of the life and belief system shaping the life of believers in
Jesus, and in that sense myth.

Both ends of the spectrum face challenges with respect to the birth narratives of Jesus: those who consider belief in the virgin birth a nonnego-
tiable test of faith should consider that among New Testament writers only
Matthew and Luke talk about it, without making it clear how important
the virginity of Mary itself is to their accounts. On the other hand, those
who think it only a theological symbol, a way of retelling a founding myth,
should ask themselves why Matthew and Luke and those who thought like
they did would have wanted to encumber their witness with a claim that
exposed them already in their own day to a great deal of misunderstanding and eventually to ridicule. After all, other New Testament writers felt
no need for this tradition in their presentation of Jesus. Moreover, the idea
that special persons were born from a sexual union between a god and a
human woman was not unheard of in wider pagan circles. To make a claim
that could be understood in the light of such pagan legends would not have
helped the cause of their witness. They themselves believed that they were
relaying something that took place in Palestine, however much they narrated
it with scriptural and traditional allusions, clearly contributing to its mythic
character and function.

These questions and the arguments they precipitate will finally not be
decided by science or historical enquiry. The toolboxes of the scientist and
the historian are ill equipped to deal with such claims. It comes down to
how one understands the gospels, revelation, miracles, truth, faith, and the
ways of God with the human community. My own position is one that
recognizes a mystery at the core of these narratives, one that neither science nor history are in a position to judge. As a believer, I acknowledge
God's ultimate agency in the birth of Jesus, but not simply in the sense in
which God is the giver (and taker) of all life. The birth of Jesus represents
God's dramatic intervention in human history in order to bring liberation.
If a dramatic and anomalous conception was the dramatic means, so be
it. However, apart from Matthew and Luke, the apostles and evangelists
who wrote the rest of the New Testament were quite capable of speaking
of Jesus's significance as the Christ, even as God incarnate (John 1), *with-*

out grounding such claims in relation to a special conception (e.g., Phil. 2:6–11; Col. 1:15–21).

In light of *both* the testimony of Matthew and Luke *and* the silence of the rest of the apostles and evangelists, it seems to me that we overstep our competence to say either that it had to be that way or that it could not have been that way. Both humility and awe in equal measure strike me as the appropriate stance. That turns out, in my reading, to be precisely the stance of the evangelists as well. If one compares their accounts with later Christian literature (e.g., the *Infancy Gospel of Thomas* or the *Protevangelium of James*), it is striking how little they speculate. It is enough for Matthew and Luke to insist that the special conception of Jesus was God's being true to the promise to send the one who would restore the people of God and to bring liberation to all humankind. It is that which they considered to be *the* miracle, the true act of divine power to change reality. And in that they are joined by all writers of the New Testament. That is why both Matthew and Luke quite consciously shape their narratives so as to maximize the symbolic aspect and so as to make as many allusions and explicit references to Scripture as possible. Contemporary preoccupation with the possibility of a virgin giving birth is thus somewhat of a distraction. For the evangelists, the big question is whether God is acting to save, not whether a virgin can conceive. That is an argument worth focusing on and, in the end, tests folks today on their openness to miracle just as much, if not more. The birth of Jesus is first and last *God's* initiative. The special nature of the birth serves to make that point—and only that point.

In Matthew the account of Jesus's birth announces his arrival as a liberator from sins, witnessed to by Gentiles and resisted by local authorities; but he is a liberator from sins not only in terms of forgiveness but in showing the way and enabling people to live a life in harmony with the will of God—hence the connections Matthew makes between Jesus's birth and that of Moses. This connection anticipates, for example, the Sermon on the Mount (see chapter 3 above).

Luke, on the other hand, tells the story of the birth of a liberator of the poor and the oppressed within Israel and beyond. That is signaled not least by placing his birth into the context of Roman imperial power over little people. His birth narrative anticipates Jesus's inaugural sermon in 4:18–21, where he announces good news to the poor and release to those in captivity (see chapter 3 above).

In short, in the ways they tell us of the birth of Jesus, both gospels anticipate in their own distinct way an adult Jesus who is to be understood in relation to Jewish hopes for redemption and liberation. As well, they anticipate an adult Jesus who comes to bring salvation to those beyond the confines of the Jewish nation. In that sense both birth narratives are overtures to their gospels, anticipating the major stresses and themes of their portrayal of Jesus. The big miracle, they insist thereby, is the arrival of the Christ—and with it salvation for the world.

For Further Reading

Brown, Raymond E. *The Birth of the Messiah*. New York: Doubleday, 1999.

Horsley, Richard A. *The Liberation of Christmas: The Infancy Narratives in Social Context*. New York: Crossroad, 1989.

Key Terms and Concepts
David
genealogy
Joseph
magi
Magnificat
Mary
Messiah
Moses
songs and hymns
virgin birth
Yeshua
Zechariah and Elizabeth (John's parents)

6

Kingdom of God

WHAT? WHERE? WHEN?

WE KNOW NEXT to nothing about Jesus's life prior to his arriving on the scene as a herald of the kingdom of God. Joseph, Mary's husband, does not play a role in the accounts of his life. The earliest tradition seems not much interested in him. Did he die early in Jesus's life? Other members of his family do appear in the accounts, especially his mother, Mary, and after his death, his brother James. Perhaps Jesus worked as a woodworker, carpenter, or contractor up until the time of his ministry, as Mark 6:3 suggests. Even if unusual for a Jewish male of Jesus's age to remain unmarried, and despite recent suggestions that he was married to Mary Magdalene, there are no good grounds for suggesting that he was married.

If we respect the evangelists' silence or lack of interest in Jesus's life prior to his public ministry, we are right to pick up the story with his appearance, together with his predecessor, John the Baptist, as a herald of the kingdom of God:

> Jesus came to Galilee, proclaiming the good news of God, and saying, "The time is fulfilled, and the kingdom of God has come near; repent, and believe in the good news." (Mark 1:14–15)

What Is the Kingdom of God?

Because the "kingdom of God" played a rich and suggestive role in the lives of John and Jesus, we must explore this concept.

Basileia—Kingdom or Reign

The English word *kingdom* translates the Greek term *basileia*, although it can just as easily be translated "rule, reign, domain, or dominion." By way of illustration, the Jesus Seminar's Scholars Version of the New Testament (*The Complete Gospels*, Polebridge Press, 1994) translates *basileia* quite accurately, if somewhat unusually, "imperial rule" and "domain." Both the territorial notion of kingdom and kingship as the exercise of power and control are implied in the concept of *basileia*. "Kingdom," while likely not the best of these various English terms, is most common in the study of Jesus, and I will for that reason alone use it most frequently. I will occasionally also employ "reign" as a reminder of how rich the overtones of *basileia* are.

Kingdom of Heaven

In distinction from the other gospels, Matthew frequently uses the term *kingdom of heaven*. This has had an enormous impact on popular understandings of *where* God's kingdom is and thus also of *when* it will happen. Many, perhaps without giving much thought to the matter, often make a distinction between "kingdom of God" and "kingdom of heaven." "Kingdom of God" is often jargon for matters of social justice in the present world, whereas "kingdom of heaven" has a transcendent meaning, a reality removed from the here and now, a place to which one goes after death, or perhaps even a concept that will become a reality only once this material universe disappears.

Stated bluntly, this distinction has no foothold in the text or in the Greek language. "Kingdom of heaven" would have been understood in the first century as completely synonymous with "kingdom of God," as seen in these examples:

Matthew 4:17	**Mark 1:14–15**
From that time Jesus began to proclaim, "Repent, for the *kingdom of heaven* has come near."	Now after John was arrested, Jesus came to Galilee, proclaiming the good news of God, and saying, "The time is fulfilled, and the *kingdom of God* has come near; repent, and believe in the good news."

Matthew 5:3	**Luke 6:20**
[Jesus said:] "Blessed are the poor in spirit, for theirs is the *kingdom of heaven*."	Then he looked up at his disciples and said: "Blessed are you who are poor, for yours is the *kingdom of God*."

Matthew 13:11	Mark 4:11	Luke 8:10
He answered, "To you it has been given to know the secrets of the *kingdom of heaven*, but to them it has not been given."	And he said to them, "To you has been given the secret of the *kingdom of God*, but for those outside, everything comes in parables."	He said, "To you it has been given to know the secrets of the *kingdom of God;* but to others I speak in parables."

Why then does Matthew usually prefer to have Jesus speak of the "kingdom of *heaven*"? The answer is not difficult to find. It is quite simply Matthew's way of expressing respect for the Jewish hesitancy to refer directly to God (see chapter 4 above). The word *heaven* would have been a circumlocution or euphemism for YHWH, similar to the use of "Lord." That Matthew is not completely consistent does not change this basic fact.

Basileia—a Symbol That Tells a Story

Despite our attempt to give some precision to the term *basileia*, we might think of "kingdom of God" less as a definable concept than as a *symbol*, a symbol that tells a *story*. What is this story? To answer that we need to go back to the very beginnings of the experience of Israel.

What drew Israelites together and forged them into a people was a conviction that the god whom they worshiped together was more than their tribal or national deity. Israel's god was none other than the creator of the universe. Not only is God the creator of the universe, God is an intervening deity, a divine liberator. The very same deity who made promises to Abraham and then liberated Abraham's offspring from slavery in Egypt gave Israel the law as part of a mutually advantageous, contractual relationship. God had subsequently offered them the gift of the land of Palestine, made promises to David, and also demanded undivided loyalty and commitment on the part of the people in return. Israel's god was jealous, reacting in anger and judgment when the people ran after other gods or did not take seriously the demands for justice and holiness, bringing upon themselves great calamity because of their sinfulness. In short, Israel's deity, whom they knew as YHWH, was not an abstract concept; God was their "king."

God as King

Several texts from the Hebrew Bible or Old Testament illustrate various dimensions of this divine kingship.

Divine King as Liberator or Savior

An ancient hymn, containing some of the oldest traditions found in the Bible, celebrates the victory over the Egyptians as a sign that "YHWH is *king* and reigns forever" (literal translation of Exod. 15:18):

> Then Moses and the Israelites sang this song to the LORD:
> "I will sing to the LORD, for he has triumphed gloriously;
>   horse and rider he has thrown into the sea.
> The LORD is my strength and my might,
>   and he has become my salvation;
> this is my God, and I will praise him,
>   my father's God, and I will exalt him.
> The LORD is a warrior;
>   the LORD is his name.
> Pharaoh's chariots and his army he cast into the sea;
>   his picked officers were sunk in the Red Sea.
> The floods covered them;
>   they went down into the depths like a stone.
> Your right hand, O LORD, glorious in power—
>   your right hand, O LORD, shattered the enemy.
> In the greatness of your majesty you overthrew your adversaries;
>   you sent out your fury, it consumed them like stubble. . . .
> Who is like you, O LORD, among the gods?
>   Who is like you, majestic in holiness,
>   awesome in splendor, doing wonders?
> You stretched out your right hand,
>   the earth swallowed them.
> In your steadfast love you led the people whom you redeemed;
>   you guided them by your strength to your holy abode. . . .
> You brought them in and planted them on the mountain of your own
>   possession,
>   the place, O LORD, that you made your abode,
>   the sanctuary, O LORD, that your hands have established.
> *The LORD will reign forever and ever.*" (Exod. 15:1–7, 11–13, 17–18,
>   emphasis added)

Divine King as Lawgiver and Judge

Psalm 95 shows clearly that God is king not only as liberator and creator, but as lawgiver and judge, one who sees to it that justice is done in the world. Given the propensity of humanity to live in a way that is contrary to the divine will, God's kingly rule is experienced also as judgment, as illustrated in Psalms 96–97:

> O sing to the LORD a new song;
>   sing to the LORD, all the earth.

Sing to the LORD, bless his name;
    tell of his salvation from day to day. . . .
Worship the LORD in holy splendor;
    tremble before him, all the earth.
Say among the nations, "The LORD is king!
    The world is firmly established; it shall never be moved.
    He will judge the peoples with equity." . . .
For he is coming to judge the earth.
He will judge the world with righteousness,
    and the peoples with his truth. (Ps. 96:1–2, 9–10, 13, emphasis added)

The LORD is king! Let the earth rejoice;
    let the many coastlands be glad!
Clouds and thick darkness are all around him;
    righteousness and justice are the foundation of his throne. . . .
For you, O LORD, are most high over all the earth;
    you are exalted far above all gods.
The LORD loves those who hate evil;
    he guards the lives of his faithful;
    he rescues them from the hand of the wicked.
Light dawns for the righteous,
    and joy for the upright in heart.
Rejoice in the LORD, O you righteous,
    and give thanks to his holy name! (Ps. 97:1–2, 9–12, emphasis added)

Both psalms relate the notion of God as "king" to creation, liberation, establishment of law and justice, and the exercise of judgment. This combination of kingly functions was, of course, known well beyond the confines of Israel, but that does not diminish its importance for understanding the thinking of Jews in relation to the kingdom of God.

DIVINE KING AS HOLY

Not surprisingly, this image of God as king—as creator, liberator, and judge—also provides the overall context in which the prophets spoke and acted, as Isaiah 6 illustrates well:

And I said: "Woe is me! I am lost, for I am a man of unclean lips, and I live among a people of unclean lips; *yet my eyes have seen the King, the LORD of hosts!"*

Then one of the seraphs flew to me, holding a live coal that had been taken from the altar with a pair of tongs. The seraph touched my mouth with it and said: "Now that this has touched your lips, your guilt has departed and your sin is blotted out." Then I heard the voice of the Lord saying, "Whom shall

I send, and who will go for us?" And I said, "Here am I; send me!" And he
said, "Go and say to this people:
   'Keep listening, but do not comprehend;
   keep looking, but do not understand.'" (Isa. 6:5–9, emphasis added)

Isaiah 6:8–9 speaks of a prophet's calling as a means by which God exercises
the kingly role as judge. Through a prophet's words and deeds, God's will
encounters a people that is sometimes receptive, but more often resistant
to God's will. This text, most particularly 6:9, finds resonance in relation
to Jesus's teaching on the parables (see Matt. 13:14 || Mark 4:12 || Luke
8:10; Acts 28:26).

Ambivalence toward Kingship in the Religion and History of Israel

MONARCHY IN ISRAEL—A COUP D'ÉTAT

As these texts show, Israel saw itself to be God's subject people, with God
as Israel's king. This conviction that God is king ran so deep in the ancient
traditions of Israel that the introduction of monarchy into Israel's story was
accompanied by considerable controversy, as the opening of 1 Samuel illustrates.
The introduction of a human king was seen by many, exemplified by the prophet
or judge Samuel, as nothing less than rebellion, as an attempt to replace the
kingly rule of God with a human monarch (1 Samuel 8–12; Judg. 9:8–15).

We find here a deep irony, one that is reflected in the ambivalence in
many parts of the Bible toward the institution of monarchy. King David,
for example, became *the* symbol of kingship for the Jewish people. In fact,
they hoped that God would enact his own royal rule in the future by sending
the "Messiah"—the "Anointed One"—who would come from the line of
David (see chapter 5 above). But early on, as we see in 1 Samuel, this was a
controversial notion. The institution of monarchy was perceived by many to
be a falling away from a central conviction, namely, that only God is king; a
human king was perceived to threaten the sole sovereignty of God.

Despite resistance from some sectors, Israel did get a king (1 Samuel
9–10). Apart from a few high points associated with David and his son
Solomon, the history of the monarchy in Israel, in both the north and the
south, was mostly a distressing one, ending in catastrophe. The storytellers
of Israel, from whom we learn about all this, did not make the story pretty.
One king after another betrayed the sacred trust to look after especially the
vulnerable, in other words, to practice justice and righteousness.

KING/MESSIAH

Somewhat to our surprise, despite early ambivalence and subsequent
failure, people did not give up on the idea of a true and just king. Their hope
for a better future included the coming of an ideal king, a messiah, a king

in the line of David, who, as God's agent, would set things right, would reestablish the kingdom or reign of God. That is, they hoped for a time when God's Anointed One would make real the kingdom of God. True, they did not agree with each other as to what that would mean, what kind of a messiah that might be (would he be a king or only a prince? would there be more than one messiah, both a royal and a priestly messiah?). Nonetheless, the idea of God sending a special agent who would fully enact God's own reign was very alive during the time of Jesus.

> **Messiah and Christ**
>
> The word *Messiah* comes from Hebrew *meshiach* ("anointed one"). Anointing was the ritual of investing a person with authority, including but not restricted to kingship. The word *Christ* comes from Greek *christos*, which is simply the translation of Hebrew *meshiach*, and is thus synonymous with *Messiah*. It is the more common appellation for Jesus because his early followers read their Bible in Greek (the Septuagint) and wrote in the common language of the far-flung communities of Jesus's followers, which was likewise Greek.

GOD IS KING OVER ALL PEOPLES, AND SO IS HIS MESSIAH!

One feature demands highlighting. As we saw in the psalms cited earlier, confessing God to be the king who created the whole universe implies that God is king not only over Israel, not only of the Jews, but of all peoples. Jews believed that God is king over *all* the earth, and that meant also ultimately king over *all* nations, including those nations that were oppressing them. This is an important point to make in trying to understand what Jesus and his contemporaries would have made of the concept of the kingdom of God. God's kingship spells trouble for those who flout his will, Jew or non-Jew.

This universalism carries the germ of yet another important aspect of the religious worldview of Jesus and his contemporaries. If God is universal king, then God's agent, the Messiah, could also be thought of as having universal importance. It is precisely this idea, one that not all Jews would have held, to be sure, that helps to explain the early missionary movement in the years immediately following Jesus's ministry in Palestine. Jesus the Messiah is Lord of all! (1 Cor. 12:3; Phil. 2:6–11). Jesus is liberator or savior and judge not only of his fellow Jews, but of all people and peoples.

To sum up: placing the kingdom of God and God's agent to bring it about against such a large universal horizon is not to abandon Jewish ways of thinking. Such a view finds its source not least in the hymnody and prayers of those Israelites who confessed that YHWH is king.

Kingship and the Hopes and Yearnings of the Oppressed

Poverty, deprivation, political oppression, injustice, illness, and possession by evil spirits (the list could be longer yet) led many in Jesus's day to yearn intensely for God to exercise his sovereignty with power. As much as they believed God to be king *now*—which they clearly did—Jesus's contemporaries believed that a time would come when God would enact his kingdom *in full*, when God would exercise his power and authority freely and completely.

But, they wondered, when will God act? How long will God put up with injustice? How long will God put up seeing his own people oppressed by foreign powers? How long will God allow disease and illness to lay waste large parts of the population? To put the question more specifically, when will God send his agent to set things right?

During Jesus's time people framed these questions in many different ways. We can guess at a sampling:

- *Poor people* asked: When will God see to our plight and raise us up out of the dust?
- *Sick folks* asked: When will the kingdom of God bring an end to debilitating and ostracizing disease and death?
- *Revolutionaries* asked: When will God free us from the hated oppression at the hands of Gentiles, specifically the heavy lid of the Roman Empire?
- *Pharisees* asked: When will people finally subject themselves to God's kingship and obey the law, thus facilitating the full appearing of God's liberating reign?
- *Essenes* asked: When will God finally enact his kingdom so that the right people are put in charge of a purified temple worthy of God's habitation?

In the minds of many of Jesus's contemporaries these questions combined in various ways. But this simple list illustrates that political, social, economic, and religious hopes and aspirations were all intertwined. Indeed politics and faith, demonic possession and political oppression, would not have been thought of or experienced as distinct or separate spheres, and as such they made for an incendiary mix. Thus, when John the Baptist and Jesus announce repentance and the arrival of the kingdom of God (e.g., Matt. 3:2; 4:17), such an announcement takes place in a context of a lively set of expectations, a keenly felt set of hopes and yearnings. To announce the arrival of the kingdom is to say that God the king is acting to set things right, and that includes forgiveness of sin, joyful and energetic exercise of righteousness, obedience to the law, relief from disease, good news for the poor, deliverance from the oppression of satanic powers, and freedom from foreign oppression.

The coming chapters will show how Jesus's announcement does or does not fit these expectations. For now it is important simply to understand something of the content of this symbol of the kingdom of God and the freight it carried for Jesus's contemporaries.

Kingdom *Now*—Kingdom *Soon*

Kingdom of God Now

We can summarize the preceding discussion in the following way: to say that God is king is to recognize God's role in creation, both in bringing it about and sustaining it in an ongoing way. To say that the divine king is creator is also to acknowledge God as the one whose will constitutes the way human beings should live. That is to say, God the king is also lawgiver and judge. Finally, this divine king cares about the creatures that inhabit this earth, especially those who recognize him as their king. As a good king, God is also a savior, a liberator when his people are victimized. These are all ways of speaking of how God is king *now*, how God's reign is a present reality. Stated differently, we can speak of these dimensions of God's power at work in the world as the *presence* of the kingdom of God.

Kingdom of God Soon

As we have also seen, however, the way history has unfolded hardly looks like God rules. Much of the talk of the kingdom of God becomes then an assertion of hope—hope that God will at some point put an end to disease, oppression, war, sin, and alienation. Seen from this perspective the kingdom of God takes on a *futuristic* meaning. It is appropriate in the light of these realities to hope in the *coming* of the kingdom of God.

One of the ongoing discussions in scholarship in the past century has been whether Jesus would have understood the kingdom of God to be essentially a present or a future reality. If future, in what sense is it future? The technical terms associated with this debate are *eschatology* and *apocalyptic*.

ESCHATOLOGY

The adjective *eschatological* and noun *eschatology* are derived from the Greek adjective *eschatos*, which means "last or final" and in that sense "the end" (*to eschaton*). Eschatology is thus the theory or doctrine of "the end" or "last things." We might well ask, the end of what? When we talk about an eschatological view of the kingdom of God, does that mean that we imply that people thought that the world, the space-time universe, would come to an end? Or does it refer to the end of life "as we know it," life, individual and corporate, marked by death, violence, and sin? Might such an "end" then also come to represent a radical new beginning?

The former view, namely, that the "end" means the end of time and matter, has been one of the prevailing views, among both scholars and the general public. There were, to be sure, many people in the ancient world who viewed material reality with a great deal of suspicion, even hostility. Death was perceived as release from captivity to materiality—that is, release into a spiritual, nonmaterial, and eternal state. Why not hope the same for the universe as a whole?

APOCALYPTIC

Related technical terms are the noun *apocalypse* and the adjective *apocalyptic*. Apocalyptic is a subcategory, one might say, of eschatology, a particular way of envisioning and articulating how God will act to bring about God's reign.

It is important to clarify the basic meaning of the term. First of all, whatever its connotation in popular speech today, it does *not* mean disaster, cataclysm, or meltdown. It means, literally, "uncovering or revelation." The last book of the Bible is thus sometimes called the Apocalypse of John, at other times the book of Revelation. The first term derives from Greek (Apocalypse=*apokalypsis*), the second from Latin (Revelation=*revelatio*)—and both mean exactly the same thing. Other obvious examples of apocalyptic writing in the Bible are the books of Daniel and Ezekiel, some sections of Isaiah (Isaiah 24–27), and, in the New Testament, Matthew 24, Mark 13, and 2 Thessalonians. Numerous Jewish apocalypses are found outside of the Bible, some from around or just preceding the time of Jesus (e.g., apocalypses associated with the ancient figures of Adam, Enoch, Abraham, Elijah, and Ezra), and from the post-Jesus era (associated with Thomas, Peter, and Paul). Importantly, even apart from writings that identify themselves as apocalypses, much of the New Testament has been shaped by what is sometimes referred to as apocalyptic thinking or apocalyptic imagery. The early followers of Jesus would not have been alone; those who produced what we call the Dead Sea Scrolls were likewise deeply influenced by such radical theology.

Dramatic Imagery

Apocalyptic writing is characterized by dramatic vocabulary and imagery, often focusing on catastrophic natural phenomena or bizarre mythological imagery of dragons and other strange animals, and sometimes exhibiting a love of mysterious numbers. For many, the Apocalypse of John will be the most familiar example. It is by no means unique.

Dualism

Apocalyptic language and thought patterns are shaped by a high degree of dualism or polar opposites—God versus Satan, angels versus demons, light versus darkness, truth versus error, good versus evil. In apocalyptic thinking the present world has fallen so far from what God intended that it cannot be fixed through gradual reformation. Only a dramatic, all-embracing intervention can bring about the kingdom of God. Often this is understood to come about through God's agent, such as a messiah or the archangel Michael, or through divine armies of angels fighting the evil powers. Not surprisingly, the vocabulary of conflict and combat marks much of this tradition. The imagery is taken from very ancient myths of the combat of the gods, shared with other peoples in the ancient Near Eastern world.

Need for Revelation

What is the importance of the term *apocalypse*, that is, why identify this kind of tradition with revelation? One obvious answer is that a central feature of this literature is that it reveals what will happen at the end. Much of this literature was written at a time when, empirically, everything pointed to God's absence and the triumph of chaos and evil. This literature is a response to such a state of affairs. It asserts that contrary to all evidence, God is king! God has known all along that there will be times of great violence and suffering—"woes," these writers called them. Such turbulence will only increase as the time of God's saving and judging intervention draws near. The saying that night is always darkest just before dawn captures this perspective well. In apocalyptic literature God reveals both that such chaos will come and his plan of intervention. God has revealed this to ancient seers or visionaries such as Enoch or Daniel and even as far back as Adam! These writers are then asked to write down what was revealed to them in their visions or dreams so that people can read it when those predicted times of chaos, judgment, and salvation arrive.

Theology and Literature of Hope

It is not difficult to see that this literature is a powerful assertion of hope and belief in God as king. God is in control, regardless of appearances. God's kingdom will surely arrive! If anything, suffering and chaos, even martyrdom, are evidence of its nearness, not of its absence. And when the kingdom of God arrives, the revolution will be dramatic, accompanied by spectacular phenomena, one of the most dramatic being the resurrection of the dead. But resurrection is only part of a larger event, namely, the re-creation of a new heaven and new earth, as the book of Revelation puts it (21:1). This has bearing on the conviction of early followers of Jesus that God raised him from the dead and with that began the process that will culminate with Christ's return and the remaking of the cosmos (see chapter 12 below).

Earth-Shattering Imagery

As indicated earlier in relation to eschatology, scholars are not of one mind as to the nature of the "end" these writers envisioned. Did Jews in Jesus's day envision the end of the created universe or the end of the world as we know it, that is, the end of evil and brokenness in the world? That same question can be asked of apocalyptic literature. Apocalyptic images are dramatic in the extreme: the sun will no longer shine, the moon will turn dark, and the mountains will melt. This language has led many to hold that apocalyptic thinking anticipates the end of the material universe, to be replaced by some sort of timeless eternity.

An increasing number of scholars, however, believe that we are closer to first-century Jewish thinking if we view apocalyptic language as expressing in highly dramatic and picturesque imagery the conviction that God will not allow injustice, oppression, disease, and sin to continue and that God will intervene forcefully through his Messiah, through the judgment of the nations, through resurrection, to bring about "a new heaven and a new earth," that is to say, God will bring *creation*—both heaven and earth—back to its intended whole. This does not bring history to a close; it brings an end to the brokenness in human history, including its relationship with God. This is not the cessation of the ages; it is the breaking in of a new age.

If such an understanding of the eschatological and specifically apocalyptic texts in the Bible is correct, and in my opinion it points in the right direction, then there is much greater continuity between the expectations of those Jews who hoped that when the kingdom comes the hated Roman oppression will end, for example, and those who expected a kingdom on a more cosmic scale of a new world in which God and humanity would live at peace, in which there would be no disease, illness, death, and oppression. The radical changes anticipated in apocalyptic imagery will be earth-shattering, regardless of how broad the horizon of change is understood to be.

This is a thumbnail sketch, collapsing into one oversimplified picture a great variety of writings and perspectives. But this sketch lets us catch a glimpse of the way many people thought about the kingdom of God during the time of Jesus.

Jesus's Understanding of the Kingdom—the Present *and* Future Powerful Presence of God

How does all this relate to Jesus? There may have been some diversity of perspective among the evangelists with respect to eschatology (see chapter 3 above). We will not be surprised, therefore, that in assessing the evidence, scholars come to rather diverse conclusions as to whether Jesus thought in apocalyptic terms and acted accordingly, or whether his eschatology was more directed to the present and its potential for realizing the kingdom of God.

We will have ample opportunity to see in the next several chapters how Jesus taught and lived in light of the kingdom of God. We will see why he could assert that God's kingship, God's sovereign rule, was present *now* in and through his activity:

> [Jesus said:] "If it is by the finger of God that I cast out demons, then the kingdom of God has come to you!" (Luke 11:20; see chapter 9 below)

> Once Jesus was asked by the Pharisees when the kingdom of God was coming, and he answered, "The kingdom of God is not coming with things that can be observed; nor will they say, 'Look, here it is!' or 'There it is!' For, in fact, the kingdom of God is among you." (Luke 17:20–21)

Moreover, Jesus's view of God as a loving parent caring for all of creation, especially the most vulnerable among them, whether sparrows or sick children, was rooted in a view of God as a benevolent divine king, a kingly father caring for his children (e.g., Matt. 6:25–34). In that sense, God's kingly rule appears, in Jesus's way of thinking and behaving, to be an ever-present reality.

We will also see, however, that when Jesus came announcing repentance in light of the good news of the *arriving* kingdom of God, he spoke directly to Jewish eschatological hopes. Many, especially those living in situations of poverty and deprivation, could not have helped but hear Jesus's proclamation of the appearance and the arrival of the kingdom of God as the assurance that God was *now* finally doing or was *about to* do what people had been eagerly anticipating for hundreds of years. Both present and future characterize Jesus's conception of the kingdom of God.

Jesus believed God to be king already *now*, a loving sovereign whose rule has always shown itself in sustaining normal everyday life—a daily miracle brought about by the love of a creator, of a divine parent, of a father—*Abba*, as Jesus repeatedly calls God. That creator's love and care comes to expression in, for example, Jesus's healings and exorcisms, but also when people forgive each other, when they do not retaliate when abused, when they love their enemies—in short, when they exercise God's will in everyday social and economic relationships. This is what is referred to in the Sermon in the Mount as "seeking first God's kingdom and its brand of justice" (Matt. 6:33, my phrasing; see chapter 10 below). At the same time, many of Jesus's parables are meant to serve as a wake-up call to be ready for the arrival of God's reign (see chapter 8 below). Moreover, to interpret Jesus's talk of the kingdom as solely a present reality and divorced from a keen expectation of what God is about to do takes the symbol of the kingdom of God out of the context of the story in which it would have made sense to Jesus and his contemporaries. Apocalyptic-like passages such as Matthew 24 and Mark 13, for example, are not alien to the views of Jesus and his followers.

Let us summarize: the kingdom of God is a comprehensive symbol that encompasses the relationship of humanity with God but also the relationships within humanity; indeed, it encompasses creation as a whole. It has a *future* dimension, necessarily so because this world is presently still deeply in need of mending. It also implies a strong *present* expression of God's reign and rule whenever the power of God comes to expression. All of these dimensions mark Jesus's ministry, in which the kingship of God as liberator, savior, creator, lawgiver, and judge comes to expression. Jesus makes sense in light of the story in which the symbol of the kingdom of God makes sense.

Key Terms and Concepts

apocalyptic

basileia ("kingdom, rule, reign, dominion")

eschatology

God as King

Messiah as King

We cannot bring this chapter to a close without reminding ourselves that mysteriously the Gospel of John does not, apart from one conversation between Jesus and a night visitor, Nicodemus (John 3), make any mention of the kingdom of God. The convictions we have surveyed in this chapter, however, are no less foundational for understanding John's Jesus. God is no less sovereign, Jesus no less God's agent of redemption and liberation, the present no less loaded with the future than in the Synoptic Gospels.

For Further Reading

Each of the major studies, most of the smaller studies, and all of the dictionaries listed in chapter 1 have excellent discussions of the "kingdom of God." In addition, see these classic and influential studies:

Perrin, Norman. *Jesus and the Language of the Kingdom: Symbol and Metaphor in New Testament Interpretation*. Philadelphia: Fortress, 1976.

———. *The Kingdom of God in the Teaching of Jesus*. Philadelphia: Westminster, 1963.

7

Announcing the Kingdom

JOHN, BAPTISM, TESTING, AND THE TWELVE

A T THE BEGINNING of all four gospels there is an imposing if somewhat mysterious figure. We know him commonly as John the Baptist,
a herald of the kingdom of God. He is best known for his activity of baptizing
masses of people—including Jesus—in preparation for that coming reign of
God. But for the evangelists, Jesus's baptism at the hands of John represents
more than his own preparation for the kingdom; it is his own special commission as herald and enactor of the kingdom. The testing in the desert, commonly
known as the "temptation of Christ," follows immediately upon Jesus's baptism
in the narratives of the Synoptic evangelists and must be viewed in relation
to his calling as enactor of God's reign, as Messiah. Finally, the choosing of
the Twelve represents a highly symbolic act, signaling the restitution of the
people of Israel, and with it the kingship of God over his people.

John the Baptist, Herald of the Kingdom

Bridge between Old and New

John the Baptist or John "the Baptizer" is present in all four gospels (Matt.
3:1–17 || Mark 1:2–11 || Luke 3:1–22 || John 1:19–34; Matt. 11:2–19
|| Luke 7:18–35; Matt. 14:1–12 || Mark 6:14–29; John 1:6–8). He is an
important bridge figure between the story of Israel and the person and mis-

139

sion of Jesus. For the evangelists he represents the last of the great prophets heralding the coming of the Messiah. All four gospels connect him with the great prophecy from Isaiah 40:3:

> A voice cries out:
> "In the wilderness prepare the way of the LORD,
>   make straight in the desert a highway for our God."

Biblical translations then as now were often approximate and lent themselves to certain adaptation. The evangelists relate the word *wilderness* not to the highway, but to the voice crying out. John, the desert prophet, is viewed by the evangelists as the herald and "advance man," so to speak, of the Lord:

> The voice of one crying out in the wilderness:
>   "Prepare the way of the Lord,
>   make his paths straight." (Mark 1:3 || Matt. 3:3 || Luke 3:4; compare John 1:23)

But who is this pivotal figure, pointing his finger to the horizon from which would come the liberator? Even though the evangelists view John as a forerunner to the main character of their story, Jesus, they nevertheless afford us some glimpses into the life and significance of this remarkable figure.

John the Baptist makes an appearance at the very beginning of each of the four gospels. Luke even intertwines an account of John's very special birth with that of Jesus in what is, in effect, a double Christmas story (Luke 1–2). John's birth is narrated as a miraculous and powerful intervention of God into the desperate circumstances of a people yearning for redemption.

We should not be surprised that scholars wonder how much of the narrative of John's birth and origin is legendary, just as they do about the stories of Jesus's birth. Regardless of how that question is answered, no one can miss the profound and radical theological assertions that are made in the narrative:

> He will be great in the sight of the Lord. He must never drink wine or strong drink; even before his birth he will be filled with the Holy Spirit. He will turn many of the people of Israel to the Lord their God. With the spirit and power of Elijah he will go before him, to turn the hearts of parents to their children, and the disobedient to the wisdom of the righteous, to make ready a people prepared for the Lord. (Luke 1:15–17)

In Luke 1:80 we read, "And the child [John] grew and became strong in spirit and he was in the wilderness until the day he appeared publicly to Israel."

Unusual birth, unusual calling, unusual life. First, John is associated with an ascetic lifestyle, most dramatically indicated by his unusual dress and food (see also Matt. 3:4) and not least by his association with the desert. This asceticism marks him as one set apart for God's exclusive use (see Numbers 6 and Judges 13). The desert represents for Jews the traditional place of encounter with God. The forty years in the wilderness (the Sinai Desert) become paradigmatic for the place where one wrestles with God, where one wrestles with the strength of one's covenant commitment and its implications. So John is a kind of "wild man of the desert" who will test the people as to their readiness to meet their God, preparing them for that encounter.

When the Dead Sea Scrolls were first discovered, there was much excitement that a connection to John had been discovered. Here was a community of people who lived celibate lives, many of them in the desert, who gave themselves to God with a passion unequaled in Palestine, all the while expecting the imminent arrival of God and the judgment of Israel and the world.

Was John one of these Essenes? Most think not. But what John does share with this community is a strong sense of the imminent arrival of God's reign. John's practice of baptism also has similarity to their ritual washings, except that there is no evidence that people went to John to be *repeatedly* baptized. While potential connections between John and Qumran are tantalizing, they remain at best historical guessing of the most tentative kind.

Second, John is identified as a prophet, one "with the spirit and power of Elijah." John's unusual behavior, appearance, and message were not seen as evidence of craziness by his contemporaries. They are intelligible within the long history of the Jewish people as the "normal" eccentricities of divine messengers, ancient and more recent (e.g., Acts 5:36; 21:38). Many of John's contemporaries, inspired by ancient prophecies such as Malachi 4:5–6, hoped for nothing less than the return of the prophet without parallel, Elijah himself, of whom Malachi says:

> Lo, I will send you the prophet Elijah before the great and terrible day of
> the LORD comes. He will turn the hearts of parents to their children and the
> hearts of children to their parents, so that I will not come and strike the land
> with a curse.

Numerous links are made between Elijah and John the Baptist in the gospels. While the Fourth Gospel gives testimony to this by having John specifically *deny* that he is Elijah (John 1:21), Matthew has Jesus state emphatically several times that John is none other than the returned Elijah (Matt. 11:14; 17:10–13; compare also Luke 1:15–17).

Third, the Baptist is identified as the forerunner of the Lord, laying the groundwork for his coming. The evangelists construct their narrative in such a way that the Lord for whom John is forerunner is Jesus, even if the biblical prophecy originally would have had YHWH more directly in mind. Nevertheless, since God and his Anointed One are often spoken of in much the same way, it is not a big stretch for the followers of Jesus to understand John to be the forerunner of *Jesus*—in hindsight, to be sure. However, as Matthew 11 hints, this was not always obvious, even at the very beginning.

Prophet of Judgment and Repentance

If John was a prophet, what did he preach? Matthew 3:1 provides an excellent summary:

> In those days John the Baptist appeared in the wilderness of Judea, proclaiming, "Repent, for the kingdom of heaven has come near [*or* is at hand]!"

The evangelists elaborate on this summary statement in several ways. All four have John identifying himself as a water baptizer and, at the same time, as a preparer of the way for someone greater, "whose sandals he is not worthy to untie," (Matt. 3:11 || Mark 1:7 || Luke 3:16). In other words, John is the advance man for the Messiah, who will baptize not with water, but with "holy wind" (or Holy Spirit), as we might translate Mark 1:8 quite literally. Matthew and Luke add "and with fire." In other words, a firestorm is coming! Get ready!

John's message is thus marked by a very sharp edge: he preaches repentance in light of the coming "wrath," Jewish and biblical shorthand for the judgment of God. Matthew and Luke record a memory of John's preaching:

> John said to the crowds that came out to be baptized by him, "You brood of vipers! Who warned you to flee from the wrath to come? Bear fruits worthy of repentance. Do not begin to say to yourselves, 'We have Abraham as our ancestor'; for I tell you, God is able from these stones to raise up children to Abraham. Even now the ax is lying at the root of the trees; every tree therefore that does not bear good fruit is cut down and thrown into the fire. . . .
>
> "His [the Messiah's] winnowing fork is in his hand, to clear his threshing floor and to gather the wheat into his granary; but the chaff he will burn with unquenchable fire." (Luke 3:7–9, 17 || Matt. 3:7–10, 12)

The motifs of axe, winnowing fork, and fire are highly symbolic allusions to the coming judgment. The Baptist's introduction of Jesus is entirely consistent with this. The "harvester"—that is how the evangelists depict John's view of Jesus—will gather the people in as grain. Those who continue their rebellious ways will experience the harvester as one who will decisively remove evil from the earth in the way a harvester separates wheat from chaff. And he will do so with wind and fire!

As is typical for biblical prophets, repentance is linked closely with judgment. The English term *repentance* can mislead us to thinking mostly of confession and regret. Since judgment is bad news for those who have done wrong, repentance represents a cessation of sin and a plea for mercy. But the Hebrew verb *shub* means literally "to turn or turn around." It implies a turning from one direction to another. John's call to repent is a call to turn in view of the coming wrath—that is, judgment of God. Clearly, for those who have been doing wrong—the "vipers"—this means to stop sinning and a need for forgiveness, a major theme in John's preaching and baptizing. For them, turning means that they prepare themselves for the coming of God so as not to get run over by it. But there were many others in Palestine who were already falling under the wheels, who were already being crushed by poverty, disease, and oppression. For such, the summons to turn meant an invitation to see the coming of the Lord, not *against* them, but *on their behalf.* Judgment is then more deliverance than threat, more vindication than punishment. There can be no doubt that John's impact provoked both deep repentance and enthusiastic anticipation among those who heeded his call.

John the Baptizer

John did more than preach, however. He is, after all, not called John the Preacher or John the Prophet but John the Baptist, the "plunger, dipper, or immerser," to translate the Greek literally. Baptism was *the* ritual characteristic of John's renewal movement. It represented a ritual of cleansing and forgiveness, but, in light of God's visitation expected in the very near future, also one of preparation for the coming of God's reign. Given John's preaching, we should expect among those gathered at the Jordan a high degree of eschatological excitement.

How should we imagine John's baptizing? It is unlikely that he personally baptized each individual the way a minister or priest might today. We should rather think of crowds of people making the trek down to the Jordan (John 1:28 identifies the place as Bethany, perhaps somewhere in the vicinity of Jericho) and immersing themselves in his presence. That would be similar to the way Jews practiced ritual bathing in a *mikvah* for purposes of purification, as happened at the temple in Jerusalem or at Qumran near the Dead Sea.

John's baptizing was, however, more than ritual purification. The Jordan was a river with enormous symbolic meaning in Jewish history. When Israel was liberated from slavery in Egypt, the people spent forty years in the desert before arriving at the Jordan. They then crossed this symbolic and physical borderline in order to enter the promised land. I find it compelling to think that, by baptizing people in the Jordan, John was in effect inviting them to reenact the liberation from Egypt and reentry into the land, into the realm or kingdom of God (interestingly, in 2 Kings 2:7–8 Elijah himself reenacts at the Jordan the splitting of the Red Sea).

It is not a big stretch to see John's baptism as a rival purity system to the temple in Jerusalem, as has been proposed, something that would have provoked considerable hostility from religious leadership. His message of the imminent arrival of the reign of God, accompanied by harsh words of warning, as well as by the offer of forgiveness at the Jordan, would surely have sent shock waves through the courts of the temple in Jerusalem as well. John's preparation of the people at the Jordan may well have been viewed as a dismissal of the temple and those in charge of it. And that would not have set John apart from fellow Jews just down the Jordan valley at Qumran or, many argue today as then, from Jesus. To compound the hostility against him, like a prophet of old, John criticized the marriage of Herod Antipas to his brother Philip's wife to his face!—a confrontation that cost him his head (Mark 6:16–29 || Matt. 14:3–12).

Significant in His Own Right

It is clear from all of this that John was a very significant person in his own right. Not only are the evangelists compelled to place him in the "opening act" of their "play," but they give witness in several ways to his significance, even though they do not allow John to eclipse Jesus (see, most noticeably, John 1:19–23; 3:23–30). During his lifetime John was immensely popular among those who were open to his message, and he was feared by those who were not (Matt. 14:5; compare Luke 3:15). Perhaps nothing witnesses more to John's importance in the eyes of his contemporaries than the suspicion that Jesus was none other than John returned from the dead (Matt. 14:2 || Mark 6:14 || Luke 9:7; Matt. 16:14 || Mark 8:28 || Luke 9:19).

The high esteem accorded John by his contemporaries is corroborated by Josephus's saying more about John the Baptist than about Jesus. Interestingly, while Josephus shares John's revulsion at the divorce and marriage of Herod Antipas and Herodias, he attributes John's execution to Herod's worries about John's popularity among the people and the possibility that he could lead them in rebellion, again testimony to John's immense importance (see *Jewish Antiquities* 18.5.1–3 §§109–29). Lastly, the Baptist's movement may not have restricted itself to Palestine. The author of the Acts of the Apostles (the same as the author of Luke's Gospel) reports the existence of followers of John in Ephesus in Asia Minor (Acts 18:25; 19:3).

John the Baptist is important for many reasons. First is the prominence given him by the evangelists, emphasizing the close connection between the Baptist and Jesus. They see him as a bridge between a long history of yearning and expectation and a present in which God is finally acting to establish his reign. He is important also because of the way he combines the anticipation of God's reign with judgment. We will need to pay close attention to how and in what ways this emphasis on repentance and imminent judgment marks Jesus's preaching and enacting of the kingdom—a ministry that apparently picked up in earnest only after John's arrest (Matt. 4:12, 17 || Mark 1:14–15).

Baptism of Jesus

John Baptizes Jesus

Even scholars who tend to be skeptical about the gospels as historical sources have little if any doubt that John baptized Jesus. Why? One reason is that John's baptizing Jesus puts Jesus in an apparently inferior position to John, clearly not where the evangelists or the followers of Jesus would have wanted to place Jesus. Among the evangelists, Matthew suggests as much in his narrative when he records John protesting that he should not be baptizing Jesus, but that Jesus should instead baptize him (Matt. 3:14). Is the absence of an explicit account of John's baptizing of Jesus in the Gospel of John a reflection of this (compare the Synoptic accounts of John's baptizing Jesus in Matt. 3:13–17 || Mark 1:9–11 || Luke 3:21–22 with John 1:29–34)? And since John's baptism was one of repentance and forgiveness, did the evangelists believe that Jesus needed forgiveness and protection from the coming judgment? Not likely. In other words, the followers of Jesus would have had no reason to invent this rather complicating episode, especially *after* Easter. There is every reason, then, to think of Jesus joining the throngs at the river in order to prepare himself for the coming reign of God. That may represent the real reason for Jesus's baptism—opening himself to the kingdom of God and identifying himself with its arrival.

Baptism as Commissioning

Jesus's baptism comes to have a meaning in the gospels, however, that sets it apart from that experienced by others being baptized along with him. Jesus not only prepares himself for the coming of God's kingdom; he experiences a divine commission to be the agent through whose words and deeds the rule or kingdom of God will be realized. Several features in these accounts of Jesus's baptism highlight his special calling. First is the motif of empowerment, captured in the image of the Spirit descending like a dove. Both the Greek (*pneuma*) and the Hebrew (*ruach*) can be translated "wind" or "spirit." "Spirit" in this case represents being filled with divine power for a particular task, that of bringing the message of the kingdom of God, and more, of making it happen.

Second are the dramatic words recounted as being spoken immediately following Jesus's baptism:

This is my Son, the Beloved, with whom I am well pleased. (Matt. 3:17)

You are my Son, the Beloved; with you I am well pleased. (Mark 1:11 || Luke 3:22)

This striking affirmation is in fact a conflation of two phrases highly familiar and suggestive to a first-century Jew. The first words are those spoken at the coronation of Israel's kings, as recorded in Psalm 2:7:

> You are my son;
> > today I have begotten you.

The king, the "Anointed One" or "Messiah," is called "Son of God" (see the previous chapter). At his coronation God acknowledges the monarch to be his son. At his baptism Jesus, as Son of God, is anointed to be the Messiah.

The other part of the sentence spoken at Jesus's baptism comes from the first of the famous Servant Songs in Isaiah (42:1):

> Here is my servant, whom I uphold,
> > my chosen, in whom my soul delights.

The bringing together of these two important and familiar texts serves two purposes: with the clear reference to the royal enthronement psalm the gospel writers wish to make us aware that Jesus is being commissioned as Son of David, the King, God's Messiah. Combining that with the Servant Song in Isaiah 42 alerts us to expect a different kind of a king, however. Isaiah 42:1–9 anticipates the very core of Jesus's identity and ministry as portrayed in the gospels (it is explicitly quoted in Matt. 12:18–21; see also the summaries of Jesus's mission in Matt. 11:5 and Luke 4:18).

Matthew 3:16 and Mark 1:10 describe this moment as a private vision of Jesus. Luke 3:21–22 makes it more publicly observable, whereas John 1:32–34 records it as the Baptist's vision.

Scholars have long argued about Jesus's sense of himself and his calling, that is, to what degree he saw himself as Messiah. The evangelists of course believe fully that he is; that is why they write their gospels! This is illustrated dramatically in the account of the transfiguration of Jesus (Matt. 17:1–9 || Mark 9:2–10 || Luke 9:28–36), where the words spoken at Jesus's baptism are sounded again. What we cannot be sure of on strictly historical grounds is to what extent *later* christological insights have affected accounts such as this one of Jesus's baptism. More than likely post-Easter convictions have helped shape the narratives regarding Jesus's messiahship. To acknowledge that in no way rules out that Jesus thought of himself as God's anointed kingdom-agent and that his baptism served as a personal summons to take up that task. Nor does it decide the merits of such a self-perception. Jesus could in theory have been deluded; some of his contemporaries clearly thought he was crazy (Mark 3:20–21). But there is little in this story that does not fit the mix of history, tradition, yearning, and expectation that marked the time of John and Jesus. And the prominence of John in the story of Jesus suggests a high degree of continuity between the two. If John was seen, and saw himself, as a prophet of the kingdom of God, then we should not be surprised that Jesus too saw himself as an agent of the kingdom. Consequently, we read in Mark 1:14–15:

> Now after John was arrested, Jesus came to Galilee, proclaiming the good news of the kingdom of God, and saying, "The time is fulfilled, and the kingdom of God has come near [or is at hand]; repent, and believe in the good news."

As Matthew makes very clear, these are unmistakable echoes of the Baptist (compare Matt. 3:2 and 4:17). There are differences, however, in the approach of these two prophets and perhaps even in their conception of how the kingdom will come and how God's agent should behave. Matthew 11 highlights the way their contemporaries would have noted the difference between the two: John was an ascetic, at home in the wilderness, wearing camel skins as clothing, and eating locusts and honey. This is not someone you invite to a party, to state it informally. Jesus, on the other hand, is both John-like in announcing the reign of God and calling to repentance in relation to it, but un-John-like in eating and drinking with those beyond the borders of a holy society, such as tax collectors and "sinners." Him you would invite to the party! Over and over again Jesus would break the mold of what one might have expected of a messenger of God's reign.

The Temptation or Testing of Jesus

With the exception of the Gospel of John, the evangelists all narrate that immediately following his baptism, Jesus went into the desert for a fast of forty days (Matt. 4:1–11 || Mark 1:12–13 || Luke 4:1–13). Mark's account is brief and stark.

> And the Spirit immediately drove him out into the wilderness. He was in the wilderness forty days, tempted by Satan; and he was with the wild beasts; and the angels waited on him. (Mark 1:12–13)

As Mark puts it, the Spirit "drove" Jesus out into the desert for forty days to be tested by Satan, who is here a figure much like the one who tested Job. As brief as it is, this is a highly symbolic account, one that has echoes of Israel's own forty years of testing in the desert, or of Elijah's sitting in the cave and having the birds bring him sustenance (1 Kings 19:8–18; see also Moses in Deut. 9:9, 18; 10:10). It is symbolic that the gospel writers place this temptation immediately after Jesus's baptism. Whereas baptism represents Jesus's commissioning as Son of God, as Messiah and King, the desert story represents the testing of Jesus on what kind of a king he would be. Given the highly symbolic features of the story, we should be careful both to attend to its symbolic significance and to be cautious about taking it as a strictly historical account. The testing lasted his whole brief working life, as we will see.

In likely dependence on an earlier source (Q), Matthew and Luke expand on Mark's brief account to describe three temptations or tests, in slightly different sequence. Whereas they agree on the first temptation having to do with turning stones into bread, they have the last two in reverse order:

Matthew 4:1–11	Luke 4:1–13
Bread and Stones	**Bread and Stones**
Then Jesus was led up by the Spirit into the wilderness to be tempted by the devil. He fasted forty days and forty nights, and afterwards he was famished. The tempter came and said to him, "If you are the Son of God, command these stones to become loaves of bread." But he answered, "It is written, 'One does not live by bread alone, but by every word that comes from the mouth of God.'"	Jesus, full of the Holy Spirit, returned from the Jordan and was led by the Spirit in the wilderness, where for forty days he was tempted by the devil. He ate nothing at all during those days, and when they were over, he was famished. The devil said to him, "If you are the Son of God, command this stone to become a loaf of bread." Jesus answered him, "It is written, 'One does not live by bread alone.'"
Pinnacle of Temple	**Kingdoms of the World**

Then the devil took him to the holy city and placed him on the pinnacle of the temple, saying to him, "If you are the Son of God, throw yourself down; for it is written,
 	
'He will command his angels concerning you,'
  and 'On their hands they will bear you up,
  so that you will not dash your foot against a stone.'"
Jesus said to him, "Again it is written, 'Do not put the Lord your God to the test.'"
	Then the devil led him up and showed him in an instant all the kingdoms of the world. And the devil said to him, "To you I will give their glory and all this authority; for it has been given over to me, and I give it to anyone I please. If you, then, will worship me, it will all be yours." Jesus answered him, "It is written,
	
	'Worship the Lord your God,
	  and serve only him.'"

Kingdoms of the World	**Pinnacle of Temple**

Again, the devil took him to a very high mountain and showed him all the kingdoms of the world and their splendor; and he said to him, "All these I will give you, if you will fall down and worship me." Jesus said to him, "Away with you, Satan! for it is written,
 	
'Worship the Lord your God,
  and serve only him.'"
Then the devil left him, and suddenly angels came and waited on him.
	Then the devil took him to Jerusalem, and placed him on the pinnacle of the temple, saying to him, "If you are the Son of God, throw yourself down from here, for it is written,
	
	'He will command his angels concerning you,
	  to protect you,'
	and
	'On their hands they will bear you up,
	  so that you will not dash your foot against a stone.'"
	Jesus answered him, "It is said, 'Do not put the Lord your God to the test.'" When the devil had finished every test, he departed from him until an opportune time.

The Tests or Temptations

TURN STONE INTO BREAD!

Both Matthew and Luke begin their narrative of the test with Satan of-fering Jesus the opportunity to turn stone into bread. After forty days and nights of fasting this would be a temptation indeed. But the symbolic nature of this narrative should make us cautious about thinking like that. This is not about hunger so much as about Jesus's sense of what it means for him to be God's agent. The aspect of hunger in this test sharpens the question as to what the point is of being God's Messiah if you cannot make nature itself a servant, in this case to serve the needs of the body. After all, part of the anticipation of the kingdom of God is that nature itself be a servant to the welfare of the people, where hunger is no more, where disease and all manner of want are eliminated. All of the evangelists provide an account of Jesus feeding the hungry by the thousands (feeding of the five thousand in Matt. 14:13–21 || Mark 6:32–44 || Luke 9:10–17 || John 6:1–15; feeding of the four thousand in Matt. 15:32–39 || Mark 8:1–10), and the Fourth Gospel highlights the connection between messiahship and the alleviation of hunger in having Jesus flee the scene after feeding the thousands because the people want to make him king (John 6:15). Satan is hardly tempting Jesus with sin, that is, with doing something immoral; he is testing him as to whether he will attempt to exercise for himself his prerogatives as God's agent, as God's Messiah.

Jesus's response is highly significant in terms of his subsequent career as Messiah, as the gospels narrate it. He responds by quoting words from Deuteronomy 8 that deal with Israel's own forty years of testing in the desert. Quoted here is the larger context from which Jesus's words are taken:

> Remember the long way that the LORD your God has led you these forty years in the wilderness, in order to humble you, *testing you to know what was in your heart*, whether or not you would keep his commandments. He humbled you by letting you hunger, then by feeding you with manna, with which neither you nor your ancestors were acquainted, in order to make you understand that *one does not live by bread alone, but by every word that comes from the mouth of the LORD*. (Deut. 8:2–3, emphasis added)

The testing in the desert or "wilderness" was designed to know "what was in the heart." In the case of ancient Israel's time in the desert, it is *God*, not Satan, who does the testing. In quoting these words in answer to Satan, Jesus in effect places himself into the ranks of Israel in the desert, reliving Israel's testing in the desert. Instead of grasping at the perks of kingship, Jesus joins the ranks of the people at their neediest and most vulnerable. This is a test not so much on whether Jesus is willing to be God's Messiah, but whether he is up to being *the kind of agent* he has been summoned to be. Not to join the people at their most vulnerable would, ironically, be a betrayal of his peculiar and surprising messiahship.

If You Are the Son of God, Jump Off!

In the next test (third in Luke) the tempter or tester takes Jesus to the highest tower in the temple and there dares him to jump off. He dares Jesus, interestingly, by quoting Psalm 91, a moving song of divine assurance of help and protection. Surely, if indeed Jesus is Son of God—as he has just been informed at his baptism—God will not allow harm to come to him.

Once again Jesus responds with a quotation from Deuteronomy, this time from Deuteronomy 6. Just as in Deuteronomy 8, the context is the desert, where Israel awaits entry into the land. Jesus is again pictured as reliving Israel's testing in the desert, placing himself with the people, subjecting himself to the sharp warnings against idolatry, summed up in 6:16: "Do not put the LORD your God to the test." But where lies the danger of idolatry for Jesus in this test? Might it lie precisely in the expected role and perks of messiahship as generally understood in Jesus's world? Might it lie in the blessings usually associated even in the Bible with divine sonship? There is a great irony in this test.

Whereas Jesus is himself being tested, his response to Satan indicates that God is not to be tested without the potential of dire consequence. The experience of the desert in the history of Israel taught that lesson well.

Worship Me! I'll Make You Ruler of the World!

The third test (second in Luke) again holds before Jesus the blessings of being King, Messiah, Son of God. The tempter takes up the promise God makes to his chosen king from Psalm 2. Psalm 2:7 was proclaimed over Jesus at his baptism, and later in this psalm we encounter the following words:

> Ask of me, and I will make the nations your heritage,
>   and the ends of the earth your possession.
> You shall break them with a rod of iron,
>   and dash them in pieces like a potter's vessel. (Ps. 2:8–9)

In effect, Satan offers Jesus the perks implied in the words of commission that Jesus received at his baptism, namely, that he is Son of God and as such he will be a great king to whom all the nations of the earth will be subject. What gives this test its power, what makes it a true temptation, is precisely its proximity to what *God* offers his Son/King/Messiah in Psalm 2: lordship over the nations of the earth.

Once again Jesus quotes from Deuteronomy 6, this time from 6:13: "The LORD your God you shall fear; him you shall serve." As the words quoted earlier, these emerge from the very center of Israel's covenant with God. They are preceded by the prayer Jews prayed daily—"Hear, O Israel: The LORD is our God, the LORD alone" (6:4)—followed by the "first commandment" in 6:5: "You shall love the LORD your God with all your heart, and with all your soul, and with all your might" (in Mark 12:29–30 Jesus combines precisely these two texts; see also Matt. 22:37 || Luke 10:27).

This is a most remarkable scene. What kind of a king will Jesus be? Matthew and Luke, by expanding the narrative of the desert testing in the way they have, prepare us to look for a messiah who will be humble, placing himself with the people of God in their vulnerability and dependence on God. He will forego the privileges and the perks of being a divine agent, of being God's royal son. Most importantly, he will fulfill the will of God with every fiber of his being. In short, he will love God with all his heart, soul, and power.

The Nature of the Tests

We need to step back and place this event into the sequence of events we have so far surveyed. We began with Matthew's and Luke's infancy narratives, which depict the birth of the Savior, of the Messiah. We sensed already there the enormous tension between the affirmation that here was the birth of the long-promised liberator of Israel, of the one who would rule the cosmos as God's Messiah, and the extremely humble and vulnerable circumstances of that birth. Then we pondered the divine commissioning and empowerment of the Messiah at Jesus's baptism. Immediately thereafter we had described for us a dramatic backing away from everything we might have thought goes with such an acclamation. We see in Jesus a messiah who says a resounding "no!" to the prerogatives of a messiah. Jesus is pitted against Satan, Scripture against Scripture, messiahship against messiahship, kingdom against kingdom.

We sense the tension in this titanic struggle regardless of how symbolic the account is and how imagery laden the narrative is. The gospel writers see this testing as marking the whole of Jesus's life and ministry. It marks the pivotal scene at the very center of the Gospel of Mark (Mark 8:27–38). Jesus's furious response to Peter in 8:33 ("get behind me, Satan!") is an indication that the testing about the nature of his messiahship lasted longer than forty days in the desert. The testing can be seen to extend, finally, to Jesus's struggle in the Garden of Gethsemane where, facing imminent death, he finds the strength to drink the "cup" in accordance with God's will (Matt. 26:36–46 || Mark 14:32–42 || Luke 22:39–46). In short, Jesus's testing, however much the tradition has collapsed this into the episode in the desert, captures with narrative force the fundamental questions that dogged Jesus and his followers, even after Easter. What kind of a messiah? What sort of a kingdom? What kind of power? The prominence given this theme in the gospel narratives, alongside Jesus's warnings to his disciples not to seek power over others (e.g., Matt. 20:25–28; Luke 22:25–27), suggests that the issues of power and privilege continued to test his followers in the decades following Jesus's Palestinian ministry.

The Twelve

In popular imagination, Jesus is usually seen traveling with twelve male "disciples" or "apostles," or simply "the Twelve" as they are at times referred to in the sources (Matt. 4:18–22 || Mark 1:16–20 || Luke 5:1–11 || John 1:35–51; Matt. 9:9 || Mark 2:13–14 || Luke 5:27–32; Matt. 10:1–42 || Mark 3:13–19 || Luke 6:12–16 and 9:1–6; Matt. 8:18–22; Luke 8:1–3; 10:1–24; John 6:66–70). Today some scholars doubt that such a group existed during the period of Jesus's Palestinian ministry. While few would deny that there was such a group, these scholars think it came into existence following Jesus's death. Paul makes mention of the Twelve in 1 Corinthians 15:5, a letter that more than likely predates the earliest gospel by at least a decade and a half. But I see no good reason to question that Jesus surrounded himself with a group called the Twelve. They were, however, by no means his only close followers.

Lists of the Twelve

There are two very similar lists of the Twelve: Matthew and Mark share one list, and Luke/Acts has another in two different places. The Gospel of John knows of the Twelve (6:67, 70; 20:24), but does not list them. Further, John mentions a person by the name of Nathanael, introduced to Jesus by Philip of Bethsaida, whom Jesus summons to follow him (1:45–51; 21:2, where he is called "Nathanael of Cana"). He is not listed by the other evangelists. The lists of the Twelve by the writers of the Synoptic Gospels look like this:

Matthew 10:2–4	Mark 3:16–19	Luke 6:14–16	Acts 1:13
Simon (Peter)	Simon (Peter)	Simon (Peter)	Peter
Andrew (Peter's brother)	James (son of Zebedee)	Andrew (Peter's brother)	John
James (son of Zebedee)	John (James's brother)	James	James
John (James's brother)	Andrew	John	Andrew
Philip	Philip	Philip	Philip
Bartholomew	Bartholomew	Bartholomew	Thomas
Thomas	Matthew	Matthew	Bartholomew
Matthew (tax collector)	Thomas	Thomas	Matthew
James (son of Alphaeus)	James (son of Alphaeus)	James (son of Alphaeus)	James (son of Alphaeus)
Thaddaeus	Thaddaeus	Simon (the Zealot)	Simon (the Zealot)

Matthew 10:2–4	Mark 3:16–19	Luke 6:14–16	Acts 1:13
Simon (the Cananaean)	Simon (the Cananaean)	Judas (son of James)	Judas (son of James)
Judas Iscariot	Judas Iscariot	Judas Iscariot	[Matthias; see Acts 1:23–26]

For the most part, the lists agree. There is some variation, however. The first nine names are identical in each of the lists except for some minor variation in sequence. Peter, or Simon, is first in all of them, which should tell us something of his importance. Judas is listed last, which should also tell us something of his standing in the years that these lists were set in the oral tradition. He is of course absent from Acts, since by then in the story he is dead (Matt. 27:5; Acts 1:18). His replacement, Matthias, is chosen by lot (Acts 1:26). Matthew and Mark list the ninth and tenth apostles as Thaddaeus and Simon the Cananaean, whereas in Luke/Acts we find Judas son of James and Simon the Zealot. Are these the same persons, remembered with different names? That is by no means impossible. After all, Peter is known as well by the names *Simon* and *Cephas*. Both the extent of agreement and ironically the slight variation suggest a strong historical reminiscence of who was part of this particular circle.

Jesus's students (which is what the term *disciple* means) were drawn from circles not usually associated with learning: fishing, tax collecting, and an assortment of folks who were as likely as not laborers. This is important for understanding the kinds of persons whom Jesus attracted and with whom he wished to be identified.

The Larger Circle of Followers and Adherents

But if we want to give an account of Jesus's followers, we must list others as well, persons who were perhaps just as close to Jesus as the Twelve. Most notable among these are women who appear at critical moments in the narrative. Luke pays especially close attention to them, but he is not alone. Luke 8:2–3 mentions women who traveled with Jesus, funding his ministry. Mary Magdalene is mentioned first, indicating her great importance among Jesus's inner circle, but so are women of means such as Joanna, the wife of a high Herodian official named Chuza. We might wonder whether the Samaritan woman in John 4 represents an important person among Samaritan followers of Jesus. John also makes much of Jesus's close friendship with the sisters Mary and Martha of Bethany and their brother Lazarus (John 11), familiar to us from Luke 10. It appears that not all close followers and friends traveled with him.

Women play a particularly significant role at the peak of the story, Jesus's crucifixion and resurrection. Luke mentions the "daughters of Jerusalem" who accompany the procession of Jesus to the place of his execution (23:27–28). But Luke and the other evangelists mention by name women who had accompanied him from Galilee and are there at the darkest and most dangerous hour of his execution, while many of his male companions have apparently fled. These include several women named Mary, including Jesus's mother. She and other members of Jesus's family are present again after Easter as part of the inner circle of his followers (Acts 1:14).

Yet others are mentioned among close followers of Jesus who do not fit any of our lists. Nathanael has already been mentioned above. Joseph of Arimathea is mentioned by all four gospel writers in relation to the events of the last days, with Matthew specifically identifying him as a disciple (Matt. 27:57–60 || Mark 15:43–46 || Luke 23:50–54 || John 19:38). We meet Nicodemus in John 3, a prominent Pharisee who does not dare to meet Jesus except by night. But John's narrative has him present during Jesus's last days, arguing Jesus's case and finally helping with the burial of Jesus (7:50–51; 19:39). And what should we make of the Gospel of John's Beloved Disciple (John 19:26; 21:20, 24)? Is he only a symbol for any number of unnamed disciples who were close to Jesus, or is he the unnamed author of the Fourth Gospel (see chapter 3 above)?

No doubt these persons are only the tip of the iceberg. Jesus likely had friends and supporters in many places. Perhaps there were cells of followers here and there in the villages and cities that heeded his message of the kingdom of God and fashioned their lives accordingly. Mary, Martha, and Lazarus may well be precisely such an example. Might this help to explain the extremely rapid spread of the early church in the years and decades after Good Friday and Easter? While this remains at best informed guesswork, we can be sure that we are entirely incorrect to imagine Jesus simply as part of a group of thirteen men wandering the roads and streets of Palestine. In Luke 10, for example, Jesus sends out seventy of his followers. Seventy is, of course, a highly symbolic number in Judaism, representing inclusiveness and completeness. Perhaps with this number Luke wishes to signal to his readers that what Jesus said to the Twelve (see 9:1–6) is valid for all his followers who became missionaries at or after Easter. Even so, by relating this event *after* also telling of Jesus sending out the Twelve, Luke wants us to know that we are mistaken if we think of twelve followers as the exclusive circle of students and followers of Jesus.

Symbolic Significance of the Twelve

What then of the special group dubbed the Twelve? Who are they? What is their function? According to biblical lore, Israel was made up of twelve tribes, originating from the twelve sons of Jacob. Twelve is thus a highly suggestive number in first-century Palestine, regardless of the tribes having disappeared from history after the catastrophic Assyrian decimation of the northern kingdom of Israel in the eighth century BCE. We should thus think of these dozen persons as a symbolic circle, demonstrating that Jesus's mission was directed to the restoration of Israel.

But, to take up again briefly the question of history, does such symbolism make more sense *before* or *after* Easter? Given that the church very quickly opened its doors to Gentiles, let me suggest that the existence of the Twelve as a living symbol makes more sense *during* the time of Jesus's ministry in Palestine, heralding the imminent arrival of God's reign and with it the redemption of the people of God. For example, the instructions to the Twelve in Matthew 10 begin as follows:

> Go nowhere among the Gentiles, and enter no town of the Samaritans, but go rather to the lost sheep of the house of Israel. (Matt. 10:5–6)

This text appears to reflect an early stage in the ministry of Jesus in which the arrival of the kingdom of God was understood to be of particular relevance to the restoration of Israel. That such a ministry carried within it the seeds of moving beyond those borders to include the Gentiles is in no way denied thereby (see chapter 6 above). In other words, beyond drawing around him circles of followers of both genders and of various classes, Jesus also signals to friend and foe alike that his is a Jewish renewal movement, a movement calling Israel back to its calling to be God's kingdom. As such, however, it is to be the harbinger of a full appearing of the universal reign of God when all nations will come to worship the one God of the cosmos. While his messiahship will be one that will not easily fit people's expectations, it nevertheless makes little if any sense outside of the convictions and yearnings of the Jewish people. Jesus's choosing exactly twelve men among the larger circle of followers illustrates that forcefully.

Circles of Jesus's Followers

The various layers or circles of supporters and followers of Jesus may be pictured with enlarging circles (see illustration 7.1)

The outer circle represents not a specific group but Jewish society in Palestine as a whole, composed of the various groups and sectors of society from which the followers of Jesus came (see chapter 4 above). The gospels suggest that they were for the most part from the humble strata of society: fishers, tax collectors, oppressed and marginalized persons, and so on. But, as we have indicated, there were also persons of means and standing who were prepared to identify with him and his mission.

The next circle toward the center represents the wide range of adherence to Jesus. There were evidently supporters, such as Mary and Martha, who did not travel with Jesus and his entourage. They should nevertheless be counted among his close followers. Others, like Nicodemus, kept a low profile, perhaps out of fear. The Apostle Paul's list of Easter witnesses is instructive here in

Illustration 7.1 The Followers of Jesus

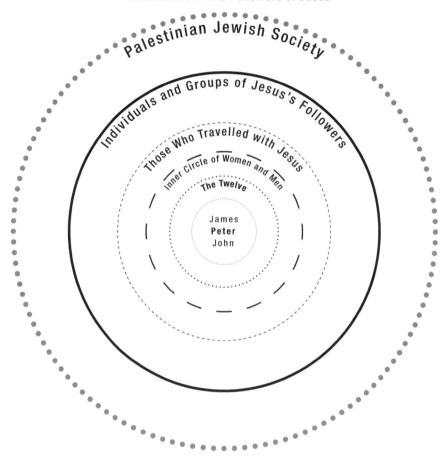

that he mentions that the risen Jesus appeared to "more than five hundred brothers and sisters at one time, most of whom are still alive" (1 Cor. 15:6). We must be sure to make these followers a part of our picture.

The third circle represents those who traveled with Jesus. Perhaps this is not a tighter circle, since it is likely that there were many who would have been hangers on for a while (John 6:66 mentions that after a particularly challenging speech by Jesus "many of his disciples turned back and no longer went about with him"). Nevertheless, as Luke 8:2–3 makes abundantly clear, there were those who traveled with him, who cared for the group, bringing with them the money needed to support such a group. And they were there when the Twelve had disbanded and gone into hiding.

The inner circle should be thought of quite naturally as including the Twelve. But it is important to include in that inner circle persons such as

Mary Magdalene and other women who are remembered in the record by name.

Of special importance within this circle of the Twelve are Peter, James, and John. They play a significant role in the narrative (e.g., at the transfiguration in Matt. 17:1 || Mark 9:2 || Luke 9:28; at Gethsemane in Matt. 26:37 || Mark 14:33). But none of the followers is as important as Peter. He carries three names in the tradition: Simon, Peter, and Cephas. Not only does he play a prominent if complex role in the gospel traditions, but Paul is fully aware of his importance for the developing church after Easter (e.g., 1 Cor. 9:5; 15:5; Galatians 1–2). Accordingly, Luke devotes a great deal of his second volume, the Acts of the Apostles, to Peter.

The Twelve represent the symbolic center of Jesus's mission. It is not at all clear, however, that the women identified above were not as close to Jesus as any of the men who play a role in the gospel narratives. Their presence in the Passion Narratives alone should alert us to that fact. Sadly, the tradition was not as respectful and hospitable toward them as was Jesus.

Conclusion

Four features help set the scene for Jesus's mission as herald and enactor of the reign of God. The gospels show him as carrying on the mission of the Baptist. But they show him as doing more. His mission is nothing less than the restoration of Israel. And that is exactly what a messiah is about. But the gospels also show us that he will be a messiah with a difference—he will refuse the road of power and force; he will refuse the safety of divine protection; he will, instead, go the road of suffering, much as did the servant of the Servant Songs of Isaiah 40–55. The enormous tension inherent in that mix will shape the narrative from here on in.

For Further Reading

See relevant articles and chapters in dictionaries and works cited in chapter 1, especially the following:

Meier, John P. *A Marginal Jew: Rethinking the Historical Jesus*, vol. 3: *Companions and Competitors*. New York: Doubleday, 2001.

Key Terms and Concepts

baptism
John the Baptist
messiahship
Satan
Suffering Servant
temptation/testing
the Twelve

8

Teaching the Kingdom

PARABLES

> With many such parables [Jesus] spoke the word to them, as they were able to hear it; *he did not speak to them except in parables*, but he explained everything in private to his disciples. (Mark 4:33–34, emphasis added)

EVEN ALLOWING FOR exaggeration, these words at the conclusion of a collection of Jesus's parables in Mark 4 indicate that he was known, among other things, as a teller of parables. It appears that Jesus found no better way to teach about the reign of God than with parables. Many of them are aphorisms or short pithy sayings, some little more than a turn of phrase. Others are longer stories, sometimes even allegories. In this chapter we will ask what parables do, what kinds of parables Jesus used, what he intended them to effect, and how they related to his overall objective of alerting his hearers to both the presence and coming of the kingdom of God.

What Are Parables?

John Dominic Crossan defines a parable as "an extended metaphor or simile frequently becoming a brief narrative, generally used in biblical times for didactic [i.e., teaching] purposes" (*Anchor Bible Dictionary* 5.146). That is as useful and expansive a definition as we might find, even if it understates the presence of short aphorisms among Jesus's word events we call parables.

Startling Analogies and Juxtapositions

Crossan's definition suggests, first of all, that a parable is intended to *teach* something, to communicate something. Jesus does not simply intend to tease his audience, but to have them learn something. At the same time, a parable does tease the listener by teaching with often startling comparisons. Many parables are little other than a comparison of one thing with another. A related and familiar term is *analogy*:

> With what can we compare the kingdom of God, or what parable will we use for it? It is like a mustard seed, which, when sown upon the ground, is the smallest of all the seeds on earth; yet when it is sown it grows up and becomes the greatest of all shrubs, and puts forth large branches, so that the birds of the air can make nests in its shade. (Mark 4:30–32)

In this case the comparison is simple: "*a is like b*"—the kingdom of God is *like* a seed. Sometimes *b* is more like an extended metaphor or even a short story:

> The kingdom of God is as if someone would scatter seed on the ground, and would sleep and rise night and day, and the seed would sprout and grow, he does not know how. The earth produces of itself, first the stalk, then the head, then the full grain in the head. (Mark 4:26–28)

As these examples illustrate, by forcing the hearer to ponder sometimes quite surprising comparisons, parables are often like riddles or puzzles. The analogies in Jesus's parables are often not at all obvious and require a certain nimbleness of mind and a free imagination to be able to catch on—much like a joke. A joke works only if it surprises the hearer with a humorous twist. And a joke is caught on to only with a sense of humor, by those nimble enough to catch the twist. People with a sense of humor are always ready to be surprised; in fact, they cannot wait. Moreover, jokes work best when there is something already familiar, such as a situation or relationship, which is then subjected to a surprising twist.

We should think similarly of the way parables work. In telling parables, Jesus is looking for the kinds of persons who have a "sense of the kingdom," that is, who are nimble enough to catch on to the surprising ways the reign of God manifests itself and who are on the lookout for the surprise. Everyone in Jesus's audience would have had an idea of what the kingdom of God is. The question is whether they are waiting for it, but in a way that leaves them open to the surprise of its appearing. I am by no means suggesting that Jesus's parables are jokes, even if there are occasional elements that might have brought a smile or a chuckle to Jesus's listeners. At the same time, some of the ways jokes function help us to listen to the parables more nimbly.

Allegories

Some parables are allegories, in which each or at least most of the parts refer symbolically to something already known by the hearers or readers. The parable of the vineyard in Matthew 21:33–41 || Mark 12:1–9 || Luke 20:9–16 provides an excellent example. The evangelists clearly understand it this way and so have Jesus tell this parable in the last days in Jerusalem when tension between him and the authorities is very high. Jesus tells of a master who had a vineyard. He went away on a journey and rented the vineyard out to tenants; whenever he would send servants to collect a certain proportion of the fruit, which were his due as owner, they all met with violence. Finally the master decided to send his own son; surely his tenants would respect him. Him they killed, thinking that without an heir the vineyard would be theirs. This served only to provoke the master to terrible retribution.

One might take this as a simple moral teaching against theft and violence. But in this case the elements of the story are loaded. It would have been difficult, if not impossible, for Jesus's hearers *not* to hear this as an allegory. The identification of Israel with the vineyard and of the master as God was already known, as is illustrated in the following parable from the prophet Isaiah:

> Let me sing for my beloved
>   my love-song concerning his vineyard:
> My beloved had a vineyard
>   on a very fertile hill.
> He dug it and cleared it of stones,
>   and planted it with choice vines;
> he built a watchtower in the midst of it,
>   and hewed out a wine vat in it;
> he expected it to yield grapes,
>   but it yielded wild grapes. (Isa. 5:1–2)

Now follows an interpretive expansion in which vineyard and the "beloved" are identified as Israel or Judah and God as the owner of the vineyard:

> And now, inhabitants of Jerusalem
>   and people of Judah,
> judge between me
>   and my vineyard.

What more was there to do for my vineyard
    that I have not done in it?
When I expected it to yield grapes,
    why did it yield wild grapes?
And now I will tell you
    what I will do to my vineyard.
I will remove its hedge,
    and it shall be devoured;
I will break down its wall,
    and it shall be trampled down.
I will make it a waste;
    it shall not be pruned or hoed,
    and it shall be overgrown with briers and thorns;
I will also command the clouds
    that they rain no rain upon it.
For the vineyard of the LORD of hosts
    is the house of Israel,
and the people of Judah
    are his pleasant planting;
he expected justice,
    but saw bloodshed;
righteousness,
    but heard a cry! (Isa. 5:3–7)

Another element of Jesus's parable of the vineyard would have been im-mediately familiar to his audience: the fate of the prophets at the hands of a rebellious nation, especially its leaders. In short, Jesus's parable is an allegory that retells in highly concentrated fashion the long history of the fate of God's messengers, and it anticipates the mortal danger that this last messenger, Jesus himself, is in. It also illustrates powerfully how a parable can function much like prophetic oracles of judgment as we find them in the Old Testament. (For another example of parable in the Old Testament, see Jotham's allegorical parable of the trees in Judg. 9:7–15.)

The question of whether parables should be interpreted as allegories is actually quite controversial in contemporary scholarship. For many centuries parables were treated strictly as allegories. An example within the New Testa-ment itself is the parable of the sower in Matthew 13:1–9 || Mark 4:1–9 || Luke 8:4–8 (*Gospel of Thomas* 9), which is followed by an allegorical inter-pretation in Matthew 13:18–23 || Mark 4:13–20 || Luke 8:11–15 (but not, interestingly, in the *Gospel of Thomas*). Most scholars treat this interpretation as *post*-Jesus, precisely because of its allegorical nature. Considerably more fanciful interpretations of the parables were developed in the centuries that followed. One of the best known is Augustine of Hippo's interpretation of the parable of the good Samaritan:

A certain man went down from Jerusalem to Jericho; Adam himself is meant; Jerusalem is the heavenly city of peace, from whose blessedness Adam fell; Jericho means the moon, and signifies our mortality, because it is born, waxes, wanes, and dies. Thieves are the devil and his angels who stripped him, namely, of his immortality; and beat him, by persuading him to sin; and left him half-dead, because in so far as man can understand and know God, he lives, but in so far as he is wasted and oppressed by sin, he is dead; he is therefore called half-dead. The priest and Levite who saw him and passed by, signify the priesthood and ministry of the Old Testament, which could profit nothing for salvation. Samaritan means Guardian, and therefore the Lord Himself is signified by this name. The binding of the wounds is the restraint of sin. Oil is the comfort of good hope; wine is the exhortation to work with fervent spirit. The beast is the flesh in which He deigned to come to us. The being set upon the beast is belief in the incarnation of Christ. The inn is the Church, where travelers returning to their heavenly country are refreshed after pilgrimage. The morrow is after the resurrection of the Lord. The two pence are either the precepts of love, or the promise of this life and of that which is to come. The innkeeper is the Apostle [Paul]. The supererogatory payment is either his counsel of celibacy, or the fact that he worked with his own hands lest he should be a burden to any of the weaker brethren when the Gospel was new, though it was lawful for him "to live by the Gospel." (Augustine, *Quaestionum evangelicarum* 2.19, quoted in Dodd, *Parables of the Kingdom*, 1–2)

In the twentieth century such elaborate interpretation rightly came under sharp criticism. Parables were taken to have one meaning, found in the twist in the story (i.e., analogous to the punch line of a joke) and not in a decoding of the hidden identities of each feature.

More recently, however, some correctly argue that allegory should *not* be rejected outright as a way of interpreting parables. Much as in the case of the parable of the vineyard or the earlier song of the vineyard in Isaiah 5 (quoted above), people would have heard many parables of Jesus as barely veiled retellings of the story of Israel. So, for example, N. T. Wright refers to the parables as "apocalyptic allegories," secretive and subversive ways of telling the story of Israel in light of the invading kingdom of God (*Jesus and the Victory of God*, 174–82). This is clearly illustrated by the parable of the vineyard discussed earlier. Wright also applies this method of interpretation to such well-known parables as the prodigal son, the good Samaritan, and the sheep and goats.

There is wisdom in being cautious about interpreting parables allegorically. At the same time, there is equal wisdom in allowing for the likelihood that Jesus's stories were heard by ears well prepared by a rich reservoir of image and symbol that the tradition would have inculcated. Perhaps the allegorical interpretation of the parable of the sower is not so unfaithful to Jesus's use of parables after all.

Extended Narratives or Stories

The longer parables of Jesus, whether allegorical or not, owe much to the ancient Hebrew form of parable called *mashal*. In addition to the song of the vineyard in Isaiah 5 quoted above, we can illustrate this with the prophet Nathan's story of the poor man with his little lamb (2 Sam. 12:1–4). With this story he confronted King David over his having taken another man's wife (Bathsheba) as his own. Fortunately, unlike John the Baptist, he did not pay with his life for "speaking truth to power." One last example is the wonderfully sarcastic parable regarding the introduction of monarchy into Israel in Judges 9:7–15. In short, Jesus's telling of loaded stories with a rich set of double meanings has a long history.

Sifting the Audience: The Parable as Judgment

To return to the analogy of the joke: jokes are fully appreciated only by those who catch on. A joke, if well told, provokes a response of laughter, but only in those who have a sense of humor. Jokes sift those with a sense of humor from those who are rather dull witted.

That is exactly how parables work. Jesus's parables have a way of sifting his audience, of separating those who have a sense of the kingdom (i.e., those alert enough to see the signs of God's reign taking shape within the everyday experiences of life) from those closed to Jesus's message (i.e., those too dim-witted to catch on to the kingdom). That is surely why Jesus ends his parable of the sower with the phrase "let anyone with ears to hear listen!" (Matt. 13:9 || Mark 4:9 || Luke 8:8). Parables are for those with ears to hear and with eyes to see the kingdom of God. Parables are for those who discover a treasure and then sell everything for the sake of that treasure. But, and this is critically important for the sifting function of parables, parables are for those who have an eye for the treasure to begin with! Whereas others might see only a field, they see the treasure.

Another word for sifting is "judgment." Immediately after the parable of the sower, and still very much in connection with it, both Matthew (13:10–16) and Mark (4:10–13) quote from Isaiah:

> And [God] said, "Go and say to this people:
> 'Keep listening, but do not comprehend;
> keep looking, but do not understand.'
> Make the mind of this people dull,
>   and stop their ears,
>   and shut their eyes,
> so that they may not look with their eyes,
>   and listen with their ears,
> and comprehend with their minds,
>   and turn and be healed." (Isa. 6:9–10)

Isaiah depicts God in a fit of anger, pronouncing judgment on the people. Mark and Matthew have Jesus referring to this oracle of judgment in order to indicate the devastating effect the parables have on those who do not hear what Jesus is saying, whose ears are closed to the kingdom. For such, parables are not grace, but judgment.

We must take a slight detour to the Gospel of John. Unlike the first three gospels, John does not contain parables (see chapter 3 above). That is somewhat of an overstatement. John 10, for example, contains a highly effective set of parabolic reflections on the shepherd, sheep, and sheepfold images, no less evocative for a Jewish audience than the vineyard discussed earlier (e.g., Ps. 23; Isa. 40:11). But John does not call this a "parable" (*parabole*), but rather a "figure of speech" (*paroimia*): "I have said these things to you in figures of speech. The hour is coming when I will no longer speak to you in figures, but will tell you plainly of the Father" (16:25; see also 10:6; 16:29). It is clear from the very way in which John uses the phrase *figure of speech* that he is aware of the way these cryptic images separate those with the ears to hear from those who do not.

Interestingly, John too has Jesus quoting Isaiah 6:9–10, but not in relation to figures of speech, but rather to Jesus's *signs*, his demonstrative miracles (John 12:37–40). Jesus performs signs, such as changing water into wine at the wedding at Cana (2:1–11) and healing the man born blind (John 9). Those who get excited about either wine or physical sight miss the point; what they are meant to see is who Jesus truly is. For those who miss the point, the signs serve as judgment.

We return to the parable of the sower. If the parable is supposed to sift those with a sense of the kingdom from those without such a sense, why then an explanation of the parable in Matthew 13:18–23 || Mark 4:13–20 || Luke 8:11–15? Does it not go against everything we have just learned about how parables are supposed to work as revelation and as judgment? To pick up the analogy from the first part of this chapter, do jokes come with an explanation? Not surprisingly, most scholars see the interpretation of this parable as secondary and thus not going back to Jesus himself. I have considerable understanding for such suspicion. Parenthetically, as indicated earlier, the *Gospel of Thomas* includes this parable but *not* the explanation (*Gospel of Thomas* 9). I think it is Mark (and also Matthew and Luke, in dependency on Mark), or the tradition that Mark draws from, who supplies the explanation for the parable. To be sure, the evangelist would not be the first to provide the key to a parable's interpretation, as seen in Isaiah 5 (quoted earlier). Nor would he be the last, as seen in the many books explaining the parables, including this chapter!

It would seem that by rendering Jesus's "joke" as an *explained* joke, Mark, to cite the earlier instance of this, has undermined the function of the parable. Or has he? Does not the very nature of this parable invite precisely such an interpretation, one that would have suggested itself over and over in the experience of early missionaries? Of course it does, and quite possibly others as well. Allegorical interpretation comes naturally, even if we recognize that the form in which we encounter it in Matthew 13, Mark 4, and Luke 8 may reflect the ongoing life of the communities of Jesus believers as they evangelized their surrounding world.

There may be another purpose, however, in Mark's offering an explanation. It may be related to the judgment function of parables. By offering an interpretation along with the scolding in 4:13, Mark is criticizing the disciples, and with them the readers of his gospel. By having Jesus needing to give an explanation of the parable, Mark insinuates that Jesus's followers are themselves too dim-witted to catch on. When Mark has the disciples requiring a great deal of impatient tutoring from Jesus, he is as much as telling his readers, then as now, that they too may have to work at developing a "sense of humor," that is, a sense of the kingdom. In offering an explanation for this parable, Mark, and in dependence on him Matthew and Luke, is both helping his readers and confronting them like a prophet.

Parables in an Unjust World

If Jesus's parables serve to sift those with an ability to catch on to the kingdom of God, and thus serve as means of judgment, we should also be alert to the way in which his parables speak to conditions of injustice and oppression, in particular, economic oppression. Indeed, their highly suggestive and at the same time unobvious nature provides Jesus with an excellent way to highlight the plight of the oppressed and at the same time to expose the callousness of the rich and powerful. The allegorical potential of some of the parables should not obscure this dimension. In the parables we meet vulnerable widows up against callous judges (Luke 18:1–8), debtors driven into a life of slavery (Matt. 18:23–35), day laborers at the mercy of the whims of estate owners (Matt. 20:1–16), and wily middlemen navigating the troubled territory between demanding estate owners and needy peasants (Luke 16:1–9). These examples resonate with the conditions of a society under the violent order of an empire in which the rich are getting richer and the poor poorer.

The riddlelike nature of Jesus's parables makes it sometimes difficult to know how to catch on to the parable. It appears, for example, that Jesus sometimes wants his listeners to identify the estate or vineyard owner or judge with God, even if they would have recognized their oppressor in that character. As bewildering as Jesus's parables sometimes are, one thing is sure: the radical social dimension of these parables tends to be ignored too often in favor of a spiritual interpretation that would have exasperated Jesus.

Specific Parables

We have already considered several parables above within a discussion about what parables are and how they work. Jesus and the evangelists are hardly concerned that we understand how parables work; they want us to hear the sayings or stories, to be prodded by them to be open to the life-changing and society-changing reign of God. We turn now to a consideration of these parables, grouped around shared characteristics or thematic stresses.

Parabolic Proverbs or Aphorisms

The Sermon on the Mount is not usually thought of as a repository of Jesus's parables. However, in Matthew 5:13–16, 39–41 and 6:22–7:27 we find a rich vein of short word pictures, analogies, and images that have a wonderful proverbial and parabolic quality about them, even if they are not always extended metaphors. That is to say, they have about them the timeless quality of everyday wisdom and a rather immediate if sometimes surprising connection with everyday life. At the same time they often serve as a wake-up call to be alert to the reign of God. Many of these pithy sayings, even if they may not be parables in the strict sense—that is, they are more like snapshots than a video—are recognizable from everyday use by people who have no idea as to their origin:

- You are the salt of the earth. (5:13)
- You are the light of the world. So let your light shine. (5:14–16)
- Turn the cheek, give your shirt, go the second mile. (5:39–41)
- The eye is the lamp of the body. (6:22–23)
- You cannot serve two masters. (6:24)
- Do not worry about life. Look at the birds and the flowers. (6:25–34)
- Take the log out of your eye before you try to take the speck out of your neighbor's eye. (7:3–5)
- Do not throw pearls before swine. (7:6)
- Knock and it will be opened. (7:7–8)
- Would you give your child a stone if he asks for bread, or a snake if she asks for a fish? Neither would God. (7:9–11)
- The wide and narrow gate and the easy and hard road. (7:13–14)
- Beware of wolves in sheep's clothing. (7:15)
- You will know them by their fruits. (7:16–20)
- Build your house on rock, not sand. (7:24–27)

Should we be surprised that Jesus would speak in the kinds of proverbs we might well use in everyday context having little to do explicitly with the kingdom of God? No—since the notion of God as king encompasses the conviction that God is creator and sustainer of *all* of life. However much Jesus anticipates the powerful intervention of God in the near future, he knows that God's sustaining and liberating power is *already* present, not least in the sun and the rain and the life they make possible (see Matt. 5:45).

And yet, many of these apparently conventional wisdom sayings are radical in their implications. To live life as called for in these images is nothing short of living *already now* in light of the *coming* reign of God—and to do so with great vulnerability. Not to worry about tomorrow is explicitly related to caring more than anything about the kingdom of God and its justice. To turn the cheek is to live vulnerably and subversively in light of the vindication the coming reign of God will bring. To live like salt and light is to walk a very hard road. There can be nothing more radical and unconventional than the life Jesus invites his audience to. But Matthew has Jesus confront his hearers with that radical summons by means of homely and easily remembered word pictures. Jesus shows himself to be a true sage, a teacher of wisdom, however subversive this wisdom might be.

Parables of God's Grace and Generosity

Several of the proverbial parables listed above portray God as a caring and sustaining father (e.g., Matt. 6:26, 32; 7:11). "Father" means in these cases "sustaining creator." The image of God as father turns out to be a major theme in Jesus's announcing of the kingdom of God.

There is today quite appropriately great sensitivity about being inclusive in the use of language. Sometimes folks are then also reluctant to talk about God as father for fear of thereby privileging maleness. As respectful as one must be of the motives behind such reluctance, there is great danger in letting the contemporary agenda cloud or even obscure what Jesus intended to teach with this appellation.

In Jesus's way of talking about God, the term *father* becomes a kind of parable, expressing God's trustworthiness, parental attentiveness to the vulnerability of life, and sustaining and uncompromising affection and love for God's creatures. More, by inviting his listeners to address God as their father, Jesus wishes his hearers and followers to know that they are nothing less than daughters and sons of the God they too can call *Abba*—"my father." Interestingly, even Gentiles in the early church retained the Aramaic form of "my father" (*Abba*) so characteristic of Jesus's own way of praying (see Mark 14:36; Rom. 8:15; Gal. 4:6). Jesus teaches his disciples to pray accordingly in Matthew 6:9–13 and Luke 11:2–4.

PRODIGAL SON OR PRODIGAL FATHER

Jesus invests the notion of God's fatherhood with much more than trust-worthiness and sustaining care. With it he also wants to teach his hearers about the depth of passion with which God loves humanity, especially when it goes astray. An unforgettable expression of such passionate love is the parable of the prodigal (Luke 15:11–32).

The word *prodigal* means "recklessly wasteful," which describes very well the younger son in the parable. But it can also mean "extravagant" and in that sense describes the *father's* generosity, his love, and his affection for a son who had betrayed and embarrassed him so thoroughly in the eyes of his peers. Whereas the son is prodigal in wasting the inheritance he demanded even before its time, in effect wishing his father dead, the generosity of this father is prodigal in that it knows no bounds. When he sees his son from afar, he runs to meet him—strange behavior for a patriarch! He forgets decorum and rushes out to meet his errant son. And then, as if his embrace were not already a gift beyond measure, he throws a massive party in celebration of the homecoming.

The response of the father, embarrassingly inappropriate in terms of com-mon, customary morality and decorum, provokes the older brother: what's the point of my staying home and doing my duty, if you throw a party for "this son of yours" who has so thoroughly offended and embarrassed you (and me!)? The generosity of the father comes to expression here again. He does not scold his older dutiful but resentful son but rather tries to have some of his generosity rub off on his son:

> Son, you are always with me, and all that is mine is yours. But we had to celebrate and rejoice, because this brother of yours was dead and has come to life; he was lost and has been found. (Luke 15:31–32)

This remarkable parable is consistent with other images of God's delight in retrieving something that was lost, in binding something that was broken. It is preceded in Luke 15:3–10, for example by "parables of recovery," if we can call them that—the parables of the lost sheep and lost coin. And Jesus attempts to capture such a God in the term *father*. That Jesus is not stuck on one gender is illustrated by the parable of the lost coin, liken-ing God to a woman—early hearers and readers would have assumed a mother—who celebrates her recovery of lost treasure. There is a party in heaven, so to speak, for every bit of recovered treasure, for every "sinner who repents" (15:10).

These notes are not dampened when the parable is heard more allegorically. Hearers will often contribute to setting the context of the parable. Spoken within the context of Jesus's ministry in Palestine and the controversy it precipitated, it will have been heard in relation to God's being father of those "sinners" (15:1–2). Heard within the context of the later spread of the Jesus movement beyond the borders of the Jewish community, it might well be heard as a retelling of Israel's story in relation to the "welcome home" offered errant Gentiles. The fatherhood of God loses no meaning when considered against the broader horizon of God's relationship to Israel and humanity as a whole.

Day Laborers in the Vineyard

Jesus tells a disturbing parable of a vineyard owner who hires workers for a day's work, some early, some just before quitting time (Matt. 20:1–16). He pays them all equally, over the protests of those who worked all day. His response is that he can do as he pleases with what he owns and that those who worked all day have not been cheated. Have they not agreed to the wage at the outset?

It is not difficult to interpret this parable similarly to the way we interpreted the prodigal son. We might see it as a further example of the scandalous nature of God's generosity, of God's "unfair" graciousness that we saw in the parable of the prodigal son. Time and again, Jesus's image of a prodigally gracious God creates resentment on the part of those who "stayed home" or on the part of those who worked "since sunrise." With such parables Jesus teaches his audience that the reign of God is marked over and over again by the unfairness of grace. That is what fathers and mothers are like; they are unfair, wasteful, and unruly in their love and generosity toward their children, especially toward the most troublesome among them. It is this wastefulness that marks God's parental reign.

Most interpretations of this parable have conformed in some rough sense to this interpretation. However, some interpreters take a very different line. Since these workers were day laborers and thus the most vulnerable among the work force ("'Why are you standing here idle all day?' They said to him, 'Because no one has hired us'" [20:6–7]) and since each was paid one denarius for a day's labor (hardly enough to live on), the picture might change from one of generosity to one of exploited vulnerability. It is interesting that the owner of the vineyard responds with the arrogance of the rich: "Am I not allowed to do what I choose with what belongs to me?" (20:15). Could it be that, perhaps before Matthew placed it into the interpretive framework of his gospel, Jesus was with this parable exposing the callousness of estate owners and, in announcing the reign of God, contrasting God with such callousness?

This parable illustrates that one is often listening to Jesus's parables with furrowed brow, and rightly so.

Parables of Urgency and Judgment

God's gracious reign is encountered in just about every context in life. That is what it means for Jesus to alert his hearers to the reign of God being "among you [*or* in your midst]" (Luke 17:21). We will not catch the full force of Jesus's understanding of the reign or kingdom of God, however, if we pay attention only to the ways God's gracious and sustaining reign is *already* present. Jesus also tells parables that emphasize alertness and urgency regarding the kingdom's imminent *arrival*. They have a heady air of anticipation and even urgent warning.

Ten Virgins

Whereas the previous parables we have considered emphasize the shocking generosity and graciousness of God's reign, in the parable of the ten virgins openness to and readiness for the reign of God is in the end a matter of life and death.

Jesus tells a whimsical story about a bridegroom and ten bridesmaids, five of whom are foolish, five of whom are wise (Matt. 25:1–13; compare Luke 13:24–30). What sets the wise and the foolish apart from each other is nothing other than the wise virgins having seen to it that they have enough oil on their lamps to last the night of waiting, whereas the five fools have given no thought to being ready. When they realize their problem, they think they can solve the problem simply by mooching off the wise. These virgins are fools in that they have given no heed to the urgency of the moment, no heed to the future.

Again, we should be reminded of the evocative nature of parables. No doubt Jesus is instructing his hearers to be ready for the moment the kingdom arrives in full. But Jesus is also making a point to those who might be tempted to take grace as a given. There is a stark note of judgment on those who presume upon God's kindness. This parable too can be heard against the backdrop of Jewish eschatology. Jesus might well have been heard forcing the question: are we ready as a people for the wedding that marks the meeting of God with his bride, Israel? Into each of these contexts, micro and macro, Jesus sounds a clear warning: God's reign comes in both grace *and* judgment. Jesus insists that one be ready for that in-breaking reign, which comes like a thief in the night (Matt. 24:42–44).

Great Banquet

The urgency of being ready for the kingdom is expressed forcefully in the parable of the great banquet (Matt. 22:1–14 || Luke 14:16–24). It comes to us in two versions:

Matthew 22:1–14

Once more Jesus spoke to them in parables, saying: "The kingdom of heaven may be compared to a king who gave a wedding banquet for his son. He sent his slaves to call those who had been invited to the wedding banquet, but they would not come. Again he sent other slaves, saying, 'Tell those who have been invited: Look, I have prepared my dinner, my oxen and my fat calves have been slaughtered, and everything is ready; come to the wedding banquet.' But they made light of it and went away, one to his farm, another to his business, while the rest seized his slaves, mistreated them, and killed them. The king was enraged. He sent his troops, destroyed those murderers, and burned their city. Then he said to his slaves, 'The wedding is ready, but those invited were not worthy. Go therefore into the main streets, and invite everyone you find to the wedding banquet.' Those slaves went out into the streets and gathered all whom they found, both good and bad; so the wedding hall was filled with guests.

"But when the king came in to see the guests, he noticed a man there who was not wearing a wedding robe, and he said to him, 'Friend, how did you get in here without a wedding robe?' And he was speechless. Then the king said to the attendants, 'Bind him hand and foot, and throw him into the outer darkness, where there will be weeping and gnashing of teeth.' For many are called, but few are chosen."

Luke 14:16–24

Then Jesus said to him, "Someone gave a great dinner and invited many. At the time for the dinner he sent his slave to say to those who had been invited, 'Come; for everything is ready now.' But they all alike began to make excuses. The first said to him, 'I have bought a piece of land, and I must go out and see it; please accept my regrets.' Another said, 'I have bought five yoke of oxen, and I am going to try them out; please accept my regrets.' Another said, 'I have just been married, and therefore I cannot come.' So the slave returned and reported this to his master. Then the owner of the house became angry and said to his slave, 'Go out at once into the streets and lanes of the town and bring in the poor, the crippled, the blind, and the lame.' And the slave said, 'Sir, what you ordered has been done, and there is still room.' Then the master said to the slave, 'Go out into the roads and lanes, and compel people to come in, so that my house may be filled. For I tell you, none of those who were invited will taste my dinner.'"

The two versions have several significant differences:

Matthew	Luke
• king	• man
• wedding banquet	• banquet
• sends servants several times	• sends one servant once with invitation
• some of those invited ignore the invitation and leave to tend to their business while others kill the servants	• those invited make excuses
• king retaliates ferociously by sending his troops to kill and burn	
• servants sent out to find whom they can to bring to the wedding feast (both the good and the bad)	• servant sent out to find whom he can (poor, maimed, blind, lame)
• visit of king to the wedding banquet and ejection of the one without proper attire	
• "Many are called; few are chosen!"	• "None of those invited shall be at the banquet!"

Our explanatory options are roughly the following:

1. These are two versions of the same parable, altered during oral transmission.
2. These are two versions of the same parable, altered by the evangelists.
3. These are two similar but different parables, or one parable told in different ways by Jesus himself.

Option 1 is in principle possible, since the sayings of Jesus lived within the oral tradition of the early church for some time before being put in writing. We often, for example, hear the same basic joke in a variety of forms and settings, even if all those variations have the same punch line.

Given the strong chance, however, that Matthew and Luke relied on a written source we call Q (see chapter 2 above), option 2 may be more likely than option 1. We might even go so far as to suspect that Matthew reworked Q more extensively than did Luke. Certainly the allegorical possibilities are exploited more fully. For example, Matthew identifies the meal as a wedding banquet, a symbol of the messianic age. The plural "servants" and their fate might well be taken to be a barely veiled allusion to the fate of missionaries spreading the word of and about Jesus in the years following Easter. The reference to the destruction of the city sounds suspiciously like a retrospective glance at the destruction of Jerusalem in 70 CE. Finally, the poor chap who arrives at the banquet without proper attire might well reflect Matthew's concern to insist on the importance of living in accordance with the will of God, rather than presuming on grace. Perhaps Matthew has even fused two distinct parables together.

Luke, in contrast, has a simpler story that fits well with his stress on Jesus's ministry to the poor and the sick. Singular "servant" may indicate that he hears and communicates the parable as a short retelling of Jesus's ministry.

But what if, as in option 3, Jesus himself told this parable in different ways in different settings to different folks? Why not repeatedly tell a parable this good? We should not assume that the only explanation for multiple versions of roughly the same story is that there was one telling that then was diversified in the subsequent oral tradition. Stated more carefully, we should assume that Jesus's repeated and varied telling of his favorite parables likely contributed to the diversification of subsequent tradition. That said, nothing keeps the evangelists from further shaping already different versions to suit their particular purposes, as we may sense most strongly in Matthew's version. In other words, perhaps all three options are at work at the same time, in ways no longer distinguishable with any degree of certainty.

Returning to the content of the parable(s), invitation and judgment are strikingly mixed. Both versions of the parable begin with an invitation to those who are typically invited to important banquets: important people. Matthew's VIPs scorn the invitation and treat the messengers with contempt and lethal violence. Luke's have a string of excuses having to do with real estate, livestock, and marriage, in that order (the humor would surely not have been lost on the audiences of either Jesus or Luke).

The response of the banquet giver is remarkable. We are not surprised by the initial reaction of anger: in anger the king or householder sends his servants (or servant) out to the highways and byways to invite those who are *not* usually invited to an important banquet: the good and the bad (Matthew); the poor, the crippled, the blind, and the lame (Luke). In both stories the banquet giver insists that the banquet hall be filled with whoever can be found, even if they have to be compelled.

The invitation to those usually not invited is an act of grace. In both versions of the parable it is also a judgment on those who refused to accept the invitation. Their access is barred. Matthew's version has an additional miniparable about someone who tries to sneak into the banquet without proper attire and who is then subsequently thrown out of the banquet. Perhaps this is yet another of Jesus's parables that in Matthew's mind fits well with the theme of judgment his version accentuates forcefully. It would fit well Matthew's concern that lived righteousness not be disparaged (see chapter 3 above).

The basic question this parable asks is: who will be at the great feast when the kingdom of God comes in full? The answer: those who are normally never asked. The coming of the kingdom, Jesus says, will be accompanied by a great reversal: those who have been on the outside will be on the inside, and those used to being on the inside will find themselves shut out. In many ways Jesus enacted this parable over and over again in anticipation of that great banquet by repeatedly eating with tax collectors and sinners, by reaching out to the poor and the sick. As did Jesus's life, this parable would have struck very different chords with different parts of his audience: the "little people" would have laughed with glee; VIPs would have been deeply insulted and angered. Grace and judgment yet again. This point is not lessened by the likelihood that audiences of Jesus or of the evangelists would have heard that message within a variety of contexts and thus related it to a variety of specific settings. That is how parables work.

INVESTED SILVER

Judgment is also a central theme in a parable that again comes to us in two versions: Matthew's parable of the talents (Matt. 25:14–30) and Luke's parable of the pounds (Luke 19:12–27). Both talents and pounds were units of silver in Jesus's day. A talent was an enormous amount of money: more than 400,000 denarii, where one denarius was a day's wage for a laborer (see above on the parable of the day laborers in the vineyard). In Matthew "a man" hands one of his slaves five such talents, another two, and a third one talent; in total he doled out 3.2 million denarii! Luke's "nobleman" hands out one pound to each of ten slaves (one talent was six hundred pounds). Perhaps it matters little for the sense of the parable whether it is talents or pounds. They were then both astronomical sums of money, especially in the eyes of Jesus's usual audience, intentionally so to increase the joke-like aspect of this parable. On the other hand, because it is so large an amount of money, perhaps early audiences would have heard in this parable an allusion to rulers who were raising huge amounts of tribute and were hated because of it (as Luke makes it explicit in 19:14).

The story is puzzling, regardless of the version. It looks like a severe lesson in capitalism: "Do business with these until I come back" (Luke 19:13). Does that fit with the reversal in fortunes the kingdom is supposed to bring with it? In Matthew, both the first and second servants succeeded in doubling their sizable amounts of money by the time the master comes to see what has happened to the money. In Luke, the investors were even more successful. The parable comes to a point with the servant who returns exactly what was given him, whether talent or pound, whether buried or wrapped up for safekeeping. He does not quite trust himself or the master. What is the master's response to the varied success of his servants? It ranges from effusive praise and reward to violent judgment. Jesus adds this cryptic statement: "To those who have, more will be given . . . ; but from those who have nothing, even what they have will be taken away" (Matt. 25:29 || Luke 19:26; *Gospel of Thomas* 41).

This is a very unsettling story, so much so that many doubt that this parable goes back to Jesus. The possible allegorical allusions in Luke's version are taken to speak against authenticity. As unsettling as it is, in either version, and as rich as it is in allegorical potential, I see no reason to question its basic authenticity. What, if it did not come from Jesus himself, would possibly commend the parable? It is unlikely that anyone would have made up this parable, and even more unlikely that it would have found acceptance in the tradition if it did not come from Jesus himself. Jesus's parables are not always appealing; they often unsettle hearers quite intentionally. In this case, hearers are surely invited to consider this parable in light of how the kingdom of God relates to human affairs or of how God relates to humanity. Just as surely those same hearers will have been deeply unsettled by being forced to identify God with such a demanding, self-interested, and violent master. Could this be the same Jesus who tells about the prodigal father and the shepherd who cares for every last lost sheep? Or was Jesus originally simply attempting to expose the way business is being done under the Romans, thus implicitly contrasting the kingdom of God to imperial economics?

To repeat the point: Jesus's parables are often teasers, unsettling "jokes," to state it provocatively. The amounts of silver doled out in this parable would surely have reminded Jesus's audience of the unjust distribution of wealth. The one handing out the wealth in both versions is not remotely attractive or fair. And the consequences meted out only accentuate the unfairness: "To those who have will be given more, from those who do not will be taken even that!"

This is clearly more than a nice story about not wasting one's talents or gifts. This is a hard saying. As much as Jesus is likely intending to draw attention to the economic realities of his day, he was forcing his audience to think about their relationship to what they had been given by their creator. By allusion Jesus depicts God as a judge before whom individuals and groups of high and low standing will need to give account as to what they did with the treasure with which they were entrusted.

While this is surely about more than money, it is also about money. If this parable is understood within the larger context of Jesus's teaching on wealth, then it becomes, ironically, the exact opposite of a lesson in capitalism. It becomes a terribly hard question about whether wealth has been invested to the benefit of the reign of God. God demands no less. The arrival of the kingdom represents not only the embrace of the wayward son and the lost sheep, but also the accounting before a demanding judge as to what was done with the treasure, whatever it may be (see below on the parable of the shrewd manager).

Sheep and Goats

The parable of the sheep and goats, one of the best known and compelling of Jesus's parables, is found only in Matthew (25:31–46). That it is found in only one gospel does not set it apart from other famous parables, such as the good Samaritan or the prodigal son.

The parable combines images drawn from various contexts: sheepherding, kingship, and apocalyptic images of the "Son of Man" coming in judgment (for Son of Man, see chapter 13). The scene is imposing: a glorious throne of judgment upon which the Son of Man sits in judgment of the nations. They are sifted and sorted according to whether they have been righteous or unrighteous, just or unjust, much like a shepherd separates sheep from goats. The sheep or the just go to the right hand of God, that is, to their reward, and the goats or the unjust to the left and to their punishment.

So far the scene is not particularly striking. Jesus's Jewish hearers would have found this familiar, even if not entirely comfortable, territory. But there are surprises. We encounter the first one in the words of the shepherd/judge/king. Whether he speaks to the sheep on his right with approval or to goats on his left with sharp disapproval, he surprises them both by informing them that he was there in their midst as a stranger and prisoner who was hungry, thirsty, naked, and sick. Both sheep and goats are shocked.

Here comes the second surprise of the parable: both sheep and goats respond identically: "When were you there as a sick and naked stranger? When did we see you hungry? When were you in prison?" The king's response is very simple: "I was there in the least of my brothers and sisters."

A parable like this is unsettling, not only because it depicts judgment as part of the coming reign of God. It is unlikely that any of Jesus's audience would have been surprised by this, however troubling they would have found the prospect. Most unsettling is that the response of the sheep and goats is identical; *both* of them are surprised that what they did or did not do in the practice of everyday ordinary justice has eternal consequence. In the case of the sheep that is of course exactly as it should be. They are righteous *not* because they recognize the Son of Man in the sick person or in the prisoner but because they see a prisoner who needs visiting, because they see a thirsty person who needs water. We might even say that they are rewarded because they did *not* look for God in the sufferer and yet did the right thing. In contrast, the goats would have done the right thing *had they only known* it was the Son of Man and not simply some hapless human victim before them—a chilling description of those who do the religiously correct thing but "have neglected the weightier matters of the law: justice and mercy and faith" (Matt. 23:23), to refer to Jesus's words in another setting.

A parable such as this would have resonated in many different settings. Jesus may well have been addressing fellow Jews on what constitutes true conformity to God's will, what it means to love the neighbor "as yourself" and in the process God himself. Jesus invites his hearers to ask themselves whether they are goats seeking to justify themselves or sheep surprised that they did something important.

But the possibilities of interpretation extend beyond such a bracing call for integrity. The judgment scene has "all the nations" appear before the judge to give account on how they treated "the least of these who are members of my family" (Matt. 25:40, 45). That suggests a much larger setting, and perhaps it is a reflection on how God's people are treated by the nations, in effect, by the Gentiles. Such a setting widens the horizon considerably and reassures those who are suffering hunger, imprisonment, and illness, perhaps at the hands of oppressing nations—Jews during Jesus's time, followers of Jesus during Matthew's—that God will judge the peoples on how they have treated the most vulnerable in whom God resides. The open-endedness of parables invites such a variety of application, including to the long and tortured history of Christian anti-Semitism. The one kind of interpretation that is excluded is one that pulls the teeth on the parable, that allows hearers and readers to escape unscathed from the encounter with the parable and, through it, with Jesus as prophet of the kingdom of God.

Ethical Parables

Several parables of urgency just discussed might have been placed here, under the heading "ethical parables." That is as it should be. A clear ethical challenge is embedded in Jesus's preaching of the kingdom of God. Nevertheless, it is useful for us to discuss a few of Jesus's parables with an eye specifically to the ethical challenge they contain or, said differently, what difference the kingdom of God makes for everyday life.

GOOD SAMARITAN

The parable of the good Samaritan is another parable that is found only once, this time in Luke (10:29–35). Its message is remarkably consistent with the parable of the sheep and goats. As discussed earlier in this chapter, the allegorical possibilities are present in abundance, as in many of Jesus's parables, even if one will not want to take them nearly as far as did Augustine in the fifth century. Nevertheless, the objective here is to discuss the parable in relation to one of the central problems of ethical reflection, namely, the extent and nature of ethical obligation.

Luke introduces the parable with a lawyer's question and Jesus's counterquestion. The frame of a parable is often suspected of being the product of either the tradition or the evangelist himself. If that is so in this case, the frame was fashioned brilliantly. A lawyer comes to Jesus and, attempting to test him, asks what he has to do to inherit eternal life. "Lawyer" here refers to someone who knows *God's* law; today we would call him a theologian, biblical scholar, or a specialist in religious ethics. "Eternal life" here is shorthand for "What do I need to do to be part of the blessings of the kingdom to come?" Jesus turns the tables on the lawyer and tests his legal acumen by asking him to recite the law. The lawyer does so by reciting the most concentrated form of the law, the so-called double commandment: "You shall love the Lord your God with all your heart, and with all your soul, and with all your strength, and with all your mind; and your neighbor as yourself" (Luke 10:27; see Deut. 6:5 and Lev. 19:18). Jesus commends him for it, telling him to live in keeping with that commandment. At this point we share the embarrassment of the lawyer. Every Jewish child would have known the answer to Jesus question! So now the lawyer "seeks to justify himself" by asking, "Who is my neighbor?" "Justify himself" means more than trying not to lose out in the repartee with Jesus. He asks an important legal question that lies at the heart of ethical reflection: What is the nature and extent of obligation?

In response Jesus tells a remarkable story. The geographical location of the story is critically important. The road between Jerusalem and Jericho was and remains inhospitable mountainous wilderness. Jesus's hearers would have understood immediately the circumstances of a traveler on that road being beaten up by robbers and left half dead on the side of the road. But the geographical location is important for another reason, as we will see.

Several persons pass by the injured person, first a priest and then a Levite (that is, one who serves in the temple). Nothing much is said explicitly about these characters, but much is said implicitly. After all, much like pastors, priests, and rabbis in our day, these figures represent the guardians of the community's values. Surely they should have stopped and offered aid!

Here is where our story takes a surprising but pivotal turn. A Samaritan comes by. Jews disdained Samaritans (see chapter 4 above), and the feeling was mutual. Both Jews and Samaritans considered themselves to be the children of Abraham, the true descendants of the promise, and both considered each other as unworthy to carry the name of Abraham. This background alerts us that Jesus places the Samaritan on what is for him foreign, indeed hostile, territory; he is not in Samaria, but in Judea. He therefore has every excuse, every reason, *not* to get involved. For him to get involved would almost certainly spell trouble for him; that much Jesus's audience would have known instinctively. He might well be suspected of having done the deed himself and thus himself be subject to attack. Nevertheless, the Samaritan stops, binds the person's wounds, puts him on his animal, and takes him to an inn. There he takes care of him. He leaves money for the innkeeper to care for him further, assuring him that he will return and pay whatever further expenses the care of the injured person might incur. The narrative is terse; there is no embellishment, no self-consciousness on the part of the Samaritan. The integrity of the Samaritan's action lies precisely in that matter-of-factness. The Samaritan will stand with the surprised sheep, to refer to the previously discussed parable.

We might think that Jesus is telling this parable as an illustration about how to take care of one's neighbor. The term *good Samaritan* has become shorthand for someone who stops to help someone in trouble. That would fit with the question the lawyer asked: Who is my neighbor? Jesus answer would then be: the neighbor is the person who was beaten up and left for dead; the Samaritan, unlike the Levite and the priest, knows what it is to love the neighbor. That would be challenge enough. Jesus would be holding up the hated Samaritan as the one who knows how to love the neighbor.

But Jesus turns the question into a very different one. He asks the lawyer: Who *was neighbor* to the one in distress? The lawyer is forced to answer: "the Samaritan." In first-century Jewish usage, "neighbor" meant fellow Jew, a member of the community to which you are obligated, a compatriot, an insider, somebody who has a legitimate covenantal claim on your attention. By having to answer Jesus's question with "the Samaritan" the lawyer is essentially declaring the Samaritan to be his neighbor. Second, he is forced by Jesus to recognize in the Samaritan a paradigm of neighborliness. It is the Samaritan who has modeled what it is to *be* neighbor. In Jesus's eyes it turns out to be more important to *be* a neighbor than to know *who* your neighbor is. *Being* a neighbor settles the question as to *when* you are obligated—always! And it settles the question as to *whom* you are obligated—everyone! By turning the question of the lawyer around, Jesus has rearranged the notion of obligation; he has also rearranged the notion of community—and thereby also boundaries of obligation. The enemy, the outsider, the nonneighbor, has become the paradigm for neighborliness. In the process, Jesus has widened the love of neighbor to include the love of the enemy (compare Matt. 5:43–48).

Shrewd Manager

The parable of the talents and the pounds should have warned us not always to take the characters in Jesus's parables as simple role models. The parables do not always depict flattering people. In fact, sometimes the evocative power of a parable, much like a joke, is dependent on the unattractiveness of the characters. The parable of the shrewd manager (often also called unjust steward), in which a crook serves as a role model, is a particularly ironic example of this—ironic because with this parable Jesus has a profound ethical lesson to teach about money and the kingdom of God (Luke 16:1–9).

As in the case of the good Samaritan, we encounter this parable only in Luke. In the verses following the parable proper, the author of Luke has added several traditions to the parable in order to provide a block of teaching on money. The saying on not serving two masters is found almost word for word also in Matthew's Sermon on the Mount (compare Luke 16:13 || Matt. 6:24).

This parable is a story of an estate owner whose administrator is accused of embezzlement. The master summons him, demands an accounting, and informs him that he is going to be fired. The corrupt manager has one big problem: "What am I going to do when I'm without a job?" He decides to ensure himself of a place to stay once his job is terminated and so shrewdly rearranges the terms of the peoples' debts, in effect continuing to squander his master's money.

The surprising twist in the story is that the master is very impressed by his dishonest steward and commends him for having acted so shrewdly. Jesus now elaborates on this story by saying that his hearers ought to take lessons from this dishonest manager: if this despicable crook, a true "son of this age" (Luke 16:8), knows how "to make friends . . . by means of dishonest wealth" (literally "unjust mammon";16:9), so also should the "children of light," especially those in some position of power with some control over money.

How should we interpret such a parable? What would it mean to catch on to this "joke"? Surely Jesus is not proposing that his listeners become shysters, is he? In what sense is the shrewd manager smarter than one normally expects the "children of light" to be? Answers to those questions are seen in Jesus's understanding and proclamation that the arrival of the kingdom of God will bring about an enormous reversal of fortunes (see chapter 6 above). We saw that theme in Mary's great hymn, the *Magnificat* (Luke 1:51–53); we saw it also in the Beatitudes (Matt. 5:3–6). Here Jesus makes the point with a particularly clever parable: the dishonest steward was smart because he bought friends with money—his master's, to be sure—for the day when he would be on the street.

The "children of light" should be smarter yet, by using unjust money (which likely covers much of what counts as money) to make friends. How? By giving wealth to the poor, as Jesus demands of the rich ruler (Matt. 19:16–22 || Mark 10:17–22 || Luke 18:18–23); by forgiving debts, as Jesus makes clear in his instructions on prayer: "Forgive us our debts, as we also have forgiven our debtors" (Matt. 6:12). In short, in anticipation of the kingdom's arrival, and as a way of *already* making it a reality, "bad" money should be put to good use for the sake of the poor. One dare not make an idol of money. After all, "you cannot serve God and mammon" (Revised Standard Version), as a saying of Jesus has it, which Luke adds to this parable (Luke 16:13). But neither does one forego the possibilities it presents to enact the reign of God *now*. One makes sure it benefits those who are in great need presently, but who shortly will be in a position of privilege.

This lesson is powerfully illustrated in the parable of the rich man and Lazarus, which follows on the heels the parable of the shrewd manager in Luke 16:19–31. Sadly, it comes to expression also in the parabolic event of Jesus's encounter with the rich young ruler cited above (Matt. 19:16–22 || Mark 10:17–22 || Luke 18:18–23). Specific practicalities are of much less interest to Jesus than the shrewdness he expects of those wanting to shape their lives in light of the kingdom. It is safe to say, I think, that kingdom ethics are less about rules than ingenuity, less about calculation than imagination. Being faithful regarding money is not a matter of honesty so much as of smart "investing" in a way that furthers the reign of God, which must *always* mean good news for the poor and the most vulnerable!

Conclusion

We have not discussed all of Jesus's parables and done little more than scratch the surface of the ones we have considered. Even such a cursory study has shown that, whether we have in mind short aphoristic proverbs or wonderfully engaging and sometimes troubling stories, Jesus's parables are the perfect vehicle with which to alert people to both the presence and coming of God's kingdom. In parables Jesus has the right means to describe in highly suggestive and imaginative ways the radically transforming dimensions of the kingdom. He also has in the parables a device with which to pry loose people's assumptions about that kingdom, inviting them to become the kinds of people who are ready to respond to the surprising nature of God's reign when it does appear, now and in the future. In the process of truly hearing the parables ("those who have ears to hear, let them hear!") Jesus's listeners become the kind of people who bring the kingdom about, who become sheep like the Samaritan, who become shrewder than the crooked manager at using money to make friends, who become ready to deal with what each day brings as opportunities to do God's will—all the while alert to discover the treasure buried in unsuspecting places and persons and to give up everything for the sake of that treasure. These are the kinds of people the parables are meant to both find and create.

Key Terms and Concepts

allegory
figure of speech (*paroimia*)
grace
judgment
mashal
metaphor
parable (*parabole*)
simile

For Further Reading

Bailey, Kenneth E. *Poet and Peasant and Through Peasant Eyes*. Grand Rapids: Eerdmans, 1994.

Dodd, C. H. *The Parables of the Kingdom*. 2nd ed. New York: Scribner, 1961.

Herzog, William R., II. *Parables as Subversive Speech: Jesus as Pedagogue of the Oppressed*. Philadelphia: Westminster John Knox, 1994.

Jeremias, Joachim. *The Parables of Jesus*. Translated by S. H. Hooke. 2nd ed. Upper Saddle River, NJ: Prentice-Hall, 1972.

Schottroff, Luise. *The Parables of Jesus*. Minneapolis: Fortress, 2006.

Wright, N. T. *Christian Origins and the Question of God*, vol. 2: *Jesus and the Victory of God*. Minneapolis: Fortress, 1996.

9

Enacting the Kingdom

HEALING, EXORCISM, AND FOOD

I n *JESUS: A Revolutionary Biography*, John Dominic Crossan makes the important point that Jesus "not only discussed the kingdom of God; he enacted it." This is the opinion of most students of Jesus today, regardless of whether they view him chiefly as a sage talking about a *present* kingdom of God or as an apocalyptic prophet anticipating the imminent intervention of God in the near future, and regardless of how they explain the phenomena associated with his activities. All acknowledge that Jesus was a healer, exorcist, and social radical.

This is no less true of the evangelists, who tell us about Jesus in the first place. Regardless of where they place the stress in their portraits of Jesus (see chapter 3 above), they *all* make clear that Jesus elicited both awe and hostility, excitement and scandal, through what he *did*, not only through what he *said*.

Urgent Actions: Healing and Exorcism

The first chapters of the Gospel of Mark recount almost breathlessly the urgency and feverish activity with which Jesus announced the kingdom. Mark does so even though in his view the character of Jesus's messiahship does not rest easily with the excitement that such powerful activism generates (see chapter 3 above). In Matthew, Jesus responds to John the Baptist's question about whether he is the awaited Messiah with these striking words:

> Go and tell John what you hear and *see*: the blind receive their sight, the lame walk, the lepers are cleansed, the deaf hear, the dead are raised, and the poor have good news brought to them. And blessed is anyone who takes no offense at me. (Matt. 11:4–6, emphasis added)

In the Gospel of Luke, Jesus's first public act is to identify himself with Isaiah's prophecy of a society transformed. Let there be no doubt, Jesus is thereby saying, that things will change—and change radically:

> "The Spirit of the Lord is upon me,
>> because he has anointed me
>>> to bring good news to the poor.
> He has sent me to proclaim release to the captives
>> and recovery of sight to the blind,
>>> to let the oppressed go free,
> to proclaim the year of the Lord's favor."...
> Today this Scripture has been fulfilled in your hearing. (Luke 4:18–21)

Signs play a special role in John's portrait of Jesus. They are revelatory *acts*, functioning no less than his words in relaying who Jesus truly is and what he is about:

> Now Jesus did many other signs in the presence of his disciples, which are not written in this book. But these are written so that you may come to believe that Jesus is the Messiah, the Son of God, and that through believing you may have life in his name. (John 20:30–31)

In short, it was inconceivable for the evangelists, and the many witnesses on whom they depended, that Jesus could be presented without recounting the acts of power, generosity, and transformation that marked his life. These powerful practices counted, in their view, as evidence that what Jesus was saying about the kingdom of God is true. More, these forceful actions counted as evidence of nothing less than the power of God! These acts of power were enactments of God's reign.

By Whose Power?

Nowhere does this come to expression more sharply than in an incident all three Synoptics relate (Mark 3:20–30 || Matt. 12:22–32 || Luke 11:14–23): Jesus's being accused of exorcising and healing by the power of the "evil one," variously called Beelzebul (in some manuscripts also called Beelzebub) or Satan. Whereas all three Synoptic Gospels relate the controversy and Jesus's response to the accusation that he is an evil sorcerer, Matthew and Luke flesh out the story with some shared traditions that Mark either does not know or does not include.

Matthew and Luke describe an incident in which a person possessed by a demon is brought to Jesus. In Matthew the "demoniac" (a person possessed by an evil spirit) is blind and unable to speak (12:22), in Luke, only mute (11:14). Jesus cures him.

This exorcism or healing creates a huge controversy. Many of those witnessing the event ask: "Can this [man] be the Son of David?" (Matt. 12:23). Their question means: Is this the Messiah? Does this mean that the kingdom of God has arrived? Others—Matthew identifies them as Pharisees—wonder whether something much more sinister is at work. For them the question is not whether Jesus has performed an "act of power," as Mark would have put it, but rather what kind of power is at work. They accuse Jesus of performing this exorcism by the power of Beelzebul, the ruler of demons.

With a series of proverbial sayings or aphorisms, Jesus responds to the accusation, intending to show how silly and self-contradictory it is. He then utters this key statement:

Matthew 12:28	Luke 11:20
But if it is by the Spirit of God that I cast out demons, then the kingdom of God has come to you.	But if it is by the finger of God that I cast out the demons, then the kingdom of God has come to you.

This statement is identical in Matthew and Luke, suggesting that they are drawing on the same tradition—with one small difference: Matthew has "spirit," whereas Luke has "finger." I suspect that Luke's version is earlier. Regardless, the meaning of both terms is "power"—God's power. In short, in Jesus's exorcisms the power, kingdom, or reign of God has arrived.

Acting with Haste, Power, and Authority

Mark's narrative is shaped by the same conviction. After Jesus's baptism and temptation and after John has been killed by Herod Antipas, Jesus appears on the scene announcing the arrival of the kingdom of God. What likely strikes most readers of the first half dozen chapters of Mark is the astonishing amount of activity marked by great haste (as seen in Mark's repeated use of the term *immediately*; see chapter 3 above). "Immediately" after the choosing of the first of his followers or disciples, the very first miracle of Jesus that Mark recounts is the exorcism of a demoniac (1:23–28), followed by the raising of Peter's mother-in-law (1:29–31), followed by a whole evening of healing and exorcising (1:32–34)—and all that on one day! Jesus is a determined and energetic activist of the kingdom.

At the same time, this activity *proclaims* something; it is itself a means of teaching. Tellingly, when the crowd sees what Jesus has *done* they say: "What is this? A new *teaching*—with authority!" (1:27, emphasis added). Jesus's powerful deeds carry such proclamatory force that even the demons obey! In other words, Jesus's *announcing* of the kingdom of God, whether through prophetic oracle or parable, is given gravity or weight by actual *demonstrations* of power. The reign of God is powerfully proclaimed by being *enacted*.

It is Mark's deep conviction that the reign of God will find its most powerful expression in that most profound expression of weakness—the cross. To miss that is to miss the scandalous heart of the gospel, Mark would insist. But it never occurs to him to obscure the miracles, the healings, and the exorcisms as representing a powerfully dramatic enactment of God's reign.

Is Jesus Crazy?

We return briefly to Mark's version of the Beelzebul controversy (Mark 3:20–21). In Mark that controversy is preceded by Jesus's appointing the twelve disciples, or apostles. Not surprisingly, given the close relationship between action and word, Jesus commissions them both to proclaim the message and to cast out demons (Mark 3:14–15).

The account of the Beelzebul controversy is introduced by a brief but significant account of Jesus's family attempting to intervene in his healing and exorcising because "they" think "he has gone out of his mind" (3:21). The identity of "they" is ambiguous in the Greek. The NRSV translates it as "people," suggesting that his family wanted to protect Jesus from the crowds that thought he was crazy. Other translations leave the text as ambiguous as it is, allowing for the possibility that Jesus's own family was among those who were scandalized by his healing and exorcising activity.

Some wonder whether the accusation of madness might not reflect something of the way Jesus went about his healing and exorcising. Crossan, for example, suggests that Jesus went into a trance, drawing the one being healed into trance as well—"contagious trance" as a form of therapeutic technique (*Jesus: A Revolutionary Biography*, 93). Such an explanation relies on anthropological studies of healers and magicians in other prescientific societies. As such, it provides a naturalistic explanation, meant to be more consistent with a modern scientific understanding of how these things actually happen.

Jesus's followers and detractors alike would clearly have rejected such an explanation. His followers would have been offended by the notion that Jesus employed magic, and they certainly would have rejected the notion that he was mad. They viewed his healing and exorcising activity as a test of whether Jesus should be trusted, whether the power at work in his activity was God's power. At stake was less Jesus than whether God's reign was now indeed asserting itself with power. They viewed these events as proof that Jesus was enacting the kingdom of God. His detractors were not interested in the mechanisms of his healing so much as ascertaining by what power he did these things. They viewed his activity as evidence of the power of Satan, the very personification of evil.

However one chooses to explain these events today, there is general agreement among scholars that Jesus made an impact on his contemporaries not only by his teaching and preaching but perhaps much more through his wonderworking. It is at least in part for purposes of combating such a perspective on Jesus that Mark works so hard at stressing the importance of the cross for understanding the full significance of Jesus (see chapter 3 above).

Actions and Deeds as a Form of Teaching

Often Jesus's healings and exorcisms precipitate occasions of teaching—"teaching moments," we might say today. Several of Jesus's actions provoke controversy around the Sabbath, for example. Permitting his disciples to pluck grain on the Sabbath or healing on the Sabbath a person who is physically impaired (e.g., Mark 2:23–3:6) become occasions to make a point about himself and about what it means to be faithful to the law.

Sometimes the very way in which Jesus performs a healing is itself an important teaching regarding the kingdom of God or regarding himself as the messenger and enactor of God's reign. One notable example is the healing of the leper:

> A leper came to him begging him, and kneeling he said to him, "If you choose, you can make me clean." Moved with pity, Jesus stretched out his hand and touched him, and said to him, "I do choose. Be made clean!" Immediately the leprosy left him, and he was made clean. After sternly warning him he sent him away at once, saying to him, "See that you say nothing to anyone; but go, show yourself to the priest, and offer for your cleansing what Moses commanded, as a testimony to them." But he went out and began to proclaim it freely, and to spread the word, so that Jesus could no longer go into a town openly, but stayed out in the country; and people came to him from every quarter. (Mark 1:40–45)

Every first-century reader would have known that leprosy—whether it was the same thing as what we today call leprosy does not matter—was a disease that had as its consequence the social and physical ostracism of those afflicted with this disease. To come into contact with such people was to become impure oneself, in effect resulting in being removed from the circle of holiness and purity. Naturally, as much as was possible, lepers were avoided. Today referring to someone as a "leper" draws on this ancient taboo of contact with a contaminating person.

What would therefore have struck the first witnesses and the readers of the gospels immediately is that Jesus *touches* the leper. At that very moment Jesus violates a taboo regarding such illness—and with it a sacred boundary. In the very act of touching this leper, Jesus steps outside the circle in order to retrieve a lost sheep, to refer back to one of the parables. Or, to state it differently, he widens the circle of acceptance to include those who have been pushed outside.

The radical nature of Jesus's action is recognized today even by those who for reasons of modern science do not believe that Jesus actually removed the leprosy. Indeed, it is common today to consider the real miracle to be that Jesus broke down the dividing wall, as it were, between insiders and outsiders, including the marginalized person in the circle of care and dignity. Crossan, for example, states baldly that Jesus "did not and could not cure that disease or any other" (*Jesus: A Revolutionary Biography*, 82). At the same time, whereas Jesus did not and could not cure the *disease*, he cured the *illness* by resocializing the outcast. This radical change in social relations is evidence of the kingdom's powerful presence.

There is no doubt that Jesus desired to draw outcasts into the circle of God's care and to reintegrate them into the community of God's people. That is reflected in many of his healing and exorcism stories. It is also abundantly clear that such restoration of the human community lies at the very core of his enactment of the kingdom. Early witnesses, however, would hardly have recognized their story in this rather pared-down modern version. For them the miracle of the kingdom of God consists most certainly in crossing the boundary and coming into contact with the outcast; but they would have insisted that evidence of the presence of the kingdom of God consists *also* in the actual physical healing of disease. Simply to deal with the social rejection of those who are ill, rather than with the physical suffering of those socially ostracized, would, in their minds, be to leave the messianic job only half done. In the view of the evangelists, the kingdom of God also addresses physical ailments, whether disease or poverty. It constitutes a recovery of the *whole* of creation. It is in the very nature of the kingdom of God that these dimensions are not separated.

Gerasene Demoniac

One of the most striking and symbolically laden of Jesus's "deeds of power" is the exorcism of the Gerasene demoniac, a story found in all three Synoptic Gospels (Mark 5:1–20 || Matt. 8:28–34 || Luke 8:26–39; Matthew uses the variant designation *Gadarenes* and has not one but two demoniacs; it is, however, quite clearly the same story). We will follow the story as told in Mark. Historians raise questions about the historicity of this story, especially given how loaded it is with allusions and connections. It remains nevertheless a powerfully compelling story, intended to bring Jesus's activity as an enactor of the reign of God into relationship with individuals caught up in the chains of oppression and the larger realities of such bondage.

The story is filled to the very brim with symbolic elements. The demoniac lives in the tombs, without clothing, beating himself constantly, out of control—a person beyond the edges of controlled society who lives in a realm of death, chaos, and self-destruction. Tombs were considered unclean to begin with, but this depiction is a stark and brutally frank image of oppression in its most awful and frightening dimensions.

The name of the demon or demons tormenting the man is "Legion," which is highly suggestive and immediately brings to mind Roman imperial military forces. A connection is thus made between oppressing spiritual forces and the military forces of an oppressive empire. This suggests that behind or within these violent structures and forces lie spiritual powers holding people in their imperial iron grip. Mark surely wishes his readers to make the connection between this demoniac and a people in bondage and oppression, knowing torture and death, but unable to transform its anger and rage into liberation. Jesus is thus pictured in highly symbolic fashion as taking on the spiritual and military bonds afflicting the people. Mark also wants us to notice that Jesus enters the territory unbidden, and is asked to leave by those he threatens.

There are other so-called mythic and symbolic features to this story. The sea, for example, is a symbol of chaos in Jewish lore. The crossing of the Red or Reed Sea during the Israelite escape from Egypt (Exodus 14–15) is recalled in mythical terms highly reminiscent of ancient Near Eastern creation myths:

> O LORD God of hosts,
> who is as mighty as you, O LORD?
> Your faithfulness surrounds you.
> You rule the raging of the sea;
> when its waves rise, you still them.
> You crushed Rahab like a carcass;
> you scattered your enemies with your mighty arm. (Ps. 89:8–10)

In Mark's Gospel, the story of Jesus's stilling the storm immediately precedes this story (Mark 4:35–41). By pronouncing the order "Peace! Be still!" Jesus binds the dragon of the deep, the primordial beast of chaos, as it were. He shows himself to be Lord over nature. Here, in the present story of exorcism, Jesus sends the demons into the swine that then drown in the sea; they return to the chaos they came from.

The swine too have symbolic meaning. Swine were for Jews unclean animals, and Jews were prohibited from eating them. The question as to why farmers were raising swine is answered by noting that this is Gentile territory just on the edge of Galilee. Even so, their presence in the story is intended to illustrate that Jesus took his enacting of the kingdom of God into the realm of uncleanness: first, a man in the tombs, and then the demons called Legion, and finally the swine. In Jesus's activity the kingdom of God is invading the realm of darkness and chaos by bringing liberation and peace, symbolized by the man now sitting quietly, "clothed and in his right mind" (Mark 5:15).

Remarkable in this story is the response of the local people who come onto the scene of quiet and order. They are upset at having lost their pigs, and they are frightened by seeing this person sitting sane, calm, and in his right mind. And they beg Jesus to leave their area. The implication is clear: the arrival of the kingdom of God is not good news for those who benefit from the status quo. It is good news for those being held in its chains.

Jesus Calls His Followers to Enact the Kingdom

We might expect that the gospels would be centered exclusively on Jesus as the messianic enactor of the kingdom of God. Remarkably, however, that is not the case. In Mark 3:14 Jesus appoints twelve apostles (ambassadors or emissaries) and gives them the tasks of proclaiming the message and of casting out demons. Jesus thereby bestows on them the authority to carry out his own dual task of announcing and enacting the reign of God. Matthew and Luke stress this dimension even more strongly. At the very center of their gospel narratives we find Jesus choosing, summoning, charging, and empowering his followers to take up the task of witnessing to the kingdom of God in word and deed (Matt. 10:1–42 || Luke 9:1–6; 10:1–20). He charges them with the task of being messengers of peace and liberation, but also warns them what awaits them:

> These twelve Jesus sent out with the following instructions: "Go nowhere among the Gentiles, and enter no town of the Samaritans, but go rather to the lost sheep of the house of Israel. As you go, proclaim the good news, 'The kingdom of heaven has come near.' Cure the sick, raise the dead, cleanse the lepers, cast out demons. You received without payment; give without payment. Take no gold, or silver, or copper in your belts, no bag for your journey, or two tunics, or sandals, or a staff; for laborers deserve their food. Whatever town or village you enter, find out who in it is worthy, and stay there until you leave. As you enter the house, greet it. If the house is worthy, let your peace come upon it; but if it is not worthy, let your peace return to you. If anyone will

not welcome you or listen to your words, shake off the dust from your feet as you leave that house or town. Truly I tell you, it will be more tolerable for the land of Sodom and Gomorrah on the day of judgment than for that town." (Matt. 10:5–15; similarly Luke 9:1–6)

The awareness that, like Jesus, his emissaries will face fierce opposition comes to powerful expression in the very next words:

See, I am sending you out like sheep into the midst of wolves; so be wise as serpents and innocent as doves. Beware of them, for they will hand you over to councils and flog you in their synagogues; and you will be dragged before governors and kings because of me, as a testimony to them and the Gentiles. When they hand you over, do not worry about how you are to speak or what you are to say; for what you are to say will be given to you at that time; for it is not you who speak, but the Spirit of your Father speaking through you. Brother will betray brother to death, and a father his child, and children will rise against parents and have them put to death; and you will be hated by all because of my name. But the one who endures to the end will be saved. (Matt. 10:16–22)

Confrontation and conflict, even violent hostility, mark the proclamation of the kingdom of God in word and deed. Being an emissary of the kingdom is nothing less than combat:

Do not think that I have come to bring peace to the earth; I have not come to bring peace, but a sword.
　　For I have come to set a man against his father,
　　and a daughter against her mother,
　　and a daughter-in-law against her mother-in-law;
　　and one's foes will be members of one's own household.
Whoever loves father or mother more than me is not worthy of me; and whoever loves son or daughter more than me is not worthy of me; and whoever does not take up the cross and follow me is not worthy of me. Those who find their life will lose it, and those who lose their life for my sake will find it. (Matt. 10:34–39)

Jesus's healing and exorcising is thus a clear demonstration of God's reign, but it is a reign marked by conflict and combat. It is a struggle with Beelzebul. While waged on the earth, it is nothing less than war in the heavens. And Jesus's followers can fully expect to participate in that struggle:

The seventy returned with joy, saying, "Lord, in your name even the demons submit to us!" He said to them, "I watched Satan fall from heaven like a flash of lightning. See, I have given you authority to tread on snakes and scorpions, and over all the power of the enemy; and nothing will hurt you. Nevertheless, do not rejoice at this, that the spirits submit to you, but rejoice that your names are written in heaven." (Luke 10:17–20)

We see that the evangelists, as much as they believe in the coming kingdom of God and as much as they see Jesus as central to that coming, are convinced that the reign of God is making its invasive appearance in the activity of his followers. They would experience both the wonder and the opposition of this participation in the decades to come. Reading carefully, it is not difficult to see that the subsequent missionary activity of the church has left its mark on these words. We may even be catching a glimpse into the early missionary activity of the Jesus movement in some of the instructions regarding going out two by two, going without provisions, or moving from town to town as itinerants. First-century readers would have nodded their heads knowingly as Jesus predicts both spectacular success in the struggle for the kingdom and great suffering—even martyrdom.

Enactment of the Kingdom in the Gospel of John

As stated earlier, the Fourth Gospel is not often taken into account in contemporary historical Jesus scholarship. There are reasons for this, some more and some less legitimate (see chapter 3 above). John's Gospel stresses more explicitly the symbolic and theological aspects of Jesus's life, ministry, and identity, but is no less insistent on the importance of Jesus's healing activity. After all, John likes to call Jesus's miracles "signs," revelations about who Jesus is and what his mission is about. As we see in the story of the healing of the paralytic at the Pool of Beth-zatha (or Bethesda) in John 5:2–18, as well in the healing of the man born blind in John 9, Jesus's healing activity serves the purpose of showing the power of God at work in him as "the Son." John refers to this activity in 6:28 as "the works of God." It is true, John's Jesus does not use kingdom vocabulary (with the one exception of his conversation with Nicodemus in John 3). But the *content* of kingdom language, intended to show the power and glory of God at work on behalf of suffering humanity, is abundantly present in the signs that Jesus performs in the Fourth Gospel. And in another echo of what we read in the Synoptics about Jesus sending out his followers as participants in his own messianic mission, John includes these remarkable words:

> Very truly, I tell you, the one who believes in me will also do the works that I do and, in fact, will do greater works than these, because I am going to the Father. (John 14:12)

Eating and the Enactment of the Kingdom of God

If Jesus created controversy with his healing and exorcising, he certainly did so also with another very important enactment of the kingdom of God—eating. Jesus appears to have been a notorious eater and drinker. There appear to have been persistent attempts to smear him with the charge of overeating and partying to excess. Jesus himself is quoted as saying:

> For John came neither eating nor drinking, and they say, "He has a demon"; the Son of Man came eating and drinking, and they say, "Look, a glutton and a drunkard, a friend of tax collectors and sinners!" Yet wisdom is vindicated by her deeds. (Matt. 11:18–19; similarly Luke 7:33–35)

Behind this accusation of gluttony and drunkenness was an even more significant reason for Jesus's notoriety: in his eating habits he was "a friend of tax collectors and sinners." If Jesus had any pretensions of being a holy man, it was this second part of the charge against him that was particularly freighted. What you eat and whom you eat with are in Jesus's world markers of holiness, that is, ways in which you enact your fidelity to God's will. You do not eat pork, and you do not eat with sinners.

Apparently it was not only his enemies who were scandalized. We should take the quotation from Matthew 11 above to suggest that the nonfeasting John the Baptist also had serious questions as to whether such a person as Jesus could possibly be the Messiah of God. We read that the Baptist sent his disciples to Jesus to inquire whether he really is "the one" or whether they should wait for another. It is in the context of such a controversy that Jesus brings up the matter of how and with whom he eats.

There can thus be no doubt that eating marked a major feature of Jesus's profile. Why? Put simply, Jesus's eating habits are a central feature of his enactment of the kingdom of God. They represent a radical and powerful expression of God's generous reign. How?

First, the hungry eat! As such, providing food is an act of generous justice. Second, by eating with social outcasts, whether rich or poor, Jesus expresses God's respect for and acceptance of them. Just as his healing of the leper represents a crossing of the boundaries in order to extend the kingdom to include those people and to offer them a new beginning, so also does his eating with extortionists and prostitutes or, as the New Testament puts it, tax collectors and sinners. Third, Jesus's eating with others, indeed his *feasting*, represents a material act of hope: it anticipates the great banquet to come, when the kingdom will come in fullness.

The last two aspects are closely related: when Jesus eats with tax collectors and sinners at meals that anticipate the kingdom of God, he expresses with an act what he also speaks of in his parables, namely, that those who hover at the edges of society, those who live in the "highways and byways," are invited to the great banquet of the kingdom (as stated in the parable of the great banquet in Matt. 22:1–14 || Luke 14:16–24, discussed in chapter 8 above).

Eating with Social Outcasts

Eating with others is thus central to Jesus's messianic activity. No incident captures this better than Jesus's retort to those who criticize his eating with a tax collector and his friends after Jesus has invited him into his circle of followers. His response is simple:

> When the scribes of the Pharisees saw that he was eating with sinners and tax collectors, they said to his disciples, "Why does he eat with tax collectors and sinners?" When Jesus heard this, he said to them, "Those who are well have no need of a physician, but those who are sick; I have come to call not the righteous but sinners." (Mark 2:16–17)

The transformative impact of this eating with sinners comes to striking expression in the story of Jesus's encounter with arguably the most famous of tax collectors, Zacchaeus (Luke 19:1–10). Among the many remarkable features in this story is that Jesus, upon seeing this man up in a tree attempting to catch a glimpse of Jesus, invites himself over for dinner. Zacchaeus's response? He promises to make restitution where he has robbed people. In short, Jesus's willingness to contaminate himself and endanger his own social standing by publicly eating in the house of a known sinner produces a change of life in the sinner and thereby a change in the community affected by his crime. As we read, this very material change in economic fortunes is nothing less than the liberation that the kingdom of God represents. Jesus does not exaggerate when he says:

> Today salvation has come to this house, because he too is a son of Abraham. For the Son of Man came to seek out and to save the lost. (Luke 19:9–10)

Feeding the Hungry

The gospels stress that Jesus used eating with others as a way to widen the sphere of God's kingdom in terms of restored relationships. Food is also a material expression of God's care for the hungry. Every Jew understood that the kingdom of God would bring relief from physical hunger. God gives food to those who need it—captured most powerfully in the image of manna in the desert (Exod. 16; see also John 6)—and so Jesus's eating and supplying food becomes itself an expression of the kingdom of God as it relates to the concrete human need for survival.

This is illustrated in a most spectacular way in two virtually identical stories of Jesus providing food for the hungry. The first is the so-called feeding of the five thousand in Matthew 14:13–21 || Mark 6:32–44 || Luke 9:10–17 || John 6:1–15. The other is found only in Matthew and Mark, the so-called feeding of the four thousand (Matt. 15:32–39 || Mark 8:1–10). As is the case in many stories in the gospels, these are heavily freighted with symbolism in the way they are narrated.

In the first story, Jesus is presented with five loaves and two fish. That is all the provisions the disciples have with which to feed a great multitude of followers, a crowd so eager to hear and see Jesus that they have not given thought to how they will eat. Or, are they following *because* they are hungry?

So, will there be enough food? Five loaves and two fish add up to seven items of food. The number seven is a biblical symbol for wholeness or completeness (as seen in the seven days of creation in Genesis). An informed reader of this story will already sense the answer to the problem of too little food and too many people: in the five loaves and two fish they have symbolically enough food to feed everyone. It turns out that they have more than enough; they feed everyone present, and there are still twelve baskets left over!

Twelve baskets of leftovers is a little over the top, but this too is highly symbolic. Twelve represents the twelve tribes of Israel. Not only does Jesus's ministry of enacting the kingdom of God have to do with meeting the real needs of the hungry, it is also about the restoration of Israel, however metaphorical that would have been understood by the time the evangelists narrate the story.

Interestingly, in the second account we again encounter the symbolism of seven. This time there are seven loaves, and that is also how many baskets of leftovers are left at the end. Once again, symbolically speaking, there was more than enough!

The Gospel of John includes a very important element in its narration of this story, one of the few stories it shares with the other gospels. The people understand the symbolic significance of what Jesus has done:

> When the people saw the sign that he had done, they began to say, "This is indeed the prophet who is to come into the world." (John 6:14)

Interestingly, here the term *prophet* is employed as the equivalent of messiah or king. The people know full well that when the Messiah comes, their hunger will be stilled. This man must be the Messiah! Rather surprisingly, Jesus does not seem to welcome this enthusiasm on the part of the crowd:

> When Jesus realized that they were about to come and take him by force to make him king, he withdrew again to the mountain by himself. (John 6:15)

On one level the people are right: Jesus *is* the Messiah, the Christ. They have correctly understood the sign embedded in his spectacular act of caring for them (John 6:14). The conviction that Jesus is the Christ lies at the very heart of the Jesus movement; without it we would not have any record of Jesus to begin with, let alone the gospels.

But have the people truly caught on to the sign? How do we explain Jesus's reluctance to accept their adulation? In the Synoptic Gospels Jesus repeatedly tells those he has healed not to tell anyone (see chapter 4 above). A similar phenomenon is observable here: the problem is *not* that healing, exorcism, and feeding the hungry is messianic activity unbecoming of Jesus. Something deeper is at issue. Jesus flees the enthusiastic crowd because they are excited not about who Jesus is, but about the food he can supply. In their view, it is his capacity to supply bread that makes him Messiah. But John's Gospel has Jesus insist: "*I* am the bread of life!" (6:35, emphasis added).

Scholars working with the tools of the historian or the scientist will have difficulty with stories of the feeding of multitudes. The symbolic richness of the narration does nothing to help them. As with other such stories in the gospels, readers of this book will differ on how such stories should be interpreted: are they fables intended to illustrate something important? Or are they historical accounts of a powerful "work of God," retold so as to highlight the symbolic significance? What is clear is that all four evangelists accord the story central importance, illustrating that Jesus's eating with others was one of the most important expressions of the kingdom's presence and also one of the most important ways of announcing its coming, of anticipating its future.

Eating in Anticipation of the Great Banquet to Come

The celebratory aspect of Jesus's eating comes to expression in several ways.

EATING LIKE TOMORROW HAS ALREADY COME

We can see the celebratory dimension of Jesus's eating habits in the controversy around fasting (Matt. 9:14–17 || Mark 2:18–22 || Luke 5:33–39). "Fasting" means doing without food as an act of worship and holiness.

Once again we observe a contrast to the way in which John the Baptist and his followers behaved. They fasted as a means of preparation for the coming of God's reign. Given Jesus's and his followers' sense that the kingdom of God was already making its presence felt in their activities, we should not be surprised that this is how they behaved. They ate, and did so frequently and joyously.

As Mark narrates the encounter, the people ask Jesus: "Why do John's disciples and the disciples of the Pharisees fast, but your disciples do not fast?" (Mark 2:18). Jesus's response is telling:

> The wedding guests cannot fast while the bridegroom is with them, can they? As long as they have the bridegroom with them, they cannot fast. The days will come when the bridegroom is taken away from them, and then they will fast on that day. (Mark 2:19–20)

Jesus identifies himself as bridegroom and his eating and drinking with people as one long wedding feast anticipating the great wedding banquet of the coming kingdom. This motif is present in Matthew's version of the parable of the great banquet (Matt. 22:1–14), as well as in the book of Revelation, also known as the Apocalypse of John: "Blessed are those who are invited to the marriage supper of the Lamb" (Rev. 19:9). In his feasting, Jesus not only expresses the generosity of God toward those on the margins; he also proclaims that what everyone is waiting for is already present around the table at which he and the sinners sit.

Eating in Anticipation of Tomorrow

Of course, in the eyes of all the evangelists Jesus's central enactment of kingdom is still looming on the horizon—his offering of his life. That act too will be marked by a special meal—the Last Supper (Matt. 26:17–29 || Mark 14:12–25 || Luke 22:1–38 || John 13–17; see chapter 11 below). Here it is enough to point out that meeting the needs of a hungry population, joyous celebration, and inclusion of outcasts are not the only dimensions of Jesus's eating. The Lord's Supper, Communion, or the Eucharist, as it is variously called in different Christian traditions, is a reenactment of that Last Supper Jesus ate with his inner circle of followers and has become in the Christian religion a ritual of great solemnity. As a time of reenacting or remembering Jesus's death on behalf of humanity, it is less a ritual of inclusion than of testing and sifting, of proving the commitments of those who identify with Jesus. No doubt the writings of the Apostle Paul have had something to do with introducing this dimension into the celebration (see 1 Cor. 11:17–34).

At the same time, the Lord's Supper retains some of the sense of anticipation that marked Jesus's feasting, as well as his Last Supper. One of the reasons Paul had to introduce some order into the celebration may well be that the Corinthians' way of eating together had too much of a party atmosphere around it, but without the concern for making that party a celebration of the coming kingdom, or for meeting the needs of the hungry among them. Paul seems to be reminding the Corinthians of exactly that point when he tells them to celebrate the Lord's Supper "until he comes"

(1 Cor. 11:26). This sense of anticipation echoes Jesus's words as recalled by the evangelists:

> Truly I tell you, I will never again drink of the fruit of the vine until that day when I drink it new in the kingdom of God. (Mark 14:25 || Matt. 26:29 || Luke 22:18)

With all its solemnity, many in Christian communities are attempting to reinvest the celebration of Communion or Eucharist with the ambience of celebration, joy, grace, and anticipation. Many churches thus celebrate love feasts in imitation of the early church, whose eating habits appear to have been marked by Jesus's ways of eating. Luke gives us a highly evocative description of early Christian eating habits, shaped, no doubt, by a living memory of the eating habits of their master:

> All who believed were together and had all things in common; they would sell their possessions and goods and distribute the proceeds to all, as any had need. Day by day, as they spent much time together in the temple, they broke bread at home [or from house to house] and ate their food with glad and generous hearts, praising God and having the goodwill of all the people. And day by day the Lord added to their number those who were being saved. (Acts 2:44–47)

Key Terms and Concepts

demoniac
exorcism
healing
leprosy
Lord's Supper
signs

Today the closest many churches come to this act of communal solidarity and generosity reminiscent of Jesus's own table fellowship is the potluck. Jesus would no doubt have insisted that such a humble event can well become nothing less than an enactment of the kingdom of God.

For Further Reading

Crossan, John Dominic. *Jesus: A Revolutionary Biography*. San Francisco: Harper, 1995.

Myers, Ched. *Binding the Strong Man: A Political Reading of Mark's Story of Jesus*. Maryknoll, NY: Orbis, 1988.

Remus, Harold. *Jesus as Healer*. Cambridge: Cambridge University Press, 1997.

Twelftree, Graham H. *Jesus, the Miracle Worker: A Historical and Theological Study*. Downers Grove, IL: InterVarsity, 1999.

10

Living the Kingdom

Seek First the Kingdom and Its Justice!

For many people, Jesus is of greatest importance for his ethical teachings. It is fitting to devote a part of our study to his teachings on how persons are to behave toward each other. But several important points need to be stated at the outset.

First, Jesus was not an ethicist. That is to say, he was not a philosopher of ethics; he did not leave behind a body of ethical writings. He was rather a prophet of the kingdom of God, calling his contemporaries to radical obedience to the will of God. He was one who announced and enacted the kingdom of God in ways that do not always lend themselves to ethical debate.

Second, Jesus was a Jew. As such, he believed that nothing was more important than to love God with heart, mind, soul and body, and one's neighbor as oneself, and thus to do God's will with undivided loyalty (Deut. 6:4–5). For Jesus that meant fidelity to the Torah, the law of God, even if Jesus's mode of interpreting and practicing such fidelity put him on a collision course with many of his fellow Jews, who also cared deeply about fidelity to the Torah.

Third, Jesus's teachings and actions imply and sometimes explicitly teach an ethic. We saw this in our consideration of his parables. This is the case especially if by the term *ethical* we mean the way people should behave toward each other and toward God in light of both the presence and the arrival of the reign or kingdom of God. Jesus taught this way by both word and action, and he expected others to follow him.

Sermon on the Mount—Sermon on the Plain

While we recognize that Jesus's teachings on how to live in light of the will and kingdom of God permeate all four gospels, we shall concentrate our survey of his ethical teaching on the most famous collection of his ethical sayings—the Sermon on the Mount (Matthew 5–7) and the briefer Sermon on the Plain (Luke 6:17–49).

Many of Jesus's teachings on how to live in light of God's kingdom or reign are concentrated in the Sermon on the Mount. This is not a sermon so much as it is a collection or compendium of Jesus's sayings, more than likely compiled and fashioned by the evangelist himself, quite possibly utilizing an earlier compendium of Jesus's ethical sayings. Luke's brief Sermon on the Plain (6:17–49) suggests as much.

Is it not only possible, but likely that Jesus taught these things more than once? But that he should have given two versions of the same sermon in the way we find them in the two gospels is less likely than that Luke preserved an earlier collection of Jesus's ethical instructions (perhaps as found in the hypothetical Q; see chapter 2 above), which Matthew augmented and shaped into what we today call the Sermon on the Mount. Since most of the Sermon on the Plain is present in the Sermon on the Mount, we will refer to this body of teaching throughout this chapter as the Sermon on the Mount or simply as the Sermon, recognizing that a good bit of what Matthew has collected into this Sermon is found in other gospels in other settings.

A Manual for Life in the Kingdom of God

A careful reading of the Sermon on the Mount suggests that Matthew has shaped traditions of Jesus's ethical teachings in a very deliberate way for a specific purpose. First, by placing Jesus on a mountain, Matthew is making obvious allusions to Moses, the great leader of Israel who, the early writings of Israel claim, received the Torah from God on Mount Sinai (Exodus 34). Matthew wants us to read this collection of instructions as coming from a "new Moses," one in and through whom God is providing *the* interpretation of his will, *the* authoritative interpretation of Torah (Matthew deliberately draws a connection between Jesus and Torah; see chapter 3 above).

Second, Matthew's Gospel is a "disciple's gospel." The followers of Jesus are "in school." He is their teacher. They are students, learning together what it means to follow Jesus, to live in keeping with the will of God, to practice the "justice of the kingdom of God" (6:33). I like to think of the Sermon as a manual for how to live under the reign or kingdom of God. "Students" of Jesus are to commit this manual to memory. They are to learn not only the particulars of the Sermon, but more importantly to learn to think and act that way, to be ready to live in light of the kingdom of God in the as-yet-unanticipated circumstances of life.

Jews knew that God's law is not simply a set of rules and commandments ("laws"), but a blueprint for how to walk through life. Torah is guidance for the way, we might say. For that reason it is to be committed to memory, to be embedded in consciousness, as we see in Israel's Scriptures:

> Hear, O Israel: The LORD is our God, the LORD alone. You shall love the LORD your God with all your heart, and with all your soul, and with all your might. Keep these words that I am commanding you today in your heart. Recite them to your children and talk about them when you are at home and when you are away, when you lie down and when you rise. Bind them as a sign on your hand, fix them as an emblem on your forehead, and write them on the doorposts of your house and on your gates. (Deut. 6:4–9)

> Happy are those
>   who do not follow the advice of the wicked,
> or take the path that sinners tread,
>   or sit in the seat of scoffers;
> but their delight is in the law of the LORD,
>   and on his law they meditate day and night. (Ps. 1:1–2)

We must think of the Sermon as composed with such delight, recitation, and commitment to deep memory, in order that "the word . . . is in your mouth and in your heart for you to observe" (Deut. 30:14). Jesus's disciples are to implant into their hearts and minds this superior way of righteousness or justice (Matt. 5:20). To be sure, to learn the Sermon is no easy delight, especially if it that means not only talk, but also walk.

How and When Is the Sermon on the Mount Relevant?

Even so, the question has persisted: Is the Sermon on the Mount a manual intended to be followed in real life, by real people? Is it a blueprint for living *now* in the kingdom? Or is Jesus laying out in rather idealized form how one will live *once* the kingdom of God comes in fullness? Or is he quite deliberately holding before us a "perfection" (Matt. 5:48) he knows no one can ever attain? If so, why? These are very live questions in communities of folks who call themselves followers of Jesus, and they have been for a long time. Much has hinged on how this set of questions is answered. What are the options?

OPTION 1: THE SERMON ON THE MOUNT IS INTENDED FOR THE PRESENT

Jesus intends his followers actually to practice what he preaches—*now*. It is enemies you have *today* that you are to love; it is women you encounter *today* whom you are not to denigrate with your lust. Jesus's demands are hard, to say the least. But they do relate to the lives that people actually live. The Sermon envisions a world in which siblings drive you crazy, beggars never repay you, oppressors abuse you, neighbors do things that offend against every value you cherish, a world in which you worry about your spouse and your children's well-being, in which you might be tempted to abandon them for greener pastures, a world in which if you try to do the right thing, you are likely to become judgmental of others. The ethic that Jesus puts forward is an alternative way of living in exactly such a world. We should make no mistake: to live according to the precepts of the Sermon on the Mount is a recipe for conflict, controversy, and suffering. Matthew surely understood this by placing the Beatitudes at the very beginning of the Sermon.

This interpretation is often criticized for being unrealistic about the way the world in fact functions. After all, say such critics, to turn the cheek does not remove violence from the world; forgiveness of debts is not the basis of sustainable economic relations; and giving no thought to how you are going to sustain yourself is a very short trip to ruin. Second, such an approach runs the risk of turning Jesus's Sermon on the Mount into a new set of laws. Attempts to live this way, it is charged, produces people and communities who become obsessed with their own perfection and in the process lose touch with the Jesus who constantly left himself open to the charge of consorting with sinners. Finally, an exclusive focus on the here and now can sever these ethical teachings from the larger context of the anticipation of the coming reign of God. It deeschatologizes Jesus's ethical teaching.

OPTION 2: THE SERMON ON THE MOUNT IS RELATED TO THE COMING OF GOD'S KINGDOM

For such reasons, others propose that the Sermon on the Mount is best understood in relation to the *future* arrival of the kingdom of God. This is a favorite interpretation among those who think of Jesus as an eschatological, or even apocalyptic, prophet. But even within that option there are several quite different suboptions.

Instructions for When the Kingdom Will Come

The Sermon is not meant for ordinary life in the present. For that it is too idealistic and impractical. Surely we must worry about what we eat and wear; surely no one can truly love enemies, even if it is sometimes possible to forego retaliation; surely no one can keep from lusting, even if they can keep from acting on it. And who has not gotten terribly angry and called someone an idiot? The Sermon's function is not to offer practical advice but, rather, to describe the way life will be lived in the future when God's reign comes in fullness. It is an ethic for the kingdom of God, not for this still-broken and conflict-ridden world.

Even a moment's thought will raise this question: why are instructions needed about loving enemies or resisting temptation in a kingdom that will be marked by the absence of conflict, violence, and lawlessness?

Instructions for the Present Short Time of Waiting before the Kingdom Comes

Another variant of a future-oriented interpretation avoids some of these difficulties. Jesus's teachings are not meant for the future, but for a *short* and *abnormal* present. While the Sermon is meant to be acted on *today*, it is not meant to make *permanent* sense. It is not timeless ethical instruction, as in option 1, but rather Jesus's call for a radical life lived *now* in anticipation of a kingdom that is coming very soon. This is an "emergency ethic," or an "interim ethic." In light of the kingdom's imminent arrival, there is no need to be realistic.

Understandably, many scholars and laypersons alike have found this to be a very persuasive interpretation. Jesus and his early followers believed they were living in the last days, and we should then not be surprised that Jesus's advice for living in that moment of transition looks different from normal life.

There is an important implication for contemporary readers of the Sermon: since Christians today live more than two millennia removed from that moment of urgent expectation and have adjusted their eschatology to suit the long haul, they should not take the Sermon too seriously as practical ethical guidance. One has to be realistic about those who do harm, about the permanence of marriage covenants, and about retirement funds.

Option 3: The Sermon on the Mount Is Not Intended as Practical Advice

One of the most venerable and widely held interpretations of the Sermon on the Mount in Christian history has been to deny that it was ever meant to have practical application, not now or in the future. True, some parts of it have some applicability in the real life of Christian individuals and groups. But the Sermon's real function is to hold up before Jesus's followers and Matthew's readers true righteousness and perfection (Matt. 5:20, 48), the kind that is not possibly attainable. Human beings are simply not capable of fulfilling the demands of God, and Jesus knows that. That was true already with the law of the Old Testament or Hebrew Bible, and it is even truer of the perfection that Jesus puts forward in the Sermon.

Why then this Sermon? Simply put, its purpose is to hold up to people a mirror in which their shortcomings become so blatantly clear that they know they have no other recourse than to throw themselves on the grace and mercy of God. As such, the Sermon on the Mount and other similar teachings of Jesus prepare the way for receiving salvation by faith.

Hand in hand with such an interpretation is the widespread suspicion that those who try to live up to the demands of Jesus in the Sermon on the Mount are practicing "works righteousness," that is, they are trying to earn their own salvation. Moreover, to place oneself under such stringent expectations can cause psychological damage to oneself and injury to social relationships.

Much could be said in response to this widespread interpretation of Jesus's teachings in the Sermon, both theologically and psychologically. While there are important insights in this perspective, the most basic question is whether Jesus as a Jew could have conceived of the will of God as something that is *not* intended to be lived out *in this life*. This option runs the serious risk of cutting Jesus off from his roots and his context.

OPTION 4: THE SERMON ON THE MOUNT IS INTENDED FOR THE PRESENT AND THE FUTURE

A final option combines important insights from each of the others. Each of them carries more than a grain of truth. The ethic of the Sermon is *not* realistic, if by the word *realistic* we mean behavior that fits prevailing assumptions about practicality and effectiveness. It *is* very future oriented. Most certainly Jesus addresses life at the intersection of a hostile present and a radical future. The Sermon surely does point to the need for grace. But, to privilege any of these insights at the expense of the others misses important dimensions of Jesus's teaching and, more fatefully, provides the means of sidestepping Jesus's call to live *now already* in light of the *coming* reign of God.

The very way in which Matthew has shaped this material into a "manual" indicates that he at least understands Jesus to mean that his words are to be heard and obeyed—*now*! When that happens, "the reign of God is in your midst" (Luke 17:21, my translation). In other words, a life lived like this is evidence that the kingdom of God is *already* making its presence felt. Such a mode of life is nothing less than enacting the reign of God, evidence as powerful as Jesus's healings, exorcisms, and table fellowship that the kingdom of God has come near. However, in a violent and oppressive present, such "seeking the kingdom and its justice" (Matt. 6:33) provokes sometimes violent resistance, clear evidence that the kingdom is *not yet* fully present. So, living by the ethic of the Sermon on the Mount in the present is always a witness, a sign, pointing *forward* to the kingdom's coming, when God's will will be done "on earth as it is in heaven" (6:10). To view the Sermon with that mix of present relevance and future anticipation is truest, I believe, to the perspective with which Matthew and Luke present Jesus's teaching on how to live.

Content of the Sermon on the Mount

Interestingly, the Sermon is framed in both Matthew and Luke by an image of Jesus not as a teacher, as we might have expected, but as a healer and exorcist! Matthew thus precedes his Sermon with a virtual inventory of Jesus's activity as a healer and a geography lesson on how far his activities as a healer went (Matt. 4:23–25). Luke makes the connection between acts of power and teaching even more explicit (Luke 6:17–19).

Perhaps the distinction between teacher and healer is a modern one. The evangelists certainly do not allow us to choose between the teacher and the doer; in Jesus, word and deed, act and teaching, are fused (see chapter 9). Jesus teaches about the kingdom of God through both instruction and transforming actions—a good reminder that in focusing on ethics we are not leaving the sphere of Jesus's enacting of the kingdom of God, but are focusing on what a life gripped by and oriented toward the reign of God might look like.

So the healer now sits down at the top of a mountain (or on the level place, as the case may be) in order to teach his followers (Matt. 5:1 || Luke 6:17).

Beatitudes

The Sermon begins with blessings, known most commonly as the Beatitudes (Matt. 5:3–12 || Luke 6:20–26; Matthew and Luke's versions are set alongside each other in chapter 3 above). The term *beatitude* is based on the Latin adjective *beatus* ("blessed"), a translation of the Greek term *makarios* ("happy, blessed"). They are thus sometimes also called "makarisms." "Blessed" is still in my view to be preferred over "happy." A blessing invokes—unleashes!—the power of God to the benefit of those who are blessed. Blessings are *acts*; they are *performative* language, just like a curse, albeit with very opposite intent (in fact, the blessings are matched by woes in Luke 6:24–26). By calling them blessed and happy, Jesus is promising a radical change for those who are poor, hungry, humble, and persecuted. His blessings are promises because they have the full weight of God's will behind them. This is true performative language because it is *God* who makes the promise as good as true. Jesus's assertions of blessing and happiness are the reign of God at work.

Kingdom Comes for the Marginalized

To whom are these blessings spoken? The answer is clear: the poor, the humble (or humbled?), the hungry, the thirsty, and the persecuted. We encounter them in Mary's magnificent hymn of liberation, the *Magnificat* (Luke 1:46–55). We see them time and again throughout the narrative of

Jesus's life: he heals these people, liberates them, and eats with them. In short, the Beatitudes are addressed to those for whom the coming kingdom represents a profound reversal. The Beatitudes promise as blessings what Jesus is already doing in his actions. Stated differently, his actions anticipate what the Beatitudes promise in full. Those who are hungry now will be filled then, those who suffer now will have it good then. And, as Luke indicates, those who are full and happy in the face of such suffering will go away empty (6:24–26).

Kingdom Marginalizes Those Who Practice Its Justice

The evangelists Matthew and Luke, however, have Jesus bestow his blessings on his *followers*, on those to whom the demands of the Sermon are addressed. In that light the Beatitudes take on a different color. They are still blessings; they still invoke the power of God upon Jesus's hearers to their benefit. But the poverty, suffering, hunger, and thirst they speak of might be the *effect* of living the Sermon. For people to be ravenous for justice, to be scandalously merciful, to inject themselves into situations of conflict as peacemakers, to be courageous in their witness to Jesus and the kingdom—this will marginalize them and bring them suffering.

The Beatitudes depict, then, not only the great reversal for those who yearn for the coming kingdom, but also what life will be like for those who choose to live in light of the kingdom already now. Therein lies the ethical challenge of the Beatitudes. As much as they are words of assurance, they also serve as a warning label for the hearers and readers of the Sermon on the Mount.

For Jesus and his fellow Jews this was, of course, an old story line. The just, that is, those who wholly and courageously live in accordance with the will of God in an evil world, often do so at the cost of their safety and even their lives. But they can count on being vindicated by the God who calls them to such a life, as the Beatitudes promise once more.

Torah

Jesus was a Jew. And Matthew and the other evangelists never let us forget that. In a particularly striking reinforcement of that point, Jesus challenges his followers to pursue righteousness or justice:

Do not think that I have come to abolish the law or the prophets; *I have come not to abolish but to fulfill.* For truly I tell you, until heaven and earth pass away, not one iota, not one stroke of a letter, will pass from the law until all is accomplished. Therefore, whoever breaks one of the least of these commandments, and teaches others to do the same, will be called least in the kingdom of heaven; but whoever does them and teaches them will be called great in the kingdom of heaven. For I tell you, *unless your righteousness exceeds that of the scribes and Pharisees, you will never enter the kingdom of heaven*. (Matt. 5:17–20, emphasis added)

The gist of this particular passage is summarized in Matthew 5:20, where Jesus calls on his followers to "exceed the scribes and the Pharisees" at righteousness, that is, in doing what the law requires.

Two things require our attention. First, "righteousness" and "justice" translate exactly the same term in the Greek (*dikaiosyne*). Second, such righteousness or justice means being obedient to God's will as encoded in Torah. That such justice is inseparable from what today would be called social justice, fairness, care for those most vulnerable, is in no way denied (e.g., the parable of the good Samaritan and Jesus's discussion with the lawyer in Luke 10:25–37). The Pharisees' concern about fulfilling the law was a concern for righteousness. Here Matthew has Jesus demanding that his followers outdo the Pharisees at practicing justice, that is, at fulfilling Torah.

We are by now sufficiently adept as students of the gospels to ask: do we hear in this call to hyperobedience the voice of Jesus or that of Matthew? If it is Matthew, has he betrayed the Jesus we think we know? If it is Jesus's words we hear, how do they fit with everything else we know of him?

First, how should we understand these words in Matthew's own setting toward the end of the first century? At this level we have two possible interpretations. One relates to Matthew's fellow Jews who did not believe in Jesus. Matthew struggled with fellow Jews who accused Jesus and his followers of unfaithfulness to the Torah (see chapter 3 above). Might Matthew be defending Jesus against the accusation of lawlessness and unfaithfulness? "Think not that I have come to abolish the law!" Matthew has Jesus calling for a fulfillment of the law that *exceeds* that of the learned interpreters of the law. The second interpretation relates to Matthew's fellow Jesus believers, many of whom were not Jews, and many of whom may have taken a stance quite critical of the ongoing relevance of the law. Is Matthew having Jesus weigh in on the side of Torah in debates raging *within* the Jesus movement? "Whoever breaks one of the least of these commandments, and teaches others to do the same, will be called least in the kingdom of heaven!" I have no doubt that Matthew 5:17–20 would have played a vital role in both settings. Perhaps, then, both interpretations are equally relevant.

But do these words make sense on the lips of Jesus? Many think not. They view Jesus as too much in conflict with fellow Jews over especially the "jots and tittles" of the law to have wanted to make such a strong plea for meticulous fidelity to Torah.

I suggest, however, that Jesus might well have said something like this, even if we should recognize that the present wording is heavily affected by later struggles of Jesus's followers. Along with other Jews, including scribes and Pharisees, Jesus believed that righteousness, obedience to the will of God, is how you love God. Pharisees, for precisely that reason, carefully planted a "hedge" around the law with what they called the "traditions of the fathers" (or "oral law"). This was to ensure that the law was obeyed to the letter in every new circumstance. This safeguarded both the doer of the law and the law itself. While, given the long history of anti-Judaism, Christians today need to learn to respect the motivation behind the "oral hedge," in his day Jesus appears to have had difficulty with many of these traditions. His ways of behaving vis-à-vis the Sabbath, for example, angered learned interpreters of the law as a deliberate flouting of the Torah. Jesus, in turn, seems to have been suspicious of ways in which interpretation and tradition can blunt the meaning of Torah, as we see in the Sermon (see also, e.g., Matt. 23:23–26).

It is not difficult, then, regardless of what one thinks of Jesus's stance, to see that he could claim to fulfill the law, to practice a superior righteousness, and at the same time to recognize that this could have introduced great tension into his relationship with other more respected interpreters of Torah. Matthew seems to have understood as much by the way he now presents Jesus's stance on such traditions.

Antitheses

The unequivocal endorsement of fidelity to law in Matthew 5:17–20 is followed by several antitheses (Matt. 5:21–48): "You have heard it said. . . . But I say to you. . . ." Comparison with Luke's Sermon on the Plain, and with other places these teachings are found in the gospels, indicates that this is Matthew's way of drawing attention to the marked difference in Jesus's way of interpreting the will of God. The basic point of the antitheses is to take issue with traditional interpretation of the law, to get to the heart of the law, and to probe what it truly means to be faithful to law and covenant. This is thus often called "Torah intensification."

MURDER, ANGER, AND RECONCILIATION

The first antithesis deals with the sixth commandment (Matt. 5:21–26): "You shall not murder" (Exod. 20:13). This is not *just* one of the traditions of the fathers; this is a central commandment of the Torah. In apparent opposition ("but I say to you . . .") Jesus now says that his hearers are not to be angry, insulting, or denigrating. Jesus minces no words: whoever calls someone a "moron" shall be liable to the fire of Gehenna (Jerusalem's garbage dump, a fitting metaphor for judgment). This is, of course, not a true antithesis, that is, a true "over against." It is rather a radical interpretation, an intensification of the command not to commit murder.

But is Jesus really equating a dismissive insult with murder? Surely this is intentional exaggeration, is it not? Knowing that Jesus assumes that his hearers are members of the covenant community—they are Jews—and that they care about the law will keep us from jumping to that conclusion. Might not the harshness of Jesus's language point to the heart of murder, namely, the destruction of the fellow member of the community, and thus to a violation of that very community? Does one not do precisely that by treating a member of one's family or community as one who is not capable of good sense and unworthy of respect? In short, one can destroy the bond between people that God intended to forge with this commandment not to murder while remaining true to the letter of the law.

Interestingly, Jesus does more than "make it impossible to obey the law" with this intensification of the commandment against murder. He demands of his hearers a positive initiative to mend broken relationships. He connects the warnings about anger and insult with the urgency to reconcile oneself with the brother or the sister whom one has offended, or better, who "has something against you." The context for this command is the community of those who go to "the altar," who worship God. Just as the Torah was intended to forge a community of loyalty under God, so too Jesus's radical interpretation of Torah is intended to forge a community of reconciliation and mutual respect.

Adultery and Lust

We see a similar pattern in the antithesis dealing with adultery (Matt. 5:27–30). First, Jesus quotes the well-known law against adultery, which follows immediately the one dealing with murder in Exodus 20:14. "Over against" it, he then speaks of lust. To lust after another is to have committed adultery "in one's heart." In fact, in light of God's judgment, one would be better off tearing out one's roving eye or cutting off one's offending hand.

As in the case of murder and anger, Jesus indicates what the spirit of the law against adultery is. Jesus seems to be living in a different universe from ours, where lust is one of the largest and most successful engines of the economy. And his solutions seem draconian in the extreme.

One should be careful, to be sure, not to mistake his picturesque language for a literal injunction. At the same time, one should hear in the harshness of the language some measure of the seriousness with which Jesus views adultery and lust. As strangely out of step Jesus seems to be with present-day values, he is remarkably in tune with our growing alarm over the dehumanization that sexual harassment represents or the objectification of women, children, or men as an objects of desire and possession. To lust after another is not only to violate that person, but to violate the covenant that person has with another and with God. And that is why the next antithesis deals with divorce.

Divorce and Remarriage

In the antithesis on divorce (Matt. 5:31–32), Jesus does not quote one of the Ten Commandments, but rather one of the *amendments* to the law, an "order of concession," as it is sometimes called. Moses gave permission to divorce one's wife if he gave her a certificate of divorce (Deut. 24:1; Matt. 19:7–8). This was no doubt intended to make divorce less than totally arbitrary, but it still allowed men to divorce their wives with ease.

In his antithesis to that tradition, Jesus essentially abrogates that concession and suggests that anyone who divorces his wife "except on the ground of unchastity" forces his wife to commit adultery, and whoever marries a divorced woman commits adultery (see also Matt. 19:9). In essence, Jesus pits the seventh commandment against the venerable tradition of divorce. It is the tradition, Jesus insists, that is in violation of Torah, not he!

To modern ears these are not only hard, but harsh words. We might wonder whether the presence of the phrase "except for unchastity" is an indication that the early followers of Jesus already found this a pill too hard to swallow undiluted (in Mark 10:11–12 || Luke 16:18 the phrase "except for unchastity" is absent; the prohibition of divorce is unqualified). However, within a culture in which women could fall victim to being divorced at the whim of their husbands and in which women were largely dependent on marriage for economic survival, Jesus is essentially weighing in on the side of women, protecting them from the vagaries of a sexist and insensitive system.

We can only wonder what he might say in our day, where the covenantal glue of marriage vows is growing ever weaker. We might also wonder what he would say about women stuck in abusive marriages. Would his words about the treatment of the vulnerable (i.e., the "little ones" in Matt. 18) apply here? What is clear is that Jesus takes the spirit of the law against adultery and, by connecting it to both lust and divorce, applies it to the *integrity* of relationships.

Swearing Oaths and Speaking Truth

The issue of integrity is addressed directly in the antithesis regarding swearing (Matt. 5:33–37). Over against commandments on swearing oaths found in Leviticus 19:12 and Numbers 30:2, Jesus prohibits swearing completely. As in the case of the previous antitheses, he goes beyond even the Mosaic code by driving to the heart of injunctions to keep one's oaths and promises. *All* of one's communication ought to be honest. "Yes" ought to mean yes and "no" ought to mean no—*always*! Otherwise *all* communication is trivialized. Attempts to dress up assurances with appeals to heaven, the throne of God, or Jerusalem have the effect of diminishing the trustworthiness of everyday communication.

Remarkably, with few exceptions, this insight has not taken hold in Christian cultures. People routinely place their hands on the Bible containing this injunction and swear their allegiance or their truthfulness. Moreover, people just as routinely consider lying under oath to be worse than everyday untruths, witnessing thereby to the way oaths devalue the currency of normal communication.

In this, as in the previous antitheses, Jesus is pushing Torah to its core. One needs to get to the core of the law in order to truly obey it; to obey the letter of the law may be good, but it is not yet the righteousness that reflects the full reign of God—it is not yet the righteousness that exceeds that of the scribes and the Pharisees (Matt. 5:20).

RETALIATION

In the next antithesis (Matt. 5:38–42) Jesus takes on a notion deeply rooted in common sense, in the laws of many nations, and in the Torah: "life for life, eye for eye, tooth for tooth, hand for hand, foot for foot, burn for burn, wound for wound, stripe for stripe" (Exod. 21:23–25; see also Lev. 24:20 and Deut. 19:21). We call this the law of "talion," from which we derive the term *retaliation*—paying back, responding in kind, tit for tat. Jesus's antithesis to this can be translated variously:

> Do not resist evil!
> Do not resist the evil one!
> Do not *violently* resist the evil one!
> Do not resist by means of evil!

Each of these lends a slightly or even dramatically different nuance to the phrase. Is Jesus suggesting a kind of stoic acquiescence to evil? Is he prohibiting not resistance so much as violence? Let's leave the question unanswered for now and allow the analysis of the rest of the antithesis, and also the next one, to suggest some answers.

Jesus follows his antithesis with examples that have become everyday idioms even among those who have no idea where they come from:

> If anyone strikes you on the right cheek, turn the other also.
> If anyone wants to sue you and take your coat, give your cloak as well.
> If anyone forces you to go one mile, go also the second mile.
> Give to everyone who begs from you, and do not refuse anyone who wants to borrow from you.

At first blush it is difficult to see how in this case Jesus is going to the heart of the law. He seems to be rejecting the notion of equivalency. Does it not undercut the notions of legal redress, of restitution, of learning that actions have consequences? The objections grow stronger among those who argue for the justifiability of war or who insist that the death penalty is a biblical mandate. Indeed, the logic Jesus is attacking here is deeply embedded in everyday notions of fairness.

So, is Jesus driving the law to its core, or is he subverting it? The answer depends to some degree on whether the law of talion in the Torah is seen as *requiring* an equivalent measure of retaliation (an eye for an eye) or as *limiting* retaliation to *no more than* equivalency (no more than an eye for an eye). Many scholars consider it to be the latter. The principle of talion had as its purpose to limit retaliation so as to break the otherwise endless cycle of violence. The preceding command in Deuteronomy 19:21 to "show no pity" makes it difficult to argue that point easily, to be sure. But in a culture of the blood feud, strict equivalency would have had the effect of ending or at least limiting violence. If limiting violence is the spirit behind the law of talion, or if that is how Jesus understood the meaning of that law, then his injunction to turn the cheek, to give the shirt, to walk the second mile might once again be a creative intensification of that law, rather than an abrogation of it. Such actions would have as their intended effect to bring an end to abuse and oppression, not their toleration.

Nonretaliation as Resistance

We can take that interpretation one step further. A closer look at the examples Jesus offers to illustrate his antithesis shows that he is not attempting to replace retaliation with inaction. The one who is abused or injured "turns," "gives," and "walks." These victims *do* something. This is important to see, since "turning the cheek," for example, has become shorthand for passivity, for a fatalism that leaves the circumstances of injustice and victimization in place.

The creativity to which Matthew's Jesus calls his audience in the face of victimization emerges clearly when we pay close attention to the specifics of his examples. The first one envisions a context in which a person is humiliated: a strike on the *right* cheek requires from a (typically) right-handed person a backhanded strike, clearly intended to humiliate and denigrate a person. The locale of the second example would be easily recognizable by especially the poor in Jesus's audience as court, the place where even what little they have is taken away by those more powerful. And no one in occupied Palestine would have missed the allusions to the humiliating demands of Roman soldiers for them to carry their packs.

Each of the responses Jesus proposes is a creative initiative, examples that might even have struck Jesus's audience as humorous, in a dark sort of way. To turn the cheek is a challenge to the insulter to treat you with dignity. Imagine this being tried by someone who has just experienced a cheap shot in a game. To give your cloak when what is being demanded of you is your coat is to disrobe totally, leaving those at the court shamed and embarrassed; today we would consider that a bit of street theater, political performance art. Since Roman soldiers were allowed to demand only one mile from someone, to offer to carry the bag for two would be to surprise the soldier with unasked for help, but also to force him into a position of breaking the law. Picture similar behavior in Palestine's Occupied Territories. *Victims* do not act like that.

With humor and hyperbole Jesus illustrates alternatives to the predictable arithmetic of retaliation. If the law of talion had as its virtue to limit injury with an ironclad rule of equivalency, Jesus is inviting his audience to push that concern much further, inviting them to find creative ways to undercut the logic of injury as a solution to injury.

Such behavior might well be called resistance in our day. And perhaps we should translate Matthew 5:39 roughly, "Resist, but not by means of evil!" Grammatically that is somewhat clumsy, but possible. That would bring Jesus's instructions here much closer to Paul's words in his letter to the Romans:

> Bless those who persecute you; bless and do not curse them. . . . Do not repay anyone evil for evil. . . . Do not be overcome by evil, but overcome evil with good. (Rom. 12:14, 17, 21)

Regardless of how we translate Matthew 5:39, Jesus offers a form of resistance that communicates to the offender that one is not victimized by the oppression one is experiencing.

Nonretaliation as Nonresistance

To be sure, one can overstress the resistance aspect in these examples. There is also real nonresistance in Jesus's counsel, rooted in the vulnerable stance of a righteous or just person who does the will of God regardless of consequence, in the full confidence that God will vindicate the righteous (see the Beatitudes). The roots of this conviction go deep in Jewish wisdom literature. Jesus's last examples have to do with giving to those who ask, without expectation of return. This is a stance of openness and defenselessness that conforms closely to the way the evangelists describe Jesus's mode of life and death. It is a stance that conforms to not giving a thought for tomorrow. What gives sense and meaning to such irresponsibility is, of course, the conviction that there is a divine father who watches and cares (Matthew 6; see chapter 8 above). Resistance and nonresistance go together in a way the translators of Matthew 5:39 have not yet succeeded in capturing.

Nonretaliation and Hatred

It is entirely possible to turn the cheek, to walk the second mile, and still to hate the enemy. Such acts can be experienced as goading, shaming, even humiliating, as anyone knows who has ever been in a fight. Nonretaliation can be an expression of hatred. This can be illustrated from Jesus's own time with a quotation from the pledge a person took in joining the community of Qumran at the Dead Sea. After assuring God that one hates all "sons of darkness" or "men of the pit," one pledged this:

> I shall not repay anyone
> with an evil reward;
> with goodness I shall pursue the man.
> For to God [belongs] the judgment
> of every living being,
> and it is he who pays man his wages. . . .
> I shall not be involved at all in any dispute
> of the men of the pit
> until the day of vengeance.
> However, *I shall not remove my anger*
> *from wicked men*
> *nor shall I be appeased*
> *until* [*God*] *carries out his judgment.* (*Rule of the Community* [1QS]
>   10.17–20, trans. García Martínez, emphasis added)

Paul's words in Romans 12, some of which were just cited above, have sometimes been read in this light—incorrectly, in my view:

> Beloved, never avenge yourselves, but leave room for the wrath of God; for it is written, "Vengeance is mine, I will repay, says the Lord." No, "if your enemies are hungry, feed them; if they are thirsty, give them something to drink; for by doing this you will heap burning coals on their heads." (Rom. 12:19–20)

For this very reason, Luke's version of the Sermon has the instruction not to retaliate fused with the positive command to love enemies. In Matthew, that command is placed in the final, crowning antithesis, to which we now turn.

LOVING ENEMIES

Matthew fashions the final antithesis in the very starkest terms (Matt. 5:43–48): inherited tradition is that one is to love one's neighbor and hate one's enemy. Over against this, Jesus calls for love not just of neighbors, but of enemies. Nothing less is required if his hearers are to be "children of [their] Father in heaven" (5:45).

With what is Jesus taking issue in this instance? Is he quoting law? Only in part: the love of neighbors is one of the central commands in the Torah, second only to the command to love God (Lev. 19:18; see also in the New Testament: Matt. 22:37–40 || Mark 12:29–34; Rom. 13:8–10; 1 Cor. 13; Gal. 5:14; James 2:8; 1 John 4). But we look in vain for a command to hate enemies. Is this a pernicious maligning of Jewish tradition, on the part of either Jesus or the shaper of the antitheses, Matthew?

One can make the case that the hatred of enemies, to state it as bluntly as our text does, is rooted in the very fabric of covenant loyalty: "Your friends are my friends, your enemies are my enemies." Anyone who has played team sports or has walked the union picket lines knows full well that the dark underside of solidarity is shared enmity toward those who threaten the bond, the covenant, the community. We can illustrate this quite dramatically from within the Scriptures. One of the most beautiful songs in Israel's hymnbook is Psalm 139. It celebrates the all-pervasive presence of the creator in unforgettable imagery, but also includes the following:

> O that you would kill the wicked, O God,
>   and that the bloodthirsty would depart from me—
> those who speak of you maliciously,
>   and lift themselves up against you for evil!
> *Do I not hate those who hate you, O LORD?*
>   *And do I not loathe those who rise up against you?*
> *I hate them with perfect hatred;*
>   *I count them my enemies.*
> Search me, O God, and know my heart;
>   test me and know my thoughts.
> See if there is any wicked way in me,
>   and lead me in the way everlasting. (Ps. 139:19–24, emphasis added)

The hatred of God's enemies is in this psalm a sign not of wickedness but of covenant fidelity, an assertion of loyalty to God who has created and sustained the psalmist through thick and thin, from conception to death. Loyalty, integrity, and fidelity lie at the root of the assurance to God that one hates those who rebel against God. The pledge of loyalty that covenanters would make on entering the community at Qumran included the promise "to hate everything that God rejects, indeed to detest all the sons of darkness and to love all the sons of light" (1QS, 1.10). Seen in this light, the characterization of the tradition of the fathers in Jesus's final antithesis is not a malicious caricature, but rather a self-evident implication of love for the covenant partner, which is what "neighbor" means. Nothing in these words would have shocked Jesus's contemporaries, other than perhaps its stark formulation.

What might have shocked them is Jesus's alternative to this tradition. Loyalty to and solidarity with God, identified as "sonship," does not mean hating those who hate God, but rather behaving like God behaves toward those who hate him: God loves his enemies! As proof Jesus points to the sun and the rain (Matt. 5:45). To love enemies is to behave as "sons of God" (today we should say "daughters and sons"). God's sons and daughters emulate the powerful creator of the universe, who *raises* the sun on the unjust and the just alike, who *rains* on the just and the unjust alike (in the Greek these are strong action verbs). For Jesus the dawn of every new day is a divine act of power meant to give God's enemies yet one more opportunity to change. In light of persistent human injustice and rebellion, every new day is a powerful act of divine grace. In the Beatitudes the term *sons of God* is reserved for peacemakers (5:9; some translations, like the NRSV, render this with a more inclusive "children of God"); here we encounter "sonship" in relation to loving enemies. Loving enemies, in Jesus's view, is at the heart of being the offspring of a God, who is himself the ultimate peacemaker, the ultimate lover of enemies.

Never far removed from Jesus's understanding of God's reign, as we saw in the parables, is the conviction that God is a judge whose grace and mercy are not to be abused. But what God's sons and daughters are to imitate, according to Jesus, is not divine wrath, but God's kindness, patience, and powerful love. They are to imitate this behavior of God because they themselves have been the recipients of God's mercy and grace. Some were one-time tax collectors and sinners, prostitutes and outcasts; others were once resentful older brothers, as in the parable of the prodigal son; still others were once wealthy landowners, practiced in the exploitation of their day laborers. As beneficiaries of divine patience and grace—love—they are to behave exactly that way toward their enemies (see Jesus's parable of the unmerciful slave in Matt. 18:23–35).

Matthew 5:48, and with it the antitheses as a whole, ends with a call to "be perfect . . . as your heavenly Father is perfect." Does this startling command mean that we were wrong earlier to reject the idea that in this Sermon Jesus is trying to set the bar of performance deliberately beyond reach? I believe not.

First, perfection should not be understood in an abstract Greek philosophical sense, which would surely remove it beyond human capability. Jesus did not, of course, originally speak these words in Greek. So, if this were said in the language of his day, Hebrew or Aramaic, the term might well have been *tamim*. Interestingly, that word in Deuteronomy 18:13 was translated in Jesus's time into the exact same Greek term we find in Matthew 5:48: *teleios*. Most often in the Bible *tamim* is translated "blameless" or "completely loyal" (in the NRSV). It often means "whole, complete, or having integrity" (concerns similar to Matthew's antitheses are found in Ps. 15:1–5). This clearly would fit well as a summary challenge of the antitheses as a whole. So "perfect" is not the best translation of Matthew's word choice. Living justly and lovingly to the very core of one's being would fit better. That helps to explain how Luke can remember Jesus's saying as a call to "be merciful, just as your Father is merciful" (Luke 6:36).

Second, the appeal to imitate God is not new. It is implied in being sons and daughters of God (Matt. 5:45). It is also an essential building block of

Torah. The so-called Holiness Code of Leviticus contains the following phrase repeatedly: "I am the LORD who brought you up from the land of Egypt, to be your God; *you shall be holy, for I am holy!*" (Lev. 11:45, emphasis added; see also 11:44; 19:2; 20:26).

The call to perfection is thus not a summons to an impossible ideal, but a way to call those who would be daughters and sons of God to emulate the merciful and scandalously gracious justice of a God who patiently shines the sun and pours the rain on the unjust as much as on the just. Strange perfection!

Such patient and loving perfection is high-risk behavior. In keeping the door open to change, enemies are at the same time dangerously given room to exercise their hostility. Such patience necessarily leaves the lovers of enemies vulnerable to having their generosity mistaken for weakness and thus exposed to abuse and suffering. But that is, as I understand Matthew's Jesus to say, the risk that the creator takes each day he puts the sun back up in the sky. God is a creator who sustains creation even in light of massive injustice, always in the interest of reconciliation. God's sons and daughters are to imitate just such high-risk behavior vis-à-vis their own enemies. The Wisdom of Solomon, a Jewish wisdom document written not long before the time of Jesus, describes God in remarkably similar terms:

> For it is always in your [God's] power to show great strength,
> and who can withstand the might of your arm?
> Because the whole world before you is like a speck that tips the
>   scales,
> and like a drop of morning dew that falls on the ground.
> *But you are merciful to all, for you can do all things,*
> *and you overlook people's sins, so that they may repent.*
> *For you love all things that exist,*
> *and detest none of the things that you have made,*
> *for you would not have made anything if you had hated it.*
> How would anything have endured if you had not willed it?
> Or how would anything not called forth by you have been preserved?
> *You spare all things, for they are yours, O Lord, you who love the*
>   *living. . . .*
> *Through such works you have taught your people*
> *that the righteous must be kind,*
> and you have filled your children with good hope,
> because you give repentance for sins. (Wisdom of Solomon 11:21–
>   26; 12:19, emphasis added)

As Wisdom of Solomon makes clear, mercy is not the withholding of power; it is the perfect exercise of sovereignty (11:23). Only if powered by such patient love—to return to the antithesis regarding nonretaliation—are turning the cheek, taking off the shirt, and walking the second mile not the behavior of humiliated victims or the means of embarrassment and goading, but inventive invitations to repentance and change and finally reconciliation, offered by those who know themselves to be daughters and sons of God. That is exactly how Luke understands these examples of subversive initiative too—which is why in his Sermon these injunctions *follow* Jesus's command to love enemies (Luke 6:27–31).

A Detour: But What About . . . ?

In contemporary ethical discussions around issues of violence and self-defense, several words and actions ascribed to Jesus elsewhere in the gospels point, in the minds of many, in another direction than the one charted in the pages above. Before bringing the discussion of the antitheses to a close, we must make a short detour outside the Sermon on the Mount to consider these.

JESUS BRINGS THE SWORD, NOT PEACE

Matthew 10:34 has often been put forward as evidence that Jesus recognizes a legitimate place for violence:

> Do not think that I have come to bring peace to the earth; I have not come to bring peace, but a sword.

It is possible to entertain such an interpretation only if one lifts the text out of its surrounding context. The context of the verse is Jesus's instructions to the Twelve when he sends them out as proclaimers and enactors of the kingdom of God (Matt. 10:1–5). The words cited above are part of his speech where he warns them of the opposition their words and activities are likely to provoke. News of the reign of God (and at the point Matthew is writing this, news of Jesus as the Christ) will bring division into the community; more, it will drive a wedge into the very heart of the family, since some will respond eagerly and openly and others will resist. Far from legitimizing the use of weapons, this saying anticipates the regrettable violence those who have *resisted* the call to take up arms have experienced in history, often at the hands of fellow Christians,

ARE TWO SWORDS ENOUGH?

In a puzzling text, Jesus calls for weaponry for his disciples:

> He said to them, "But now, the one who has a purse must take it, and likewise a bag. And the one who has no sword must sell his cloak and buy one. For I tell you, this scripture must be fulfilled in me, 'And he was counted among

the lawless'; and indeed what is written about me is being fulfilled." They said, "Lord, look, here are two swords." He replied, "It is enough." (Luke 22:36–38)

Is Jesus telling his disciples to buy a sword? Is he summoning them to fight? How does that fit with everything we have been reading? One explanation is that we just barely see the tip of an iceberg here. Jesus and his followers were revolutionaries engaged in a struggle that came to a terrible end with his own crucifixion. The evangelists for the most part have succeeded in covering that up, but here in Luke a tiny bit of evidence still exists. That line of interpretation has not been widely accepted.

Another possibility presents itself when we pay close attention to the quotation from the prophet Isaiah in Luke 22:37. It comes from Isaiah 53:12, a long hymnlike poem about God's Servant who gives his life for the sins of others and in the process is "counted among the lawless," that is, he is treated like a criminal. Early followers of Jesus read the song in Isaiah 53 with Jesus's own ministry and death in mind. There is no reason to think that Jesus did not also think of his ministry as leading to a dark end. The command to buy a sword would then be a highly metaphorical reference to the coming struggle of Jesus's last days, a struggle that would lead not to the death of *others* but to his *own*. The brief phrase at the end, spoken in Jesus's response to disciples who assure him that they have two swords—"it is enough!"—is not to be taken as assurance that two swords should do, but rather as a rather impatient, "Enough already! You are misunderstanding me again!"

Jesus's Temple Demonstration

A favorite counterexample to Jesus's teaching of patient and creative love for enemies has been the so-called cleansing of the temple (Matt. 21:12–13 || Mark 11:15–17 || Luke 19:45–46; and esp. John 2:13–16; see chapter 11 below). This episode has long been an important element in the debate regarding Jesus and violence. The Synoptic Gospels all relate briefly Jesus's "prophetic demonstration" in the temple shortly before his death. John, however, places this event at the very beginning of Jesus's ministry and gives a more extensive account. John's account figures most prominently in the debate:

> In the temple he found people selling cattle, sheep, and doves, and the money changers seated at their tables. Making a whip of cords, he drove all of them out of the temple, both the sheep and the cattle. He also poured out the coins of the money changers and overturned their tables. (John 2:14–15)

The Synoptic Gospels all agree that Jesus entered the temple grounds and "threw out" all those who sold and bought in the temple, overturning tables of moneychangers and sellers of pigeons. A ruckus indeed, one sure to have inflamed the ire of the authorities. John's account has drawn a great deal of attention in that Jesus is said to have fashioned a whip with which to accomplish his "cleansing." The image of Jesus in the tradition is one of using the whip on the people as well as on the animals, as many translations carelessly suggest. The Greek text makes it clear that the phrase is not "with the sheep and oxen," as the older Revised Standard Version has it, but "both the sheep and the cattle," as above. This may seem like quibbling, were it not that Jesus is often depicted in this episode as using a weapon on persons, rather than herding animals out of the grounds. Whereas we should not downplay the provocative nature of Jesus's prophetic act (see chapter 11 below), nothing in the story supports taking up arms with Jesus's blessing.

To return to our discussion of the last two antitheses in Matthew 5: none of the texts considered in this detour indicate that Jesus was inconsistent in his behavior or in his teachings on the question of how to deal with injury or enmity. The last two antitheses in Matthew 5 regarding nonretaliation and love of enemies reflect his stance clearly and powerfully.

By shaping some of Jesus's teachings as antitheses, Matthew has placed Jesus in considerable tension with many of his fellow Jews. At the same time, it is just as clear that Matthew views Jesus as standing fully *within* Jewish tradition as a forceful and authoritative interpreter and reinterpreter of Torah. To admit that not many Jews agreed with Jesus or with his witness, Matthew, does not change for a moment that both Matthew and Jesus would have wanted to be located fully *within* the story of God's relationship with Israel and to be fully faithful to the will of God.

Other Topics in the Sermon on the Mount

ALMSGIVING AND FASTING

The teaching on almsgiving gets to the heart of what it means to practice righteousness or justice with integrity (Matt. 6:1–4). Sometimes "justice" is unfortunately translated, as in the NRSV, as "piety"—I say unfortunate because "piety" often has more limited, even negative, connotations in our time than does "justice." Jesus's concern here is that the only righteousness or justice that counts is one that is performed in relation to human need. Justice is not about the person practicing it so much as about that to which or whom it responds. That is entirely biblical and Jewish. It corresponds to words attributed to Jesus's brother James: "Religion that is pure and undefiled before God, the Father, is this: to care for orphans and widows in their distress, and to keep oneself unstained by the world" (James 1:27). Jesus is after true righteousness, one that is prompted by need and love for God, not by the need to be seen. Secrecy, in the sense of integrity, lies at the core of such righteousness.

The same spirit pervades Jesus's teaching on fasting (Matt. 6:16–18). Jesus does not disparage fasting. But if someone fasts, make sure that no one but God can see the fasting. Jesus is deeply suspicious of the social benefits of obvious piety, benefits that too easily lead to hypocrisy.

Jesus does not mean, however, that religion is a private matter, one between only you and your God. Everything we know about Jesus shows his concern about the actual socially concrete manifestations of the kingdom of God, public and observable by their very nature. But Jesus hates showing off. The need to show off one's religion is a reflection of the lack of integrity and true love for God; the desire for public approval is odious to God.

In the parable of the sheep and goats in Matthew 25:31–46 (see chapter 8 above), the sheep are as surprised at the significance of their acts of love and care as the goats are at their own failure. Something quite similar lies at the roots of these words: "Do not worry about who sees what you are doing. Hide it even from yourself!" That is what it means to say that the left hand should not know what the right is doing (6:3). God sees everything, God is judge, God will pay attention to the acts of kindness that people do and reward accordingly. But if your left hand does not pay attention at all, then even that promise of reward will be forgotten. Meeting of human need should happen even when no one is watching—especially when one is not watching *oneself*. Jesus is clearly out of step with much of what propels philanthropy. He deliberately intends to subvert a religious culture in which levels of true piety and love of God can be judged by outward behavior.

Lord's Prayer

One of the most widely known teachings of Jesus is the prayer that he taught his followers. It is recited in many schools and public events and, of course, in worship services. It may be that some readers will have learned this prayer by memory. If so, they may wish to compare their memorized version with the versions found in Matthew and Luke (see below). Several differences will likely have become obvious: the popularly memorized version seems more ornate in its language, and the text is fuller, ending on a grand flourish: "For yours is the kingdom and the power and the glory, for ever and ever, AMEN!" This should be a reminder that the prayer had its origin in instructions on how to pray, and that it has been expanded for liturgical use.

Mark does not include the prayer itself, and it is entirely absent from the Gospel of John. Naturally there is debate among scholars as to whether the prayer goes back to Jesus or whether it emerged in the early communities of his followers as the routines of worship developed. My strong hunch is that the instructions on prayer go back to Jesus, even if the exact shape was strongly affected over time by the worship habits of early Christians. Rather ironically, Jesus's instructions on prayer, as remembered by the evangelists, are intended to take issue directly with wordy formal prayers that are a performance rather than a direct appeal to a trustworthy divine parent with whom one does not need to mince words or dress up one's language. That in itself speaks strongly in favor of Jesus being behind these instructions on prayer. The "menu" that the prayer offers is highly instructive, and tells us a great deal about Jesus:

Matthew 6:9–13	Luke 11:2–4	Mark 11:25
Our Father in heaven,	Father,	
hallowed be your name.	hallowed be your name.	
Your kingdom come.	Your kingdom come.	
Your will be done,		
on earth as it is in heaven.		
Give us this day our daily bread.	Give us each day our daily bread.	
And forgive us our debts,	And forgive us our sins,	
as we also have forgiven our debtors.	for we ourselves forgive everyone indebted to us.	
And do not bring us to the time of trial	And do not bring us to the time of trial.	
but rescue us from the evil one.		
		Whenever you stand praying, forgive, if you have anything against anyone; so that your Father in heaven may also forgive you your trespasses.

While we are considering this prayer here within the context of a discussion of Jesus's ethics, much more could be said from other perspectives. The ethical implications of this prayer are rather unsettling. First, the prayer is directed to *our* rather than *my* father. In Jesus's view, prayer is not only directed to God as a trustworthy parent, but God is parent to "us" and not just to "me." Prayer, as Jesus taught it, is not a selfish act, but an act of solidarity with those around.

To illustrate: "give *us* our daily bread!" is a request to give bread enough for the day, evoking in every Jew memories of the years in the wilderness, where the people received manna, also called "bread from heaven" (e.g., Exodus 16). At the end of each day it needed to be shared because nothing survived to the next day. Might Jesus be asking his followers to pray for bread with just such an assumption in mind? Prayer becomes then a prelude to an ethical act, because it is always spoken within the context of sharing of one's plenty in face of others' scarcity.

Second, after an expression of respect and awe ("your name be holy!") comes the request that God's kingdom come—in effect that God's reign be established. This is, of course, shorthand in the extreme. This prayer is for justice, healing, liberation, and wholeness in relationships among human beings and their relationship to God (see chapter 6 above). But it is also very much an eschatological prayer. It cries out to God to establish the kingdom in full. It is the request made by the kinds of folk we meet in the Beatitudes, who hunger and thirst for justice, but who then express with their lives already now what that kingdom will bring in fullness. Such folks cannot wait to see God's reign of "new creation," as they liked to say in Paul's churches, come in fullness. But, this request that the kingdom come is not a request to be freed from this earth and to be removed to heaven: "Your will be done on *earth*!" Everything Jesus taught about how much the kingdom will change when it comes makes this request nothing less than a plea for a revolution in the affairs of humanity.

Perhaps the most unsettling ethical implication in this prayer is the plea that God treat those who are praying the way they treat others: "Forgive us as we forgive" or, as Matthew has it, "as we have forgiven." One might have expected something like: "Teach us to forgive as you have forgiven us." Instead, Jesus tells his disciples to obligate God to treat them in the way they themselves behave toward those who injure them. This is either the height of brazenness or an ingenious way Jesus has of alerting us to the importance of forgiveness. It also once again speaks to this issue of integrity. You cannot ask God to forgive unless you yourself are prepared to forgive—more strongly, unless you have *already* forgiven!

Close reading of the prayer shows us that in Luke the plea is "forgive us our *sins*," whereas in Matthew the term is *debts*. Perhaps they are interchangeable, since sins become debts that offenders "owe" God or the person they have wronged, as Luke's version implies: "As we forgive everyone *indebted* to us."

As true as such a reading is, is it also possible that the debts are real, that is, monetary? Behind this emphasis on forgiveness of debts may well lie the Old Testament notion of the Jubilee (Leviticus 25). During the Jubilee year—which was to happen every fifty years—debts were to be forgiven, slaves were to be given their freedom, even the land was to be allowed to catch its breath. Isaiah 61:1–4 catches well this vision of a jubilary renewal of the world. Jesus quotes this text in his first sermon in the synagogue in Nazareth, as we read in Luke 4:18, echoed also in Matthew 11:4–6. A few scholars go so far as to suggest that Jesus was announcing the year of Jubilee, that he actually expected the kingdom of God to find expression in people forgiving debts, releasing slaves, and allowing the land to lie fallow. One need not be persuaded that 28 CE (or whatever the year might have been when Jesus was active in Palestine) was the year of Jubilee to recognize how concretely Jesus expects his followers to live in a jubilary fashion. The recent discussion about forgiving the crippling debt load of the world's poorest nations, expressed in the campaign called "Jubilee 2000," is a force-ful contemporary illustration of the relevance of Jesus's teaching on debt forgiveness as required by the kingdom of God. Forgiveness of debts is a way of giving people, families, and nations a chance to start afresh. Such forgiveness is an integral part of the fabric of a society being renewed; it is part of the socially concrete way in which the kingdom of God is making its presence felt; that is why it is gospel—"good news" for the *poor*. That is part of why Jesus stresses forgiveness so much. And what is true of money is no less true of any other form of incurred indebtedness.

EARTHLY TREASURE

The interpretation of the Lord's Prayer given above puts in perspective the saying about not storing up treasures (Matt. 6:19–21, 24; Luke 12:33–34; 16:13). Matthew understands Jesus to suggest that people ought to look to stuff that lasts and not to transient goods. This should not be mistaken for downplaying the importance of material existence; everything about Jesus's way of behaving points very much in the direction of addressing *real* pov-erty and *real* illness. In an admittedly provocative way Jesus is saying that true treasure is not found in the accumulation of wealth; it is heaped up in responding to human need.

At the same time, if this is done with integrity, with love for God and neighbor, then it will not be done for the sake of a reward, as an investment. Once again, the parable in Matthew 25 is relevant, where the sheep are as surprised as the goats are when informed of the significance of what they done or not done. This kind of righteousness or justice (see 5:20; 6:1) requires singleness of heart (6:21), a single-hearted devotion to God's reign: "You cannot be a slave to two masters. You cannot serve both God and Money" (6:24, my paraphrase). (Luke 16 places this saying in immediate proximity to the parable of the shrewd manager; see chapter 9 above.)

Both Matthew and Luke see this principle as central to a life that is open to the kingdom of God. In Matthew 6:25–34 Jesus calls for a mode of living that is released from anxiety about material goods and totally devoted to the justice of the kingdom (see chapter 9 above). True sons and daughters of God are free of greed and at the same time consumed with passion and hunger to see justice done for those who are poor. This is not antimaterialism; this is a very different vision of *why* one is involved with material issues.

ADVICE FOR THOSE WHO LIVE THE JUSTICE OF THE KINGDOM

Assurance of God's Care

Jesus does not simply put these stringent demands before his followers as injunctions to be obeyed. Accompanying them are assurances that God will take care of them (Matt. 6:25–34), as pointed out earlier in connection with nonresistance. The summons to "seek first the kingdom of God and its justice" in 6:33 (my translation) is *preceded* by assurances that the God who cares for the birds and the flowers will—just like an attentive parent—care for those who seek to live out the kingdom. This assurance is *followed* by an equally reassuring phrase: "And all these things will be given to you as well."

This is a very radical ethic. It is also radical theology, even as its roots lie in the earliest experiences of Israel. To relinquish one's anxieties about material things and to give oneself wholly to the justice of the reign of God presuppose a God who pays meticulous attention to the welfare of God's sons and daughters. That is why Jesus calls God "father"—*Abba*, and also why he invites his followers to call God *Abba*. It explains why Jesus stresses God as one who answers prayer: "If you, then, who are evil, know how to give good gifts to your children, how much more will your Father in heaven give good gifts to those who ask him!" (7:11).

Warning against Judging

There is very special vulnerability to which all are prone who give themselves wholeheartedly to living an ethical life: judging others around you who fall short of what you yourself are striving to live up to (Matt. 7:1–5 || Luke 6:37–42). We might call it the occupational hazard of striving for holiness.

We are familiar with Jesus's harsh words for Pharisees on this score: his charge of hypocrisy has stuck. Hypocrisy, judgmentalism, and legalism have become virtual synonyms in many religious and nonreligious circles. The Pharisees should not be judged as being different from anyone else who makes righteousness a prime objective in their everyday existence (see chapter 4 above). Without doubt, Jesus would today have harsh words for those who claim to be his followers who in their commitment to goodness and justice have fallen prey to judgmentalism. Jesus captures this with a very clever parabolic picture of having a plank in one's own eye as one seeks to remove the sliver from the eye of the other (7:3). As little as Jesus has patience with hypocrisy and judgmentalism, he has even less for not putting heart and soul into being righteous, as stressed unambiguously in 5:20. It is just that righteousness is best achieved when it is not itself the object of one's energies. Better to love, which is to say, better to care about God and neighbor than one's own justice or righteousness. Ironically, that is what it means to be righteous (as seen in the surprise of the righteous in Jesus's parable of the sheep and goats in Matt. 25). That is, incidentally, how the plank is removed from one's own eyes.

Warning to Choose the Road Less Traveled

In contemporary culture, being nonjudgmental often goes hand in hand with a kind of ethical relativism, a hands-off policy of tolerance. Whatever the social value of such tolerance in a pluralistic society, this is entirely foreign to Jesus's mentality, as it was to his contemporaries. What is right is clear: rightness and righteousness are not abstractions; they are defined by what is consistent with the will of God (Matt. 7:13–23). As we saw in the antitheses, Jesus not only does not qualify that in any way, he intensifies that point.

The manner in which Matthew has constructed the Sermon, specifically in the way he has Jesus conclude it, expresses this clearly. Matthew chooses several striking parabolic word pictures from the tradition of Jesus's teaching to illustrate the choice facing the followers or students of Jesus, in a way highly reminiscent of Deuteronomy:

> I call heaven and earth to witness against you today that I have set before you life and death, blessings and curses. Choose life so that you and your descendants may live, loving the LORD your God, obeying him, and holding fast to him; for that means life to you and length of days. (Deut. 30:19–20)

In Matthew's Sermon on the Mount the importance of committing oneself to the attitudes and practices of the kingdom of God comes to expression in the time-tested metaphor of the "two ways." The choice between good and evil, reward and punishment, going with the majority or the minority, choosing life or death, is depicted with the images of two ways, two roads, two gates or doors (e.g., Deut. 30:15–20; Psalm 1; Prov. 4:10–19). Familiar from biblical literature too is the metaphor of good and bad fruit. Jesus here relates it to true and false prophets. But no one in the first century would have had any doubts that in this instance "fruit" relates to what kind of behavior a life exhibits, what kinds of consequences such behavior elicits. Interestingly, Paul the apostle uses this image in a way that brings it very close to the two-ways metaphor. In his letter to the Galatians Paul speaks of "the works of the flesh," among them fornication, idolatry, and enmity, and then pits them against "the fruit of the Spirit"—love, joy, peace, patience, generosity (Gal. 5:13–26). Paul captures well the agenda underlying this part of the Sermon on the Mount.

The seriousness of the choice implied in these images comes to expression in the motif of judgment in Matthew 7:21–23. Once again we are reminded of the parable of the sheep and goats. Only this time Jesus uses another parable: two men who build houses, one on sand, the other on rock. "Building on rock," constructing a life that will withstand the onslaughts of life and especially scrutiny by the great judge, is done by heeding the words of Jesus. "Heeding" means "hearing" and "doing" (7:24).

Conclusion

As the gospels narrate the teaching and activity of Jesus, they portray him as exemplifying the peculiar righteousness or justice of the kingdom, one that expresses radical hospitality to sinners and enemies in imitation of a merciful and loving creator; one that takes with deadly seriousness the demands that hunger for justice places on life's choices. The Jesus who sits down and has lunch with tax collectors and prostitutes is the same Jesus who preaches the justice and holiness of the Sermon on the Mount and who asks of his followers that they take up *their own* cross. Conversely, the Jesus who asks people not to diminish in any way the demands of Torah is the same Jesus who has lunch with the tax collectors and sinners. That astonishing, even baffling, fusion of holiness and hospitality marks Jesus's life and his teaching. The justice of the kingdom of God is marked precisely by that same fusion of dogged adherence to the will of God as expressed in Torah and equally persistent practice of a self-giving and sacrificial love, a love that gives its own life for the sake of those who are not yet part of God's reconciled community of daughters and sons. The ethic of the Sermon on the Mount is remarkable in being at the same time daunting in its demands and thrilling in its generosity.

> **Key Terms and Concepts**
>
> antitheses
> Beatitudes
> interim ethic
> Sermon on the Mount
> Sermon on the Plain
> talion

For Further Reading

Betz, Hans Dieter. *The Sermon on the Mount: A Commentary on the Sermon on the Mount, Including the Sermon on the Plain (Matthew 5:3–7:27 and Luke 6:20–49)*. Hermeneia. Minneapolis: Fortress, 1995.

Hays, Richard B. *The Moral Vision of the New Testament: Community, Cross, New Creation: A Contemporary Introduction to New Testament Ethics*. New York: HarperCollins, 1996.

Klassen, William. *Love of Enemies: The Way to Peace*. Overtures to Biblical Theology 15. Philadelphia: Fortress, 1984.

Perkins, Pheme. *Love Commands in the New Testament*. Ramsey, NJ: Paulist, 1982.

Swartley, Willard M. *Covenant of Peace: The Missing Peace in New Testament Theology and Ethics* (Grand Rapids: Eerdmans, 2006).

Wink, Walter. *Engaging the Powers: Discernment and Resistance in a World of Domination*. Minneapolis: Fortress, 1992 (esp. pp. 175–277).

Yoder, John H. *The Politics of Jesus*. 2nd ed. Grand Rapids: Eerdmans, 1994.

11

Death of Jesus

T HE SPACE THAT all four evangelists allot to the death of Jesus and surrounding circumstances rightly leads us to draw the conclusion that we have arrived at the apex of the story of Jesus. His death has been of such great importance in the history and belief system of Christianity that it can easily overwhelm the rest of the story of Jesus. Previous chapters of this book have illustrated amply that there is so much more to Jesus than that he died. At the same time, his death has enormous significance, not least in the eyes of New Testament writers.

In the first part of this chapter we will explore the questions as to *why and by whom* Jesus was killed. We will do so by following the narrative and drawing conclusions that will necessarily remain tentative. In the second part we will explore the meaning and significance of Jesus's death as perceived by his followers. In short, we will explore how a miscarriage of justice, the death of an innocent man, the potentially catastrophic end to the dreams of his followers, could have become a central element of the Christian religion.

Sources

We are largely dependent on the four evangelists for information on Jesus's death. They, in turn, appear to draw on widely shared traditions, which we see reflected, for example, in Paul's traditions of Jesus's last meal with his followers prior to his death (1 Cor. 11:23–26). Comparing the four gospel accounts shows that Matthew and Luke seem to draw heavily on Mark and that John is dependent on other, if very similar, traditions.

Similarities

The gospel writers agree for the most part on the main elements of the story:

- All use biblical citations or allusions liberally in how they narrate the death of Jesus. In fact, many of the elements of the Passion Narrative appear to have strong echoes of earlier biblical passages, much as in the case of the infancy narratives in Matthew and Luke. What is different from the birth narratives, however, is that the Passion Narrative exists in all *four* gospels, not only in Matthew and Luke.
- All four evangelists show Jesus very much aware that his days were numbered and that he was about to be put to death.
- The evangelists all make a connection between Passover and Jesus's last meal with his followers.
- All agree that Jesus was brought before the Roman governor Pontius Pilate by Jewish authorities.
- All writers agree that Jesus was crucified as a purported "king of the Jews," that he was executed on a cross in full view of the populace, a form of state terror the Romans employed against political troublemakers.
- The sources also agree that Jesus was put to death the day before the Sabbath.

Differences

There are some significant differences in the accounts of the evangelists, some dealing with sequence and chronology and some being quite distinct elements in how the evangelists narrate the death of Jesus. The biggest differences are once again found between the Synoptic Gospels and John:

- Whereas the evangelists all agree that Jesus ate a very solemn meal with his intimate circle of followers on the Thursday evening before he was executed, they appear to disagree on whether this was a Passover meal. Matthew and Luke agree with Mark that Jesus celebrated the Passover meal with his disciples (Mark 14:12–17 and Synoptic parallels). John, on the other hand, states clearly that his meal took place "before the festival of the Passover" (John 13:1). Further, John identifies the day of Jesus's crucifixion as "the day of Preparation for the Passover"

(John 19:14), that is, the day *before* the Passover, implying that in that particular year the Passover fell on the Sabbath.

- The Synoptic Gospels specifically identify the Last Supper as a Passover meal, inviting reflection on the relationship of Jesus's impending death and the slaughter of lambs in commemoration of liberation. John, in contrast, places Jesus's death and not his last meal at the time of the slaughter of lambs, connecting Jesus's death and Passover in that way. While both traditions bring Jesus's meal into some connection with Passover, the temporal discrepancies are difficult to harmonize.

- Traditions regarding the supper itself also differ. The words Jesus speaks over cup and bread in Matthew and Mark diverge somewhat from Luke's (Luke agrees more closely with the tradition Paul inherited; 1 Cor. 11:23–26). John, rather surprisingly, records no such tradition at all. The only "eucharistic" words in John are found in connection with the feeding of the multitudes (John 6:22–59). In John's Gospel the last meal provides the occasion for a long speech by Jesus not recounted by the Synoptic writers, often referred to as the Farewell Discourse (John 13–17). John narrates the central action of Jesus at the meal not as breaking bread and blessing the cup but as his washing of the disciples' feet, again entirely absent in the Synoptic Gospels.

- There are some differences regarding the proceedings against Jesus. Whereas all the gospels have Jesus brought first before the Jewish authorities and then before Pilate, John adds an appearance of Jesus before Annas prior to his being brought before Caiaphas. Luke adds an episode in which Pilate sends Jesus to Herod, who at that time is presumably visiting the city from Galilee.

- Jesus's "words on the cross" differ significantly from one gospel to the other, with the exception that Matthew appears to have taken over Mark's tradition.

To summarize, with all their differences the gospels agree on the essential aspects of the passion to a very significant degree. Was there a common source, edited variously by the evangelists? Was there an earlier written Passion Narrative? These questions highlight the high degree of agreement in the various layers of the Christian tradition as to how Jesus died, even as the exact nature of this complex of tradition continues to perplex scholars.

Passion Narrative(s)

Perhaps we should not speak of *the* narrative of Jesus's passion and death, since several items appear in only one or two gospels. Perhaps it would be better to speak of "elements" of a narrative tradition. Just as in the case of the birth narratives, we should be careful about boiling the various traditions into one soup, so to speak. Aware of the problem of harmonization, we will nevertheless identify the most important elements in the Passion Narrative(s).

Raising of Lazarus and the Ensuing Controversy

Before going on to what many Jesus scholars consider the actual trigger that brought about the death of Jesus, namely, Jesus's disruptive demonstration in the temple, we must discuss the distinctness of John's Gospel. The author of the Fourth Gospel places the temple demonstration at the beginning of his gospel, immediately after the wedding at Cana (John 2:13–22). In John's Gospel the trigger that leads to Jesus's execution is the raising of Jesus's friend Lazarus from the dead (John 11). This "sign," as John calls it, leads directly to the firm resolve on the part of the authorities to kill Jesus (11:53). According to John they are afraid of what the Romans will do if all the people believe in Jesus because of the "signs" he performs (11:47–48).

Connecting the sign of a raising from the dead with fear of Roman imperial violence points to Jesus's contemporaries having identified his activities, including reports of such an episode, with "enacting the kingdom of God" in a way that would, in our terminology, have political implications troubling to the imperial authorities. "Better that one man die for the nation," the Jewish leaders reason, "than that the whole nation should perish"—an oft-employed calculation throughout history, which, given the meaning accorded Jesus's death by his followers, becomes in John's way of telling the story a prophetic utterance with a very different spin (11:49–52).

Triumphal Entry into Jerusalem

All four gospels tell of a highly symbolic entry of Jesus into Jerusalem (Matt. 21:1–11 || Mark 11:1–10 || Luke 19:28–38 || John 12:12–18). He rides into Jerusalem on a young donkey, accompanied by enthusiastic crowds euphorically proclaiming Jesus to be the king of Israel—the Messiah. A biblically informed Jew would have understood immediately what this signifies, given the words of the prophet Zechariah:

> Rejoice greatly, O daughter Zion!
>   Shout aloud, O daughter Jerusalem!
> Lo, your *king* comes to you;
>   triumphant and victorious is he,
> humble and riding on a *donkey*,
>   on a colt, the foal of a donkey. (Zech. 9:9, emphasis added)

Has the whole episode of Jesus's entry into Jerusalem been constructed with Zechariah's prophecy in mind, in order to illustrate that Jesus was in fact the promised peaceful Messiah? Despite the evident difficulties such data present the historian, there is no reason to think Jesus could not have deliberately wanted to signal to his followers his mission as a peaceable messiah. People often act in deliberately suggestive ways that presuppose knowledge of symbolism. As often in our study, we should be wary of claiming too much, either thinking we can prove this event took place with the tools of the historian or, just as importantly, believing that we can dismiss it as fiction just because it is recounted with Zechariah 9 in mind.

Parenthetically, dependency on the specific wording of the prophecy from Zechariah is particularly obvious in that in Matthew Jesus rides into Jerusalem on both a donkey and on its colt. While puzzling, it is unlikely that Matthew intended for us to think of Jesus awkwardly riding on two animals at once. It is clear, however, that the presence of two animals in Matthew derives from his literal use of the Greek translation of Zechariah 9. Hebrew writers often employed parallelism, in which the second phrase reiterates the first with slightly different wording, sometimes giving greater precision. So, "riding on a donkey" is reiterated with "on the foal of a donkey," clarifying that the donkey was young (a point picked up clearly by the other three evangelists). The Greek translation of the Hebrew, the Septuagint, obscures the parallelism by tying the phrases together with the word *and*. Matthew evidently has shaped the specifics of his version of the story on the basis of the Greek translation of Zechariah 9, and so he has Jesus asking his disciples to find a donkey and a foal and bring "them" to him (Matt. 21:2).

Once again we are in the presence of an event that has been heavily shaped by allusion to Scripture. The point of this story is to announce Jesus's arrival in Jerusalem as that of a king, a king who comes in peace, a king who is ironically the exact opposite of a military conqueror. The story also intensifies another level of irony: while Jesus the Messiah is here greeted enthusiastically, the reader already knows that this enthusiasm will bring great trouble as well.

Demonstration at the Temple

Many scholars give priority to the Synoptic evangelists in considering the actual precipitating event leading to Jesus's death to have been his so-called cleansing of the temple (Matt. 21:12–17 || Mark 11:11, 15–19 || Luke 19:45–48 || John 2:13–22). I prefer to call it the "demonstration" at the temple, for reasons that will become clear. The incident is recounted in all four gospels (as we have seen, John discusses it at the very beginning of his account in 2:13–22; see chapter 10 above).

What exactly took place? As always, historians will wish for more information than we have. Regardless of motivation and significance, one thing seems certain: Jesus created a ruckus in the temple. He and his followers went into the temple, and, with the zeal and rage of an ancient prophet, Jesus overturned the tables of the moneychangers and chased the animals out of the temple. Thousands of pilgrims would have been in the city for the Passover festival. A great deal of activity would have been taking place on the temple grounds, so Jesus's action would likely have had major crowd-control implications. Temple authorities would naturally have been extremely nervous, and the Romans would have been wary in the extreme of any signs of trouble. Concern for the safety of the thousands of pilgrims would have been enough for the Jewish authorities to want to avoid a confrontation with the Roman troops.

Such was the tinderbox into which Jesus threw the match of his prophetic protest or demonstration. Was this yet another of his enactments of the kingdom? What exactly was Jesus saying by overturning the tables of the moneychangers and driving livestock out of the temple precincts? Several suggestions have been offered.

Symbolic Destruction of the Temple

More than one scholar refers to this as Jesus's "symbolic destruction of the temple." Jesus is seen as attempting to show that the temple has no place in the kingdom of God. The kingdom is here *now*; there is no longer a need for a brokered relationship between God and humanity. Jesus is symbolically ending the system that the temple represented.

Other explanations stress eschatology more strongly than brokerage. To state it baldly, the temple will no longer be needed when the kingdom comes, and so with his action Jesus is symbolically anticipating the new messianic age.

Relatedly, some think that in Jesus's view the temple would not so much be done away with as radically reconceived when the kingdom of God comes in full. In John's account Jesus identifies himself as the real temple (2:21). In a related fashion, the Apostle Paul could speak of a "temple" made up of the people of God, a people that is at the same time also the "body" of Christ (1 Cor. 3:16–17; see also 12:12–26 and Eph. 2:19–22).

One should be cautious with lines of analysis that pit Jesus against the temple. We will want, for example, to be careful not to demonize the temple by treating it as a symbol of everything that had gone wrong in Judaism. After all, the gospel writers depict Jesus as teaching "day after day . . . in the temple" (e.g., Mark 14:49). Further, preserved in as late a writing as the Acts of the Apostles is a remarkable characterization of the earliest followers of

Jesus as being "day by day . . . together in the temple" (2:46). However critical Jesus's attitude may have been toward what was going on in the temple, and however much it appears that some of his adherents in later years were viewed as deeply hostile to the temple (see Stephen's martyrdom in Acts 6–7), it did not translate into wholesale hostility toward the temple on the part of his followers, even after Jesus's death. This leads us to another line of interpretation, in which Jesus is not pitted so much against the temple per se, but against its abuses.

Cleansing of the Temple

Did Jesus wish less to destroy the temple than to cleanse or reform it? There were other Jews who shared with him a high degree of disquiet over what had happened to the temple, whether that means the degree of commercialism associated with it or the degree of moral and spiritual cynicism many of them saw in the leadership in charge of the temple. The covenanters at the Dead Sea (Qumran), for example, were very much opposed to what was going on in Jerusalem and yearned for a new temple.

The virtue of interpreting Jesus's action in this light is that it seems to agree with the way the evangelists themselves portray the event. After Jesus performs his prophetic act of outrage, the Synoptic evangelists all have him recite a combination of phrases from the prophets Isaiah and Jeremiah (Matt. 21:13 || Mark 11:17 || Luke 19:46):

My house [i.e., temple] shall be called a house of prayer for all peoples. (Isa. 56:7)

Has this house, which is called by my name, become a den of robbers in your sight? (Jer. 7:11)

The use of these texts from the prophets suggest outrage over what has happened to the house of God precisely because the temple is God's abode, however symbolically. It needs to be cleansed of the abuses perpetrated within its walls and practices, not only because God lives there, but because it is to be a place of prayer for "all peoples," for "all Gentiles," as it can be translated. The temple is not to be destroyed; it is to be rendered holy again, with doors flung wide open to the nations, Jew and non-Jew alike.

Like the other evangelists, John also has Jesus quoting words of Scripture to explain the vehemence of his actions (John 2:17). Only now it is not one of the prophets but a psalm that expresses the intensity of Jesus's fidelity to the traditions of Israel:

It is zeal for your house that has consumed me;
the insults of those who insult you have fallen on me. (Ps. 69:9)

This text also does not speak of hostility to the temple per se, but is intended to express the white-hot intensity of Jesus's concern for the integrity of the temple as a place of prayer.

Much of this temple demonstration and the motivation behind it will of necessity remain shrouded in mystery. Even if Jesus was not concerned to destroy the temple per se, the sharpness of his words and the vehemence of his actions apparently left him open to the charge that he was hostile to the temple in the extreme. According to Matthew and Mark, one of the charges brought against Jesus at his hearing before the Jewish authorities was that he had claimed that he would destroy the temple of God (Matt. 26:61 || Mark 14:58). So, if we are looking for immediate reasons why the Jewish authorities would have wanted Jesus out of the way, we have found at least one.

Anointing of Jesus by a Woman

In three of the gospels (Matt. 26:6–13 || Mark 14:3–9 || John 12:1–8) the story of the anointing of Jesus is an important part of the opening scenes of the passion. In Luke, interestingly, this tradition is placed early in Jesus's ministry in Galilee, where it serves to illustrate the love that "sinners" have for Jesus who offers them forgiveness (Luke 7:36–50). In Matthew, Mark, and John, however, this anointing is placed in the Passion Narrative and thereby comes to allude to two Jewish practices: anointing of a king, a Messiah, and anointing for burial. In making these twin connections, the gospel writers draw attention to the connection between Jesus's death and his role as Messiah.

In all strands of this tradition the woman's action provokes shock on the part of those present. In Luke, a Pharisee named Simon, Jesus's dinner host, is scandalized by Jesus's letting himself be touched by a woman from the streets (Luke 7:39). In the other gospels, the reaction is one of resentment at the spendthriftiness of the woman who "wastes" precious ointment on Jesus, when the oil could have been sold and the money given to the poor (Matt. 26:8–9 || Mark 14:4–5 || John 12:4–6; John specifies that it was Judas Iscariot who was scandalized). Jesus is remembered as having responded with the famous but too often misinterpreted statement, roughly rendered: "Let her be! She is preparing me for burial! The poor you always have with you." Rather than downplaying concern for the poor, this episode is intended to highlight rather the central importance of Jesus's death in the story the evangelists are narrating.

In John's Gospel the woman who anoints Jesus is identified as Mary, the sister of Martha and Lazarus. Other variations and discrepancies are item-ized below for purposes of comparison:

Gospel	Time	Person	Location	Means	Anointing
Matthew	last week, two days before Passover, outside Jerusalem	a woman	home of Simon the leper, in Bethany	ointment	on head
Mark	last week	a woman	home of Simon the leper, in Bethany	ointment	on head
Luke	early in Jesus's ministry	a woman of the city	home of Simon the Pharisee, in Galilee	tears and ointment	on feet
John	last week, six days before Passover	Mary, sister of Martha and Lazarus	home of Mary, Martha, and Lazarus in Bethany	ointment	on feet

Matthew and Mark recount words of Jesus to the effect that "wherever this good news is proclaimed in the whole world, what she has done will be told in remembrance of her" (Matt. 26:13 || Mark 14:9). The episode is indeed remembered in all four gospels, but, interestingly, not in the same way. It is obvious from the table above that this is one and the same tradition, despite the differences in the telling and the location, perhaps as a result of the telling and retelling "whenever this good news is proclaimed." Even so, the story sensitizes us to an important feature of the whole of the Passion Narrative, namely, the highly symbolic way in which this last week of Jesus is recounted.

Last Supper

Before moving on to the public events related to Jesus's death, we must retreat with Jesus and his disciples to the solemn occasion of their final meal together (Matt. 26:17–29 || Mark 14:12–25 || Luke 22:7–20 || John 13–17).

While scholars debate whether this supper was indeed a Passover celebration or even whether such a meal even took place, most observe correctly that the association with the Passover meal is intended by the evangelists to provide meaning for the account of the Last Supper. N. T. Wright suggests that Jesus deliberately celebrated the meal before the normal time for the Passover meal in order to highlight that he himself was the lamb that was to be slain (*Jesus and the Victory of God*, 555–59). Regardless, the evangelists all agree on the connection between this meal and Passover. At the celebration of a Passover meal Jews slaughtered and ate a lamb. The blood of the lamb, according to the original story in Exodus, served to avert divine judgment for the Israelites. The association of the Last Supper with the Passover meal provides a context in which Jesus's death is not simply a result of a miscarriage of justice but becomes a means of salvation for the people.

It is of course precisely these resonant overtones that lead many to doubt the historicity of the event. But I see little difficulty with Jesus understanding that his actions would bring about his death and symbolically anticipating it in some such fashion, however much the present narrative also bears the signs of the Jesus movement's reflection on his death, of the churches' practice of worship, and of the development of its rituals.

Judas and Peter

Two of the best known of Jesus's disciples figure strongly in the Passion Narrative—Judas and Peter. Both are remarkable figures, one because of his terrible reputation for treachery and betrayal, the other for his role as one of the great "pillars" of the early church (Paul's word in Gal. 2:9), revered in the Roman Catholic tradition as the first pope, the "rock" (Greek *petra*) on whom Christ would build his church. Both come off rather poorly in the story of Jesus's passion.

JUDAS ISCARIOT

Judas Iscariot is one of history's most notorious figures, a byword for evil and treachery and a potent arrow in the quiver of anti-Judaism and anti-Semitism. Judas was hardly a rare name. "Yehudah" was, like countless other Jewish boys, named after the great patriarch of the tribe of Judah (there are several in the New Testament, including the brother of Jesus [Matt. 13:55 || Mark 6:3] and another member of the Twelve [Luke 6:16; Acts 1:13]). "Iscariot" thus serves to distinguish him from the many other Judases. But what Iscariot means is up for grabs, possibly referring to his town of origin or to his belonging to a group of assassins called Sicarii, or possibly serving as a transliteration of a Semitic word for "one handing over."

We have encountered Judas in the present part of the story at the anointing at Bethany, concerned about the waste of fine ointment, only to be called a "thief" by the author of the Fourth Gospel (John 12:4–6). We observe him immediately after the anointing at Bethany going to the religious authorities, offering to "hand over" Jesus to them, to translate very carefully (Matt. 26:14–16 || Mark 14:10–11 || Luke 22:3–6). He is mentioned in all of the accounts as being present at the Last Supper.

Many translations render the Greek *paradidomi* "to betray." That reflects a view of Judas as a symbol of treachery. In recent years it has been suggested that the Greek language is less malignant and should be properly translated "to hand over" or "to deliver" rather than "to betray." William Klassen even suggests that far from wishing to betray Jesus, Judas was doing what he thought was the right thing, "handing over" Jesus to the duly constituted religious authorities in order for him to be tested as to his faithfulness to God (*Judas: Betrayer or Friend of Jesus?*). Perhaps Judas believed he was doing a favor to Jesus, helping him to fulfill his mission. That appears to be the interpretation as well in the recently recovered second-century gnostic

Gospel of Judas, where Jesus asks Judas to hand him over to the authorities so that he can be delivered of his material body.

Judas's motivations have been the subject of a great deal of popular and scholarly speculation—and will remain so. He remains a tantalizing subject for novelists and moviemakers alike. It is important to recognize that in their present form the Passion Narratives allow little access to the personal motivations and thoughts of persons like Judas Iscariot. At the same time, it is abundantly obvious that the evangelists do not have a particularly nuanced or empathetic view of Judas. Both Luke (22:3) and John (13:27) in fact speak of Satan entering Judas at the point of his "handing over" Jesus to the authorities. Thus, even if they do not say "betray" but rather "hand over" (Luke 6:16 is a sole exception, where "traitor" or "betrayer" is the appropriate translation), the effect of Judas's action is to "deliver" Jesus into (not out of!) the hands of those who want to do away with him. The *Gospel of Judas* recognizes this as well, even if that act is seen as precipitating the deliverance of Jesus from his embodied existence. While the evangelists share a negative view of Judas, they also preserve a hint that Judas may not have fully appreciated the consequences of his actions (accounts of his violent end seem to indicate serious second thoughts; Matt. 27:3–10; Acts 1:15–20).

PETER

Peter's denial, on the other hand, predicted by Jesus on the way to the Mount of Olives following the Last Supper, is unambiguously negative. It might well be called a "betrayal" (Matt. 26:30–35 || Mark 14:26–31 || Luke 22:31–34 || John 13:36–38). Three times Peter is given an opportunity to own up to his connection to Jesus, and three times he fails to do so (Matt. 26:69–75 || Mark 14:66–72 || Luke 22:56–62 || John 18:15–18, 25–27).

It is remarkable, given Peter's stature at the time the gospels were written a half century after the events recounted, that his cowardice at the moment of Jesus's trial and death is not in any way camouflaged. Unlike Jesus, Peter and his fellow disciples fail at the moment of Satan's "sifting" (Luke 22:31). The evangelists know full well that Peter is one disciple, unlike Judas Iscariot, with whom readers of the gospels will quite readily wish to identify. What question are the evangelists asking readers to ponder? Might it be that if Peter could not find the courage when it counted to own up to his allegiance to Jesus, will they? Both Peter and Judas represent troubling mirror images for readers of the gospels to ponder.

Gethsemane—Prayerful Struggle and Arrest

After the supper Jesus and his disciples retreat to a garden called Gethsemane (Matt. 26:36–56 || Mark 14:32–52 || Luke 22:39–53 || John 18:1–12).

Jesus takes Peter, James, and John aside and asks them to go with him to pray.

The story of Jesus's intense struggle to accept his coming ordeal and death is well known. We might justifiably view this event as continuing the temptation or testing that began immediately after his baptism (see chapter 7 above). Here in the garden Jesus is pictured as again struggling with the implications of his baptism and his calling. Interestingly, in Mark 10:38 Jesus refers to his coming suffering as "baptism."

Those who believe that Jesus did not think of himself as Messiah or that he did not anticipate his death as part of his mission will view this traditional episode as a theologically motivated after-the-fact construction. While the narrative is again shaped by theological reflection on the part of the evangelists and the sources they rely on, there is no compelling reason to deny Jesus a degree of self-awareness and sense of mission within which he had to struggle intensely with whether he had the courage to go this route. It is entirely understandable in terms of the struggle anyone faces who knows full well that a certain course of action will likely lead to death.

By way of illustration with regard to the question of whether Jesus anticipated his own death, I recall a lecture I was preparing on this very topic and text in 1997. As I typically do when I work, I had the radio on. On this particular day a Canadian Broadcasting Corporation feature commemorated the second anniversary of the death of Ken Saro-Wiwa, the Nigerian poet and playwright who was executed by Nigerian authorities on November 10, 1995. For years he had led the resistance to the military crackdown on his fellow indigenous people, who were protesting the exploitation of their land by oil companies such as Shell and Chevron. As part of the 1997 broadcast, CBC presented a dramatization of Saro-Wiwa's trial, execution, and funeral entitled "On the Death of Ken Saro-Wiwa." What jolted me was not that this play dealt with Saro-Wiwa's resistance, trial, and execution, but that Saro-Wiwa *himself* had written the drama while awaiting his death in prison. The short drama, performed only once on May 31, 1996, in London, anticipates and describes his own coming death. Saro-Wiwa knew exactly why he was going to die; in fact, he was able to predict largely how he would die and what role each of the actors would play in it. He was able to anticipate quite accurately his coming death because he knew—given his actions, given the nature of the authorities, and given the nature of the political and economic interests at stake in the living drama in which he was playing out his protest—what would likely transpire. The way the events transpired may not have been predetermined, but they were anticipated as being certain. Is it out of the question, then, that Jesus too understood the role he himself was playing in a larger drama? Did not Mahatma Gandhi? Or Martin Luther King Jr.? Or Bishop Oscar Romero of El Salvador?

Whether we think of Jesus's last meal with his followers or his praying in Gethsemane, we should most certainly recognize the degree to which these accounts are heavily shaped by later church memory, recollection, worship, ritual, and theology. At the same time, we should resist the temptation to deny that these accounts might well be grounded in a memory of the historical struggle of Jesus in his last days to summon the courage and resolve to complete his mission.

The narration of the episode in the garden of Gethsemane ends with Jesus's arrest, a storied scene in which Judas is given a central role of handing Jesus over with a kiss. It is also the scene in which Jesus explicitly rejects the violence of his followers in their attempt to protect him, culminating in his scolding of Peter with the words Matthew recalls: "Put your sword back into its place; for all who take the sword will perish by the sword" (26:52).

Jesus before the Jewish Authorities

Much ink has been spilled on the historical validity of the gospel accounts of Jesus's hearings before the authorities, including the Sanhedrin, the leading council (Matt. 26:57–68 || Mark 14:53–65 || Luke 22:54–71 || John 18:13–24). The exact descriptions vary between the gospels, and it is difficult to determine what exactly transpired. The evangelists suggest that matters were handled in a rather extraordinary fashion, in the night, out of the glare of public scrutiny. They suggest, moreover, that the Jewish authorities were particularly exercised by Jesus's claims to having a special and unique link to God—"Are you the Son of God?" (e.g., Matt. 26:63 || Luke 22:69)—and by his criticism of the temple, in particular the charge that Jesus had promised to destroy the temple. These were indeed critically important charges. It should not surprise us that the authorities would want to take action.

The objection has been repeatedly raised that the kind of a trial described by the evangelists is not the same as Sanhedrin trials described in the Talmud, the compendium of Jewish legal teaching. That may well be the case. It is also true, however, that the Talmud was put into writing many years *after* the events described in the gospels, and Jewish scholars themselves argue about how accurately the Talmud describes the Sanhedrin's dealings in the first century. But even if the Talmud reflects first-century practice, history is replete with examples in which people act in extralegal fashion, especially when the religious, political, and military stakes are extremely high. Whereas the gospel accounts are heavily affected by later traditions and vary on some details, they agree that Jesus's fate was fundamentally a *miscarriage of justice*. To find elements, then, within the story of Jesus's passion that from a Jewish legal perspective are irregular and anomalous does not discredit the account of the gospel writers. We might even expect to find such anomalies in the story and see them as lending authenticity to the accounts.

Jesus before Pilate

The evangelists all agree that the Jewish authorities subsequently brought Jesus before Pontius Pilate, the Roman imperial authority in Judea (Matt. 27:1–2, 11–26 || Mark 15:1–15 || Luke 23:1–25 || John 18:28–19:16). Why? Here again there is considerable debate. Did Jews have the right to exercise capital punishment? If they did, then why did they not just stone Jesus, in accordance with Jewish law, given that they were convinced he had committed blasphemy? Many scholars believe they did indeed have this authority, as the Talmud suggests. The account of the death of Stephen by stoning, recounted in Acts 7, would lend some support to this. It is thus telling that Jesus was not executed by stoning but rather by crucifixion. It was Pilate who ordered Jesus's execution because he spelled trouble for the imperial authorities—hence the prominence of the issue of Jesus's being a "king of the Jews," that is, a challenger to Roman authority, an insurrectionist, or an insurgent. In the view of these scholars, crucifixion hints at the real reasons for Jesus's death.

Others, no less concerned about the murderous legacy of blaming "the Jews" for the death of Jesus, argue differently. They believe that Rome considered capital punishment as coming under its imperial domain, even if some exceptions seem to have occurred (again, the stoning of Stephen in Acts 7 is an illustration). The Talmud, put into writing several centuries after these events, may in this instance not reflect the reality of early-first-century Roman Palestine. Pilate would have had the sole authority to order Jesus's execution. If the Jewish authorities had simply accused Jesus before Pilate as a false prophet leading Jews astray religiously, this would not have convinced Pilate to approve the execution. What would matter to Pilate is if Jesus were presented to him as potential political trouble. This is indeed how the evangelists narrate the story. The appellation "King of the Jews," nailed to the cross as the reason for his execution, speaks volumes.

We cannot determine the exact degree to which the story as we find it in the gospels is shaped by historical reminiscence or by attempts to depict characters and events in a way that suits the agenda of the writers. What is clear is that no one comes off well in the Passion Narratives: Jewish leaders nervously plot against Jesus, Jesus's followers fearfully abandon him, and Romans callously torture and kill him. What is also clear is that, whatever the levels of collusion by Jerusalem authorities, Jesus was *crucified*, that is, he was to put death by the Romans for insurrection, accused of claiming to be a king. Jesus was put to death by means of state terror, the way terrorists would have been put to death, sometimes by tens, sometimes by hundreds.

Jesus Executed and Buried

SCENE

The depiction of Jesus's death is bleak. Among Jesus's followers it is especially the women who have followed him from Galilee who are present, even if from afar, to witness his execution (Matt. 27:55–56 || Mark 15:40–41 || Luke 23:49 [Luke mentions others with the collective "all his acquaintances"]). John, uniquely, places the women, specifically his mother Mary, Mary Magdalene, another Mary, and the Beloved Disciple at the foot of the cross (John 19:25–27). Apparently most of the men who have been part of his inner circle have abandoned him. They have either participated in his arrest (Judas) or denied all connection with him (Peter) or gone into hiding (Matt. 26:56 || Mark 14:50–52), frightened, disappointed, and no doubt shell-shocked by the turn of events, despite, as the evangelists insist, Jesus's repeated warnings that this would happen.

MODE OF CRUCIFIXION

Jesus dies the tortuous death of crucifixion as an insurrectionist, as one who claimed to be the true ruler of his Jewish people. He dies outside the city gate, on the city dump called *Golgotha*—the Place of the Skull—where the Romans no doubt crucified other hapless revolutionaries (Matt. 27:33 || Mark 15:22 || Luke 23:33 || John 19:17). In countless paintings the superscription "INRI" can be seen attached to the cross above Jesus's bowed and bloody head. INRI is simply the acronym of the Latin version of the phrase *Jesus of Nazareth, King of the Jews* (Matt. 27:37 || Mark 15:26 || Luke 23:38 || John 19:19).

Death by crucifixion was execution by prolonged torture, in which death always came much too late. Often people would be hung on crosses, sometimes nailed to them, sometimes impaled, at times through their genitals, left to die in full view of callous, more often terrorized, crowds. And then the wild scavenger animals would eat the corpses, oftentimes feeding on those almost dead. Today crosses adorn countless buildings or, as jewelry, countless ears and necks. In Jesus's day it could not have occurred to people to see the cross as anything but a horrifying symbol of state terror.

WORDS OF DERISION AT THE CROSS

The details in the gospel narratives of Jesus's death owe much to scriptural traditions. That is particularly striking in the way the crowds surrounding the cross are described. Whereas Jesus's followers, most notably the women who had come with him from Galilee, stand far off, there are those who taunt him:

Those who passed by derided him, shaking their heads and saying, "Aha! You who would destroy the temple and build it in three days, save yourself, and come down from the cross!" In the same way the chief priests, along with the scribes, were also mocking him among themselves and saying, "He saved others; he cannot save himself. Let the Messiah, the King of Israel, come down from the cross now, so that we may see and believe." (Mark 15:29–32; see also Matt. 27:40–43)

And the people stood by, watching; but the leaders scoffed at him, saying, "He saved others; let him save himself if he is the Messiah of God, his chosen one!" (Luke 23:35)

These taunts are comparable to passages in the Wisdom of Solomon and the book of Psalms:

> He calls the last end of the righteous happy,
> and boasts that God is his father.
> Let us see if his words are true,
> and let us test what will happen at the end of his life;
> for if the righteous man is God's child, he will help him,
> and will deliver him from the hand of his adversaries.
> Let us test him with insult and torture,
> so that we may find out how gentle he is,
> and make trial of his forbearance.
> Let us condemn him to a shameful death,
> for, according to what he says, he will be protected. (Wisdom of
>   Solomon 2:16–20)

> All who see me mock at me;
>   they make mouths at me, they shake their heads;
> "Commit your cause to the LORD; let him deliver—
>   let him rescue the one in whom he delights!" (Ps. 22:7–8)

And all the while soldiers are mocking Jesus, callously casting lots to see who will get his clothing (Matt. 27:35 || Mark 15:24 || Luke 23:34 || John 19:23–24). That too is an allusion to Scripture:

> They divide my clothes among themselves,
>   and for my clothing they cast lots. (Ps. 22:18)

And when Jesus cries out in thirst, a soldier runs to give him some vinegar to drink (John 19:28–29 and Synoptic parallels), also linked to the Old Testament:

> They gave me poison for food,
>   and for my thirst they gave me vinegar to drink. (Ps. 69:21)

It is evident that the account of Jesus's death has been recalled in the vivid images and language of Scripture, in particular the paradigmatic tradition of the torture and death of a just and faithful person. The early witnesses, especially the evangelists, are intent on making sure we do not miss the significance of what transpired. As stated repeatedly, this is not a dispassionate account, but a narrative that is as scripturally and theologically resonant as possible. The historian will thus naturally have difficulty getting at the raw data. We should be wary at the same time of drawing the conclusion that the events of the passion are created whole from the Scriptures that are employed in shaping the narrative. To willingly acknowledge the historian's difficulties in controlling the evidence is one thing; to know with enough certainty to dismiss the accounts as fiction is quite another.

Jesus's Last Words on the Cross

Jesus's last words on the cross in his final hours are recounted variously in the gospels. They have been melded in the tradition of the church, rehearsed in liturgy, and set to music. It is worth sorting them out briefly.

First is Jesus's conversation with the thieves (we should likely think of these less as criminals than as guerilla fighters) crucified along with him. Whereas Matthew and Mark depict both as hostile to Jesus, Luke recounts Jesus promising paradise to the one who appears to recognize Jesus as Messiah (Luke 23:39–43):

> Truly I tell you, today you will be with me in Paradise. (Luke 23:43)

Mark and Matthew (who depends on Mark) record only a few profoundly chilling words of Jesus, quoted first in Aramaic, and then in Greek:

> "Eloi, Eloi, lema sabachthani?" which means, "My God, my God, why have you forsaken me?" (Mark 15:34 || Matt. 27:46)

As bitter as these words are, as unforgettably vivid in expressing unfathomable anguish, they are found verbatim in Psalm 22:1, a psalm mentioned above as a source of imagery and language for this account.

Luke's account is less bleak. He includes Jesus's promise of paradise to the one being crucified with him, and he does *not* record the anguished words from Psalm 22:1. Instead we hear Jesus express a plea that God might forgive his tormentors:

> Then Jesus said, "Father, forgive them; for they do not know what they are doing." (Luke 23:34)

In Luke, Jesus ends his life by crying out in a loud and confident voice:

Father, into your hands I commend my spirit. (Luke 23:46)

John's account is different yet. Jesus speaks words not to those who are being crucified with him, but to his mother and his Beloved Disciple, commending them to each other as mother and son (19:26–27). Jesus's very last words are as simple as they are eloquent: "It is finished!" or "It is accomplished!" The author of the Fourth Gospel signals to us not only that Jesus's ministry has been brought to completion, but that his suffering and death are constituent elements in that task.

ROMAN CENTURION'S RECOGNITION

The narration of Jesus's death in the Synoptic Gospels concludes with a brief but significant item. The earth-shattering and reality-transforming significance of the death of Jesus is marked in the Synoptic Gospels with a report of a darkening sky and the tearing of the curtain in the temple at the moment of his passing (Mark 15:33–38; Luke 23:44–46). Matthew adds that an earthquake took place, in which the tombs of the "the saints" were opened, anticipating symbolically the resurrection to come (Matt. 27:45–53). It is left to a Roman officer to find the words to capture the full weight of the event:

Now when the centurion, who stood facing him, saw that in this way he breathed his last, he said, "Truly this man was God's Son!" (Mark 15:39; similarly Matt. 27:54)

When the centurion saw what had taken place, he praised God and said, "Certainly this man was innocent." (Luke 23:47)

This text is important for Christology (see chapter 13 below). Mark, Matthew, and Luke are evidently relaying the same saying, albeit it in slightly different versions. Where Mark (and, in dependency on him, Matthew) has "God's Son," Luke has "innocent." That is how the NRSV renders the texts. The translation obscures how close these variations are to each other. Luke's should, in my view, be translated more accurately: "This man was a just or righteous one." Mark's should be translated more carefully "a son of God." Wisdom of Solomon 2:16–20 (quoted above) shows that being a "righteous one" is synonymous with being "a son of God." Quite understandably, by the time the evangelists wrote their gospels, Jesus had long been venerated as *the* Righteous One and especially as *the* Son of God. Even so, to translate carefully lets us observe from where this language has emerged and what meaning it carries.

Buried by Secret Disciples

The evangelists state that Jesus is buried by Joseph of Arimathea, a member of the Sanhedrin (Mark 15:43 || Luke 23:50–51), a "secret disciple" of Jesus, according to John (19:38). Joseph buries Jesus in a newly dug tomb, after receiving permission from Pilate (Mark 15:45; John 19:38). In the Fourth Gospel a man named Nicodemus, also a "leader" and "teacher of Israel" (John 3:1, 10), perhaps a member of the Sanhedrin, suspected also of being a secret follower of Jesus (7:50–51), joins Joseph in burying Jesus. Strange, is it not? Two high-ranking members of the Jewish leadership, men who have been secret supporters of Jesus throughout his ministry, now express their loyalty to Jesus by recovering his body, taking it down off the cross, preparing it for burial, and laying it in a newly hewn out tomb. Their presence in the narrative makes it difficult to resist the urge to wonder what would have been going through the minds of such leaders during these terrible days. Their presence, as that of the Roman centurion earlier, is a timely warning not to stereotype any of the groups within the narrative. Reality is always messy, and despite the evident stylization of the gospel narratives, that messiness is not obscured.

In the Synoptic Gospels the curtain goes down on this act in the drama with the women following the body of Jesus to where it is laid in a newly hewn tomb.

The overall picture the evangelists paint is bleak and unspeakably sad: Jesus is executed between two thieves; the Twelve are apparently in hiding or dead (Judas); women who had followed Jesus from Galilee are present but watch from a (safe?) distance; up close, according to John are only the three Marys (Jesus's mother, the wife of Clopas, and Magdalene) and the Beloved Disciple; and Jesus is buried by two highly placed disciples who apparently did not during Jesus's lifetime find it possible to live out their allegiance to him publicly. This would hardly seem to be the raw material for a significant moment in the history of the world. What could possibly make this Friday a "good" Friday? Before attempting to answer that question, we must first return briefly to the question, "Who killed Jesus?"

Who Did It and Why?

Given the narratives the evangelists provide us of Jesus's passion, and given what we might be able to surmise based on what we know of the time, can we now answer the question as to who killed Jesus and why? Let me summarize what I have already suggested above.

Jews

First, did the Jews do it? This is an important question, because in the history of the Jews since the time of Jesus, there is probably no more dangerous a question than this. Accusing the Jewish people as a whole of killing Jesus, and thus of deicide ("killing God"), has contributed to countless pogroms and finally to the horror of the Holocaust. Much hinges, then, on how this question is answered. Humility, always fitting, is especially so here.

We should not be surprised that since the Holocaust many scholars, both Jewish and non-Jewish, have attempted to set the record straight. As I indicate above, that Jesus was crucified rather than stoned is seen by many as placing the blame squarely on the Romans. They attribute the highly negative accounts of the Jewish role in Jesus's death to the growing mutual hostility between an early Christianity and the Judaism from which it was separating—or more accurately, between Jews believing in Jesus as Messiah and those Jews rejecting the notion as preposterous. The gospel accounts are thus seen to reflect the level of hostility present at the time of the writing of the gospels, rather than at the time of Jesus's death. The weeping of the women in Luke 23:26–31 might, for example, be taken as a hint that Jesus did not die without significant public support from the Jewish populace. The evangelists have also been suspected of wishing to downplay Roman culpability in order to protect believers in Jesus from Roman hostility to Jews. Note, for example, the apparent reluctance of Pilate to have Jesus crucified (Matt. 27:15–26 || Mark 15:6–15 || Luke 23:13–25 || John 18:29–19:16).

Others are not so sure one can rule out at least some Jewish participation in Jesus's death, even as they are equally concerned not to fuel the anti-Judaism that adheres to the traditional rehearsal of the events. They point to the gospel writers being clearly of one mind that the instigators of the plot against Jesus were Jewish leaders. But that hardly permits tarring the whole Jewish community with this brush or even the whole of the leadership (as seen in the presence in the gospel narratives of Nicodemus and Joseph of Arimathea, both identified as members of the upper echelons of Jewish leadership). Populations are not homogeneous, and that was true in the first century. Populations under occupation are not homogenous, as can be observed in Palestine in our own day. Jesus was unrepentantly Jewish, as we have seen throughout our investigation and as the gospels make every attempt to show; his followers were Jewish, believing him to be the Jewish Messiah. Jewish authorities were nervous about Jesus not least because of broad public enthusiasm for Jesus. But to say that hostility between Jesus and at least some very important Jewish leaders had reached lethal levels is in no way to speak of Jesus's fate as *the* Jewish response to Jesus.

If Jewish authorities did have a hand in Jesus's death, why would they have opposed him to such an extent? One issue would have been that Jesus announced the imminent arrival of the kingdom of God. What would have made the authorities particularly nervous was that Jesus, according to the gospel narratives, did so in a way that produced in the crowds that followed him an enthusiasm that he himself might be the Messiah. Apart from many of the leadership no doubt thinking that was simply crazy, they would have been justifiably nervous about how the Romans would react. To announce the arrival of God's kingdom was easily understood by many of the Jewish population to mean the end, among other radical changes, of Roman occupation and imperial oppression. And to claim to be Messiah, or even just to be thought by others to be Messiah, was to make a political claim to which the Romans would respond violently.

Second, for Jesus to be heard announcing the end of the temple, and then to create a ruckus on the temple mount during a holy festival when the city was packed with pilgrims, would have created a great deal of alarm and resentment.

Third, perhaps nothing offended and alarmed the religious authorities more than Jesus's claim that he had a very special relationship to God, one that allowed him to call God "father" and to claim on the basis of that authority the freedom to challenge their interpretation of how God's will, Torah, should be lived out. This made him vulnerable to the charge that he was a false prophet, that he was enticing the people into apostasy. Such a charge could not be taken lightly by any Jewish leader. The book of Deuteronomy, for example, views misleading the people under the guise of divine authority as such a grievous affront that the people are to eliminate such a person: "Show them no pity or compassion and do not shield them" (13:8). According to all of the evangelists, Jesus *did* say and do many things that were very provocative and thus he was surely not surprised by the hostility his words and actions provoked.

So it should not be surprising to us that there would have been at least significant elements within the Jewish leadership that would have wanted Jesus out of the way.

ROMANS

Did the Romans do it? Here again, the sources all agree that Pontius Pilate, the Roman prefect or proconsul, ordered the crucifixion. But why would the imperial authorities have wanted Jesus out of the way? Again the answer is hardly difficult to come by. Great empires, old and recent, are remarkably callous in the exercise of their power. They are equally paranoid about challenges to that power and control. Pilate would not have needed a great deal of knowledge about Jesus to order his execution. It was enough that Jesus was accused of being a troublemaker, of having designs on power, for Pilate to have him put to death as an example. That Pilate is described as vacillating and finally caving in under the pressures of Jewish leadership may well fit his rather terrible reputation for both brutality and lack of principle. Luke 13:1 alludes all too briefly to an episode in which Pilate is said to have slaughtered Galileans while they were sacrificing in the Jerusalem temple. Josephus several times relates an episode in which Jews protested Pilate's use of Jerusalem temple treasury funds to finance an aqueduct and that many were brutally killed in the attempt to put down the demonstration (*Jewish Antiquities* 18.3.2 §§60–62; *Jewish War* 2.9.4 §§175–77). The picture of Pilate in the gospels is consistent with Josephus's account. His role has been reprised countless times in history, most particularly in times and places of callous imperial aggression and occupation.

I find it most plausible to view the death of Jesus as a result of a volatile mix of violent imperial arrogance and the nervous hostility of religious leaders. *Both* Roman and Jewish authorities had plausible reasons to wish Jesus away. And that is exactly how the evangelists, for all their differences, depict the event. Jesus was an innocent man, killed for no good reason, but for understandable, even predictable ones. His death was no accident.

God

It turns out, however, that in the view of the early followers of Jesus such analysis cannot possibly fully explain the *meaning* of Jesus's death. The rehearsal of the injustice and brutality of callous powers becomes an essential part of what Jesus's followers called "good news"—*gospel*. While depicting Jesus's death as the result of a miscarriage of justice, as a result of human treachery and callousness, the evangelists also all assert that Jesus's death was in some sense God's deed. To explore this more fully we will need to pay close attention to the meaning the early followers of Jesus saw in his death (see below).

Jesus Himself

This question is related to how Jesus thought of himself, what role he thought his death would play in the larger story of God's salvation of the world. The gospel writers depict Jesus's crucifixion as an act of treachery and brutality, as we have seen. At the very same time they also show Jesus predicting his death and acting in a way that was not designed to avoid a confrontation (e.g., Mark 8:31; 9:31; 10:33 and parallels). More, the "demonstration in the temple" might even be called the "provocation in the temple." Jesus is shown as fully aware of the potential hostility his actions would elicit. Did he deliberately choose death? This may not be suicide exactly, but we can imagine his disciples suggesting that the road he has chosen will lead there. "Let us also go, that we may die with him," says one disciple as they head for Jerusalem (John 11:16).

Second, as much as the writers in the New Testament talk about Jesus's death as God's act of reconciliation, they also speak of Jesus's *self*-offering (apart from the accounts of the Last Supper, see also Gal. 2:19–21; Eph. 2:14–16; 5:2; Titus 2:14).

The gospel writers do not describe Jesus's death as a suicide, but rather as a crime against him. At the same time, they depict Jesus as fully aware of what lies before him, what significance it will have, and thus a road he fully chooses in obedience to his divine father's will. Is there a contradiction in the story the evangelists tell? Or is this mysterious tension between a crime against an innocent man and his having deliberately chosen this road one that made sense within the tradition informing Jesus, his followers, and the evangelists who tell us the story of his passion? To this we now turn.

Meaning of Jesus's Death

Surely one of the biggest questions those who had banked on Jesus as being the one to liberate the Jews was whether his death at the hands of the Romans implied his failure. The surprise is that the answer early believers gave to the question very quickly became a very resounding, "No, Jesus did not fail!" Indeed, Jesus's death became a core symbol of their faith and thus of Jesus's success!

No doubt the conviction that God raised Jesus from the dead played an important role in laying the groundwork for this remarkable perspective. God vindicated this righteous man and thereby expressed approval for what Jesus had done and said. Such a conviction would no doubt have awakened in Jesus's followers a deep desire to revisit the circumstances of his death and ponder its meaning. Several notes of caution need to be sounded, however:

1. We have to be careful not to assume uniformity of perspective among the followers of Jesus regarding the meaning of his death. For example, some scholars treat the hypothetical Q, which may not have contained a Passion Narrative, like a *gospel*, thereby implying that early communities of Jesus followers could proclaim Jesus without making his death a central part of their proclamation (see chapter 2 above). The *Gospel of Thomas* is a further example of presenting Jesus as a sage, a teacher of saving wisdom, rather than as a crucified savior. One must be careful about using a hypothetically reconstructed Q to argue for a "crossless" Christianity at the beginnings of the Jesus movement. The date for the *Gospel of Thomas* is too uncertain to provide strong support for such a proposal. Even so, whatever sets the canonical witnesses apart from each other, they all share the conviction that the cross is of central importance for understanding Jesus; and they all place it at the very climax of their story of who Jesus is and why he matters.

2. To argue that Easter plays a central role in the process of discovery of how and why the cross is important does not mean that people got up on Easter Monday morning and immediately came to a full-blown

understanding of Jesus's death as an atoning offering or ransom for the sins of the world, or a decisive victory over the powers of evil and death. We should assume considerable growth in understanding. The many allusions to Scripture in the way Jesus's last days and death are narrated suggests a process of reflection and discernment.

3. The evangelists all express their convictions about the meaning of Jesus's death as an essential part of a lengthy story of Jesus's words and deeds. They want readers to reflect on the meaning of Jesus's death in relation to his life. The importance of this can hardly be overstated, since in the history of the Christian religion the cross has been so central to forgiveness and salvation that Jesus's life, teachings, and actions function too often as little more than a preamble to his death. This way of thinking of Jesus's death can also distance Jesus from his role in the story of Israel and estrange him from his own Judaism.

4. To focus on Jesus's death as solely God's act reduces the historical persons we encounter in the story of Jesus's death to playing little more than bit parts in a drama in which God is the only real actor. That is exactly how the gospel writers do not tell the story. As much as they come to view Jesus's death as not a tragedy but a central expression of what he was about, they nevertheless narrate that event in a way that lets characters like Peter, Judas, Caiaphas, Pilate—and Jesus himself!—emerge as real historical actors.

With those cautions in mind, we nevertheless recognize that the gospel accounts were all written "on this side of Easter." That is to say, early followers of Jesus, including the authors of the gospels, had the benefit of looking back on an event and seeing in it the working of God. In addition to the cross being an act of human treachery and brutality, they were able to see the crucifixion of Jesus as also *God's* act. The crucifixion was viewed not only as an act of hostility on the part of human beings toward God's messenger, but also an act of immeasurable love on the part of the one who had sent that messenger. Listen to Paul in his letter to the Romans:

> For while we were still weak, at the right time Christ died for the ungodly. Indeed . . . God proves his love for us in that while we still were sinners Christ died for us. . . . If while we were enemies, we were reconciled to God through the death of his Son, much more surely, having been reconciled, will we be saved by his life. (Rom. 5:6, 8, 10)

What were the building blocks of such an understanding of Jesus's death as God's powerful act of love? To answer that, we need to go back once again to the traditions of Israel. We will discover that to understand Jesus's death as good news for rebellious human beings is not a foreign imposition on a Jewish story of a Jewish wonderworker and sage; it emerges from the very heart of Israel's tradition. To say that does not, of course, deny that it was very much a minority reading of that tradition.

Suffering and Divine Sovereignty

Suffering includes both the fate of those who do God's will in a world in rebellion against God, and also as a means of bringing wholeness and reconciliation to those caught up in that rebellion. There is much in the Bible, of course, that deals with suffering as a consequence of sin and rebellion against God. The evangelists are of one mind that Jesus did not suffer for his own sins. As we will see, they were able to integrate that kind of suffering into their view of his suffering when they show him suffering "on behalf of" his tormenters, taking on himself the judgment that would normally be falling on them. But first, we need to explore the suffering of the innocent messenger of God.

Suffering—the Predictable Fate of a Prophet

Suffering, sometimes even death, is biblically the predictable fate of a prophet. One way to see Jesus's life and work is as that of a "prophet of the kingdom." Why should a prophet expect to suffer? Simply stated, in the Bible prophets are needed especially when society or its leaders must hear God's uncomfortable and inconvenient truth regarding injustice, oppression, or religious idolatry. The opening chapters of the book of Jeremiah show how deeply interwoven the theme of suffering was in the typical life of a prophet, as seen in the parable of the vineyard in Matthew 21:33–46 (discussed in chapter 8 above). That parable is a succinct snapshot of the fate of prophets. And we cannot forget the end of that other prophet of the kingdom of God in the gospel accounts, John the Baptist. In short, prophets who speak the truth of God into a broken and rebellious world can expect to suffer.

Suffering—the Predictable Fate of a Righteous or Just Person

More broadly, suffering is understood in the Jewish Scriptures to be the plight of a righteous or just person, one who does God's will consistently, courageously, and without fail in a world where people resist God's will (as seen in the Beatitudes in the Sermon on the Mount, discussed in chapter 10 above). They reflect both what the coming revolution of the kingdom will mean for those who suffer injustice and what life will be like for those who practice the justice of the kingdom now already in this unjust world: they will necessarily face great opposition and persecution.

Such teaching is not unique to Jesus, but runs through much Jewish literature, especially in the wisdom literature (e.g., Wisdom of Solomon 2 and 2 Maccabees 7). In the years leading up to the time of Jesus this set of insights developed into what is often called "martyr theology."

A Suffering Messiah

So far we have been on familiar territory in terms of Jewish faith and tradition. But what about a suffering *messiah*? This was a very rare theme, since for the most part messiahs, anointed kings, are understood to be the *solution* to the suffering of the just. The righteous people of God can endure suffering only because they can count on the intervention of God. The Messiah, as God's intervening agent, will bring suffering and oppression to an end by being victorious over the foes of God and the enemies of God's people. So is this idea of a suffering and dying Messiah a complete innovation introduced by the followers of Jesus? Perhaps not quite.

The Suffering Servant of Isaiah 53

We encounter a strange figure in one of the famous poetic passages called Servant Songs in so-called Second Isaiah (chapters 40–55), specifically the fourth Servant Song in Isaiah 53:

> He was despised and rejected by others;
> > a man of suffering and acquainted with infirmity. . . .
> Surely he has borne our infirmities
> > and carried our diseases;
> yet we accounted him stricken,
> > struck down by God, and afflicted.
> But he was wounded for our transgressions . . .
> upon him was the punishment that made us whole,
> > and by his bruises we are healed.
> All we like sheep have gone astray;
> > we have all turned to our own way,
> and the Lord has laid on him
> > the iniquity of us all.
> He was oppressed, and he was afflicted,
> > yet he did not open his mouth;
> like a lamb that is led to the slaughter,
> > and like a sheep that before its shearers is silent,
> > so he did not open his mouth.
> By a perversion of justice he was taken away . . .
> > stricken for the transgression of my people. . . .
> although he had done no violence,
> > and there was no deceit in his mouth.
> Yet it was the will of the Lord to crush him with pain . . .
> > his life an offering for sin. (Isa. 53:3–10)

Who is Isaiah's "servant"? There are several possibilities:

- Isaiah might be thinking of the servant as the king taken away by the Babylonians into exile. Kings, especially David and his offspring, were sometimes referred to as servants of YHWH (e.g., 2 Sam. 7:18–29; 1 Kings 3:5–9; Luke 1:69; and frequently in the Psalms). It is not much of a stretch to think of the servant as the "Anointed One," the Messiah (e.g., Zech. 3:8; Matt. 12:18; Acts 3:18; 4:27).
- Isaiah's servant might be a prophet, much as Moses is repeatedly referred to as "servant of YHWH" (e.g., Deut. 34:5; Josh. 1:2; Isa. 20:3; Rev. 15:3; 22:9). Some medieval Jewish sages argued that the servant was none other than the prophet Jeremiah. Whether Moses or Jeremiah, the prophet might well suffer at the hands of his own people.
- Isaiah's servant might more generally be a righteous or just person (Isa. 50:10; 53:11; see also Acts 3:13–14).
- Isaiah's servant might be the people of God as a whole (e.g., Isa. 42:19; 44:1, 8; see also Ps. 136:22; Jer. 30:10).

Perhaps this ambiguity and the suggestiveness of the poetry allow us to think of all of these possibilities at once. We have seen throughout our study of Jesus that the evangelists depict him as king, messiah, prophet, Moses-like figure, and representative of the people as a whole, without any need to choose one designation at the exclusion of another. That might serve as a warning for us not to determine the identity of the servant too carefully either. What is important is that the variety of possibilities leaves room for a Jewish writer who believes Jesus to be the Messiah to relate this poem to him and his experience of suffering. In short, here we have a well from which one can draw for reflection on Jesus as a messiah who suffers on behalf of others. Further, we here find a source for the idea that Jesus's suffering and death brings healing and reconciliation to the very ones who have brought that suffering and death upon him.

Several features in Isaiah's poem play a significant role in how Jesus's death is depicted in the gospels, helping us to get at the meaning that Jesus's death had for early followers.

Suffering of the Servant a Result of Human Injustice

Isaiah 53:8 calls the servant's suffering a "perversion of justice." Nothing in the song suggests that human beings are not culpable in the suffering of the Servant of God (Isa. 53:3, 7–9). This corresponds very well to the way in which the evangelists tell the story of Jesus's death. The servant's death comes as a result of a travesty and a perversion of justice, as does Jesus's.

Suffering of the Servant a Result of God's Act

At the same time, the servant's suffering is from another perspective the doing of God, as stated most dramatically in Isaiah 53:4, 6, 10. The death of the servant is not only an act of human treachery; it is God offering a sacrifice. This too is an essential element in the understanding of Jesus's death (e.g., Romans 5).

Suffering as Willing Act of the Servant

The servant is depicted as a victim—a victim at the hands of his tormentors and in some sense a victim at the hands of a God who "crushes him with pain" (Isa. 53:10). And yet, in the end, the servant "pour[s] *himself* out to death" and "[bears] the sins of many, making intercession for the transgressors" (53:12; also 53:4, 7, 11).

COMBINATION OF DIVINE AND HUMAN VOLITION

How do we explain this strange combination: the suffering of the servant as *at the same time* the result of human treachery, divine will, and voluntary service? It turns out that this tension-riddled set of convictions is quite typical of Jewish thinking about God and humans. The solution to this riddle does not lie in a philosophical attempt to explain the relationship between divine intervention and human culpability or, stated differently, between determinism and free will. Rather, we come to an understanding of this puzzle by paying attention to two apparently contradictory convictions that sit side by side in the Scriptures and other writings of Jesus's contemporaries.

Divine Sovereignty

The first conviction is that God is creator and lord of the cosmos (see chapter 6 above). "YHWH our God is one" lies at the heart of Jewish theology and worship and is expressed several times a day in the Jewish prayer called the Shema. There can finally be nothing and no one who operates outside of the sovereign lordship of God. We listen again to the prophet Isaiah:

> I am the LORD, and there is no other;
>   besides me there is no god.
> I arm you, though you do not know me,
> so that they may know, from the rising of the sun
>   and from the west, that there is no one besides me;
>   I am the LORD, and there is no other.
> I form light and create darkness,
>   I make weal and create woe;
>   I the LORD do all these things. (Isa. 45:5–7)

We might add the well-known words of Paul regarding God's hardening of Pharaoh's heart. Anticipating protests, Paul says:

> But who indeed are you, a human being, to argue with God? Will what is molded say to the one who molds it, "Why have you made me like this?" Has the potter no right over the clay, to make out of the same lump one object for special use and another for ordinary use? (Rom. 9:20–21)

Many other examples within and outside the Bible could be found to illustrate this point. God is free to act and intervene even in ways that lie beyond human understanding, rationality, and calculations of justice. Ultimately it is exactly the conviction that God is an intervening God that explains why Jews prayed, hoped, exulted in the promise of salvation, and why they shuddered at the prospect of judgment. They believed in an active and intervening divine sovereign.

Human Beings Bear God's Image and Are Therefore Agents

What keeps this conviction about the sovereignty of God from rendering human behavior inconsequential? Paul's words quoted above are a response to a question he anticipates: "Why then does [God] still find fault? For who can resist his will?" (Rom. 9:19). There is a second conviction, alongside the sovereignty of God, namely, that human beings are responsible and accountable. This conviction is critical for understanding the mix of causation in Isaiah 53, as also in the Passion Narrative. As God's creatures, human beings bear the image of this God (Genesis 1). They are therefore to exercise "dominion" (1:26, 28); they are to be responsible. Their misdeeds are thus *sins* and not simply engineering mistakes; their acts of justice are the exercise of love, not simply divine control (as seen in the parable of the sheep and goats in Matthew 25).

Given this set of convictions, the poet of the Servant Song and the evangelists narrating the death of Jesus were able to observe the circumstances of the servant's and of Jesus's death as *both* a result of human injustice *and* as the work of God. Indeed, the evangelists saw Jesus as that servant, acting freely and selflessly at the behest of God for the sake of his tormenters.

On one hand, we hear Jesus's cry on the cross: "My God, my God, why have you forsaken me!?" We see in this cry the depth of human suffering, of a person suffering unspeakable injustice at the hands of his fellow human beings, to the point of experiencing this as abandonment by God. On the other hand, the evangelists show us also a Jesus who knows that he will die, who at his Last Supper anticipates his death. More, he provides his disciples with the rudiments of making sense of his death:

> While they were eating, Jesus took a loaf of bread, and after blessing it he broke it, gave it to the disciples, and said, "Take, eat; this is my body." Then he took a cup, and after giving thanks he gave it to them, saying, "Drink from it, all of you; for this is my blood of the covenant, which is poured out for many for the forgiveness of sins." (Matt. 26:26–28)

Many readers of this book will have heard these words from the Lord's Supper over and over again in the celebration of Communion or the Eucharist. But is this not a retrojection of later church practice into the story of Jesus's life prior to his death? That is a legitimate question, especially since the gospel accounts are symbolic in virtually all details of the Passion Narrative. However, if Jesus was familiar with traditions such as Isaiah 53—and there is no reason to think he was not—then there is also little reason to question the evangelists in their conviction that Jesus knew full well that his activities would lead to his death and that he viewed his coming death within a larger divine scenario of reconciliation, forgiveness, and restoration. Jesus would then have understood his fate as being *both* a result of murderous treachery *and* the path of faithfulness he needed to take for the sake of his people. To say that Jesus could well, from a historical point of view, have thought this way does not for even a moment deny that the way and manner in which the evangelists tell the story is heavily shaped and influenced by the ongoing reflections and practices of the early church. The post-Easter fingerprints of the early believers are all over the accounts.

Theological Significance of Jesus's Death

Viewing the story of Jesus's death as both the story of *human* injustice and an act of *God* leads us to the heart of the theological significance early followers of Jesus saw in his death. In the view of the evangelists the great miracle of the cross is nothing less than God transforming the most intense expression of human rebellion against God into God's own act of reconciliation toward those very same rebels. It is the ultimate expression of God's ingenious and persistent love for God's own enemies.

Even though we have shown how deeply rooted this understanding of Jesus's death is in the traditions of Israel, the early followers of Jesus nevertheless experienced this as "*good news*"—*gospel*. That terrible Friday becomes "Good Friday." This news is at the same time entirely consistent with Jesus's enacting the kingdom during his lifetime—eating and drinking with tax collectors and sinners, drawing disreputable characters into his inner circle of followers, introducing them to God as a loving parent, and teaching them to live vulnerably, to trust a loving divine parent, and to imitate God by loving their enemies. The very way in which the evangelists construct their narratives means that they believe that the cross must never be severed from the life Jesus lived that got him onto the cross. The cross is thus an essential part of the enactment of God's strange kingdom.

The Rest of the New Testament

We have so far restricted the discussion to the Passion Narratives in the four gospels. The evangelists were, of course, not alone in reflecting on the central importance of Jesus's death for the fate of humanity. Indeed, they inherited their views in large measure from a rich and varied tradition that preceded them, that paralleled their writing, and that succeeded their efforts at the same time, as is reflected in the other parts of the New Testament.

But first a brief comment: the saving significance of Jesus's death is often cast in Christian theology, both formal and popular, in forensic terms. Jesus's death represents the price paid for human sin and is therefore a kind of insurance against God's judgment, safety from the wrath of a judging God. Two problems often accompany this way of treating Jesus's death. The first is that it casts God as an angry judge, with Jesus absorbing God's fury on behalf of sinful humanity. Second, Jesus's death can easily be reduced to a principle, rule, or formula, which easily obscures the degree to which New Testament writers see the cross-as-means-of-salvation as a surprise, as good *news*. It also obscures the degree to which those writers give parabolic expression to their conviction that the cross represents *God's* act of peacemaking, the ultimate expression of God's *love* of enemies. The various metaphors that express the meaning of the cross might be best thought of as parables intended to help us appreciate that love.

JESUS AS LAMB OF GOD

Jews who went to the temple to offer sacrifices to God and who celebrated the Passover meal knew the importance of the symbol of the lamb in relation to deliverance and forgiveness. To speak of Jesus as "the lamb of God who takes away the sins of the world" expresses the conviction that the cross represents *God's* act of atonement—God's offering of his own "lamb" for the sake of the world. This theme comes to expression already at the very beginning of the Gospel of John at the occasion of Jesus's baptism (John 1:29, 36). It also finds expression in the Last Supper, where Jesus presents himself, in effect, as the Passover lamb (see also Rev. 5:6, 12).

This image of the lamb as applied to Jesus's death may well reflect an atonement theology that took some time to develop fully. Even if it is a development, it is not simply an imposition on the story of Jesus's death.

ACTS OF THE APOSTLES

Even though Acts was written after Luke's Gospel, it may preserve some early views of how the followers of Jesus would have understood his death and its meaning in the very first years after Good Friday and Easter. Lengthy sermons make up a good proportion of Acts, one example of which is Peter's famous sermon at Pentecost (Acts 2:14–36). The sermon shows a remarkable, but by now familiar, mix of stresses on human culpability and divine will in the death of Jesus. As a result of Peter's sermon, the people "were cut to the heart and said to Peter and to the other apostles, 'Brothers, what should we do?'" Peter's response is very illuminating:

> Repent, and be baptized every one of you in the name of Jesus Christ so that your sins may be forgiven; and you will receive the gift of the Holy Spirit. For the promise is for you, for your children, and for all who are far away, everyone whom the Lord our God calls to him. (Acts 2:38–39)

What we do not find here is a fully articulated theology of atonement. But the very people whom Peter has just accused of having collaborated in Jesus's death are here offered the gift of forgiveness and the gift of the Holy Spirit. Articulated in embryonic form (or in highly curtailed form, depending on when we date such a tradition) is the fundamental understanding of the meaning of Jesus's death as an act of divine reconciliation with rebellious humanity. An act of treachery is transformed into an embrace of the enemy. Rejection is transformed into an offer of forgiveness.

PAUL'S LETTERS

No New Testament author reflected more deeply on the cross than Paul. No New Testament writer has done more to shape the understanding of the cross as being at the very center of the gospel. Quoted earlier were the unforgettable words from Romans 5, which speak of the death of Christ as *God's* act of loving enemies, the very enemies who put Jesus on the cross to begin with. Elsewhere in Romans, Paul says:

> But now . . . the righteousness of God has been disclosed, . . . the righteousness of God through faith in Jesus Christ for all who believe. . . . They are now justified by his grace as a gift, through the redemption that is in Christ Jesus, *whom God put forward as a sacrifice of atonement by his blood*, effective through faith. He did this to show his righteousness . . . ; it was to prove at the present time that he himself is righteous and that he justifies the one who has faith in Jesus. (Rom. 3:21–26, emphasis added)

Important also is 1 Corinthians 1, where Paul acknowledges both the scandalous nature of the cross and also its ironic power:

> For the message about the cross is foolishness to those who are perishing, but to us who are being saved it is the power of God. . . . For since, in the wisdom of God, the world did not know God through wisdom, God decided, through

the foolishness of our proclamation to save those who believe. For Jews demand signs and Greeks desire wisdom, but we proclaim Christ crucified, a stumbling block to Jews and foolishness to Gentiles, but to those who are the called, both Jews and Greeks, Christ is the power of God and the wisdom of God. For God's foolishness is wiser than human wisdom, and God's weakness is stronger than human strength. (1 Cor. 1:18, 21–25)

This text goes to the very heart of the problem and the genius of early proclamation: there was at that time no romance associated with the cross. It was in no way a religious symbol, but rather a symbol of degradation, oppression, and terror—a scandal, an offense. In this passage Paul is very aware of the affront of his message. And yet, to his own surprise, the cross represents the power of God in that it is at once an expression of weakness and vulnerability in the face of human hostility and at the same time the most profound expression of divine power to start things anew. It is that twist that lies at the heart of Paul's gospel.

A later letter, Ephesians, quite possibly penned by one of Paul's students or co-workers, shows yet another dimension of the power of the cross. In this instance the cross is interpreted in relation to divisions and enmities in human society as a whole, most particularly the division between Jews and non-Jews:

Remember that at one time you ... were ... without Christ [or without the Messiah], being aliens from the commonwealth of Israel, and strangers to the covenants of promise, having no hope and without God in the world. But now in Christ Jesus you who once were far off have been brought near *by the blood of Christ*. For he is our peace; in his flesh he has made both groups into one and has broken down the dividing wall, that is, the hostility between us. He has abolished the law with its commandments and ordinances, that he might create in himself one new humanity in place of the two, thus making peace, and might reconcile both groups to God in one body *through the cross*, thus putting to death that hostility through it. (Eph. 2:11–16, emphasis added)

As we see, early followers of Jesus did not think of the effects of his death only in relation to an individual's relationship to God. Jesus's death was understood as reconciling and restoring God's community, God's people, in fact re-creating all of humanity. Ephesians 2 goes on to describe wonderfully the ultimate effects of peace with God, which results in the constructing of a new temple, a temple made up of human beings, of old enemies, of Jews and Gentiles, fused together into a new humanity in Christ (Eph. 2:19–22).

LETTER TO THE HEBREWS

The letter to the Hebrews is a particularly rich set of reflections on the death of Jesus and its meaning. Perhaps that is so because it is not so much a letter as an anonymous sermon, with only some of the trappings of a letter. It was likely written toward the end of the first century when Paul's letters, among others, had apparently begun to set a pattern for how to circulate teachings in the church. While the whole letter is relevant, related themes are succinctly captured in concentrated fashion in Hebrews 2:

> But we do see Jesus, who for a little while was made lower than the angels, now crowned with glory and honor because of the suffering of death, so that by the grace of God he might taste death for everyone.
>
> It was fitting that God, for whom and through whom all things exist, in bringing many children to glory, should make the pioneer of their salvation perfect through sufferings. . . .
>
> Since, therefore, the children share flesh and blood, he himself likewise shared the same things, so that through death he might destroy the one who has the power of death, that is, the devil, and free those who all their lives were held in slavery by the fear of death. . . . Therefore he had to become like his brothers and sisters in every respect, so that he might be a merciful and faithful high priest in the service of God, to make a sacrifice of atonement for the sins of the people. (Heb. 2:9–10, 14–15, 17)

On one hand, Jesus's suffering and death are an act of self-giving, of self-offering—an act of liberation of those who have been held under the grip of evil. Jesus's own death is the price of liberation, as it were, breaking the very power of death and evil. He is celebrated in these words as the great liberator, the great savior. The means of this liberation? Jesus's *own* death. On the other hand, as much as Jesus is celebrated as the one to whom God has "subjected all things," in other words, as Messiah, as Son of God (Heb. 1–2), and as much as his death sets Jesus apart from normal humanity, the preacher goes to great lengths to show how much Jesus's suffering and death make him "just like us in every way" (2:17).

First, Jesus's own suffering is related to *his own* perfection (Heb. 2:10). Second, he is not ashamed to call those who have benefited from his offering of himself his brothers and sisters (2:11, 17), since both he and they share the same Father (2:11). So, not only is Jesus a savior, but in being "like us" he is the "pioneer of [our] salvation." Finally, he is not only a pioneer, but in solidarity with broken and sinful humanity in need of forgiveness, he is a "high priest" offering a sacrifice of atonement—his own life (2:17).

The story of Jesus's being tested through suffering and death is thus rehearsed by the preacher of Hebrews as not only an act of liberation, but an act of solidarity with those who themselves experience suffering and death. These would surely have been comforting and reassuring words for early followers of Jesus who, in confessing their faith in him, made themselves vulnerable to suffering and death. Just as he was in solidarity with them in his suffering, so now they are to be in solidarity with him in his passion. With a remarkable allusion both to the figure of the scapegoat in the Hebrew Scriptures (e.g., Lev. 16:21–22) and to Jesus's crucifixion on the garbage heap at Golgotha just outside Jerusalem city limits, the preacher says this:

> Jesus suffered outside the city gate in order to sanctify the people by his own blood. Let us then go to him outside the camp and bear the abuse he endured. (Heb. 13:12–13; see also 12:1–4)

The temptation should be resisted to read this rich sermon in a strictly forensic way, to the effect that Jesus had to die in order to meet some requirement in a sacrificial system of restitution. Instead, the imagery of sacrifice is here employed in a very parabolic fashion: Jesus is sacrifice, scapegoat, and high priest all at once. He is Savior and Messiah, placed above everything in the universe, but also "just like us," a "pioneer" whom one can follow and imitate, even in the act of self-giving and death for the sake of others. In this the preacher of this sermon echoes the challenge that the Jesus of the gospels puts to his listeners, namely, that they are to take up their own cross and follow him (e.g., Mark 8:34 and parallels; see also Col. 1:24).

JOHN'S APOCALYPSE

The Apocalypse of John (also called the book of Revelation) presents the reader with a remarkably ironic image of Jesus. After introducing us in Revelation 1 to the exalted Christ who rules the universe, in Revelation 4 we are taken along by the seer into the heavenly throne room of God, where we witness an astonishing drama. A profound question is asked of the grand assembly around the divine throne: "Who is worthy to open the scroll and break its seals?" (5:2). Who holds the key to the will of God for the universe? Initially no one comes forward, and the seer is about to despair:

> Then one of the elders said to me, "Do not weep. See, the Lion of the tribe of Judah, the Root of David, has conquered, so that he can open the scroll and its seven seals." (Rev. 5:5)

The reference to the Lion of Judah and the Root of David is of course to the Messiah, to Jesus. This is a very militaristic image, one of conquest and victory (as in Heb. 2:14–15).

But now comes the twist, one for which we are by now prepared: the seer looks up to see the lion, and what does he see?

> Then I saw between the throne and the four living creatures and among the elders a *Lamb standing as if it had been slaughtered*, having seven horns and seven eyes, which are the seven spirits of God sent out into all the earth. He went and took the scroll from the right hand of the one who was seated on

the throne. When he had taken the scroll, the four living creatures and the twenty-four elders fell before the Lamb, each holding a harp and golden bowls full of incense, which are the prayers of the saints. They sing a new song:

> "You are worthy to take the scroll
>   and to open its seals,
> for you were slaughtered and by your blood you ransomed for God
>   saints from every tribe and language and people and nation;
> you have made them to be a kingdom and priests serving our God,
>   and they will reign on earth."

Then I looked, and I heard the voice of many angels surrounding the throne and the living creatures and the elders; they numbered myriads of myriads and thousands of thousands, singing with full voice,

> *"Worthy is the Lamb that was slaughtered*
> *to receive power and wealth and wisdom and might*
> *and honor and glory and blessing!"* (Rev. 5:6–12, emphasis added)

The means with which to open the scroll, the keys to the meaning of history and the designs of God for the cosmos, are held by the slain Lamb. By giving his own life for humanity, the one whom the Romans tortured to death on a cross has, by going that road willingly, exercised the power of God to break the back of evil and death. However difficult it might be after two millennia to recover a sense of the wonder of this insight, in the early days of the Jesus movement it was still "news," shocking news. Indeed, it was a brazen claim hurled by a small suffering community at an overwhelming and self-confident empire: "The one you thought you had ground in the dust has won the victory over you!"

Key Terms and Concepts
atonement
crucifixion
Gethsemane
high priest
Judas
Lamb of God
Last Supper
Lazarus
Passion Narrative
Pilate
sacrifice
Sanhedrin
Suffering Servant
temple
temple demonstration (cleansing)
triumphal entry

Conclusion

No account of the Jesus of the New Testament is able to ignore the centrality of his death. His followers saw in the miscarriage of justice that led to his death the power of God to reconcile, to make new, to start all over again with humanity. They found in their own traditions the vocabulary, the language, and the imagery with which to express that insight. They found parablelike vocabulary to express what they experienced as a love that surpasses knowledge, to paraphrase Ephesians 3:19, and thus finally dwarfs words. One thing remains very clear, however: the structure of the gospel narratives of the New Testament is intended to show that one does not fully appreciate the meaning of Jesus's death if one divorces it from his life, from his words and his deeds, or, as we will see in the next chapter, from his resurrection.

For Further Reading

Brown, Raymond E. *The Death of the Messiah*. 2 vols. New York: Doubleday, 1999.

Hengel, Martin. *The Atonement: The Origins of the Doctrine in the New Testament*. Philadelphia: Fortress, 1981.

Klassen, William. *Judas: Betrayer or Friend of Jesus?* Minneapolis: Fortress, 1996.

McKnight, Scot. *Jesus and His Death: Historiography, the Historical Jesus, and Atonement Theory*. Waco: Baylor University Press, 2005.

Sloyan, Gerard Stephen. *The Crucifixion of Jesus: History, Myth, Faith*. Minneapolis: Fortress, 1995.

——— *Jesus on Trial: A Study of the Gospels*, 2nd ed. Minneapolis: Fortress, 2006.

Wright, N. T. *Christian Origins and the Question of God*, vol. 2: *Jesus and the Victory of God*. Minneapolis: Fortress, 1996.

12

Resurrection of Jesus

E ASTER IS ARGUABLY the most important event in the Christian tradition. This is especially true for Eastern or Orthodox traditions. From Greece to Russia, Christians will greet each other at Easter with a forceful "Christ is risen!" and an equally forceful "He is risen indeed!" It was, if anything, even more important for the early followers of Jesus.

The reasons for the significance of the resurrection of Jesus are manifold and complex, but can be summarized as follows. First, the resurrection represents God's vindication of Jesus. By his being raised from the dead, what Jesus said and did received God's ultimate sign of approval. Jesus turns out to have spoken the truth when he said the kingdom is coming. His peculiar brand of holiness, so easily misunderstood by his contemporaries, proved to be the righteousness or justice of God. Resurrection is the ultimate declaration that Jesus is "Son of God," as Paul says in Romans 1:4.

Second, Jesus's resurrection is inextricably linked to Jewish eschatological, particularly apocalyptic, expectations. Jews understood resurrection to be one of the central features of God's renewing of the cosmos. The raising of Jesus was thus viewed by his followers as a sign that the new age has broken into this present dark age, that the kingdom of God is finally appearing in full force. These two features are inextricably bound up with each other. One without the other would not have made any sense to the early followers of Jesus.

We do not exaggerate when we say that in the minds of those first Jesus believers the truth of their faith rests on the truth of Easter. The apostle Paul says so succinctly in his correspondence with the Corinthians:

267

If Christ has not been raised, then our proclamation has been in vain and your faith has been in vain. . . . If Christ has not been raised, then your faith is futile and you are still in your sins. . . . If for this life only we have hoped in Christ, we are of all people most to be pitied. (1 Cor. 15:14, 17, 19)

None of this implies that the writers of the New Testament are consistent about the details of Christ's resurrection, either on exactly what transpired or on what his resurrected body was or, better, is like. Striking, however, is that they do not argue over these differences. What matters most to them is that it happened—it matters for Jesus, for their faith, and, importantly, for the fate of the cosmos.

Sources

The conviction that Jesus rose or that he was raised from the dead informs all of the writings of the New Testament. In their final chapters, each gospel furnishes us with an account of the resurrection: Matthew 28; Mark 16; Luke 24; and John 20–21. John 21 is quite obviously an addition to an already completed gospel (see chapter 3 above). We ought to think, then, of John 20 and John 21 as two separate resurrection texts. Further, we find outside the gospels a sustained discussion of the issue in Paul's first letter to the Corinthians (1 Corinthians 15).

A good argument can be made to begin with Paul, since he likely wrote a decade and a half prior to the writing of the earliest gospel in the New Testament (Mark). Given, however, that we have been exploring primarily the gospels in our study of Jesus, and given further that the evangelists draw on traditions that predate their writing (as does Paul, to be sure), it is beyond our ability to determine whose ideas or traditions are older. We shall thus proceed by looking first at the gospels, knowing that we could just as easily have begun with Paul.

Gospels

As with other special moments in the narratives of Jesus's life, we encounter the familiar phenomenon of both unity and diversity in the evangelists' accounts. We begin with what is arguably the earliest of the gospel accounts, that of Mark (see chapter 3 above).

MARK

Mark offers the least amount of information on the resurrection. On the day following the Sabbath, three women visit the tomb where Jesus was laid after being taken down from the cross (16:1). Upon finding the stone serving as a door to the tomb rolled away, they enter the tomb. There they meet a young man dressed in white, who tells them that Jesus is alive and that they are to pass on that startling news to Peter and the other disciples and inform them that Jesus will meet them in Galilee (16:6–7). The women leave the tomb terrified, saying nothing to anyone (16:8).

This is exactly how abruptly the best manuscripts end the Gospel of Mark (see chapter 3 above). Some early manuscripts furnish endings of Mark that include either a concluding sentence attached to 16:8 that rounds off the gospel or a longer ending that provides more extensive Easter appearances in Galilee (16:9–20). There is rough agreement today that these verses were created by a scribe or scribes who were sure that the abrupt and strange ending at 16:8 was not in keeping with the evangelist's intentions. Either to fix what had disappeared due to an accident or to correct what was deemed to be theologically unacceptable, they fused together several known Easter traditions to provide a proper ending to the gospel.

At the time of its writing and initial dissemination, the Gospel of Mark was not yet deemed to be Scripture, with all that implies in terms of status and immutability. Mark's Gospel was part of the still-unfolding traditions about Jesus. The rewriting of Mark by such additions is little different from the rewriting of Mark represented by gospels such as Matthew and Luke (see chapter 3 above).

MATTHEW

Matthew follows Mark in beginning his account of the resurrection with the visit of women to the tomb. But he prepares the reader for the unusual event by relating that Jewish authorities were worried that someone would steal Jesus's body only to claim that he had been raised to life and that they therefore requested to have guards posted at the tomb (27:62–66).

Matthew knows of only two women witnesses, both named Mary, one of them Mary Magdalene (28:1). They are met by an angel, who tells them much the same thing we read in Mark; again they are to tell his disciples to meet the risen Jesus in Galilee (28:5–7). Only now their fear is tempered by joy (28:8). Not only that, Jesus himself meets them (28:9–10; this is only briefly mentioned but not described in Mark 16:9, likely an addition to that gospel). The two women named Mary thus become the very first witnesses to the risen Lord, an enormous honor in the eyes of early believers.

Interlacing his brief narration of the women, Matthew introduces into his narrative another earthquake, during which a heavenly angel descends to remove the stone before Jesus's tomb, terrifying the guards. After the angel addresses the women, Matthew returns to the guards who, after relaying their bizarre experience, are bribed by the authorities and ordered to spread a rumor that Jesus's disciples stole his body. Matthew 28:15 suggests that such stories were in the air during the time in which Matthew's Gospel was written.

The episodes of earthquake and guards are not the only elements unique to Matthew's narration of Easter. As we noted in the previous chapter, Matthew mentions the puzzling and mysterious event of the tombs opening at the time of Jesus's death, and then at the moment of his resurrection, appearing to many in Jerusalem (27:52–53). It is mysterious that Matthew does not integrate this into his narrative of Easter itself—mysterious also because it runs the risk of undermining the singularity of Jesus's own resurrection. We may stand before a puzzle we cannot easily solve. We can of course dismiss it as no more than a legend. But, if so, what would its origin be? Does it recall Ezekiel's reviving of the dead bones in Ezekiel 37? Is it intended to point forward to the resurrection of the dead in the future, as suggested earlier? Perhaps Matthew himself inherited the tradition he uses primarily to make a connection between Jesus's resurrection and the general resurrection of the saints to come. Even so, it remains difficult.

Matthew concludes his account with Jesus meeting his disciples in Galilee, as promised. They are now the Eleven rather than the Twelve (Judas is missing). Jesus meets them on a mountain and instructs them to go everywhere, making disciples, baptizing, and instructing them in his teachings (28:18–19). This is usually referred to as the Great Commission, a tradition that has played a major role in the history of Christianity's missionary efforts. Matthew concludes his narrative, indeed his whole gospel, with the risen Christ's assurance that he will be present with his followers to the "end of the age" (28:20).

LUKE

Luke's account differs in some respects from those of Mark and Matthew. Luke implies a larger number of women visitors than any of the other evangelists (23:55–24:1, 10). Moreover, they meet two "men" rather than angels at the empty tomb (24:4; it is of course possible that Luke thinks of these men as angels, since the term *angel* literally means "messenger").

Of greater interest is that Luke goes on to describe the appearances of the risen Jesus to his disciples as all taking place in and around Jerusalem, rather than in Galilee as in Matthew and as implied in Mark. First is the all-day Bible study that Jesus holds with two of his followers on a road to the village of Emmaus (24:13–35). Opinions vary as to exactly where this village was, but it is clear that Luke believes it to be in the vicinity of Jerusalem. Jesus then meets the Eleven and other disciples, gathered in Jerusalem, still trying to come to grips with the reports of his being alive. Jesus shows them that it is he—Jesus—who is alive, with real flesh and bones (24:39–40). Just to prove it, he eats some broiled fish in their presence (24:41–43).

Luke's account ends with Jesus's final words of assurance and blessing (24:44–49). Jesus tells the assembled disciples that they are to stay in Jerusalem in order to receive power—a reference to Pentecost, an event that

Luke describes in his next volume, the Acts of the Apostles (Acts 2). Jesus leads his disciples to Bethany, across the Kidron valley from Jerusalem, and is there taken up to heaven (Luke 24:50–51), a story rehearsed again at the beginning of Luke's second volume (Acts 1:6–11).

John

As stated at the outset of this chapter, John's Gospel has two sets of Easter traditions. In John 20 the appearances of the risen Jesus are in and around Jerusalem, and that chapter indicates clearly that the gospel was intended to conclude at this point:

> Now Jesus did many other signs in the presence of his disciples, which are not written in this book. But these are written so that you may come to believe that Jesus is the Messiah, the Son of God, and that through believing you may have life in his name. (John 20:30–31)

John 21 is thus quite clearly an addition to the gospel. This time the appearances are in Galilee, suggesting the existence of two sets of traditions, some set in Galilee (as also in Matthew and Mark) and others in and around Jerusalem (as in Luke).

John 20 features several traditions that have played a very important role in Christian devotion. First, unlike in the other gospels, only one woman shows up at the tomb—Mary Magdalene. She is present also in the other Easter accounts, but here she is alone. It is she who tells Peter and the Beloved Disciple about the empty tomb (20:2). Those two race to the tomb and, upon checking it out, go home "believing" but not yet understanding what has taken place (20:8–10). Mary remains at the tomb and there first meets two angels inside the tomb, and then encounters the "gardener," who turns out to be the risen Jesus (20:11–18). The evangelist thus accords her the honor of being the very first to witness the risen Christ (see Mark 16:9; Matt. 28:9).

Another important element of the tradition John transmits is Jesus's joining his disciples in Jerusalem. They are meeting behind closed doors "for fear of the Jews [*or* Judeans]," John's shorthand for the Judean leadership hostile to Jesus (John 20:19–23). Unlike in Luke, where Jesus tells his disciples to wait in Jerusalem for the coming of the Spirit at Pentecost (Acts 2), in John Jesus "breathes" the Spirit onto his disciples, giving them authority to forgive and retain the sins of others (John 20:23). If Matthew's Great Commission bestows on his followers the messianic task of bringing the Gentiles into the kingdom (Matt. 28:16–20), so too the authority to forgive sins in John is nothing less than the bestowal of the messianic task onto Jesus's followers. This carrying on with the messianic task is the essential gist of the Farewell Discourses in John 13–16 (see esp. 14:12; see also Matt. 18:15–20).

A third distinct tradition in John 20 is the famous exchange between "Doubting Thomas" and the risen Jesus (20:24–29). Thomas has been absent from the encounters with the risen Jesus and evidently doubts the veracity of the reports. He wants proof: "Unless I see the mark of the nails in his hands, and put my finger in the mark of the nails and my hand in his side, I will not believe" (20:25). When Jesus appears to him with the still-fresh wounds in his hands and his side, Thomas utters the loftiest confession we encounter anywhere in the gospels: "My Lord and my God!" (20:28). The risen Jesus is recognized as being nothing less than "Lord" and "God." This illustrates the importance of the belief in the resurrection in the development of the respect accorded Jesus by his followers following his Palestinian ministry. Poor Thomas. He is remembered more for his doubt than for his faith.

The addition of John 21 to this gospel has added several remarkable resurrection appearances, this time on the shore of Lake Tiberias, otherwise known as the Sea of Galilee. Seven of the disciples, including Peter and Thomas, have gone fishing. In a way highly reminiscent of a similar episode described in Luke 5:1–11 (which some scholars suspect of being a misplaced resurrection appearance), their efforts are futile until someone on the beach—they do not yet know who it is—tells them to fish on the other side of the boat, resulting in a miraculously large catch. Then they know! "It is the Lord!" (John 21:7). Again reminiscent of the miraculous feeding of the five thousand, Jesus gives them bread and fish to eat for breakfast (21:13).

This is followed by an exchange between Jesus and Peter (here also called Simon), where Jesus presses Peter on whether he loves him (21:15–17). Three times the question is asked. Is Peter being offered an opportunity to right the wrong of his triple denial (18:15–18, 25–27)? Simon Peter assures Jesus that he does indeed love him and receives the mandate, "Feed my sheep!" and a prediction that he, like Jesus, will die the death of a martyr (21:17–18). There is subsequently a rather puzzling exchange between Peter and Jesus regarding the Beloved Disciple and the rumor that this disciple would not die, giving us a tantalizing but too-scanty glimpse into the development of early traditions regarding the church's leaders.

John 21 concludes with an assurance that these traditions are true, going back to trustworthy witnesses (21:24), and the literary exaggeration that all the books in the world could not contain all that Jesus did. In other words, this account, however adequate to communicate the full truth about Jesus, only scratches the surface as a record of words and deeds. Incidentally, the fourth evangelist evidently does not find it necessary to allude to, let alone describe, the departure of Jesus.

We can conveniently summarize the similarities and diversities in the gospel narratives in tabular form:

Matthew 28	Mark 16	Luke 24	John 20–21
guards at tomb			
• Mary Magdalene • "other" Mary	• Mary Magdalene • Mary mother of James • Salome	• Mary Magdalene • Mary mother of James • Joanna	• Mary Magdalene
an angel/messenger from heaven	young man in white	two men in brilliant clothes	
earthquake			
dead come out of tombs (27:52)			
			Peter and Beloved Disciple run to tomb
women encounter Jesus	women do not encounter Jesus, but are told by a "man" that Jesus will meet Peter and the others in Galilee; they say nothing to anyone		Mary Magdalene meets two angels in white and Jesus himself
bribing of the guards			
		Jesus encounters disciples in and around Jerusalem: (a) Emmaus (b) "flesh and bones" risen Jesus meets followers in Jerusalem and eats broiled fish (c) ascension at Bethany outside Jerusalem	Jesus meets disciples meeting in secret in Jerusalem: (a) shows them scars of crucifixion (b) commissions them (c) second meeting with disciples; Thomas comes to believe
Jesus meets the Eleven on mountain in Galilee and commissions them to teach, baptize, and make disciples (no ascension account)	appearance of Jesus in Galilee is implied by words to women (no ascension account)	ascension recounted again in Acts 1, specifying Mount Olivet, outside Jerusalem, as the place of Jesus's departure	Jesus meets his disciples at lake in Galilee where they are fishing; miraculous catch of fish; Jesus shares breakfast with them; conversation with Peter (no ascension report)

Other Easter Texts

Passages outside of the gospels also figure in our reconstruction of how the early followers of Jesus would have understood the phenomenon of Jesus's resurrection.

ACTS 1:1–11

In volume two of Luke's grand work we find the description of the ascension of Christ, which we should add to the list of resurrection appearances. Several items are worth noting briefly.

First, Luke tells us that the appearances of the risen Jesus continued over a period of "forty days" (1:3). The number forty is one with which we have become familiar. It designates the length of Jesus's testing in the desert (see chapter 7 above). Given the highly symbolic nature of this number we will want to be careful not to take it as an exact chronological indicator.

Second, Jesus's ascension takes place at Bethany, just outside Jerusalem, here specified as "Olivet" (i.e., the Mount of Olives; 1:12). This is impossible to harmonize with the tradition Matthew recounts and to which Mark alludes, namely, that Jesus ascended from a mountain in Galilee (see above).

Third, Luke accords prominence to the theme of the kingdom of God in relation to Easter. The risen Jesus offers many proofs of his being alive and continues, characteristically, to speak of the reign of God (1:3). And Jesus's promise of the coming gift of the Spirit at Pentecost comes in response to the question his disciples ask: "Lord, is this the time when you will restore the kingdom to Israel?" (1:6).

Finally, Jesus's ascension is described in very physical terms, as a bodily ascension into the clouds. The similarities to the resurrection itself should not be missed. "Two men" again meet the disciples, as at the empty tomb. At the tomb the question was:

> Why do you look for the living among the dead? He is not here, but has risen. (Luke 24:5)

Like an echo it is again "two men" who now ask:

> Why do you stand looking up toward heaven? This Jesus, who has been taken up from you into heaven, will come in the same way as you saw him go into heaven. (Acts 1:11)

This brief text in Acts alerts us to an important aspect of Easter in the mind of early Christians: *Easter points forward*. It is not simply an event in the life of Jesus of Nazareth. His resurrection is part of a larger scenario in which the sovereign rule of God, the kingdom of God, will be instituted fully and finally. The reference to clouds does not simply make for good storytelling, but represents an important symbol in relation to this eschatological expectation of the coming of the kingdom of God:

> As I watched in the night visions,
> I saw one like a human being [*or* son of man]
>   *coming with the clouds of heaven.*

> And he came to the Ancient One
>   and was presented before him.
> To him was given dominion
>   and glory and kingship,
> that all peoples, nations, and languages
>   should serve him.
> His dominion is an everlasting dominion
>   that shall not pass away,
> and his kingship is one
>   that shall never be destroyed. (Dan. 7:13–14, emphasis added)

Just a few chapters later Daniel furnishes us with an important early Jewish witness to belief in the resurrection:

> Many of those who sleep in the dust of the earth shall awake, some to everlasting life, and some to shame and everlasting contempt. Those who are wise shall shine like the brightness of the sky, and those who lead many to righteousness, like the stars forever and ever. But you, Daniel, keep the words secret and the book sealed until the time of the end. (Dan. 12:2–4)

These texts illustrate that when early believers in Jesus read accounts such as Acts 1:1–11 they read them through the prism of loaded texts such as Daniel 7 and Daniel 12—texts that point to the day when God will establish his rule throughout the cosmos. Jesus's resurrection and ascension are in this way placed within that larger scenario of the end, when the dead will be raised to life in a renewed creation.

1 Corinthians 15

Paul's first letter to the Corinthians, usually dated around the middle of the sixth decade of the first century, is important in a very different way. First Corinthians 15 affords us the earliest written glimpse into the tradition of Easter and its meaning.

Witnesses

First Corinthians 15:3–8 is likely the earliest recorded tradition of encounters with the risen Christ. The tradition is, of course, earlier than the letter in which it is found, since Paul clearly identifies his comments as something he himself "received" (15:3). He is providing his readers with an inherited list of witnesses to the risen Jesus. Like concentric circles moving outward, Paul begins with Peter (here called Cephas) and moves outward to the Twelve, "five hundred," James (Jesus's brother, who had by the time of writing taken over leadership of the movement in Jerusalem), and to all the "apostles" (the "sent ones," that is, missionaries); last, but not least among them (despite his disclaimers), Paul lists himself as a latecomer, as one "untimely born" (15:8–10).

This list contains several features: one is that Paul identifies his own en-counter with Christ by "revelation" (e.g., Gal. 1:11–17), perhaps identified in Acts as his "Damascus Road" experience (see the various accounts in Acts 9:3–9; 22:6–11; 26:12–18), as an appearance of the risen Christ. Earlier in this letter Paul asks rhetorically: "Have I not seen Jesus our Lord?" (1 Cor. 9:1). Interestingly, Paul's experience of the risen Jesus clearly does not fall into the category of appearances immediately after Easter. Perhaps Acts' "forty days" (1:3) was intended to suggest an indeterminate period of time.

Second, Paul does not mention any women witnesses. We should not chalk that up to Paul's attitude toward women, since he does not hesitate at all to identify women as his coworkers, even as fellow apostles (e.g., Rom. 16:1, 3, 7). If there is misogynism at work in this list of witnesses, it was already at work in the formation of the tradition Paul received.

Resurrection Essential to the Faith

What motivates Paul's arguments in 1 Corinthians 15:12–28 is his desire to impress on the Corinthians that the resurrection, however much they find the notion difficult or even bizarre, is of critical importance to faith in Christ. On the surface it would appear that for many of these Greek-speaking Gentile believers the resurrection makes little sense (see Acts 17:22–34). Why raise the body, when the body is little else than a material prison from which the soul, the true person, is to be liberated?

Perhaps some in the Corinthian assembly, especially those from a pagan background, have so thoroughly reconceptualized resurrection as to make it unrecognizable to Paul. In particular, there is reason to think that they have spiritualized it in a way that lets them claim that *their* resurrection has already happened, that they have already been "raised" and are behaving ac-cordingly. That would mean, in Paul's view, that they are thereby making a claim that *the* resurrection, and with it the full transformation of the cosmos, has already taken place (the Corinthians were apparently not alone; see the warnings in 2 Thess. 2:1–3 and 2 Tim. 2:17–18). In Paul's view this is noth-ing less than to "deny the resurrection." Clearly Paul and the Corinthians need to get some things cleared up.

While this is no occasion to go into a careful analysis of Paul's response, much is at stake here. It would be too quick simply to pit a Jewish understand-ing of resurrection of the body against a Greek notion of the immortality of the soul, although there is more than a grain of truth in that.

Many Jews were able to combine a belief in the future resurrection of the body (which might be understood to be part of the "raising" of Israel [see Ezekiel 37] and in turn of the cosmos as a whole) with some notion of the ongoing disembodied repose of the soul until that "day of resurrection" when it would receive the body fit for immortality, to use Paul's language (e.g., the quotations from the Wisdom of Solomon below). Conversely, myths and legends in Greek or Hellenistic culture(s) spoke of persons who appeared to have been dead but were not in actuality or who were "translated" into the pantheon of the gods. But the "resurrection of the body" would not have made sense to Greeks, in whose view the soul is liberated at death from the confines of the earthly body that is subject to decay. For the Corinthians to deny the resurrection is, in the view of Paul, not only a denial of personal hope after death, but tantamount to a denial of the larger story of salvation of which resurrection is but one element.

Paul speaks tellingly of the kingdom. He does not do so often. Paul speaks of *Christ's* kingdom or reign as marked by the struggle with and final subjugation of the powers that resist God's will. Once all things are "subjected" to the "Son," then he will hand over the kingdom or reign to God the Father (1 Cor. 15:24). In other words, Easter makes sense only within the larger story of the reestablishment of God's reign over the cosmos. The process began with Christ's resurrection and will culminate in the resurrection of all at the great turning of the ages, something Paul believes to be just around the corner, if it is not already taking place (see 1 Corinthians 7).

To summarize, at the heart of the resurrection faith is finally nothing less than belief in the radical renewal of the cosmos. Christ is the "firstfruits" of those who have died (15:20), and his resurrection means resurrection for all who belong to Christ (15:21–23). For Christ this has already happened; for those who belong to him this will be a *future* event, one that will culminate in the elimination of evil and finally death itself (15:24–28). Any fool, in Paul's view, can tell that that has not yet fully taken place. The sorry state of the Corinthian church is proof enough!

Body Fit for Immortality

In 1 Corinthians 15:35–57 Paul attempts to explain what resurrection is to Gentile believers, for whom, as I said above, the concept is difficult if not unintelligible. Paul makes arguments that are in some ways quite different from what the gospel narratives by themselves might have led us to expect. Paul insists that people should *not* think in terms of resuscitation of bodies. He states it bluntly: "Flesh and blood cannot inherit the kingdom of God" (15:50). Yes, the resurrected person is embodied. But it will be a spiritual body, no longer subject to death (15:42–50). We should be cautious not to equate the term *spiritual* with *invisible*. That would be to betray Paul's view. The resurrected body will bear the image of the "last Adam," the "man … from heaven" (15:45, 47). Implied in this is continuity between a good creation the way God intended it before sin and death entered the picture (see Genesis 1–3) and the new creation, of which resurrection is the opening act. Even so, as much as he insists on its actuality and its crucial importance, Paul leaves the nature of resurrection and the nature of its embodiment firmly anchored in mystery.

Paul concludes his euphoric reflection on the resurrection with a taunt, quoting Hosea 13:14:

> Where, O death, is your victory?
> Where, O death, is your sting? (1 Cor. 15:55)

Evidence

One of the features of the New Testament accounts is the insistence that Jesus's resurrection actually took place. Several kinds of evidence are offered in evidence, and, as 1 Corinthians 15 makes clear, evidence mattered to the writers of the New Testament: the empty tomb, the witnesses who claimed to have encountered the risen Jesus, and the proofs offered by those who testify to having encountered the risen Jesus. To call these evidence does not mean that a skeptic cannot dismiss them or that they pass the bar of historical verification. They were believed to be persuasive by those who offer them on the pages of the New Testament. What do the earliest witnesses claim to have seen or experienced?

Empty Tomb

Prominent in every gospel is the insistence that the tomb into which the body of Jesus was laid was empty on that early Sunday morning. Scholars differ on the historical value of this tradition. Some argue that the empty tomb is one of those bedrock historical facts that demand an explanation. The explanation that early followers of Jesus give is that he was raised to life. His was, they insisted, a bodily resurrection.

That is, of course, not the only explanation possible, and the followers of Jesus knew that very well. Matthew, for example, informs us of the rumor that the disciples had themselves stolen the body and then claimed that he had risen (Matt. 28:11–15; see also 27:62–66). This may be a hint that the story of the empty tomb was known and believed not only among those who followed Jesus, but also among those who did not. Hence the competing explanations. Other scholars nevertheless consider the tradition of the empty tomb a tale fashioned largely to support the *prior* conviction that Jesus had been resurrected and a particular view of what resurrection means for bodies.

Without denying the evident difficulties the historian will have in weighing this tradition, it appears that the empty tomb figured for Jesus's followers as evidence that Jesus had been raised. To put it baldly, had someone discovered the bones of Jesus it would have constituted clear evidence in the minds of these followers that God had *not* raised Jesus from the dead. To say that still leaves unresolved the historical and scientific questions with which contemporary readers of the gospels struggle. It also leaves unanswered the question as to how an empty tomb—with its implications of considerable continuity between the pre-Easter and post-Easter Jesus—fits with how Paul, and with him no doubt many other Jews, thought about resurrection. Does it matter that Paul makes no mention of an empty tomb? In a recent major study of the resurrection, N. T. Wright suggests that when Paul specifies that Jesus was "buried" (1 Cor. 15:4) he implies what need not be said, namely, that when Jesus was raised he left the tomb empty (*Resurrection of the Son of God*, 321, 626). That may be correct, but it is worth pondering whether Paul's discussion of resurrection, especially in 1 Corinthians 15:35–57 with analogies of seed and plant, mortal and immortal clothing, requires an empty tomb.

It is clear, to summarize, that the prominence of the resurrection in the gospel accounts witnesses to the empty tomb being of considerable importance to at least a significant number of early followers of Jesus as a crucial bit piece of evidence supporting their belief in Jesus's resurrection.

Encounters/Witnesses

Witnesses are important in the early announcements of the resurrection of Jesus. They testify to what they have experienced, giving support to the faith of adherents and a challenge to detractors. Paul suggests as much in 1 Corinthians 15:6, when he tells his readers that most of the witnesses he lists "are still alive"—and thus persons who can vouch for the truth of the claims. The Corinthians do not need simply to take Paul's word for it.

Even a cursory reading of the gospels shows that women play a very important role in their accounts of Jesus's resurrection. That said, apart from the consistent presence of Mary Magdalene, the names of the other women vary to some degree. Further, as seen earlier, women are entirely absent from the tradition in 1 Corinthians 15.

In 1 Corinthians 15:5, Cephas (also called Peter and Simon) is the first one to whom the risen Jesus appears. His priority is hinted at in some of the gospel accounts as well. In John 20, for example, Peter and the Beloved Disciple race to the tomb. It appears to matter to the gospel writer who wins the race: the other disciple does, but, perhaps tellingly, does not enter the tomb. That honor is given to Simon Peter, who actually enters the tomb first. In a reference that has weak manuscript support, Luke also mentions Peter going to the tomb (24:12). Peter's role as "first witness" shows up later in Luke's account, however, in connection with the Emmaus road incident. Before Cleopas and another disciple can report to the gathered disciples on their encounter with the risen Jesus, the disciples themselves report to them that the Lord has appeared to Simon (24:34).

The interest in who was first and the complete absence of women in the tradition Paul passes on in 1 Corinthians 15:3–8 has raised the question as to whether these accounts and lists are something like status reports. Do they reflect the relative importance of these various people in the early churches? Is that why Peter and James are mentioned in the list in 1 Corinthians? Is this also why Paul adds himself to the list in 1 Corinthians 15? We get the impression from other places in the New Testament (e.g., Gal. 1:18–24) that Peter and James were two of the most important leaders in the early church. Is the issue of relative status or importance behind John's Gospel's having the Beloved Disciple accompany Peter to the tomb and get there before Peter? Was that Beloved Disciple an important leader in a part of the Jesus movement in which this particular tradition emerged or was preserved (see chapter 3 above)?

Whatever the merit of this line of enquiry, it raises some tantalizing possibilities for why women are so prominent in the four gospel accounts. Given what would have been a prevailing suspicion against women as reliable witnesses, does the prominence of Mary Magdalene in the narratives, for example, tell us something about her importance in circles of Jesus believers? And would that hold true of the other women mentioned and named, to such a degree that the tradition could not expunge their presence as the very earliest witnesses? I am convinced that it does reflect their importance, even if we must temper our enthusiasm for this possibility with the recognition that we are at best reading between the lines.

Jesus Movement/Church

Strange as it may seem, we can infer that the very existence of the church was seen as evidence for the raising of Jesus. The term *church* is a rather unfortunate translation of the term usually used for the early gatherings of those devoted to Jesus—*ekklesia*. It means, quite literally, the assembly of those called out or selected. It was a term used widely in the culture of the day and had no necessary religious connotations, as does the word *church*.

In the early decades of the Jesus movement, the surprising phenomenon of a community made up of those who were once "strangers" (Eph. 2:11–12), that is, Jews and Gentiles, slaves and free, men and women (Gal. 3:28), sharing belief, hope, food, and mutual caring, was considered nothing less than evidence of the work of the Spirit of the risen Christ, the power that raised Christ from the dead (Eph. 1:19–23). The Apostle Paul, to name only one member of the community of early witnesses and messengers, understood these small, still weak and struggling assemblies to be the body of the risen Christ, living by the power of the resurrection even as they are still very much in this present age marked by opposition to the God who raises the dead. Paul understood the church to be the daily sign of the resurrection and baptism to be the ritual of the resurrection it both lives by and still anticipates (e.g., Rom. 6:1–4; Eph. 2:1–10; 4:22–24).

To offer these assemblies we now call "church" as proof of the resurrection is both profoundly true in the mind of first-century believers and, in the eyes of most of our contemporaries, foolish in the extreme. But not to mention the sociological phenomenon of assemblies of believers in Jesus in this context would be to miss an important piece of the way the early followers of Jesus witnessed to their experience of the resurrection of Jesus.

What Was the Risen Jesus Like?

A curious person may well be interested to know what the risen Jesus was thought to have been like. Is there information to be gleaned from the accounts in the New Testament that would allow us to reconstruct what the early followers of Jesus believed they witnessed?

The data are somewhat bewildering. At times Jesus shows the marks of his crucifixion on his hands and side (John 20:27) or his hands and feet (Luke 24:36–42). At other times he eats with his disciples, just to prove he has "flesh and bones" (Luke 24:39, 42). These texts suggest at least a quasi-physical continuity between the pre-Easter and post-Easter Jesus. In these same texts, this flesh-and-bones, non-ghost, post-death Jesus (Luke 24:39) can emerge in rooms with locked doors (Luke 24:36; John 20:19, 26). What does the term *flesh and bones* mean then?

At other times, sometimes within the same narratives already mentioned, there is no obvious physical recognizability to the risen Jesus, even to his most intimate followers. For example, Jesus spends the whole day with two of his disciples on the road to Emmaus (Luke 24:13–35); they recognize him only after a characteristic *action*: their "hearts were warmed" (24:32) when they recognized him "in the breaking of the bread" (24:31, 35). This is similar to the experience of Peter and the other disciples catching fish in Galilee: when their catch is suddenly huge, they recognize Jesus on the shore (compare John 21:1–14 with Luke 5:1–11). In these Easter stories Jesus is not recognizable *physically* so much as he is recognizable in the typical or characteristic *action*. What does that imply for the concept *bodily resurrection*? What level of continuity does that suggest between the pre-Easter and the risen Jesus?

Paul, as we saw, lists himself as one of the witnesses who too has "*seen* Jesus" (1 Cor. 9:1). In 1 Corinthians 15:35–57, where Paul carries on a sustained discussion of how a resurrection body is different from a mortal body, he argues that one should be careful *not* to imagine the resurrection as a matter of resuscitation of the bodies we know. Clearly Paul understands the resurrection body to be a body, that is, an embodied self, but he is very careful to make a distinction between that kind of a body and the body that he and the Corinthians presently inhabit (Paul speaks of a "tent" in 2 Cor. 5:1–5, possibly speaking of earthly embodiment). Resurrection represents a radical *re*-creation of the person in an entirely different mode, one fit for immortality. In Paul's view such resurrection is part of the restoration and re-creation of the cosmos as a whole. And to bewilder us even more, the resurrected body of Jesus is in some mysterious way one that encompasses the assemblies of believers. How that goes together with the accounts in the gospels of a Jesus who has scars and who eats with his disciples gives us reason to ponder.

Most interesting, there is no argument among these various New Testament witnesses and writers, little if any apparent attempt to get their stories to agree with respect to the details. What this resurrected person was exactly like seems to take a back seat to *whether* the resurrection took place—and *everything* depends on that! The gospel writers and Paul are unequivocal that the raising of Jesus was a *bodily* resurrection, even if with that they do not imply that this is in any simple sense the *resuscitation* of his earthly Palestinian body. It is safe to say that in their view resurrection is not giving Jesus's body another chance; resurrection is *re*-creation, so to speak, the first installment of the major *re*-creation of the cosmos they anticipate as the full coming of the kingdom of God, "fit for immortality," as Paul puts it.

Parenthetically, support for the distinctness of Jesus's resurrection is seen in the raising of the young girl (Mark 5) and of Lazarus (John 11). They are not viewed by the gospel writers as in any sense equivalent to the raising of Jesus, even if those "resuscitations" are clearly harbingers of the great awakening they associate with the full appearing of the kingdom of God (see the emptying of the tombs in Matt. 27:52–53 and Dan. 12:2–3).

To sum up, we encounter considerable obstacles to reconstructing one coherent picture of what the New Testament writers would have understood the resurrected Christ to be like: was he physical? was he spiritual? or both? What is certain, and clearly visible to modern readers of these texts, is that there is an astonishing level of agreement among all of the gospel writers, as well as Paul, that it is *Jesus*, the man from Galilee, executed by the Romans in Jerusalem, who was encountered in these appearances. In other words, however difficult they find it to describe the exact nature of the continuity between the Jesus they knew *then* and the risen Christ they know *now*, early witnesses were of one mind that it is the *same person*. Paul does not ask his rhetorical question as, "Have I not seen Christ?" but, "Have I not seen *Jesus?*" (1 Cor. 9:1). In fact, it is both that continuity and the radical difference in the way that same person appeared to them and is now present to them that lies at the root of their insistence that this is not a matter of resuscitation but a matter of *resurrection*. Easter, they believed, was an early hint of what the world will be like when God's kingdom comes in full (as seen in Paul's use of the term *firstfruits* in 1 Cor. 15:20, 23).

The Meaning of Easter

In conclusion, let me pick up again the comments made at the outset of this study of Easter. What does Easter mean? What did it mean?

Resurrection as Vindication of Jesus

First of all, Easter is of enormous importance in relation to Jesus and how he comes to be perceived by his followers. Early followers would have seen Easter as God's final word of approval regarding what Jesus said and did and regarding his willingness to give himself even in death.

Current in the Judaism of Jesus's day was what we today call "martyr theology." A central element of this theology is the conviction that God will vindicate those who have paid with their lives for their faithfulness to God. The Wisdom of Solomon, likely written not long before the time of Jesus (see chapter 11 above), describes the vindication of the just person through God's intervention:

> Then the righteous one will stand with great confidence
> in the presence of those who have oppressed him. . . .
> [The unrighteous will speak to one another:]
> "This is one whom we once held in derision
> and made a byword of reproach—fools that we were!
> We thought that his life was madness
> and that his end was without honor.
> Why has he been numbered among the sons of God?
> And why is his lot among the saints?
> So it was we who strayed from the way of truth,
> and the light of righteousness did not shine on us,
> and the sun did not rise upon us. . . .
> But the righteous one will live forever,
> and his reward is with the Lord;
> the Most High takes care of him.
> Therefore he will receive a glorious crown
> and a beautiful diadem from the hand of the Lord,
> because with his right hand [God] will cover him,
> and with his arm [God] will shield him." (Wisdom of Solomon 5:1,
>   4–6, 15–16, adapted from NRSV)

This passage should be read in relation to Wisdom of Solomon 3, where the echoes to Isaiah 53 are quite discernable:

> But the souls of the righteous are in the hand of God,
> and no torment will ever touch them.
> In the eyes of the foolish they seemed to have died,
> and their departure was thought to be a disaster,
> and their going from us to be their destruction;
> but they are at peace.
> For though in the sight of others they were punished,
> their hope is full of immortality. . . .
> In the time of their visitation they will shine forth,
> and will run like sparks through the stubble.
> They will govern nations and rule over peoples,
> and the Lord will reign over them forever. (Wisdom of Solomon
>   3:1–4, 7–8)

The same relationship between costly faithfulness and divine vindication is illuminated more specifically in 2 Maccabees, roughly contemporaneous with the beginnings of the Jesus movement. A pagan king attempts to get Jews to eat pork, forbidden by Torah. A mother and her seven sons are cruelly tortured on the orders of the king. Their stubborn, dying words speak volumes to us of resurrection as divine vindication:

> And when he was at his last breath, [the second brother] said, "You accursed wretch, you dismiss us from this present life, but the King of the universe will raise us up to an everlasting renewal of life, because we have died for his laws." (2 Maccabees 7:9)

The mother speaks to her dying sons in the following way:

> I do not know how you came into being in my womb. It was not I who gave you life and breath, nor I who set in order the elements within each of you. Therefore the Creator of the world, who shaped the beginning of humankind and devised the origin of all things, will in his mercy give life and breath back to you again, since you now forget yourselves for the sake of his laws. (2 Maccabees 7:22–23)

We see that those who die in selfless obedience to God's will receive not only divine approval but exaltation to the status of monarch (see especially Wisdom of Solomon 5:16). This comes to expression in 1 Corinthians 15:25, where Paul borrows a phrase from a hymn sung at the enthronement of a king, Psalm 110:1, to the effect that God "has put all his enemies under his feet," implying that resurrection was for Jesus the enthronement and victory of a monarch. A fragment of one of the earliest creeds or confessions of the followers of Jesus is embedded in Paul's letter to the Romans, where Paul speaks of Jesus as "descended from David according to the flesh and . . . declared to be Son of God with power according the spirit of holiness by resurrection from the dead, Jesus Christ our Lord" (Rom. 1:4). This early creed suggests that Jesus's divine sonship is made fully manifest in the resurrection. Resurrection, vindication, and exaltation are part of one large, encompassing scenario of divine intervention. They bring together the theme of the enthronement of a monarch in Israel with the vindication and resurrection of a faithful and just person who has suffered to the point of death in the exercise of righteousness.

The importance of this can hardly be overstressed. Anticipating the next chapter, the resurrection of Jesus lies at the basis of the early followers becoming more than followers. They become devotees and believers in Jesus, confessing and proclaiming him to be Son of God, Lord of the cosmos. In short, we cannot account for the faith of the movement centered on Jesus apart from the conviction that he had been raised.

Resurrection as Eschatological and Cosmic Event

Easter is fundamentally an eschatological event. That is, it has meaning within the big story of God's salvation of the whole cosmos, of what will happen when God finally (at the end of this age) brings about the full appearing of the kingdom of God. Death will be defeated and finally banished from the scene (1 Corinthians 15). The righteous dead will be raised to their eternal reward (2 Maccabees 7). This notion was eventually broadened to include the raising of *all* people, both the good and the bad. The good will be rewarded, the evil condemned (as in the parable of the sheep and goats in Matthew 25; see chapter 8 above). So, more than only the vindication and exaltation of that one man from Nazareth, Jesus's resurrection is the signal that God has begun the remaking of the cosmos. The revolution has started.

The New Testament gives witness to a level of eschatological, specifically apocalyptic, anticipation among many of Jesus's early followers. Paul's letters attest to this, as we have already seen. Indeed, his earliest known letter illustrates in striking imagery the vivid nature of this anticipation:

> But we do not want you to be uninformed, brothers and sisters, about those who have died, so that you may not grieve as others do who have no hope. For since we believe that Jesus died and rose again, even so, through Jesus, God will bring with him those who have died. For this we declare to you by the word of the Lord, that we who are alive, who are left until the coming of the Lord, will by no means precede those who have died. For the Lord himself, with a cry of command, with the archangel's call and with the sound of God's trumpet, will descend from heaven, and the dead in Christ will rise first. Then we who are alive, who are left, will be caught up in the clouds together with them to meet the Lord in the air; and so we will be with the Lord forever. Therefore encourage one another with these words. (1 Thess. 4:13–18)

This all means that Jesus's resurrection is not seen as an isolated event. Rather, the resurrection identifies him as Son of God and agent—God's Messiah. It also identifies him as *the* primal human who was the first to experience the remaking of humanity—the "firstfruits of the resurrection," as Paul puts it (1 Cor. 15:20, 23, 42–49). In short, for early believers the resurrection of Jesus spells good news for all human beings. It represents a way of setting Jesus apart, in terms of exaltation, but it also represents good news for what was in store for the rest of humanity. This is captured in Jesus's instructions to Mary Magdalene. She is to say to Jesus's "brothers": "I am ascending to my Father and your Father, to my God and your God" (John 20:17).

That the resurrection is an inherently *eschatological* event cannot be stressed too strongly. Easter oriented the church to the future. In the eyes of his followers Jesus turns out to have been right despite his apparent failure on the cross: the kingdom of God is coming, and it has already shown its powerful presence not only in the life of Jesus, but also in his death, and most dramatically now in his resurrection. As such it announces *what is to come*!

Resurrection and the Present Life

I have so far stressed the relationship of Jesus's resurrection to the anticipation of the future resurrection of all as part of the remaking of the cosmos. The Corinthians were wrong in denying that, whether by outright denial of resurrection or through reconceptualizing to such a degree that it could be said to having already happened. Given their newness to the movement and the novelty for them of the notion of the resurrection, they might be forgiven.

They might also be forgiven for another reason: early Jesus believers were not simply in a waiting mode. They believed that what happened in the case of Jesus has a profound impact on the present. Baptism reminded every believer that she or he has said no to the old way of being human and yes to the new:

> How can we who died to sin go on living in it? Do you not know that all of us who have been baptized into Christ Jesus were baptized into his death? Therefore we have been buried with him by baptism into death, so that, just as Christ was raised from the dead by the glory of the Father, *so we too might walk in newness of life.*
>
> For if we have been united with him in a death like his, we will certainly be united with him in a resurrection like his. (Rom. 6:2–5, emphasis added)

Sometimes the insistence on the *present* relevance of the resurrection for those still awaiting the full revealing of the sons and daughters of God, the "redemption of the body" (Rom. 8:18–25) in the *future*, can sound almost like the resurrection has already taken place:

If anyone is in Christ, there is a new creation: everything old has passed away; see, everything has become new! (2 Cor. 5:17)

God, who is rich in mercy, out of the great love with which he loved us even when we were dead through our trespasses, *made us alive* together with Christ—by grace you *have been saved*—and *raised us up with him* and *seated us with him* in the heavenly places in Christ Jesus. (Eph. 2:4–6, emphasis added)

New Testament writers thus understand the resurrection of Jesus to have a decisive effect on the practice, on the ethics of believers, individually and in community (see, e.g., Col. 2:1–17). Not only do they act in *hope* and with *patience* but they act with *power*:

So it is with the resurrection of the dead. What is sown is *perishable*, what is raised is *imperishable*. It is sown in *dishonor*, it is raised in *glory*. It is sown in *weakness*, it is raised in *power*. (1 Cor. 15:42–43, emphasis added)

Implicitly, resurrection is about revolution, about the bringing to an end of injustice, oppression, poverty—death. New Testament writers see their assemblies as places where this world-changing revolution is already taking hold. We cannot likely explain the resilience of the early communities of followers of Jesus in the face of opposition, even death, and their willingness to face the empire as an alternative community apart from their resurrection faith (e.g., 1 Thess. 5:1–11, where "peace and security" is an obvious imperial slogan).

Contemporary Interpretations of Easter

A considerable range of views as to how the resurrection of Jesus should be interpreted meets us in contemporary literature and public discourse. Many fall well short, in my view, of capturing the depth and range of convictions and hopes that mark the faith of New Testament writers and their coreligionists.

At one end of the spectrum are many who take the New Testament accounts as the rough equivalent of a scientific report. They imagine the resurrection as essentially a supernatural resuscitation of Jesus's body. They are often unwilling to acknowledge the mysterious variety of data in the New Testament texts ill suited to one coherent scientific explanation. The focus on the miraculous also tends to crowd out the larger eschatological framework within which these accounts make sense, as well as the metaphorical and allusive nature of many elements in the accounts.

Many others today think of the resurrection as a mythological way of expressing the ongoing relevance of Jesus. Resurrection may remain an important way theologically to express the power of God over defeat and despair, but it would be wrong to look for some historical event behind this rather ornate myth, other than the historical event of this belief among die-hard followers of Jesus. Some suggest therefore that the true Easter miracle is that there were those who continued to hold fast to the teachings and way of life of an executed troublemaker. Easter means not that *Jesus* rose from the dead but, in effect, that the *movement* rose after his death.

Early followers of Jesus would have distanced themselves from an understanding of resurrection as resuscitation. Resurrection was of a different order, as we have seen. But they would most assuredly also have distanced themselves from an interpretation of Easter, increasingly popular at present, that sees it as a powerful myth expressing indomitable hope and resilience. They would have said—and did! (see Paul at the beginning of this chapter)—that the veracity of their faith was dependent on whether *God* raised *Jesus* and had begun the re-creation of the cosmos. Their faith rested on God's action in raising Jesus, with all that that implies for the world and for the kingdom of God, not on having given them the confidence to go on despite Jesus's absence. To say that is not to dismiss the importance of the Easter faith on the daily lives of Jesus's followers, then as now (see Rom. 6:1–14; Eph. 2:1–10). Early followers of Jesus would have insisted on tethering Easter's importance to its having happened and because it happened, to the present and, most importantly, to what will happen in the future.

Conclusion

I have attempted in this chapter to show how centrally important Easter is to the faith that Jesus is the Christ. The Christian religion becomes something very different if Easter is taken out of the picture or when it is so radically redefined as to stretch the term beyond recognition. Was resurrection an event in real history? Jesus's early followers would have insisted on that without hesitation. Everything depends on that being true. I return once more to the words of Paul:

> If there is no resurrection of the dead, then Christ has not been raised; and if Christ has not been raised, then our proclamation has been in vain and your faith has been in vain. . . . If Christ has not been raised, your faith is futile and you are still in your sins. Then those also who have died in Christ have perished. *If for this life only we have hoped in Christ, we are of all people most to be pitied.* (1 Cor. 15:13–14, 17–19, emphasis added)

*If you confess with your lips that Jesus is Lord and believe in your heart that
God raised him from the dead, you will be saved.* (Rom. 10:9, emphasis added)

To claim that for early followers of Jesus everything depended on the
truth of Easter, that is, whether Christ had been raised from the dead, does
not mean that it lends itself in any obvious way to historical verification.
Proofs or evidence that were once "convincing" (Acts 1:3) may be so no
longer. Proving something by the exacting standards of the modern scientist or historian is an entirely different matter. The scientific toolbox of the
historian is hardly equipped for such an enterprise (Wright would wish
to expand the toolbox of historians to permit a serious wrestling with the
claims of resurrection in his *Resurrection of the Son of God*). With respect to
Easter, I suspect that historical toolboxes contain tools only to verify that
there were people who believed this to be true and who banked everything
on it being true.

That is an important finding, to be sure. But it leaves the historian before
another set of questions: did apocalyptic anticipation give birth to the belief
in the resurrection of Jesus? Or was it an entirely surprising experience in
which his followers believed they met Jesus *after* his crucifixion that precipitated or at least spurred on the anticipation that the full coming of God's
kingdom had indeed begun? I believe the second explanation is the more
plausible. After all, it would have been entirely consistent with a belief in
the resurrection *to come* that Jesus's followers would have waited together for
the raising of the Righteous One at some point in the future. Anomalous
entirely within any of the sets of expectations that first-century believers
were in possession of is the belief that Jesus had been raised, the firstfruits
of the resurrection to come in the future.

The controversies over Easter will continue both because of the importance of Easter for the Christian religion and because of the historical and
scientific difficulties attending the claim that God raised Jesus of Nazareth
from the dead. Despite their desire to reassure their readers that there were
witnesses who could vouch for the truth of their momentous claims, both
Paul and the evangelists appear to have been aware that historical enquiry,
then as now, can take us only so far. Matthew lets it slip that, even at the
final moment of the risen Jesus's commissioning of his followers, "some
doubted" (28:17). And Thomas, despite his being the very first to recognize
and confess Jesus as divine (John 20:28), has been forever tarred in popular
culture with the label *doubting*. Jesus's words to him and to all who struggle
mightily with the resurrection and who would wish for empirical proof are
a fitting conclusion to this chapter:

Blessed are those who have not seen and yet have come to believe! (John
20:29)

**Key Terms
and Concepts**

empty tomb
eschatology
resurrection
witnesses to the
resurrection

For Further Reading

Marxen, Willi. *The Resurrection of Jesus of Nazareth*. Philadelphia: Fortress, 1970.

Stewart, Robert B. *The Resurrection of Jesus: John Dominic Crossan and N. T. Wright in Dialogue*. Minneapolis: Fortress, 2006.

Wright, N. T. *Christian Origins and the Question of God*, vol. 3: *The Resurrection of the Son of God*. Minneapolis: Fortress, 2003.

13

Jesus—Christ and Lord

W̲ᴇ ᴡɪʟʟ ꜰᴏᴄᴜꜱ in this final chapter on how early followers of Jesus understood and expressed their devotion to and convictions about who Jesus *was* and, importantly, *is*. This is typically referred to as Christology. Larry Hurtado recently proposed that we speak less of Christology, which focuses on ideas or concepts, and more of "devotion to Jesus," which takes in practice, worship, and, I would add, ethics. This is an important insight. To confess Jesus as "Lord" and "Christ" thus expresses not only a way of thinking about Jesus, but also a pledge of obedience, a commitment to a way of life. This is exactly what we see in the New Testament.

One illustration will suffice: in Mark 8:27–31 || Matthew 16:13–21 || Luke 9:18–22, Jesus asks his followers, "Who do you say that I am?" Peter answers, "You are the Messiah, the Son of the living God!" This episode represents the climax in the narrative up to that point (see chapter 3 above). It is also a shocking moment in that Peter turns out not to catch on that this will mean that Jesus, the "Son of Man," will die. To compound matters, Jesus insists immediately thereafter that his followers take up *their own* cross and "follow" him (Mark 8:34–9:1 || Matt. 16:24–28 || Luke 9:23–27). In this pivotal episode Mark recalls for his readers not only the tenuousness of the grasp that Jesus's followers had of his identity and mission during his time with them in Galilee, but also his understanding some four decades later of the indissoluble relationship between christological insight and living like Jesus.

In this chapter the titles attributed to Jesus typically carry with them an implicit summons to a way of life. Indeed, the ancient creeds that insisted that Jesus is both divine and human (see chapter 2 above) thus link Jesus not only with God, making him an "icon" of God, as Colossians 1:15 puts it, but also an icon of humanity as God intended it, and thus implicitly a model for how humans are to live in conformity to the Creator's will. Readers should keep that double identity and its implicit challenge in mind when working through this chapter.

We began in chapter 2 by digging down from the present to the beginnings, using the metaphor of archeology. Now, we are going in the other direction. Perhaps we should switch the metaphor from one of retrieval to one of growth, from archeology to botany. A fitting biblical metaphor, often recalled at Christmastime, is a shoot growing out of an old stump or root. The prophet Isaiah anticipates the coming of an ideal king, a messiah, as a branch from the stump or root of Jesse (King David's father):

> A shoot shall come out from the stump of Jesse,
>   and a branch shall grow out of his roots.
> The spirit of the LORD shall rest on him,
>   the spirit of wisdom and understanding,
>   the spirit of counsel and might,
>   the spirit of knowledge and the fear of the LORD. . . .
> With righteousness he shall judge the poor,
>   and decide with equity for the meek of the earth;
> he shall strike the earth with the rod of his mouth,
>   and with the breath of his lips he shall kill the wicked.
> Righteousness shall be the belt around his waist,
>   and faithfulness the belt around his loins. . . .
> On that day the root of Jesse shall stand as a signal to the peoples; the nations shall inquire of him, and his dwelling shall be glorious. (Isa. 11:1–2, 4–5, 10)

Paul quotes this prophecy in his letter to the Romans:

> The root of Jesse shall come,
>   the one who rises to rule the Gentiles;
> in him the Gentiles [or nations] shall hope. (Rom. 15:12)

Throughout this study we have attempted to view Jesus within the context of his own Jewish world and piety, a piety with deep roots in history and ritual. But we also know that over the past two millennia Jesus has become the centerpiece of the faith of millions who have come to think of him as Messiah, as Son of God, as Lord, indeed as God, often with little awareness of Jesus's Jewish roots. Is such devotion rooted in the story of Jesus? Is it the outgrowth of the story we have uncovered or a graft—or even another plant altogether?

In this chapter we will try to show that Christology, or, more broadly, devotion to Jesus, is not an alien phenomenon, but the natural growth and development of the ministry, teaching, death, and resurrection of Jesus. Borrowing language from Isaiah, it is the flowering of the shoot that has grown out of stump of an old tree, nourished by the deep roots of experience, tradition, and scripture.

Background and Context

Monotheism and Christology

One of the thorny issues in any discussion of Christology is the relationship between Jewish monotheism and the veneration of Jesus. This issue has been a vexing one between Christians and both Jews and Muslims, who find the Christian assertions at best puzzling and at worst a violation of the oneness of God. Perplexing as it may be, early followers of Jesus insisted that in their devotion to Jesus they were fully in line with the Jewish prayer, the Shema, from Deuteronomy 6:4:

> Listen, Israel: YHWH our God, YHWH is one. (literal translation)
> Hear, O Israel: The LORD our God, the LORD alone. (NIV)
> Hear, O Israel: The LORD is our God, the LORD alone. (NRSV)

These various translations illustrate the issue at stake. Nothing could be more important to a Jew but to insist that only YHWH is God. The name of the sole deity was so sacrosanct that it was typically referred to as "the Name" or replaced with "Lord" (see chapter 4 above). Imagine then what consternation would have struck fellow Jews when devotees of Jesus called him "Lord" in ways that Jews were used to speaking of and to only YHWH. Even so, followers of Jesus did not see themselves stepping over the line, whatever their contemporaries thought they were doing. Listen, for example, to the Apostle Paul:

> Even though there may be so-called gods in heaven or on earth—as in fact there are many gods and many lords—yet for us there is one God, the Father, from whom are all things and for whom we exist, and one Lord, Jesus Christ, through whom are all things and through whom we exist. (1 Cor. 8:5–6)

However we might assess the success of early Jesus believers in staying true to their Jewish monotheistic moorings, any attempt to understand early Christian language about Jesus will need to wrestle with this issue: post-Easter devotees of Jesus *both* insisted on the oneness of God *and* often

deliberately applied language traditionally used in relation to this one God
to express their respect for and devotion of Jesus—and they did so very soon
after Easter. They did so in the choice of vocabulary with which to express
their devotion in confession and worship, but also in the way they attempted
with varying success to imitate the life of Jesus and heed his teachings in
their dealings with each other and the world. In Jesus's teachings they heard
the word of God; in his life they saw the will of God expressed; and with
their own lives they attempted to venerate him in the very way they had
learned to venerate God.

Jews and Gentiles

Within a few years, at most a few decades, the Jesus movement had become a varied amalgam of Jews and non-Jews (or Gentiles). The non-Jews
were by no means a homogenous group, but were likely Gentiles attracted
already earlier to Judaism ("God fearers") and pagans engaged to one degree
or another in any number of Greco-Roman religions. Language means
different things to different folks. This very diverse community would thus
have shaped the development of the language of devotion for Jesus. We
should not expect that it would be any different with language once fully
at home in a Jewish matrix being brought into contexts not at all familiar
with that context.

Mediator

The ancient world was familiar with so-called mediator figures who bridged
the gap between human beings and deities. As later Trinitarian formulations
would also show (see chapter 2 above), Jesus was understood to bridge the
gap between humanity and God. This is anticipated in the New Testament:

> There is one God;
>   there is also one mediator between God and humankind,
> Christ Jesus, himself human,
>   who gave himself a ransom for all. (1 Tim. 2:5–6)

The nature of this bridge was a highly controversial one. Was Jesus someone who had access to God in a special way? Was he God's agent to bring
about salvation for humanity? Was he thus a very special human being? Or
was he divine, but not in a way so as to infringe on the oneness of God? If
he was fully divine, fully God, how could one continue to insist that "the
Lord our God is one"?

It is easy to see why these questions would become a source of intense
controversy. As today's vast literature on Jesus illustrates amply, the contro-

versy has not abated. What would enliven the debate in the first century was, once again, the mix of traditions that came together in the community of those devoted to following and worshiping Jesus, made up of both Jews and Gentiles.

Impetus for Christological Development

What got the christological ball rolling? What precipitated the belief in Jesus as more than a teacher from Galilee, a Jewish healer and exorcist, and as more than a prophet of the kingdom of God? To put it that way is not in any sense to downplay the importance of those aspects of Jesus's life and ministry. They are, after all, an essential and necessary aspect of the record the evangelists have left us.

EASTER

The first impetus, if not in chronological order then perhaps in order of importance, was Easter. We saw in the last chapter that Easter combines two intersecting story lines: the first story line is that God looks after the righteous even if they die in the practice of faithfulness. Resurrection was understood by eschatologically oriented Jews to be part of how God looks after the righteous, how the just are vindicated. The second story line is related: the resurrection of the dead is not only the vindication of the just, but is a part of the larger story of God's addressing the brokenness of the whole cosmos. In short, the resurrection of the dead is a part of the great world-transforming event of the full and complete arrival of the kingdom of God.

Applied to Jesus, these two intersecting story lines signified for early followers of Jesus that in raising him from the dead God vindicated this just man. Easter represents a dramatic and decisive affirmation that the one who was accused of lawlessness, of contaminating himself with sinners, of identifying himself illegitimately with God's will—he spoke truth, acted justly, and did God's will without qualification. To say that God vindicated Jesus is to say that God exalted him, raised him up, and enthroned him.

The early followers of Jesus insisted that his resurrection must not be isolated from the larger picture of God's redemption of the cosmos. Jesus's resurrection is thus the firstfruits of the resurrection of all, as Paul says in 1 Corinthians 15:20–26 (see chapter 12 above). God put his stamp of approval on Jesus, and with the resurrection of Jesus God's dramatic transformation of the cosmos has begun.

JESUS HIMSELF

A further impetus for christological development was Jesus himself. Through his words and actions, especially as focused on the kingdom of

God, Jesus prepared his followers for the christological explosion that Easter precipitated. With (1) his authoritative and daring announcement in word and deed that God's reign was appearing, (2) his very intimate and strong bond with God as his father, and (3) his own sense of mission that informed the anticipation of his own death (see chapter 11 above), he left his followers with basic building blocks for their christological constructions. In other words, Jesus prepared the ground even if at the time, as the evangelists insist, his disciples understood too little of what he was saying or doing. Easter *confirmed* that Jesus had been right, and thus it *precipitated* the process of remembering in earnest.

Such a claim is today controversial. Many scholars are not so sure that Jesus believed himself to be as special as later Christology would suggest; he may have understood himself to be a man with a mission, the mission being to announce what he called the kingdom of God. Scholars who doubt or even deny Jesus had a "messianic self-consciousness" typically credit Easter—or, if not Easter, then the conviction that Jesus had been raised—for precipitating the veneration of Jesus. As the church became less and less Jewish, and thus more open to pagan influence, the christological train gained speed, we might say. Scholars approaching the matter from this perspective are understandably reluctant, or more likely opposed, to making Jesus responsible for what they consider to be later Christian myth.

Some years ago I heard one of the leading Jesus scholars, John Dominic Crossan, muse in public that if Jesus truly preached and enacted the kingdom of God then people would *necessarily* have asked him, "Who do you think you are?" That is: "Do you think you are the Messiah?" But if that is so self-evident, is it plausible that Jesus would not *himself* have been conscious of that question and that he would not have addressed it, even if circumspectly, and even if it did not register fully in the minds of his followers until *after* Easter?

Surely Jesus could not have sidestepped questions about his identity and mission during his own life. His message and his activity made him a lightning rod precisely for the kinds of questions to which Christology then becomes a post-Easter answer. The gospels, the only relevant records we have, indicate that Jesus was very much aware of his calling and his mission (see chapters 7 and 11 above). At the same time, the evangelists to varying degrees also depict Jesus as rather nervous about being identified in such lofty terms as Messiah and Son of God. That said, the gospels are clear that the issue lay not with whether Jesus thought himself to be God's Messiah; his nervousness arose out of the difference in his understanding of how that was to be done and the expectations of the people (see chapter 3 above).

There is no doubt that post-Easter Christology affects the way the pre-Easter Jesus is described in the gospels, making it sometimes difficult to sort out what is pre-Easter and what is post-Easter. Most dramatically this appears to be the case with John's Gospel. It is therefore all the more remarkable how much the pre-Easter Jesus acts and speaks in ways that put severe strain on christological language. In short, as much as the gospel writers are writing *after* Easter about what came *before* Easter and as much as they wish to have their readers encounter the post-Easter living Christ, they are very careful to allow readers to experience the mystery and bewilderment the pre-Easter Jesus evoked in his contemporaries. In doing so, readers are forced to identify with the bumbling and confused disciples, trying to sort it all out until Jesus's resurrection makes it clear that he is indeed the Messiah, the Son of God. In no way does that undermine the strong likelihood, as I have suggested earlier, that Jesus himself was in some way responsible for precipitating later christological development.

To sum up, unless we want to drive a major wedge between Jesus and his followers—as much present Jesus scholarship does—we should think of Jesus as laying the groundwork for Christology, even if we will want to credit his followers with a great deal of inspired creativity in the process.

Christology and a Multitude of Titles

The term *Christology*, the technical term for making sense of the significance and identity of Jesus, highlights especially the title *Christ* or *Messiah*. It is used, however, for the study of the whole field of how Jesus is perceived and venerated, and thus it covers the study of all titles or designations for Jesus.

The basic question this chapter attempts to explore is this: how did the man from Nazareth come to be venerated as Son of God, or even as God? *How did the one with a message become the message?*

The answer is not at all simple. First is the multitude of titles for Jesus:

Lord	Icon (or Image)
Messiah	Wisdom
Son of God	High Priest
Servant of God	True Vine
Son of Man	Good Shepherd
Son of David	Door
Righteous One	Truth
Lamb of God	Way
New Adam (or True Human)	Life
Word	Resurrection

These names are obviously metaphorical or parabolic, used within the euphoria of worship more than as tools of doctrinal precision. They express both veneration and allegiance, both worship and obedience. Each of the titles or names tells a story. None of these titles were invented on the spot to suit Jesus. They all root Jesus's identity in the traditions and anticipations of Judaism and at the same time make enormous tradition-shattering claims about him. They carry the freight of veneration, hope, and faith, born and nurtured within the long history of suffering and expectation. And, as the movement centered on Jesus as the Christ became more and more open to Gentiles and took hold throughout the Greco-Roman Mediterranean world, these terms of respect, honor, and veneration would take on yet-further hues of meaning.

Second, we should not imagine that everyone used all of these ways of giving expression to devotion to Jesus. The early Jesus movement was from the beginning diverse in terms of religious background, class, and region. We should thus not be surprised if different ways of addressing and confessing Jesus found greater acceptance among some early believers than among others. Urbanized Jews living in Rome or Athens might have had different sensitivities from rural Palestinian Jews. Gentiles whose culture of origin was decidedly polytheistic might have been more attracted to some vocabulary than those coming out of strict monotheism. That much we should assume. But how should we assess these differences? Do these titles reflect mutually exclusive views of Jesus or only different emphases?

It is striking that early believers used many titles side by side, even if they tell different stories and reflect varying perspectives and claims. This is important for the study of Christology since the taxonomical interests of scholars often collide with the actual use of these varying titles in the worship life of real communities of faith. This is the vocabulary of worship, veneration, devotion, and obedience. We should then not be surprised if we find a certain piling on of expressions of veneration, without a concern for whether these terms carry different doctrinal freight or are drawn from various parts of the tradition.

Development from Low Christology to High Christology

As stressed often in this book, Easter represented in the thinking of early Christians a major turning point in God's dealings with not only humanity but the world as a whole. The early followers of Jesus were therefore essentially *forward-looking*, eagerly anticipating the completion of this great revolution in the very near future. This also affected, quite naturally, their Christology. We should then not be surprised that the earliest christological emphasis falls, first, on the vindication of Jesus as the messenger of the kingdom, as the Righteous One, and second, on his coming in the very near future as Lord and Son of Man, coming to save and to judge (e.g., 1 Thess. 4:13–18; Acts 1).

When we get to later writings in the New Testament, such as the gospels, especially the Gospel of John, or the later Pauline writings such as Colossians and Ephesians (quite possibly penned by Paul's followers), the eschatological stance appears to have shifted somewhat. People took stock of Jesus's having not yet returned. They responded in two rather different ways.

Some drew the inference that the general resurrection of the dead must already have taken place. That means, of course, that they needed to radically recast their understanding of their own resurrection as an inward spiritual reality (see chapter 12 above). New Testament writers warn of such views (e.g., 2 Thess. 2:1–3; 2 Tim. 2:18). Some New Testament writers, like the Gospel of John or the author of the letter to the Ephesians (e.g., 2:1–10), reflect some of this reconceptualization while retaining a future orientation (see chapter 3 above). Others thought in quite different terms: Christ will indeed come at some indeterminate point in the future; our task is to be ready for that moment, however far away it seems to us (e.g., 2 Peter 3:8–10).

Regardless of which way they sorted out the return of Christ and the nature of the future hope, the question grew in importance and urgency: who is Christ *now*? So, as attention shifted from the future to the present and then to the past, we find a growing interest in elaborating who Christ truly *is* and *always has been*. In the process, christological claims became more all-encompassing. Scholarship speaks in terms of an increasingly high Christology. The repertoire expands and deepens and moves up the scale of respect and status.

A word of caution: we should not oversimplify the development from a low Christology to a high Christology or stretch it out over so long a period. Nor should we think in oversimplified terms of a Jewish low Christology and a Gentile high Christology. What we might consider low and high quite happily *coexisted* in the worship life of early communities of Jesus believers. The letter to the Hebrews, for example, is a virtual storehouse of christological titles and concepts, some of which imply that Jesus is a human being, others a heavenly being without beginning or end. The author of Acts too can place Righteous One, Prophet, Servant, Messiah, and the Author of Life next to each other without hesitation (see the sermons of Peter and Stephen in Acts 2 and Acts 7). No doubt some of this messiness or lack of taxonomical fastidiousness is a result of the euphoria of respect and worship. Even so, one should be cautious about assuming too rigid a pattern of development.

Christological Titles and Names: Do They Imply Deity or Divinity?

In our day there is a great deal of controversy about whether one should talk about Jesus as being God. Each of the symbolic titles or names for Jesus is somewhat fuzzy—to varying degrees, to be sure—on whether they imply the divinity or deity of Jesus. As we will see, some clearly do not *by themselves* imply divinity; others suggest it but do not necessitate it; yet others leave that question completely ambiguous; and some make the inference virtually unavoidable.

New Testament scholar James Dunn suggests that we peg the various designations along a "spectrum of respect" (*Unity and Diversity in the New Testament*). At one end of the spectrum Jesus is only human, however special; at the other end, he is solely divine (see illustration 13.1).

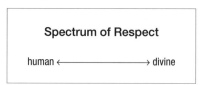

As we will see, it is difficult to peg any of the titles for Jesus on this spectrum with any certainty, because they all enjoy a range of meaning. It is precisely this mix of signals that plays a role in the later Trinitarian formulations (quoted in chapter 2 above), in which church leaders insisted that Jesus was *both fully* human and *fully* divine. How else is it possible to accommodate the bewildering data we are about to survey?

Titles, Names, and Symbols

Each symbolic title or name conveys important information about Jesus (see illustration 13.2).

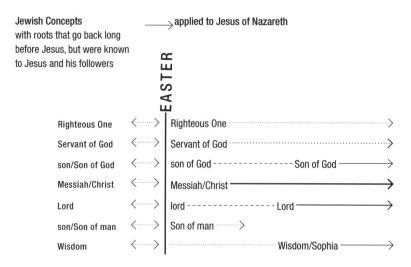

Note: Arrow strength indicates the relative holding power of the language of devotion and allegiance.

Righteous One (or Just One)

Referring to Jesus as Righteous One (or Just One) has already emerged in our discussion of his death and resurrection. "Righteous" or "just" translates the Greek adjective *dikaios*. We cannot be sure how widely this term was used for Jesus as a title, but it does appear in several key places, especially in Luke's writings. Inexplicably, translations sometimes obscure its presence by translating it "innocent." While quoting the NRSV I am rendering *dikaios* with Righteous One:

> While he was sitting on the judgment seat, [Pilate's] wife sent word to him, "Have nothing to do with that Righteous One [NRSV: innocent man], for today I have suffered a great deal because of a dream about him." (Matt. 27:19)

> When the centurion saw what had taken place, he praised God and said, "Certainly this man was a Righteous One [NRSV: innocent]." (Luke 23:47)

> But you rejected the Holy and Righteous One and asked to have a murderer given to you. (Acts 3:14)

> Which of the prophets did your ancestors not persecute? They killed those who foretold the coming of the Righteous One, and now you have become his betrayers and murderers. (Acts 7:52)

> The God of our ancestors has chosen you to know his will, to see the Righteous One and to hear his own voice. (Acts 22:14)

> You have condemned and murdered the Righteous One [NRSV: righteous one, not restricting it to Jesus], who does not resist you. (James 5:6)

> For Christ also suffered for sins once for all, a Righteous One [NRSV: the righteous] for the unrighteous. (1 Pet. 3:18)

This designation places Jesus into the familiar story line of the faithful one who gives his life in the practice of God's will, who suffers for it, and who can then count on God's vindication. The hymn of the Suffering Servant in Isaiah 53 gives a good sense of this paradigmatic character, as does Wisdom of Solomon 2–5 (see chapter 11 above).

Where should this christological designation be placed on our spectrum of respect? As we shall see in the case of the closely related terms *servant* and *son*, to be a righteous or just person is to be a very remarkable individual, one whose faithfulness to God sets him or her apart from those who fall short. As we see from the Wisdom of Solomon 2, the righteous person has a very special and intimate relationship with God, reflected both in his special character and in his exaltation and enthronement as reward for his faithfulness (see chapter 12 above). But it would be stretching the conceptual framework beyond the breaking point to see it as implying divinity. True, through the quality of his faithfulness to God, the righteous person shows "what he's made of," so to speak, but divine status, if that is how one should interpret the ultimate fate of the righteous person, is at best a gift, a reward for faithfulness.

Given Jesus's suffering and death, and especially given the conviction of early followers that God had raised Jesus from the dead, we should not be surprised that this term should have been richly resonant for them. It goes a long way in telling the story of Jesus's life and fate at the hands of humanity and, importantly, of God. It just as clearly identifies him, his teachings, and his way of life as normative for all those who believe him to come from God. He is not so much uniquely righteous as he is thereby a model for all who wish to practice justice. That said, this designation is not adequate *by itself* to carry the full freight of christological significance.

Servant of God

Very closely related to the concept of the Righteous One is the designation *servant*, translating Greek *pais* and Hebrew *ebed*. Interestingly, *pais* is sometimes translated "child" (the genitive form of *pais* is *paidos*, from which we derive the term *pedagogy*, which means "leading a child"), indicating something of the social status of both servants and children. But when translated "child," it can also suggest a relationship of care and intimacy. Some of this semantic stretch can be observed in Luke's writings: Luke is able to use *pais* for the twelve-year-old "boy" Jesus in the temple (Luke 2:43) and identically but with a fuller sense for Jesus as God's "servant" (Acts 4:27, 30).

The designation "servant," especially when combined with "of the LORD," has deep roots within Jewish tradition. It suggests being completely and absolutely at the disposal of God—being a *slave* of YHWH. It also suggests status—being a slave of the *LORD*. These various connotations are captured well in Isaiah 42:1 (quoted in Matt. 12:18–21), a text discussed together with Psalm 2 in relation to Jesus's baptism (see chapter 7 above):

> Here is my *servant*, whom I uphold,
>   my *chosen*, in whom my soul delights;
> I have put *my* spirit upon him;
>   *he* will bring forth justice to the nations. (Isa. 42:1, emphasis added)

This text comes from the so-called Servant Songs of Isaiah (found in Isaiah 40–55), which capture perfectly the meaning of being the servant of the LORD. They describe and celebrate the life, fate, and suffering of God's Servant (see chapter 11 above).

Of special relevance to our discussion of Christology is the ongoing debate as to the identity of the servant in Isaiah. Is the Servant of God a suffering prophet? a suffering king? a suffering people, sent into exile, but called to be God's agent of reconciliation and renewal in the world? all of these? We should respect the ambiguity of the language as very fruitful (e.g., Luke calls Jesus *pais*, meaning both "boy" and "servant of God," and he also employs the term to refer both to Israel as a whole [Luke 1:54] and specifically to David [1:69]; see also Acts 4:25).

The ambiguity of the term fits the strange but for us now understandable mix of vulnerability and status in the evangelists' depiction of Jesus. It also fits the strange mix of early Christians' insistence on the special status of Jesus *and* their own participation in that status and mission. It thus identifies again the inextricable relationship between Christology and ethics.

The identity in Isaiah of the *servant-as-prophet* fits well the "biography of a prophet" seen in the Gospel of Mark (see chapter 3 above). The *servant-as-king* anticipates the tensions inherent in the way Jesus was Messiah, a suffering king who gives himself for the sake not only of his people, but also for the sake of his and God's enemies. The *servant-as-people* anticipates the way in which Jesus's vocation would be democratized and picked up by his followers (Matt. 10; Luke 10) and then by the church as his body (1 Corinthians 12; Romans 12). Christology turns out, as we see, to have implications not only for how one thinks of Jesus, but also the identity and task of his followers. That mix turns out to have roots at least as deep as Isaiah.

Where do we place the servant on our christological spectrum of respect? This is not so easy to answer. It depends on who the servant is and on how we translate the term. We see that it functions within the traditions of Israel as a way of speaking of prophet, king, and people. And how does it relate to the question of divinity? Most naturally, to identify Jesus as a faithful *servant* of God is to speak of him not as God, but as someone who is fully at the disposal of God. To be sure, if a servant fully does the will of the lord, then the master is acting or speaking in and through the servant. The term implies complete subservience—subservience so great that one can also speak of identification. To put it cutely, we cannot get the needle on our christological spectrometer to come to rest.

son of God/Son of God

The instability of the needle on our christological spectrometer only increases as we move to the next, but still related way of signifying who Jesus is, illustrated by my capitalization: *son of God* or *Son of God*. Capitalization is a function, in this case, of the English language. In some languages, such as German, all nouns are capitalized. In the Greek either all or no words are capitalized. In other words, capitalization or the lack of it reflects interpretive possibilities, not Greek usage.

In Wisdom of Solomon 2:13 the "righteous one" professes to have knowledge of God and calls himself a *pais* ("child or servant") of the Lord. And in Acts 3:13–14 "Righteous One" and "servant" are placed next to each other as virtual synonyms. But then, in Wisdom of Solomon 2:16–18, the evil tormentors and oppressors of the righteous say this:

> He calls the last end of the righteous happy,
> and boasts that God is his *father*.
> Let us see if his words are true,
> and let us test what will happen at the end of his life;
> for if the *righteous man* is God's *son* [NRSV: child], he will help him,
> and will deliver him from the hand of his adversaries. (Wisdom of
>   Solomon 2:16–18, emphasis added)

We have thus added to *righteous one* and *servant* a third and very closely related term: *son of God*. What does it imply? First, it signifies a high degree of intimacy with God as father, an intensely close bond that finds expression in the character of the *righteous one*: his way of life shows what he is made of. Second, his bond with God also implies that he can count on God's protection or at least vindication beyond the suffering of the moment (see chapter 12 above). This is recognized in Wisdom of Solomon 2, interestingly, by none other than his tormentors. They reason that

> if the righteous man is *God's son*, he will *help* him,
> and will *deliver* him from the hand of his adversaries. . . .
> Let us condemn him to a shameful death,
> for, according to what he says, he will be *protected*. (Wisdom of Solo-
>   mon 2:18, 20, emphasis added)

This taunt is echoed in the testing of Jesus in the desert: "If you are [a] son of God" (Matt. 4:3, 6 || Luke 4:3, 9). It comes to most forceful expression in the Passion Narrative: "If you are [a] son of God, come down from the cross!" (Matt. 27:40). In each of these cases the NRSV has "the Son of God" rather than "a son of God." Strictly speaking, "son" comes without the article, thus minimally allowing a translation of "a son" rather than "the Son." The capitalized version pushes an important christological point; a noncapitalized version allows us to place Jesus within the story line of the tested, suffering, but faithful righteous person. A final example, already referred to, serves to illustrate this. Translated very carefully in line with the point I have just made, the words of the Roman centurion at the scene of the crucifixion in Matthew 27:54 || Mark 15:39 read: "Truly this one was a son of God!" In light of what we have just said, this is a virtual equivalent to Luke 23:47, which when translated very carefully reads: "Truly this one was a righteous one!"

Lowercase "son of God" expresses in a broad paradigmatic way the character of the righteous or just person and the bond of this person with God. It also makes a connection between the experience and fate of Jesus and the righteous person's vulnerability in an evil and violent world and, as son, to being able to count on God's protection and vindication. Jesus's temptation or testing in the desert and his passion are painted by the evangelists in the already known forms and pigments of the paradigmatic experience of the righteous person/servant/son of God.

Such sonship is not about one solitary divine/human individual's experience, but of all truly righteous persons, however few there may be in the world. In the Sermon on the Mount Jesus calls peacemakers and lovers of enemies "sons of God" (Matt. 5:9, 45; the NRSV obscures this somewhat with the more inclusive "children of God"). Being sons (and daughters) of God became a favorite way of referring to members of the assemblies of believers in Jesus. To refer to Jesus in this way as a "son of God" serves not to distinguish him from other righteous people, but to depict his life and fate in light of that larger paradigm. It further highlights a theme in this chapter, namely, that christological titles often carry within them an ethical challenge to the followers of Jesus.

With respect to our spectrum of dignity or respect it would seem that this usage of "son of God/Son of God" does *not* imply deity. That said, careful reading of the New Testament makes clear that Jesus is often called "Son of God" in a way that has us capitalizing "Son," even if that is only a convention of the English language. In the following examples, the term *Son* clearly implies singular status:

Simon Peter answered, "You are the Messiah, the Son of the living God." (Matt. 16:16)

But Jesus was silent. Then the high priest said to him, "I put you under oath before the living God, tell us if you are the Messiah, the Son of God." (Matt. 26:63)

Nathanael replied, "Rabbi, you are the Son of God! You are the King of Israel!" (John 1:49)

She said to him, "Yes, Lord, I believe that you are the Messiah, the Son of God, the one coming into the world." (John 11:27)

Since, then, we have a great high priest who has passed through the heavens, Jesus, the Son of God, let us hold fast to our confession. (Heb. 4:14)

God abides in those who confess that Jesus is the Son of God, and they abide in God (1 John 4:15)

One of the most striking examples from within the gospel narrative is the so-called transfiguration of Jesus. At the high point of the story, and echoing Jesus's baptism, a heavenly voice announces, "This is my beloved Son. Listen to him! (Mark 9:7 || Matt. 17:5 || Luke 9:35).

These texts exhibit a very close identification between "Son of God" and "Messiah." That tells us much about another level of significance to the appellation "Son of God." It was part of the *royal* vocabulary, we might say, a way of speaking of the kings of Israel. They were "anointed" (to translate "Messiah" or "Christ") and as such "adopted" as "son" by God, as seen at Jesus's baptism and the use of Psalm 2 in his commissioning (see chapter 7 above):

> You are my son;
>> today I have begotten you. (Ps. 2:7)

Ancient Near Eastern kings and queens were believed to be representatives of deities, often even gods themselves. In Jesus's day, the Roman emperor Caesar Augustus was celebrated as a *divi filius* ("son of god" or "son of the divinized one"). Does the identification of Messiah (King) and Son of God owe something to such notions?

We should not be hasty in drawing such conclusions. The enormous respect Jews had for the one God, reiterated in their prayers daily ("Hear, O Israel: The LORD is our God, the LORD *alone*"), would have made speaking of a king or messiah as a "son of God" a term of great respect, but hardly an attribution of deity.

Even so, among the followers of Jesus such language does sometimes make exactly the claim that Jesus is divine. This is especially the case in the Johannine writings, both in the gospel and letters of John:

> The one who comes from above *is above all*. ... The one who comes from heaven *is above all*. ... He whom *God has sent* speaks the *words of God*, for he *gives the Spirit* without measure. The Father loves the *Son* and has *placed all things in his hands*. Whoever believes in the *Son* has eternal life; whoever disobeys the *Son* will not see life, but must endure God's wrath. (John 3:31, 34–36, emphasis added)

> And we know that the *Son of God* has come and has given us understanding so that we may know him who is true; and we are in him who is true, in his *Son* Jesus *Christ. He [Jesus] is the true God and eternal life*. (1 John 5:20, emphasis added)

Clearly in these texts the needle on our spectrometer has moved dramatically in the direction of divinity. Given that Christians have always read the whole of the Bible as their Scripture, we should not be surprised that these high-Christology texts also tend to elevate what might in isolation have been read as low-Christology texts. Hence we see the repeated capitalization and addition of articles ("*the* Son of God") by translators where more cautious translation would have suggested otherwise. That should not obscure the fact that in and of itself being a "son of God" fits just about everywhere on the spectrum.

Messiah/Christ

The designation *Messiah* or *Christ* has became the title of choice in Christian history. While we have already addressed it to some degree in the discussion of "son of God/Son of God" above, a few more comments on the term as applied to Jesus are in order.

Messiah is an adaptation of the Hebrew *meshiach* ("anointed one"). *Christ* is an adaptation of *christos*, which is the Greek translation of *meshiach*. Lexically "Messiah" and "Christ" thus mean exactly the same thing (see chapter 6 above). This is important, since in popular usage the two words sometimes have different connotative meaning. It is safe to say that in the first century, especially among Jewish followers of Jesus, the two terms meant exactly the same thing. His followers were convinced, of course, that Jesus, and *only* Jesus, was the Messiah, the Christ. Small wonder, then, that the term came to be associated with Jesus in an exclusive way. But the claim that he was the Messiah was given meaning by its rich associations in Jewish memory and hope.

Anointing was the typical way in which the kings of Israel and Judah were crowned (e.g., Ps. 2:2; 89:19–29; 1 Sam. 9:16; 16:12–13; 2 Sam. 5:3; 1 Kings 1:34). In these contexts "messiah" means "king." The most famous king was, of course, David. Whereas the long history of monarchy in Israel's history is, for the most part, a sorry tale, God's promise to sustain the dynasty of David forever was not forgotten (see, e.g., Ps. 89:19–37). It became a central part of the hope that sustained Jews for hundreds of years. At some time God would send the "Son of David," the "Messiah," to redeem Israel and restore it to its promised glory. The hope for the realization of this promise was strong during Jesus's day as well. It should not surprise us that the excitement Jesus generates in the gospels results in his being called "Son of David" (e.g., Matt. 12:23; 15:22; 21:9; Mark 10:47–48).

Messiah is thus associated with God's intervening in the history of the people to restore their fortunes. For some, this would have meant getting rid of the hated Romans; for others, it would have entailed the end of disease, hunger, and all other forms of physical, economic, and spiritual oppression. The Messiah was thus conceived of as a warrior, redeemer, savior, and healer.

To call Jesus *meshiach* is thus to say that he is the king through and in whom God's liberating reign is asserting itself. During and after Jesus's life this was highly charged language, to say the least.

Before leaving this topic, we should point out that anointing was also used in the commissioning of priests (e.g., Exod. 30:30; 40:13). The anonymous letter or sermon to the Hebrews combines the role of king and priest in the anointed Jesus (1:9). He is a *priest* in the order of Melchizedek, *king* of Salem, a "high priest" offering up himself as the ultimate sacrifice for the sake of humanity, but also continuing in his priestly service of offering intercession for the faithful (Heb. 5:7, 9). Interestingly, the covenanters at Qumran at the Dead Sea looked forward to two messiahs, "the anointed of Aaron and Israel," one priestly and the other royal (*Rule of the Community* [1QS] 9.11).

Prophets too were anointed (Ps. 105:15; Isa. 61:1), even if sometimes metaphorically, much as is suggested when in Luke's account of Jesus's inaugural sermon in Nazareth in 4:18 Jesus quotes Isaiah 61:

> The spirit of the Lord GOD is upon me,
>   because the LORD has anointed me;
> he has sent me to bring good news to the oppressed,
>   to bind up the brokenhearted,
> to proclaim liberty to the captives,
>   and release to the prisoners. (Isa. 61:1)

Anointing has in this instance less to do with royal status or priestly service than it does with the empowerment and authority of the prophet of the kingdom of God. Anointing with oil thus had ritual significance as well as the metaphorical meaning of investing with divine authority and power.

The term *meshiach* is thus laden with Jewish hope and faith, rich in biblical and extrabiblical allusion. It was also intensely controversial when applied to Jesus, both before and after his life. Both the tradition of his testing in the desert and the circumstances and charges related to his death illustrate this (see chapters 7 and 11 above).

Did Jesus think of himself as *meshiach*? If so, what did he mean by it, and why is he depicted in the gospels as so ambivalent about being the Messiah? Did he say no to the title and all it entailed? The gospels show the crowds following him around, waiting for food and healing (John 6:14–15), insisting on seeing Jesus as a messiah, most dramatically in those final days where they welcomed him to Jerusalem as a king with shouts of "Hosanna" (Matt. 21:9, 15 || Mark 11:9–10 || John 12:13). If Jesus refused to accept the job, so to speak, did his followers, including the evangelists, betray him when, especially after Easter, they came to confess their commitment to him and their boundless respect for him with this very title?

What we do know is that once the followers of Jesus became convinced that God had raised him from the dead, the reticence around calling Jesus Messiah disappeared. We might even say that in their experience Easter made the messiahship of Jesus an unavoidable conclusion. As clear as that confession became, both within and beyond the Jewish part of the community of devotees, the evangelists do not forget or obscure in their accounts that Jesus's messiahship did not fit well what most expected from a messiah. On the one hand, by referring to Jesus unabashedly as Messiah or Christ, they place him in direct continuity with Jewish hopes; the Messiah is, after all, God's agent to make things new, to bring an end to oppression. Jesus's healings, exorcisms, and other works of power fit messianic traditions well. On the other hand, it was a real stretch to apply such a title to a man who lived in poverty, who behaved in a way to bring repeated charges of unfaithfulness, and who finally died an ignominious death at the hands of imperial powers. This messianic "warrior" himself died rather than kill his enemies; this messiah left largely intact (for now) a world of disease, oppression, and violence. But, and this is critically important for an understanding of early confessions that Jesus is the Christ, this messiah would come again in power to finish the job (e.g., Matt. 24:30; 26:64 and parallels; 1 Cor. 15:23–28; 1 Thess. 4:13–5:11; Rev. 1:7). So, while the term *messiah* comes to be redefined in relation to Jesus's life of humble service and to his suffering to the point of death, it retains its overtones of power and victory by being associated with his resurrection, exaltation, and his return at the end of the age. Indeed, it pushes these into the stratosphere of cosmic transformation.

What it means to be a messiah was thus quite radically reformulated vis-à-vis other Jewish ideas, but it would also need to be translated into vocabulary intelligible to Gentile followers of Jesus in years to come. And here we encounter yet further surprises. The Apostle Paul, for example, made the Greek word for Messiah—*christos*—a regular part of Jesus's name: "Jesus Christ" or "Christ Jesus." A measure of the creativity of this Jewish missionary to Gentiles is his idea of the gathered followers of this messiah as "the body of Christ" (Rom. 12:3–8; 1 Corinthians 12; Eph. 2:16; 4:1–16). In other words, to call Jesus the "Christ" is not to separate him from his followers; as Messiah he provides the identity and task for his followers. In Paul's view, communities of believers in Jesus are messianic cells, so to speak, made up of people who are together "in Christ" as men and women, slaves and free, Jews and Gentiles (Gal. 3:28). Jesus the Messiah's task becomes in an important sense theirs too.

We return to our question of what level of respect this title implies. It is clear from many of the texts we have cited that *meshiach* and its Greek translation *christos* are sometimes very closely related to the other titles we have observed, most particularly Servant and Son. Much as in those instances, the term *need* mean no more than king, prophet, or priest. It *can*, however, point to the agent of God's decisive and final intervention to bring evil and corruption to an end and to inaugurate a new or at least renewed creation, the kingdom of God. A Jew would not assume that that means the Messiah *is* God. He is God's agent, in and through whom God is at work. *By itself* this term does not imply divinity.

lord/Lord

With the title *lord* (Greek *kyrios*) we come to a christological title that is both tantalizing in its suggestiveness and complex in its definition. It is by its very nature both a term of respect and one of submission and obedience.

First, as the title of this chapter intimates, in many early circles of Jesus followers it enjoyed pride of place in how they confessed their allegiance to Jesus:

> If you confess with your lips that Jesus is Lord and believe in your heart that God raised him from the dead, you will be saved. (Rom. 10:9)

> Therefore I want you to understand that no one speaking by the Spirit of God ever says "Let Jesus be cursed!" and no one can say "Jesus is Lord" except by the Holy Spirit. (1 Cor. 12:3)

But what exactly were they confessing? After all, the word *lord* need mean no more than master, teacher, boss, leader, or just a polite "sir." The translators all capitalize "Lord" in the verses quoted above (again, this is a feature of the English language—not Greek), but a low usage is exhibited throughout the gospels, for example, in the many parables that deal with master and slaves or servants. The Samaritan woman in John 4 constantly addresses Jesus with *kyrios*, without of course making the confession that "Jesus is Lord!" Sometimes it means "teacher," someone with the authority to teach followers or disciples (e.g., Matt. 10:24–25; Luke 9:61; John 13:13–16). In these cases it is a title of honor without christological significance.

As a title of respect and honor, *kyrios* quite naturally implies superiority and authority and is thus related to the royal titles we have been looking at. Of note is Psalm 110:1, quoted repeatedly in the New Testament as a way of celebrating the exalted Jesus as king (e.g., Matt. 22:44 || Mark 12:36 || Luke 20:42; Acts 2:34; 1 Cor. 15:25; Heb. 1:3, 13):

> The LORD says to my lord,
>   "Sit at my right hand
> until I make your enemies your footstool." (Ps. 110:1)

The first instance of this word in this verse stands for YHWH and is thus the typical Jewish euphemism or circumlocution for God (see below). The second instance of this word has messianic, that is royal, significance. So, the first and last terms in the phrase *Lord Jesus Christ*, frequent in the New Testament, are virtually synonymous messianic designations. The New Testament usage of Psalm 110 expresses that Jesus is King, Messiah, the one to whom God has given great status and authority. To confess Jesus as "Lord" is to express allegiance and loyalty to Jesus as the Messiah, as the King.

Such a use of the term also played a significant role in the expectations for Jesus to come again in power and glory to finish the messianic task of judging, saving, and renewing the cosmos. The Aramaic *Marana tha!* ("Our Lord, come!") in a Greek-speaking setting witnesses to how early this acclamation became a part of Christian worship:

> Let anyone be accursed who has no love for the Lord. *Marana tha!* (1 Cor. 16:22)

It also appears as the final plea, albeit in Greek translation, after the closing "Amen!" in Revelation:

> The one who testifies to these things says, "Surely I am coming soon." Amen. *Come, Lord Jesus!* (Rev. 22:20, emphasis added)

"Lord" is thus part of the vocabulary not only of respect and allegiance, but also of expectation, testifying to the forward-looking orientation of early followers of Jesus. He was their Lord in the present, but he was also the Lord whose coming again they looked to with eager anticipation.

Even though this is lofty language, enthusiastic in its reverence, and vivid in its expectancy, the designation "lord" does not in and of itself imply divinity. However, in this case we have a special problem in that "Lord" was the predominant way in which Jews referred to God, as we have just seen in Psalm 110:1 (see chapter 4 above). Behind the capitalized "LORD" is the tetragrammaton (or "four-letter-word") YHWH. For reasons of respect, Jews did not pronounce God's name, but said *adonai*, Hebrew for "lord." They took the third commandment prohibiting wrongful use of God's name very seriously (Exod. 20:7), preferring not a name with which to refer to God but an attribution of honor and authority. The NRSV and the NIV follow Jewish practice and render YHWH as "LORD," using capitalization in order to set it off from all other uses of the term. In the Greek translation of the Hebrew Bible used by early Christians, YHWH is always translated *kyrios*, as if *adonai* is the Hebrew word being translated. Thus in the New Testament, written by persons who apparently used mostly the Greek translation of the Old Testament, "Lord" is often the way to refer to God. The typical way in which Matthew avoids the name *God* is by referring to the "kingdom of heaven" rather than "kingdom of God." He could just as easily have said "kingdom of the Lord."

To call Jesus "Lord" is thus potentially highly charged language. Early followers of Jesus took the huge step of using the otherwise quite normal term of respect to express their belief in his divinity. If they did not intend to do so, they were unconscionably sloppy. They were not, of course, in that they quite deliberately adapted biblical texts referring to YHWH to Jesus, as seen in Isaiah's prophecy of the coming of God:

> A voice cries out:
> "In the wilderness prepare the way of the Lord,
>   make straight in the desert a highway for our God." (Isa. 40:3)

This verse is quoted several times in the New Testament in relation to John the Baptizer's paving the way for *Jesus* (Mark 1:3 || Matt. 3:3 || Luke 3:4 || John 1:23; see chapter 7 above).

Further, Paul usually uses the title "Lord" together with Jesus Christ alongside a reference to "God the Father" ("God the Father and our Lord Jesus Christ"), leaving the impression that "Lord" is a title of authority for Jesus rather than a euphemism for God. But that is too simple, as shown by the two texts below. In the first, Paul applies to Jesus a biblical text every Jew would have understood as referring to God. In the second, he attributes to Jesus the act of creation itself:

> If you confess with your lips that Jesus is Lord and believe in your heart that God raised him from the dead, you will be saved. For one believes with the heart and so is justified, and one confesses with the mouth and so is saved. . . . For there is no distinction between Jew and Greek; the same Lord is Lord of all and is generous to all who call on him. For, "Everyone who calls on the name of the Lord shall be saved." (Rom. 10:9–10, 12–13, quoting Joel 2:32, where "Lord" clearly refers to God)

> For us there is one God, the Father, from whom are all things and for whom we exist, and one Lord, Jesus Christ, through whom are all things and through whom we exist. (1 Cor. 8:6)

What is puzzling, as seen in the second text, is that Paul seems unperturbed *as a Jew* to insist that there is *"one* God, the father" while at the same to draw Jesus into what every Jew understood "God" to mean. One of the most dramatic examples in Paul's writings is the great christological hymn in his letter to the Philippians (2:6–11; see below). Christ is depicted in the hymn as a slave who does *not* "grasp at" or "exploit" being like God, itself a remarkable statement within a christological hymn. He is nevertheless given "the name above all names," clearly a reference to God, a name at which every knee will bow and every tongue exclaim: "Jesus Christ is Lord!" Isaiah 45, which furnishes at least some of the vocabulary for this hymn, makes this very clear.

> Thus says the LORD,
>   the Holy One of Israel, and its Maker: . . .
> I made the earth,
>   and created humankind upon it;
> it was my hands that stretched out the heavens,
>   and I commanded all their host. . . .
> For thus says the LORD,
> who created the heavens
>   (he is God!),
> *I am the LORD, and there is no other. . . .*
> For I am God, and there is no other. . . .
> *"To me every knee shall bow,*
>   *every tongue shall swear."* (Isa. 45:11–12, 18, 22–23, emphasis added)

At the outset of this chapter the point was made that Christology is not to be separated from ethics if one wishes to appreciate fully what it meant for Jesus's early followers; in this instance, Paul employs the euphoria of a hymn acclaiming Jesus as Lord, even as LORD, precisely in order to make Jesus's way of self-denial and servanthood absolutely normative for those so worshiping him (Phil. 2:1–5).

We could cite other such examples in the New Testament where texts in which "Lord" refers to YHWH in the Hebrew Bible are taken over and attributed to Jesus or in which language or phrases associated with God are applied to Jesus. On a few occasions the attribution of deity to Jesus is breathtakingly direct. Perhaps the most famous incident is Thomas's confession. Upon meeting the risen Jesus he exclaims:

My Lord and my God! (John 20:28)

When "Lord" is used in that way, the needle has moved unambiguously over to the divine end of the spectrum of respect.

son of man/Son of Man

In this survey of christological titles, we have observed them slowly inching up the respect ledger, so to speak. It seems strange that we should take up the designation "Son of Man" at this point. Is it not the opposite of "Son of God"? Yes and no. This designation is once again difficult to peg on our spectrum. It can mean relatively little, but can also mean very, very much.

"Son of man" is a very literal translation of the Aramaic *bar enosh* (Greek *huios tou anthropou*). This is simply one way to say "human being." Psalm 8, for example, speaks of God as having created all things, including the "human being," and placed them in a certain order (quoted here from the NIV since, in the interest of gender inclusiveness, the NRSV has obscured this particular aspect of the text):

> O LORD, our Lord,
>   how majestic is your name in all the earth!
> You have set your glory
>   above the heavens. . . .
> When I consider your heavens,
>   the work of your fingers,
> the moon and the stars,
>   which you have set in place,
> what is man that you are mindful of him,
>   the *son of man* that you care for him?
> You made him a little lower than the heavenly beings [*literally* the
>   gods *or* God]
>   and crowned him with glory and honor.
> You made him ruler over the works of your hands;
>   you put everything under his feet:
> all flocks and herds,
>   and the beasts of the field,
> the birds of the air,
>   and the fish of the sea,
>   all that swim the paths of the seas.
> O LORD, our Lord,
>   how majestic is your name in all the earth! (Ps. 8:1, 3–9 NIV,
>   emphasis added)

Hebrew poets often used poetic parallelism. So, in Psalm 8:4 the first line has the term *man*, the second, making much the same point: *son of man*. They mean exactly the same thing: human being. There are a few instances in the gospels in which Jesus might speak of "son of man" in such a humble way, although we cannot be sure:

> Jesus said to him, "Foxes have holes, and birds of the air have nests; but the Son of Man [*or* son of man] has nowhere to lay his head." (Matt. 8:20 || Luke 9:58; see also Matt. 9:6 and parallels; Matt. 12:8 and parallels)

Is Jesus making a comment about the vulnerability of human life, in effect turning Psalm 8 on its head? Or is he referring obliquely to himself, as the translators into English obviously think when they capitalize the term? The NIV did not capitalize "son of man" in Psalm 8:4, and the NRSV in fact there translates the term "mortals."

For the most part the term is *not* used in the gospels to point to the "humble humanity" of Jesus, even when in connection with his suffering (e.g., Matt. 17:12, 22; 20:18, 28; Mark 8:31; Luke 9:22). Remarkably, Psalm 8:6 appears in several christological texts celebrating Christ's status as ruler of the cosmos (1 Cor. 15:27; Eph. 1:22; see also Heb. 2:6). This is surprising, since Psalm 8 is meant to identify the place of *humanity as a whole* within God's order of creation. But in the New Testament it is employed to celebrate *Jesus's* exaltation to the position of cosmic ruler. In such a setting the term *Son of Man* comes to take on great and superhuman significance.

Another text from the sacred literature of Israel, Daniel 7, has played a decisive role in lending the term such gravity:

> In my vision at night I looked, and there before me was *one like a son of man*, coming with the clouds of heaven. He approached the Ancient of Days and was led into his presence. He was given authority, glory and sovereign power; all peoples, nations and men of every language worshiped him. His dominion is an everlasting dominion that will not pass away, and his kingdom is one that will never be destroyed. (Dan. 7:13–14 NIV, emphasis added)

On one hand, we see in this text a strong similarity to Psalm 8:5–8, in that one like a "son of man" is given dominion over everything. On the other, it is clear that Daniel's "son of man" is not so much a human being as a heavenly being who in this visionary episode *looks like* a human being. Suddenly the term is more than simply an anthropological term; it now ascribes great and profound status to a humanlike heavenly figure. But just when it appears that we have left the human sphere, we read in 7:27 that the everlasting kingdom is given to the "people of the Most High." The heavenly drama appears to envision nothing less than the establishment of the kingdom of God in fullness on a cosmic scale.

There is little doubt that Daniel 7 and the meaning it lends to this term colors the New Testament use of the term as applied to Jesus:

> From now on you will see the Son of Man
>   seated at the right hand of Power
>   and coming on the clouds of heaven. (Matt. 26:64)

This is echoed in John 1:51 (Matt. 16:27–28 || Luke 9:26; Matt. 24:27–44 || Mark 13:26; Matt. 19:28; Mark 14:62; Luke 17:22–30; 21:27). Indeed, John, a gospel with a very high Christology, employs the term very dramatically. For example, Jesus's suffering is anticipated as the Son of Man being "lifted up," a striking way of alluding both to his being hung up on a cross and to his exaltation (John 3:14; 8:28; 12:34). The Eucharist or Lord's Supper is anticipated as "munching" the flesh and drinking the blood of the Son of Man (6:53), who is nothing less than the manna, the divine food from heaven

(6:26–51). Should we be surprised that in John there is even reference to the preexistence of the Son of Man (3:13; 6:62)?

Very puzzling is that "son of man" or "human one" is found only on Jesus's *own* lips (the only exceptions in the New Testament are Acts 7:56; Rev. 1:13; 14:14). In other words, it is almost never used as a term of respect or devotion by others. Should we then refrain from using it as one of the titles, since it appears that early communities of Jesus believers did not use it in worship? I think we should consider it a title precisely because the evangelists retain it in their memory of Jesus and use the term as a way of describing Jesus and his role. Moreover, the gospels draw on rehearsed oral traditions and were themselves read in settings of worship. In that way "Son of Man" did play a role in devotion. Even so, it is important to recognize the unique nature of this title. It is more eschatological symbol than personal title.

What adds to the mystery is that Jesus speaks of the Son of Man in the third person. Is he speaking of himself? Is he being deliberately coy? Or is he speaking of the heavenly messiah who will come, without identifying himself with that heavenly agent? Is it only after Easter that his followers identify Jesus unambiguously with the Son of Man, John no less than the Synoptic evangelists? As they narrate the story of Jesus, the evangelists record him as referring to his *present* activity as the "son of man" or perhaps "Son of Man" (e.g., Matt. 11:19 and parallels). They also have Jesus predict his own suffering as that of the Son of Man (e.g., Matt. 20:18–19 and parallels), implying that he sees himself as that person. And finally it is clear that they believe he is speaking of his own coming in power to judge the nations. That they understand the Son of Man to be none other than Jesus himself is illustrated nicely in the comparison between Matthew 19:28 and Luke 22:28–30. In Matthew, Jesus speaks of the "Son of Man," whereas in Luke he refers directly to himself:

Matthew 19:28	Luke 22:28–30
Jesus said to them, "Truly I tell you, at the renewal of all things, when the *Son of Man* is seated on the throne of his glory, you who have followed me will also sit on twelve thrones, judging the twelve tribes of Israel."	[Jesus said:] "You are those who have stood by me in my trials; and I confer on you, just as my Father has conferred on *me*, a kingdom, so that you may eat and drink at my table in my kingdom, and you will sit on thrones judging the twelve tribes of Israel."

Despite its importance in the gospel narratives, the evangelists seem to recall the designation "son of man/Son of Man" not as a *current* way of speaking of Jesus, but as a characteristic way *he* spoke of himself and his role in present and future. Perhaps the designation did not carry over well beyond the Semitic context of Palestine. Or, perhaps the term became too closely identified with the very heated expectations of Christ's return "on the clouds of heaven," as Daniel 7 has it—expectations that necessarily became less intense. When Jesus did not return as expected, the term may have quickly fallen into disuse. But then why use it in the gospels? Perhaps its presence in all four gospels, even if John uses it somewhat differently, points to the characteristic way Jesus himself spoke, so much so that it became an inextricable part of the memory of Jesus.

After all this, does "son of man/Son of Man" imply divinity? Once again we are up against an element of ambiguity: on one hand, as Psalm 8 shows us, it need mean no more than human being, in which case the answer is a clear no. But when we see how the New Testament writers use Psalm 8, especially Psalm 8:6, the no becomes more qualified (e.g., 1 Cor. 15:27; Eph. 1:22). And when connected with Jesus's role as enactor of the kingdom, as one who suffers and dies for humanity and finally as one who will come on the clouds to save and to judge all of humanity together with his followers à la Daniel 7, then the needle on our meter moves far in the direction of divinity. One thing is clear: "Son of Man" is potentially every bit as lofty a title as is "Son of God."

Wisdom

I have reserved the grandest of the christological titles for last: Wisdom. With this title we connect not so much with the messianic, royal, military, or even eschatological traditions of Israel and Judaism, but with Israel's wisdom tradition. Of course, as always, we are well advised not to think in terms of hermetically sealed compartments of tradition. As the followers of Jesus themselves illustrate, it was entirely possible for Jews of Jesus's day to combine and reconceptualize elements of tradition in sometimes radically new ways. Even so, with wisdom we enter an identifiable sphere of Jewish tradition central to the development of Christology.

Matthew has a special fondness for this tradition (see chapter 3 above). I will highlight here only the important features and discuss how they affect the christological development, especially in the great christological hymns we find in the New Testament.

Two important story lines come from the wisdom tradition that early followers of Jesus saw as shedding light on him. The story line of the suffering Righteous One who is vindicated by God (see chapter 11 above and earlier in this chapter) plays a particularly important role in the Passion Narratives. The other story line is that of the personified figure of Wisdom, a female character called Ḥokma in Hebrew and Sophia in Greek.

Contemporary theology, especially feminist theology, is very interested in the figure Sophia. Previous discussion of the Gospel of Matthew highlighted in particular the identification of personified Sophia with Torah, with the law, accompanying the people of God in their relationship with God, enabling them to know God's will and to live it (see Sirach 24, quoted in chapter 3 above).

Of particular importance for the development of Christology are two further aspects: one is the way Ḥokma/Sophia is involved in creation. Sophia is said to have been there at the beginning when all things were made; she was God's architect, the one in charge of creation. The other aspect relevant to the development of Christology is the way Jews poetically, and maybe even playfully, borrowed from the cultures around them to describe Wisdom/Sophia as virtually a goddess. What these Jewish monotheists desired to express with this bracing language was that the wisdom of God permeating creation and accompanying the human family as Torah was nothing other than God's own presence up close. Let Sophia speak for herself:

> The LORD created me at [*or* as] the beginning of his work,
>   the first of his acts of long ago. . . .
> When he established the heavens, I was there,
>   when he drew a circle on the face of the deep,
> when he made firm the skies above,
>   when he established the fountains of the deep,
> when he assigned to the sea its limit,
>   so that the waters might not transgress his command,
> when he marked out the foundations of the earth,
>   then I was beside him, like a master worker [*literally* architect];
> and I was daily his delight,
>   rejoicing before him always,
> rejoicing in his inhabited world
>   and delighting in the human race. (Prov. 8:22, 27–31)

This view of Sophia comes to forceful expression in the Wisdom of Solomon 6:12–9:4, a Jewish wisdom document written in Greek within a century of Christian beginnings and included in the Catholic canon as the Book of Wisdom. "Solomon" sings the praises of Sophia:

> Wisdom, the fashioner of all things, taught me.
> There is in her a spirit that is intelligent, holy,
> unique, manifold, subtle,
> mobile, clear, unpolluted,
> distinct, invulnerable, loving the good, keen,
> irresistible, beneficent, humane,
> steadfast, sure, free from anxiety,
> all-powerful, overseeing all,
> and penetrating through all spirits
> that are intelligent, pure, and altogether subtle.
> For wisdom is more mobile than any motion;
> because of her pureness she pervades and penetrates all things.
> For *she is a breath of the power* of God,
> and a pure emanation of the glory of the Almighty;
> therefore nothing defiled gains entrance into her.

> For she is a *reflection of eternal light,*
> *a spotless mirror of the working of God,*
> *and an image of his goodness.*
> *Although she is but one, she can do all things,*
> *and while remaining in herself, she renews all things;*
> *in every generation she passes into holy souls*
> *and makes them friends of God, and prophets;*
> for God loves nothing so much as the person who lives with wisdom.
> She is more beautiful than the sun,
> and excels every constellation of the stars.
> Compared with the light she is found to be superior,
> for it is succeeded by the night,
> but against wisdom evil does not prevail.
> *She reaches mightily from one end of the earth to the other,*
> *and she orders all things well.* (Wisdom of Solomon 7:22–8:1, emphasis added)

This text combines the various elements we have identified: Sophia bears the image of God, creates the world, pervades all that is, inhabits God's human creatures, and thus befriends them with God, making them prophets (i.e., persons able to hear God's word and to speak it). Sophia is the one through whom God and humans meet. Can we miss the similarity to how Jesus is celebrated in the New Testament?

Christological Hymns

In the New Testament Jesus is explicitly identified as the wisdom of God: in Matthew 11 (see chapter 3 above) and by the Apostle Paul in 1 Corinthians 1:18–31 (especially 1:24). Further, there are several texts in which we find much the same ambience we sense in the texts from Proverbs and the Wisdom of Solomon. Not surprisingly, they too are poetic, more than likely wisdom hymns that New Testament writers created or hymns in praise of Wisdom that they adapted for celebrating Jesus as the wisdom of God. We will briefly consider three of these great christological hymns—or should we say "wisdom hymns"?—John 1:1–18, Philippians 2:6–11, and Colossians 1:15–20. They are discussed in the order in which the documents appear in the New Testament. They are likely older than the documents in which we find them.

JOHN 1:1–18: CHRIST THE LOGOS

The Gospel of John opens with the famous words:

> In the beginning was the Word,
> and the Word was with God,
> and *the Word was God.*

He was in the beginning with God.
All things came into being through him,
and without him not one thing came into being.
What has come into being in him was life,
and the life was the light of all people. (John 1:1–4, emphasis and
    poetic scansion added)

While the important term here is Word (*Logos*) and not Wisdom (*Sophia*), the similarities to what we read above in Wisdom of Solomon regarding Sophia are surely obvious. Were we to replace *logos* for *sophia*, this text would read just as well. Even in the Wisdom of Solomon the two terms function quite similarly at times (compare Wisdom of Solomon 10:15–21 and 18:14–16). But precisely because we know what this vocabulary means, a real shock awaits us in John 1:14: "*The Word became flesh and lived among us*, and we have seen his glory, the glory as of a father's only son, full of grace and truth" (emphasis added).

In the view of the hymn writer, Jesus is Word/Wisdom incarnate. This is very similar to what we see in Matthew 11, except that in John the connection to creation is made more explicit. More, the Word that has become flesh was not only *with* God, but *was* God. The implication is as clear as it would have been shocking: Jesus is God incarnate! The metaphor of Wisdom as used in John's hymn has pushed the needle on our spectrum as far in the direction of divinity as it can go.

Several factors require our attention. One is that this text is poetry. It is the poetry of wonder and awe, not mathematical or scientific precision. (Our image of the spectrometer should be used very playfully!) It is the euphoric language of worship and gratitude. The poet wants to say that in the flesh—Jesus, the man from Nazareth—*God* has entered the sphere of alienated and broken human life. Light has entered darkness (John 1:5, 9). The Logos has become flesh. God's glory has come to live "in a tent," as 1:14 should be carefully translated. Any attribution of deity to Jesus must keep this element of irony very sharp or else it will downplay the flesh, the "tent," and the full humanity of Jesus. To forget that renders much of the Gospel of John unintelligible.

The second factor is that this text is quite late. The Gospel of John was likely written as late as the last decade of the first century CE (see chapter 3 above). However, there is a good chance that this particular poem or hymn predates the gospel. It may even be that it was originally a hymn to Sophia, radically adapted by the followers of Jesus for their worship. So we cannot be sure how early already the followers of Jesus worshiped him as God in the flesh, as it were, but this hymn suggests they were certainly doing so within the first century.

Philippians 2:6–11: Christ the Exalted Slave

How early the followers of Jesus were making the loftiest of claims about Jesus in their worship is seen in the hymn embedded in Paul's letter to the Philippians. It predates John's Gospel by at least three decades. The hymn was discussed above when considering the title "Lord." A few further comments need to be made, however. As stated earlier, this is a hymn that celebrates the exaltation of Jesus to such an extent that he is given the name to which every knee should bow in heaven and on earth:

> Therefore God also highly exalted him
> > and gave him the name
> > that is *above every name*,
> so that at the name of *Jesus*
> > every knee should bend,
> > in heaven and on earth and under the earth,
> and every tongue should confess
> > that Jesus Christ is *Lord*,
> > to the glory of God the Father. (Phil. 2:9–11, emphasis added)

This is biblical language reserved only for God. The phrase about "every knee" bending in adoration is taken directly from Isaiah 45:23, where it refers unambiguously to God and is preceded in 45:22 by the assertion: "I am God, and there is no other." The implication? Jesus is exalted by God to the status of deity. "Jesus" becomes "the Name," a Jewish euphemism or circumlocution for YHWH, much like "Lord."

The hymn, however, does not allow us to draw this implication without some qualification. For example, the attribution to Jesus of the title "Lord" is followed by "to the glory of God the Father," suggesting some distinction between God who is Father and Jesus who is given the name of God ("the name above every name"). The mystery deepens in the earlier part of the hymn:

> [Jesus Christ], though he was in the form of God,
> > did not regard equality with God
> > as something to be exploited [*or* grasped],
> but emptied himself,
> > taking the form of a slave,
> > being born in human likeness.
> And being found in human form,
> > he humbled himself
> > and became obedient to the point of death—
> > even death on a cross. (Phil. 2:6–8)

The hymn begins with the assertion that Christ was in the form (*morphe*) of God, but that he did not regard equality with God as something to be "exploited" or "grasped." The Greek noun *harpagmos* is ambiguous; it means either "something to be taken by force or grasped" or "something to be held on to or exploited." How this is translated is important for understanding the Christology of this hymn. The NRSV translates the term "something to be exploited." If "equality with God" is not something to be exploited then it implies that Jesus already enjoyed equality with God. Philippians 2:6 then implies preexistence as God ("in the form of God"). We would then take 2:7 to read that Christ emptied himself of the perks of divinity, taking on the "form" of a slave, of a human, to the point of dying on the cross (Paul speaks of this as Christ's self-impoverishment for the sake of others in 2 Cor. 8:9). As a reward for Jesus's faithful service as a servant or slave of God he is then restored by God to the status of deity (Phil. 2:9–11). Understood this way, this hymn retells in highly concentrated form the story of preexistence, incarnation, death, and resurrection of Jesus. And it does so in a way reminiscent of Wisdom's being asked to find a home among humans in Sirach 24 or of the Logos becoming flesh and "tenting" with humanity in John 1.

The NIV translates *harpagmos* as "something to be grasped." Can a case be made that the hymn also makes good sense if translated that way? I believe it can. It is still a wisdom hymn, but one with a different story line. The hymn refers less to Wisdom than to Adam, the first human, who, as we read at the beginning of Genesis, sinned precisely by wanting to be like God (Gen. 3:1–7, esp. 3:5). Unlike the first Adam, Jesus as the "new Adam" did *not* grasp at being like God. He behaved the way human beings are supposed to behave. *As a reward* Jesus was offered precisely what he did not grasp at—the privilege of being like God, more, of being given "the name that is above every name."

There is support for such an interpretation elsewhere in the New Testament. The most obvious is that Jesus was recognized as the Righteous One (see earlier in this chapter), who fulfilled the will of God fully and unreservedly. Thus God raised him up, vindicating him, through the resurrection. Further, in the Pauline letters there is an explicit reference to Jesus as the "last Adam" (1 Cor. 15:45; see also Romans 5) or the "perfect man" (Eph. 4:13; translations typically obscure this). The letter to the Hebrews speaks of Jesus as being "in every respect . . . tested as we are, yet without sin" (4:15). Such an interpretation would fit well with why Paul integrates the hymn into his argument in Philippians 2. After all, he is holding up to his readers the behavior of Jesus as a model human being, with special stress on his humble servanthood, to be emulated by those who follow him (see 2:1–5).

Both interpretations are possible linguistically. Both make sense in terms of what else we read in the New Testament. And, to be sure, in both cases the hymn concludes with a clear attribution to Jesus of the title "Lord" and the honor of having all of creation treat him as God. We can read this hymn, then, as a celebration of Jesus as the perfect human, the perfect Servant of

God, who is then rewarded with the status of being treated as God, and we can also read it as celebrating Wisdom's emptying herself and coming to live with humanity, only to return to her true state as part of the Godhead.

Perhaps we should refuse to choose and rather hold on to both interpretations, even if they are in some tension with each other christologically. After all, as we have seen, the tension between humanity and divinity is inherent in virtually every one of the titles we have surveyed. And, as we have also seen, early witnesses felt no inhibition in using a variety of titles to express their devotion to Jesus. What is important to observe in this hymn is that this tension is present even when the needle on our so-called respect meter moves far in the direction of divinity. After all, Paul uses the hymn celebrating Christ's unequalled greatness to reinforce his call to radical humility.

That tension serves to highlight the other theme stressed in this chapter. To bend the knee and to acclaim Jesus as "Lord," even as "LORD," is to pledge oneself to live in imitation of him. To recognize God in Jesus gives the life and words of the slave ultimate authority; to recognize his full humanity is to acknowledge in that life and those words the template of what humanity should be and live like. Jesus is alike true God and true Adam.

COLOSSIANS 1:15–20: CHRIST THE ICON OF GOD

The impact of the wisdom tradition on Christology comes to expression in yet another hymn, this one embedded in the letter to the Colossians. Scholars disagree on whether Paul himself wrote this letter, as it claims to have been, or whether it was written some time after his death by one of his coworkers. In my opinion the latter is likely. The possibility thus exists that this letter too is quite late. However, as in the case of the hymn embedded in John 1, we cannot know how old the hymn is (was it composed by the author of Colossians or adapted for present purposes?) or whether it was a christological hymn from the start. In the opinion of many, including mine, this was a hymn to Wisdom freely modified to speak of Jesus. Whatever the case may be, it sheds light on the way the wisdom tradition, not least the tradition of personified Sophia, gave early followers the means with which to express their convictions about Jesus:

> He is the image [*eikon*] of the invisible God,
> the firstborn of all creation;
> for in [*or* by] him all things in heaven and on earth were created,
> things visible and invisible,
> whether thrones or dominions
> or rulers or powers—
> all things have been created through him and for him.
> He himself is before all things,
> and in [*or* by] him all things hold together.
> He is the head of the body, the church;

he is the beginning,
the firstborn from the dead,
so that he might come to have first place in everything.
For in him all the fullness of God was pleased to dwell,
and through him God was pleased to reconcile to himself all things,
whether on earth or in heaven,
by making peace through the blood of his cross. (Col. 1:15–20, poetic
    scansion added)

The wisdom roots of this hymn are seen when it is compared to Wisdom
of Solomon 7 quoted earlier. Phrases singing the praises of Wisdom find
resonance in Colossians 1. Wisdom is . . .

- the fashioner of all things
- all-powerful, overseeing all
- the pervador and penetrator of all things
- the breath of the power of God
- a pure emanation of the glory of the Almighty
- a reflection of eternal light
- a spotless mirror of the working of God
- an image of his goodness
- able to do all things
- able to renew all things
- able to excel every constellation of the stars
- compared with the light and found to be superior
- able to order all things well

The similarities are obvious, especially with the first verses of the Colossian hymn (1:15–17). Christ is described as "the image of the invisible God,
the firstborn of all creation; for in him all things in heaven and on earth are
created, things visible and invisible." Colossians 1:19 sums up it up: "For in
him all the fullness of God was pleased to dwell." Here are echoes not only
of Wisdom of Solomon 7, but also of Proverbs 8 and more immediately of
John 1.

As in John 1, the Colossian hymn in its present form connects the wisdom
tradition with the story of Jesus and with his relationship with his church.
For example, in Colossians 1:18 Christ is identified as "the head of the body,
the church." In short, Christ cannot be conceived of apart from the community of Jesus's followers. The way that relationship is envisioned owes a
great deal to the tradition of Lady Wisdom or Sophia (compare Jesus as
Wisdom in the Gospel of Matthew; see chapter 3 above). In that instance
Jesus *as Wisdom* invites all to come to him and to take up his (her) yoke
(Matt. 11:28–30; see also Sirach 6:23–31; 51:26). Wisdom of Solomon 7:27
says that Wisdom "in every generation . . . passes into holy souls and makes
them friends of God, and prophets."

But Colossians 1 becomes even more explicitly a celebration of *Jesus*: "Through *him* God was pleased to reconcile to himself all things . . . by making peace through the blood of *his* cross" (1:20, emphasis added). Whereas in John 1 Wisdom as Logos becomes flesh, that is, enters into history in and through Jesus, so here the celebration of Christ as Wisdom is inextricably linked to the specific story of the crucified man from Nazareth. The hymn composer (or adaptor) has effectively fused the notion of Wisdom as creator of the world with the Wisdom of the cross, the Wisdom through whom the world is being reconciled (see 1 Cor. 1:18–25).

Again we find the needle on our spectrometer very far in the direction of divinity. Even so, the language is still somewhat fuzzy: on the one hand, Christ is "preeminent," the one through whom "all things were created," in whom "all the fullness of God was pleased to dwell." This speaks of divinity. On the other hand, it is still the case that he is the one "in whom" or "through whom" *God* both creates the world and reconciles it to himself. That suggests the language of agency and mediation more than identity. As in other high christological texts, it appears that the writers deliberately want to have it both ways. Jesus is no longer only the Righteous One or the Servant, but the way in which *God* is active in the cosmos.

Conclusion

We have surveyed a tantalizing mix of designations and titles. Is it any wonder that two and a half centuries later the bishops of the church will have little choice if they want to be true to the New Testament but to declare that Jesus the Christ is *both* fully human *and* fully divine? They will argue their case in ways earlier biblical writers do not. The apostles and evangelists express their convictions about Jesus in a way that does not seek philosophical or even theological precision. For them poetry and faithful living are fully adequate. For them it is enough to claim that in the *man* Jesus, the one whom they knew and followed in Palestine, ate with, suffered with, and whose death they witnessed, they encountered none other than the living *God*. Of enormous importance is that as much as their narratives are shaped by the excitement of that encounter, the writers of the New Testament never let their conviction that God has met them in Jesus—and continues to be present with believers through his Spirit—stop them from telling the story of a man who lived, spoke, acted, and died among them. As much as they are awed by the power of the creator God to raise that man from the dead, they never downplay the terrible human vulnerability of that life. As much as they describe that life in all its vulnerability, it never keeps them from seeing in it the will of God for all who want to be faithful. And as excited as they get about who Jesus turned out to be, their excitement always serves to buttress their resolve to be like Jesus in the way they themselves live and act. So they call *each other* sons and daughters of God, sisters and brothers, imitators of a lord who showed his authority by washing their feet.

This is a great mystery and the genius of early Christology: at the very moment early believers in Jesus celebrate God's drawing near to them in Jesus they also celebrate humanity drawing near to God in Jesus. Jesus becomes a bridge, a meeting ground between God and humanity. Jesus becomes the mediator, facilitating the encounter between the divine and the human, between God and humanity, as seen in three further texts, the first another hymn:

> For [Jesus] is our peace;
> in his flesh he has made both groups into one
> and has broken down the dividing wall, that is, the hostility between
>   us.
> He has abolished the law in its commandments and ordinances,
> that he might create in himself one new human in place of the two,
>   thus making peace,
> and might reconcile both groups to God in one body through the
>   cross,
> thus putting to death that hostility through it.
> So he came and proclaimed peace to you who were far off and peace
>   to those who were near;
> for through him both of us have access in one Spirit to the Father.
>   (Eph. 2:14–18, poetic scansion added)

> We do see Jesus, who for a little while was made lower than the
>   angels, now crowned with glory and honor because of the suffer-
>   ing of death, so that by the grace of God he might taste death for
>   everyone.
> It was fitting that God, for whom and through whom all things exist,
>   in bringing many children [*literally* sons] to glory, should make
>   the pioneer of their salvation perfect through sufferings. For the
>   one who sanctifies and those who are sanctified all have one Fa-
>   ther. For this reason Jesus is not ashamed to call them brothers
>   and sisters. . . .
> Since, therefore, the children share flesh and blood, he himself like-
>   wise shared the same things, so that through death he might de-
>   stroy the one who has the power of death, that is, the devil. (Heb.
>   2:9–11, 14)

> There is one God;
>   there is also one mediator between God and humankind,
> Christ Jesus, himself human,
>   who gave himself a ransom for all
> —this was attested at the right time. (1 Tim. 2:5–6)

This fusion of human and divine has turned out historically to be extremely difficult to maintain, not only conceptually but, more importantly, in terms of veneration and imitation. Many Christians came to view Jesus as a divine human being and therefore as only *seemingly* human. Others insisted on his humanity and thus felt compelled to downplay his divinity. The creeds of the church were intended to tackle both of these tendencies as inadequate ways of coming to a full appreciation of Jesus (see chapter 2 above). They did so with the doctrine of the Trinity, namely, that there is one God in three persons, the Father, the Son, and the Holy Spirit. The longevity of the solution the bishops found at Nicea and Chalcedon in the fourth and fifth centuries speaks volumes regarding its profundity, if for no other reason than that it has never allowed the Christian community to solve the mystery of Jesus.

It should be acknowledged that the creeds emerged in their present form at a time when the Roman emperor decided to recognize Christianity as the official religion of the empire. This Roman imperial context would have a considerable effect on Christology. Jesus became the cosmic emperor. In a world in which Christianity enjoyed the status of official imperial religion, it would become extremely difficult to remember Jesus the slave, the servant who is most at home with those at the edges of society, who was not born in a palace and did not live in a palace, and who died on the killing field at the hands of Roman imperial might.

In that time and in subsequent centuries the emperor crowded out the servant, divinity crowded out his humanity, even if not completely. The fact that the canon of the New Testament enshrined four versions of the bracing story of Jesus, along with Paul's radical gospel of the cross, would result in countless movements and persons who followed Jesus to the margins of society, to the poor, the ill, and the oppressed. For many moderns and postmoderns, in contrast, at least in Europe and North America, the christological enthusiasm of Jesus's early followers is difficult to understand. Jesus as vulnerable sage, teacher, social activist, prophet of an ethically defined kingdom of God is more palatable than a divine Jesus who empties himself to the point of dying for others' salvation.

Our investigation has shown that *both* humanity *and* divinity are required to give a faithful rendering of the Jesus who emerges in the New Testament. Jesus is Lord, but precisely as Servant—and vice versa. Jesus is God in his humanity—and vice versa. The cosmic emperor has new clothes indeed, and they look exactly like those of a slave. This "emperor" can be trusted because he cares about prostitutes and tax collectors, about beggars, lepers, and demoniacs, and eats with them. Conversely, the slave is to be emulated and imitated precisely because he is lord. He can be followed because his fate is in the hands of a God who finally has the last laugh over injustice and oppression, over sin, and even over death.

It is difficult to hold these extremes together, but that is the strange and wonderful mix of New Testament Christology and devotion. One without the other—humanity and divinity—renders the early Jesus movement unintelligible. Only by holding them together can we understand why the New Testament writers did not tell us only who Jesus *is* but also who he *was*. Stated differently, it is impossible for the evangelists and apostles to tell us who Jesus *is* as the Christ, the divine Son, without telling us who he *was* as the man from Nazareth, his life, his death, and his resurrection.

Whether their christological project is faithful to who Jesus was, as I contend, or is an imposition on the Jesus of history, as many contemporary Jesus scholars maintain, will continue to be a matter of intense debate. This chapter, indeed this book, will hopefully have provided readers with the raw materials and some of the skills with which to jump into the fray of that debate.

For Further Reading

Bauckham, Richard. *God Crucified: Monotheism and Christology in the New Testament.* Grand Rapids: Eerdmans, 1999.

Brown, Raymond E. *Jesus: God and Man.* New York: Macmillan, 1967.

Dunn, James D. G. *Christology in the Making.* Philadelphia: Westminster, 1980.

———. *Unity and Diversity in the New Testament.* Philadelphia: Trinity, 1990.

Fredriksen, Paula. *From Jesus to Christ: The Origins of the New Testament Images of Christ.* 2nd ed. New Haven: Yale University Press, 2000.

Hurtado, Larry W. *Lord Jesus Christ: Devotion to Jesus in Earliest Christianity.* Grand Rapids: Eerdmans, 2003.

———. *One God, One Lord: Early Christian Devotion and Ancient Jewish Monotheism.* Philadelphia: Fortress, 1988.

Johnson, Elizabeth A. *Consider Jesus: Waves of Renewal in Christology.* New York: Crossroad, 1993.

Powell, Mark Allan, and David R. Bauer, eds. *Who Do You Say That I Am? Essays on Christology.* Louisville: Westminster John Knox, 1999.

Schüssler Fiorenza, Elisabeth. *Jesus: Miriam's Child, Sophia's Prophet: Critical Issues in Feminist Christology.* New York: Continuum, 1994.

Index